Graham Taylor

Graham Taylor

Pioneer for Social Justice

1851-1938

Louise C. Wade

The University of Chicago Press • *Chicago and London*

Library of Congress Catalog Card Number: 64-24976

THE UNIVERSITY OF CHICAGO PRESS, CHICAGO & LONDON
The University of Toronto Press, Toronto 5, Canada

for Dick

Foreword

A few years before his death Graham Taylor remarked to his daughter, "If any biography is thought of after I am gone," it should be a "symposium by someone on the settlement connections, another, the church and so on — No one person could cover it." In defiance of this warning, I have tried to tell the complete story of Taylor's pioneer activities for social justice. Any failure to interpret Taylor's life adequately is, of course, my responsibility.

Any virtues the book may have are due in large part to the help and cooperation of Lea Demarest Taylor and Katharine Taylor. They presented the bulk of their father's papers to the Newberry Library, generously granted me permission to use the personal family letters still in their possession, answered numerous inquiries, and read the manuscript with care. Mrs. Amy Nyholm expertly catalogued the Taylor Collection, and she, along with Mrs. Gertrude L. Woodward and Stanley Pargellis, did everything possible to make my research at the Newberry Library both pleasant and productive.

At the University of Chicago I was aided by Helen R. Wright at the School of Social Service Administration and by the staff at Harper Library. I am also grateful to the people at Hammond Library, Chicago Theological Seminary. Miss Vera Tweddell and the staff at Rush Rhees Library, University of Rochester, gave valuable assistance in the search for documents and microfilms. So too did librarians at the Chicago Historical Society and the Chicago Public Library; the Columbia University School of Social Work and the Manuscript Division of the New York Public Library; the Congregational Library in Boston; the Connecticut State Library and Case Memorial Library of the Hartford Seminary Foundation in Hartford, Connecticut; the State Historical Society, Madison, Wisconsin; and the Library of Congress.

Professor Merle Curti, Professor Glyndon G. Van Deusen, and Dr. Blake McKelvey offered helpful suggestions at several stages in the preparation of the manuscript. I am grateful to all of these people for so willingly contributing their time and their talents. The most vital contributions, however, were the persistent encouragement, sound advice, and good-natured forbearance of my husband, Richard C. Wade.

L.C.W.

Contents

Illustrations

One ❧ *The Rural Apprenticeship*

The generation which came of age in the 1870's and 1880's lived through a tumultuous period in America's growth. In their lifetime they saw the face of the country transformed from a landscape of small farms and quiet villages into an industrial patchwork of smoking factories and noisy, crowded cities. They witnessed the constant flow of people into the burgeoning urban centers, some of them drawn from the American countryside, but many more fleeing political or religious oppression in central and eastern Europe or escaping from economic stagnation in the Mediterranean lands. Difficult indeed was the adjustment of these newcomers to the harsh demands of the factory machines which so many of them tended and to the cruel restrictions of the slums where they had to live.

That *fin de siècle* generation provided a perfect example of the paradox of poverty amidst progress. While technological advances and mass production held out the opportunity of a higher living standard for all Americans, the blight of urban tenements and heavily mortgaged farms disfigured the American scene. At the same time that a few men amassed enormous fortunes, the majority of the country's farmers and wage-earners considered themselves fortunate if they could command a living wage. When these men complained about exploitation, as they did at Haymarket Square, Chicago, or when they took bolder action at Homestead, Pennsylvania, or Pullman, Illinois, they achieved little. For most employers at the end of the nineteenth century were convinced that poverty was the poor man's fault. Any concession to the demands of the laborers or their organizations would bring a halt to industrial progress.

This point of view was shared during the 1870's and 1880's by most of the leading politicians, churchmen, and educators. The federal government, whether controlled by Democrats or Republicans, showed little concern for the discontented wage-earner and farmer. Widespread corruption in state and city administrations at the end of the century meant that few legislators or aldermen thought much about the destitute. Nor were the Christian churches greatly disturbed. The Protestant clergy followed their congregations out of the heart of the city, and though Catholic churches remained in the slums, they too were slow to respond to the immigrants' needs. Complacency and acceptance of the status quo characterized most of the college and university courses in political economy during these decades. For the laissez faire theory of government then prevalent discouraged inquiry into the cause and effect of poverty.

In the 1890's, however, a growing number of middle-class men and women began to heed the protests of disgruntled farmers and wage-earners. Shocked by the stark contrast between social and economic classes in America and frightened by the deep chasm separating the beneficiaries of progress from the victims of poverty, they boldly demanded social justice for all. And their call for reform brought a prompt and energetic response from a wide variety of people. Journalists probed the sharp edges of class conflict and explored the economic differential between employers and employees. Political reformers turned to the progressive factions of the two major parties in the early twentieth century and to the non-partisan movements that reformed municipal government. In time they routed the worst of the spoilsmen, making city, state, and national administrations more responsive to the demands of social justice. The Protestant clergy adjusted to the new climate of opinion by preaching the social gospel to their upper-class parishioners and establishing missions and institutional churches for the lower classes. Non-sectarian social settlements provided still another attempt by the middle classes to bridge the gap between the privileged and the under-privileged in American cities.

Graham Taylor was one of the versatile, energetic reformers of this generation. His college and theological training had been thoroughly conservative, but his first parish in Dutchess County, New York, introduced him to rural poverty and set him thinking about the social causes of sin. When in 1880 he went to the Fourth Congregational Church in Hartford, Connecticut, he found that some of his church members were derelicts of urban, industrial life. Deeply sympathetic with their plight, he was convinced that religion could salvage them. Moreover, he went in search of other victims of vice, drink, and poverty despite the criticism of ministerial colleagues. His missionary work with these men and women was so successful that Hartford Theological Seminary, long a conservative stronghold, appointed Taylor to its faculty in 1888.

Taylor's reputation in Congregational circles spread rapidly, and in 1892 he agreed to head the new Department of Christian Sociology at the Chicago Theological Seminary, the first such department in any religious institution in the United States. It was during his three decades of teaching in Chicago that Taylor recast his theological concepts, breaking away at last from the rigid orthodoxy that had been riveted on him in the 1870's and adopting instead the social gospel tenet that not only individuals but entire communities committed sin or won salvation. He argued, furthermore, that it was the broad function of the church to Christianize all aspects of life and to admit that "other groups and agencies were essentially religious and constituted along with the church the kingdom of God on earth."[1] This social Christianity is what Taylor taught his students at the seminary, wrote about in numerous magazine articles, and defined in his first book, *Religion in Social Action*.

Yet preaching social justice was not enough for Graham Taylor. He was eager to promote understanding between divergent classes, races, and religions, and the social settlement appealed to him as an excellent instrument for achieving this goal. Thus in 1894 he installed his family and four students in a dilapidated old house on Chicago's west side. Chicago Commons, as the settlement was soon named, conducted clubs and classes for its neighbors, opened a nursery school, a playground, and sponsored adult discussion groups. Constantly adjusting its program to the changing character of the neighborhood, Chicago Commons worked successively with Germans, Irish, and Scandinavians in the 1890's, Italians in the early years of the twentieth century, and later with Poles, Greeks, Mexicans, Armenians, and Turks. By the time the Commons celebrated its twenty-fifth anniversary in 1919, its founder had been honored with the presidency of both the National Conference of Charities and Correction and the National Federation of Settlements. Throughout these years Taylor's many other reform activities were, as he put it, "pivoted" on Chicago Commons. In addition, the settlement gave him the opportunity to cross class lines and work for more harmonious civic and industrial relations.[2]

His teaching, writings, and experience in settlement work made Taylor an ideal propagandist for social justice. He pioneered in this area with his usual energy and enthusiasm. From 1896 until 1905, Taylor published *The Commons*, a small magazine devoted to interpreting the settlement movement. It merged with *Charities*, and, in 1909, *Charities and The Commons* became *The Survey*, an influential bimonthly of which Taylor was both an editor and a frequent contributor. In addition, Taylor wrote a weekly column for the Chicago *Daily News* from 1902 until his death in 1938. In these columns he explained social legislation, supported clean politics, discussed the rights and abuses of labor unions and employers' organizations, defended the immigrants, and in general sought to convert his readers to social justice. To train young men and women for positions in settlements and social agen-

---

[1] Graham Taylor, *Pioneering on Social Frontiers* (Chicago, 1930), pp. 357, 398.
[2] Taylor, *Pioneering*, pp. 9, 6.

cies, Taylor established the Chicago School of Civics and Philanthropy, an independent institution from 1908 until its absorption by the University of Chicago twelve years later. The Chicago Civic Federation, the Municipal Voters' League, the Chicago Plan Commission, and the Vice Commission were only a few of the many organizations that were glad to have Taylor as an active member and an effective advocate.

Like the other reformers of his generation Taylor was motivated by the broad goal of social justice for all groups in American society. He was not the first to establish a social settlement or training school for social workers, nor was he the earliest spokesman for social Christianity or civic reform. But in each of these areas he was a courageous, energetic, and remarkably successful pioneer. The fruits of his "pioneering on social frontiers," as he referred to his life work, constituted an important contribution to American reform. As a result, a study of Taylor's career affords an interesting perspective on that tumultuous period of the late nineteenth and early twentieth centuries. Indeed, as Alexander Johnson, former secretary of the National Conference of Charities and Correction, predicted: when "the history of the social movement in the United States of the most socially fruitful forty years in the nation's life, those from 1880 to 1920, shall be written, the work of Graham Taylor will fill a wonderful chapter. No more socially-minded man has ever lived." [3]

II

Taylor's social-mindedness was not the product of his inheritance, his youth, or his formal education. He was born into a conservative, ministerial family, four generations of which had served the Dutch Reformed Church. The line began in the early part of the eighteenth century with Thomas Romeyn. His son, James Van Campen Romeyn, was a minister, and his granddaughter married Benjamin Cook Taylor, pastor for forty-two years of the Dutch Reformed Church in Bergen, New York. The offspring of this union, William James Romeyn Taylor, served the church as did three of his sons, Graham, William Rivers, and Livingston Ludlow. Graham Taylor took pride in this "apostolic succession" and in the achievements of the Taylor and Romeyn families. By contrast, he said little about his mother's parents except that they were "farmer folks, Cowenhoven by name, descendants of old Holland-Dutch settlers of the soil." [4]

William James Romeyn Taylor and his wife, Katharine Cowenhoven, were living in Schenectady, New York, when their second son was born on

[3] Alexander Johnson, *Adventures in Social Welfare: Being Reminiscences of Things, Thoughts and Folks During Forty Years of Social Work* (Fort Wayne, 1923), p. 379.

[4] Taylor, *Pioneering*, p. 346.

May 2, 1851. Contrary to the family predilection for long names, they simply called him Graham. Shortly afterwards William Taylor took his family to Philadelphia where his wife died in June, 1852. Later he married Maria Cowenhoven, sister of his first wife, and she gave him two more sons, William Rivers and Livingston Ludlow.

The second Mrs. Taylor treated Graham and his brother Van Campen with as much tenderness as she did her own sons. Years later Graham wrote to her, "You *never* made any distinction between us. You were Mother to all of us." It must have tested her patience at times, for Van Campen was a mischievous child and Graham a sickly one. While the family lived in Philadelphia, Graham was carefully kept indoors all winter to guard his health. Every summer, however, he and the three other boys lived with their aunts and uncles and seven cousins in New Brunswick, New Jersey. It was a "city boy's paradise" and many years later Taylor could still recall the "good out-of-doors times we all had in playing under the pear tree in our NB home and on Bishop Hill with our cousins." At the age of eighty-five he reminded his brother Will of the day "you were chasing me after I dropped that rotten pear on you from the 3rd story . . . I have never failed to laugh aloud over my unseemly behavior *even now*."[5]

Taylor corresponded with his New Brunswick cousins during the winter months and his earliest extant letter, written in April, 1862, informed them of the latest developments in Philadelphia. He, Livingston, and Will had just recovered from measles and whooping cough. Then the eleven-year-old casually continued, "There is no news here but the war news and that I suppose you get. The news of victory comes in most every day. I guess Jeff Davis and co. will soon be played out. What do you think about it? . . . Ma . . . is tired out with nursing. Papa is too."[6] That same year, 1862, Taylor's parents moved to New Brunswick. In 1868, William Taylor was called to a church in Newark, New Jersey, where he and his wife spent the remainder of their lives. Their son Graham, however, always considered New Brunswick home.

Religion in the Taylor household was a happy, joyful, natural expression. The family worshiped together daily, with responsive readings, Bible stories, and hymns. Taylor was especially impressed by the easy way in which his parents blended religious training with family life. He remembered Sunday as "the gladdest time of the week . . . because in the afternoon and early

[5] Graham Taylor to Mrs. William J. R. Taylor, November 29, 1894, Taylor Collection, Newberry Library, Chicago, Ill. Unless otherwise stated, all manuscript citations come from the Taylor Collection.

Fred Eastman, *Men of Power* (Nashville, 1939), IV, 181; Taylor, *Pioneering*, pp. 339, 340; Graham Taylor to William R. Taylor and Livingston L. Taylor, September 26, 1936.

[6] Graham Taylor to "Benny," April 1, 1862.

evening play and merriment mingled with instruction, story-telling, vesper hymns, and dear home-companionship."[7]

Very different were Taylor's recollections of Dutch Reformed church services in his childhood. The pulpit was a forbidding "judgment bar" and preachers acted "like prosecutors of their fellow-men before the high court of heaven." He learned at an early age that he was not a person, but rather a "soul" at church. Though he shared a pew with other members of his family, he was acutely conscious of his "isolation and loneliness." Nor could he find any consolation in the hymns, for most of them were "attuned to death."[8]

Two people helped young Taylor reconcile the stern doctrines of the church service with the happy religious experience of his home. One was his Sunday school teacher, a carpenter who "knew little of the Bible as a student," but "knew it well as the way of life." Taylor learned from him the difference between right and wrong and the reasons why man needed help from above to make the choice. The other person was his father. The elder Taylor's gentle yet strong spirit, his example of humanized religion at home, and his calm words of encouragement aided his son during trying periods of religious doubt. In the spring of 1866 when the boy was attending Rutgers College Grammar School, his father wrote regularly urging him to read his Bible, repent of his sins, "use the means of grace," and pray "that God will bring you out of darkness into light & that your troubled soul may soon find peace in believing in Jesus."[9]

Young Taylor did eventually find religious peace, but only after he accepted God as a merciful father rather than a stern judge, and only after he discovered these reassuring lines in the liturgy: "no sin or infirmity which still remaineth against our will in us can hinder us from being received of God in mercy." Thus, at the age of fifteen, he was able to partake of communion and become a full member of the Taylor and Romeyn families' Dutch Reformed Church.[10]

III

It was natural for Taylor to enroll at Rutgers College in the fall of 1866. He had spent four years at the Rutgers College Grammar School in New Brunswick, his brother Van Campen was a senior at the College, and his grandfather Benjamin Cook Taylor was a trustee of that Dutch Reformed educational stronghold. Graham Taylor passed the entrance examinations in

---

[7] Taylor, *Pioneering*, p. 340.

[8] Taylor, *Pioneering*, pp. 341, 340, 343.

[9] Taylor, *Pioneering*, pp. 344, 339; Graham Taylor, "To Prof. L. L. Bernard at request for data," no date; William J. R. Taylor to Graham Taylor, March 8, 28, 1866.

[10] Quoted in Taylor, *Pioneering*, p. 342; note written by Graham Taylor, May 18, 1866, in the possession of Lea Taylor, Highland Park, Ill.

Latin, Greek, mathematics, and geography, and the president accepted his "testimonials of . . . good moral character." In September, he and Van Campen each paid their $45 annual tuition and moved into rented rooms at 54 Somerset Street, New Brunswick.[11]

Taylor was a good, but not spectacular, student at Rutgers. Of the seven compulsory courses during his freshman year he did his best work in elocution and Latin, his worst in mathematics. A sophomore slump sent his mathematics grade plummeting to 64, but he recovered after the Christmas vacation and finished the year with an average of 89⅜. During his junior and senior years his marks were consistently in the 90's. Yet the strong finish was not enough to overcome his slow start, and, as a result, Taylor was not elected to the new Phi Beta Kappa chapter at Rutgers or awarded any of the academic prizes at graduation.[12]

In addition to pursuing his academic studies, Taylor participated in a number of campus organizations. He entered several oratorical contests, was an enthusiastic member of the Peithessophian Literary Society, and devoted many afternoons to editorial work on the student newspaper, *The Targum*. The Raritan River, which wound through the town and along the edge of the campus, made boating a popular sport with everyone in New Brunswick. Even the ministers had their own boat club. During his senior year Taylor was a member of the White Caps crew and every morning of that fall and spring he rose at 5:00 A.M. to join his teammates in practice before breakfast. On Friday evenings he made a ritual of consuming oysters with a secret fraternal organization, cryptically referred to in his diary as "No. 28."[13]

Taylor also had time for various activities in the town. He took piano lessons at the conservatory and sang with the choral society of the Second Reformed Church, where Dr. Chester D. Hartranft, the main force behind the ministers' boat club, was the pastor and choral director. With his spirited cousin Bella Bishop and her friends, Taylor played backgammon and croquet and went to parties and receptions that lasted until the early hours. With the more serious Leah Demarest, daughter of the professor at the Theological Seminary in New Brunswick, he attended musicals, lectures, prayer meetings, and social gatherings of the church's young people.[14]

Taylor's graduation in June, 1870, coincided with Rutgers' one-hundredth

[11] Rutgers College, *Catalogue, 1866–67*.

[12] Rutgers College, *Catalogues, 1866–67, 1867–68, 1868–69, 1869–70, 1870–71*; Rutgers College, report cards issued to Graham Taylor, 1866–67, 1867–68, 1868–69, 1869–70.

[13] Rutgers College, *Catalogues, 1867–68, 1868–69*; William H. S. Demarest, *A History of Rutgers College, 1766–1924* (New Brunswick, 1924), pp. 422–23, 425–26; Graham Taylor, "Writes of His Ins and Outs with the Press," *Press Impressions*, VIII (May, 1930), 1–2, 5; Graham Taylor, Diary, *passim*.

[14] Taylor, Diary, *passim*.

anniversary. Justice Joseph P. Bradley of the United States Supreme Court, a graduate of the class of 1836 at Rutgers, was the main speaker at the commencement ceremony. Graham Taylor delivered a brief address entitled "Our Charter" in which he thanked the founders of the college for insisting upon a classical curriculum: they "saw what the utilitarian upstarts of this exceedingly practical, and marvelously progressive age have not the ability to see or comprehend." When he had finished speaking, Taylor received "the kindly floral remembrances of my lady friends. After taking our sheepskins and hearing the Valedictory . . . we went out into the 'Wide, wide world.'" [15]

A few months later, with all the aplomb of a recent graduate, Taylor reflected upon his years at Rutgers. "Four happy years," he called them, "Years frought with privileges and blessings. Years of progress and development. Years made bright by careless joys and freedom of student life and hallowed by many sweet, solemn hours of prayer . . . Years of manly friendship, of the gentler, softer, cheering sympathy of woman's heart and of the sacred ties of Christian love." [16]

In Taylor's diary there is evidence to suggest that he was developing these "sacred ties of Christian love." In April, 1870, he began to keep a volume entitled "Vagae Meditationes," which he dedicated "to the poor 'wandering thoughts' and straying meditations of my mind." This was designed "to educate — lead up — my low & groveling thoughts toward the Holy, the Just & True." He does not say in this book or in his diary exactly when he decided to prepare for the ministry. But given the "apostolic succession" in his family and the personal influence of his father and his pastor, Dr. Hartranft, it was understandable that Graham Taylor would choose to serve the Dutch Reformed Church. In September, 1870 he was back in New Brunswick and enrolled at the seminary. His "Thoughts upon entering the Theological Seminary" were preserved in "Vagae Meditationes": "To lead the immortal soul . . . blighted by sin and doomed by the law to dismal punishment to seek forgiveness from the offended yet merciful Deity; To preach the glad tidings of Salvation to a fallen world . . . To be the servant of the Most High God . . . What earthly honor can compare with this or what service has a greater reward?" [17]

The course of study required three years to complete. There were twelve students in Taylor's class, and they received intensive training in Hebrew

---

[15] Demarest, *ibid.,* p. 432; Graham Taylor, "Our Charter" (manuscript); Taylor, Diary, June 22, 1870.

[16] Graham Taylor, "Thoughts upon entering the Theological Seminary," Vagae Meditationes (manuscript).

[17] Taylor, "Dedicatio" and "Thoughts upon entering the Theological Seminary," in Vagae Meditationes.

and Greek, sacred history and chronology, church government, and the constitution of the Reformed Church. In addition, there were courses in the Chaldee and Syriac languages, as well as biblical geography and biblical criticism. Throughout these three years they studied theology — didactic, polemic, and pastoral — and they were drilled in elocution, extempore preaching, and the composition and delivery of sermons.[18]

In later years Taylor changed his mind about the value of the education he received both at Rutgers College and at the seminary. He realized that his college courses in classics gave him little if any appreciation of literary content. He had studied ancient and medieval but not modern history. As for political economy, "systems of government were taught, from the top down, while the practice of citizenship was ignored. Economics whipped facts into line with theory, ignoring industrial history and human experience." At the seminary he heard nothing about the Bible as literature, or as a guide to character and conduct. Nor was there any mention of the obligation or opportunity for the clergy to be "influential in the workaday world or in the ways in which men, women and children work for a living." Professors at both schools relied heavily upon lectures and recitations, and demanded little "collateral reading, original inquiry, first-hand observation, or independent thought upon the part of the student." Consequently, as Taylor remarked in the 1930's, "I entered upon adult life and the work of the ministry" with "no practical knowledge of my own self and immediate surroundings." [19]

Taylor aired these criticisms in his autobiography, *Pioneering on Social Frontiers*, which he wrote from the vantage point of fifty years of participation in American reform movements. He was quite right in saying that the conservative political and economic theories he learned at Rutgers and the equally conservative theological concepts drilled into him at the seminary were not the best preparation for a lifetime of social pioneering. But few schools and few professors in the 1860's or 1870's offered the type of education which Taylor would have found useful.

Although no teacher seems to have exerted much influence on Taylor, he was deeply affected by two individuals whom he met during his student days in New Brunswick. One was Dr. Chester Hartranft, pastor of the Second Reformed Church. Taylor attended his services, sang in his choral society, and as a seminary student joined Hartranft's Septemviri boat club. The two men exercised daily, with Taylor at the bow oar and Hartranft the stroke oar of their shell. Many years later Taylor could remember their walks to

[18] New Brunswick Theological Seminary, *Catalogue, 1875–76.*
[19] Taylor, *Pioneering*, pp. 349, 108; Graham Taylor, manuscript, no title, dated 1936

and from the Raritan, when Hartranft "talked to me as no one else ever did, of the humanity of God and the divinity of man, as naturally as about the joy of our recreational fellowship." Taylor admired his pastor's eloquent preaching, deep learning, and broad culture, and he marveled at the older man's ability to stand "in the breach between religion and life, church and world, interpreting and serving both." Hartranft's many achievements furnished the impressionable seminary student with a lofty goal.[20] Furthermore, it was Hartranft who a few years later brought Taylor to the Fourth Congregational Church in Hartford, where he first tangled with urban religious problems, and it was Hartranft who was instrumental in getting Taylor appointed to the Hartford Theological Seminary, a position which proved to be the stepping-stone for his Chicago career.

The other person Taylor met in New Brunswick was Leah Demarest, oldest child of Dr. David D. Demarest, Professor of Pastoral Theology and Sacred Rhetoric at the seminary. Taylor dated her occasionally during his years at Rutgers, but as a first year seminary student he saw her much more frequently. In April, 1871, he chose a balmy spring night to call upon "Miss Lillie,"

> with whom I spent the evening sitting in the moonlight by the window of the sitting room overlooking the Raritan and revealed to her my deep & devoted love and the fond hopes which I have cherished for more than a year, all of which were kindly received & taken into consideration. This action was taken after the most careful & prayerful consideration & with the certainty of success upon the same grounds — if we ask anything in the name of Jesus in accordance to the divine will and in faith believing we have G's word, we shall receive it.

He spent an anxious spring vacation with his parents in Newark, not knowing whether God would answer his prayer or not. The end of April brought "No light yet — but hope on hope ever." Then on his twentieth birthday, May 2, 1871, he took Lillie to prayer meeting, and afterwards they engaged in earnest conversation "on the Sofa in the Parlor where at 10:45 my prayer was answered and Lillie revealed her love to me." Not until the next day did he remember to add in his diary: "the thought that God has heard and answered the earnest and longing prayer of the soul gives rest & confidence."[21]

In January, 1873, during his last semester at the seminary, Taylor received an invitation to preach at the Dutch Reformed Church in Hopewell, New

[20] Graham Taylor, manuscript, no title, no date; Taylor, *Pioneering*, pp. 349, 350.

[21] Taylor, Diary, April 5, 29, May 2, 3, 1871. The Demarests were descendants of David Des Marest who came to America in 1663. Leah's brother, William H. S. Demarest, later became president of Rutgers. William H. S. Demarest and Mary A. Demarest (comp.), *The Demarest Family* (New Brunswick, 1938), pp. 13, 316.

York. He made a good impression, for the consistory offered to pay him $1,200 a year, plus the use of the parsonage, a comfortable old house with ten acres of land, and the customary annual donation by the congregation. Taylor discussed the matter with Lillie, Dr. Demarest, and Dr. Hartranft, and he corresponded with his father and grandfather. With the approval of all these people, Taylor accepted the position.[22]

In May he received his professional certificate from the Theological Seminary; he then had to prepare for the rigorous oral examinations by the Reformed Church classis in Newark and also in Poughkeepsie. He wrote to Lillie about the examination in theology: "Old Dr. Van Cleif went through nearly the whole system from everlasting to everlasting including all between." Taylor passed both examinations and answered some inquiries about the Belgic Confession of 1561 which had stumped all previous candidates. When the ordeal was over, he and his friends went off "on a final 'spree,' a ministerial one of course," he assured his fiancé. Taylor's formal ordination took place on July 1, 1873, in the Hopewell Church, with his father, grandfather, and prospective father-in-law all participating. To Lillie, who was not present, the newly-ordained minister confided, "The services were very solemn and impressive. . . . All the exercises passed off finely but you may imagine were very exhausting to me. Last night I was really sick with weariness."[23]

IV

The weariness soon wore off as Taylor began to acquaint himself with his new surroundings. Hopewell was located in the southwestern part of Dutchess County, about ten miles from the Hudson River and twelve from Poughkeepsie, the county's seat and largest town. Both Poughkeepsie and the neighboring town of Fishkill had been settled in the 1680's; two centuries later they were utilizing their rail connections and water routes to encourage manufacturing. Taylor's parish of 120 square miles lay to the east, an area of rich farmland and prosperous dairies supplying primarily the Poughkeepsie and New York City markets. The town of Hopewell, founded in 1750, was the oldest in the parish. Nearby Hopewell Junction, the youngest, owed its origin to the intersection of the Central New England and the Newburgh, Dutchess & Connecticut railroad lines in 1869. The Junction, however, promptly became the transportation and business center for the surrounding

[22] Graham Taylor to Leah Demarest, January 27, 1873, in the possession of Lea Taylor; Consistory of Hopewell Church to Graham Taylor, February 11, 1873.

[23] Graham Taylor to Leah Demarest, May 30, 1873, in the possession of Lea Taylor; Taylor, Diary, May 21, 26, 28, 1873; Taylor, *Pioneering*, p. 351; Graham Taylor to Leah Demarest, July 2, 1873.

farm community, and within a decade its population outstripped the much older town of Hopewell.[24]

Taylor's parish included seven villages: Hopewell, Upper Hopewell, the Junction, Johnsville, Stormville, East Fishkill, and Fishkill Plains. Each of these villages constituted a separate neighborhood, though many of the families were closely related. Some of them, such as the Van Wycks, Storms, Adriances, or Brinckerhoffs, could trace their lineage back to the pre-Revolutionary period, and as they hastened to tell their new minister they were farming the very soil which their ancestors had settled.[25]

The Dutch Reformed congregation of Hopewell was organized in 1757 and its first church completed seven years later. A larger building was constructed on the same site during 1833 and 1834, and this was the only church serving the Hopewell community when Taylor arrived in 1873. He described it to Lillie as "a fine old brick building with some cappings, nicely fitted up inside, and able to accommodate about 600 people." During the summer Taylor called on as many families in the parish as he could reach, including wealthy landowners and professional people, tenant-farmers, and even field-hands. He urged all of them to come to church services if they could, or to the Sunday afternoon and evening prayer meetings which he conducted in the village schoolhouses.[26]

In mid-September Taylor returned to New Brunswick to claim Leah Demarest as his bride. Dr. Hartranft married them on September 18, and their ten-day honeymoon to Niagara Falls, Toronto, and Montreal cost $225 according to the groom's account book. As soon as the Taylors reached Hopewell, members of the congregation came calling on the dominie's bride, bringing donations which more than filled the pantry. Before the winter weather set in, they presented Taylor with a horse and buggy and found that they also had to teach their new pastor how to harness the horse.[27]

The Taylors enjoyed their seven years at the Hopewell parsonage. In the evenings they sang and played the piano or took turns reading aloud from the historians Prescott, Motley, or Gibbon, selections from Greek and Latin literature, the sermons of Horace Bushnell and Phillips Brooks, or such periodicals as *Harper's Monthly* and the *Independent*. The young minister

[24] Frank Hasbrouck, *The History of Dutchess County, New York* (Poughkeepsie, 1909), p. 293; *Dutchess County* ("American Guide Series" [Philadelphia, 1937]), pp. 31, 79, 81, 115.

[25] Taylor, *Pioneering*, p. 354.

[26] Hasbrouck, *Dutchess County*, p. 294; *Dutchess County* ("American Guide Series"), p. 115; Graham Taylor to Leah Demarest, January 27, 1873.

[27] Graham Taylor, Account Book (manuscript); Taylor, Diary, October 10, 18, 25, 1873; interview with Lea Taylor, February 29, 1964.

told his father, "History is recreation for me which I enjoy far more than fiction." Taylor planted a garden and carefully noted in his diary his success at raising celery, raking hay, gathering strawberries, and even poisoning potato bugs. Although the food from the garden helped to cut living expenses, Taylor still found that he could not afford a new overcoat at the "up-river prices" asked by the Newburgh and Poughkeepsie merchants. Two of the Taylor's four children were born while they were living in the Hopewell parsonage: Helen, in September, 1876, and Graham Romeyn, their only son, on March 17, 1880.[28]

During his Hopewell and Hartford ministries Taylor kept a journal of his church activities and also a "Private Record of Services Rendered as Minister of the Gospel of the Lord Jesus Christ." These two documents together with his diary and letters to his father give an interesting picture of the young minister's trials. He kept a keen eye on church attendance and recorded such disheartening events as "only 5 people" on a fine Sunday in August. That particular day Taylor decided "to lay aside the sermon on 'Jesus' which had cost me so much trouble & dissatisfaction and preach from Isaiah 4:38 . . . God bless it to the few." Bad weather also cut down the size of the congregation: "Rain, snow & hail—found no one at church." There were trials in the pulpit too. Taylor was often dissatisfied with his sermon manuscripts and sometimes he found it "hard to break through the embarrassment I feel, and cannot seem to get rid of." Not until January, 1875 did he dare speak from notes, and it took another five years before he "trusted the Lord" enough to deliver impromptu sermons.[29]

Realizing that not all of his parishioners came to the regular services, Taylor decided to call on every family. He refused to make any distinction between the wealthy landowners who occupied the pews on the main floor of the church and the tenants and field hands, both Negro and white, who had to sit in the cramped gallery when they attended services. Taylor was amazed to find that the field hands lived in wretched tenant-houses, some of which were dangerously overcrowded. Their children received only desultory instruction in rundown schoolhouses. By searching out and inviting these families to participate in church affairs, Taylor antagonized the landowners. One pillar of the church "admonished me to 'confine my attentions

[28] Graham Taylor to William J. R. Taylor, February 18, 1880, in the possession of Lea Taylor; Taylor, Diary, June 19, 1877; Graham Taylor to William J. R. Taylor, October 31, 1879, in the possession of Lea Taylor.

[29] Taylor, Journal, August 9, November 29, February 15, 1874, January 31, 1875; Graham Taylor to William J. R. Taylor, September 19, [1879], April, 1880, in the possession of Lea Taylor; Taylor, Diary, February 1, 1880.

to those who paid my salary, instead of calling upon every household in the community.' I meekly replied that 'I presumed that I was the minister of the whole parish and never imagined that I was only the pastor of the subscription list.' "[30]

To make it easier for all parish families to attend some kind of weekly religious service, Taylor inaugurated Sunday afternoon meetings in the schoolhouses of the outlying villages. The response was so satisfactory that he added Sunday evening prayer meetings and week-night Bible classes. It meant, however, that the dominie did a great deal of traveling by horse and buggy to reach these distant schools. He was exposed to rain, snow, and piercing winds, and he struggled all year round with "the awful mud" of Dutchess County roads. At the end of one severe winter he wrote to his grandfather that he had "done little but bounce over the rough roads, and recover from the effects of the bouncing . . . it costs me just about twice the time, strength, and patience ordinarily required to do the same work." Yet Taylor, felt that this strenuous schedule was imperative if he wanted to be "minister of the whole parish" and not just of the village of Hopewell.[31]

In the 1870's many clergymen measured the success of their sermons by the number of conversions and the emotional response of the congregation. Initially Taylor shared this criterion, and he watched with interest the careers of contemporary revivalists. He spent his 1875 vacation in Brooklyn observing the techniques of Dwight L. Moody and Ira Sankey. That fall Taylor was pleased by an increase in his church attendance, and he felt that the people "manifested more feeling." His predecessor heard of these developments and sent Taylor a note of congratulations, praying for "a yet more plentiful harvest." But no harvest ripened in Hopewell, and by March Taylor sadly concluded, "though we may plant and water God gives the increase . . . it is not for us to know the times or the reasons which the Father has put in his own power."[32]

Eventually Taylor stopped trying "to be Moody and Sankey together" and cast about for other ways to make religion relevant for his parishioners. He knew that his Sunday sermons were not as effective as his pastoral work, Bible classes, or evening prayer meetings. And this realization was painful. In his journal he attributed the trouble to lack of time. Many years later,

[30] Taylor, *Pioneering*, pp. 358, 359.

[31] Taylor, *Pioneering*, pp. 356, 357; Graham Taylor to William J. R. Taylor, November 18, 1879, in the possession of Lea Taylor; Taylor, Diary, March 17, 1879; Graham Taylor to Benjamin Cook Taylor, February 21, 1880.

[32] Taylor, Journal, October 31, 1875; Rev. Oliver E. Cobb to Graham Taylor, March 9, 1875; Taylor, Journal, March 5, 1876.

however, he said that his early "pulpit inhibition" was due to the "framework riveted upon my faith by my theological training." [33]

It was difficult for Taylor to make the transition from rigid Dutch Reformed orthodoxy to a more liberal theology. His seminary training had emphasized the Calvinist doctrines of predestination and divine election. He had been taught that life on this earth was tinged with evil, and that nature must always be subordinated to revelation. Taylor was able to modify these concepts only when he became aware of the personal presence of Jesus. By seeking to emulate Christ's life and to understand the meaning of the Savior's sacrifice, the young minister arrived at "a more natural and vital view of relationship with the Father." During his years in Hopewell he acquired for the first time a "reverence for the world of nature as the handiwork of God." Turning back to his Bible, he shunned the Old Testament which had been emphasized at the seminary and concentrated instead upon the New Testament. There he discovered "how to preach and teach that the world is the subject of redemption as the object of God's love." [34]

Unfortunately, it is impossible to see how Taylor applied these new ideas in his Hopewell sermons. He apparently saved most of his early manuscripts, but upon rereading them in the 1920's he was so embarrassed by the fire and brimstone that he destroyed them all. Occasionally he discussed an outline for a sermon in the letters to his father. But in *Pioneering on Social Frontiers* the only reference to these early efforts was to ask forgiveness "for having preached such a sermon as my nature-loving farmer folk once endured, on the terror of being 'in the world' — the world of nature, 'red in tooth and claw,' the world wholly possessed by evil and hurrying to complete destruction — the terror being used as a persuasive warning to risk no longer being 'without Christ.' " [35]

Taylor's theological concepts did change, however, during his Hopewell ministry. That he was placing less emphasis on divine election and more on Christian action can be seen in an article which he wrote in 1878. Entitled "The Heresy of Life" and published in the *Christian Intelligencer*, it was widely quoted in other religious journals. Taylor defined the heresy of life as the deliberate "choice of actions which are not only in known opposition to the law of God and the practice of the Church, but also in conflict with one's own conscience." His key assertion was that "More heresy is lived

<hr>

[33] Graham Taylor to Mr. and Mrs. William J. R. Taylor, January 9, 1880, in the possession of Lea Taylor; Taylor, *Pioneering*, pp. 350, 357; Taylor, Journal, February 15, 1874.

[34] Taylor, *Pioneering*, pp. 349–50, 357–58.

[35] Taylor, *Pioneering*, p. 358.

than is written or believed" and that the "Gospel has suffered more from the underestimate of the one than from the overrated influence of the other." "Worse is it," he continued,

> to live heresy than to believe it, not only because the intrinsic wrong is greater, but because the resulting evils are more widespread and disastrous. . . . Well nigh futile is the preaching of the pulpit to sinners which is contradicted by the daily life of the membership in the pews. For fact will always outweigh profession, deed will always counterbalance word in the scales of human judgment.

Taylor concluded with an urgent plea for the church to be "as orthodox in life as in faith" and to guard "as jealously against heretical living as against disbelief." [36]

In his own church Taylor fought against "heretical living." On one occasion he refused to accept as deacon a prominent young man who frankly admitted that he had purchased his father-in-law's election as county commissioner. Taylor's strong condemnation created a furor in the community where it was assumed that the dominie would not interfere with politics. Naturally Taylor was "much worried about the possible issue in regard to personal & ch[urch] friends — but duty 1st." The upshot of this unpleasant incident was the withdrawal from the church of the young man and all of his "influential and deeply offended family." [37]

Church finances constituted another vexatious problem which Taylor met head-on. The Hopewell congregation was known in Dutch Reformed circles as tight-fisted because of its long-standing debt and its insignificant contributions to benevolent and missionary work. By constantly emphasizing the saintliness of giving, Taylor was able to retire the $1200 church debt in 1875. He introduced the system of envelopes for donations, and, despite one angry church member who made "a bitter attack upon it and me as despoiling of the community," the size of Hopewell's gifts increased sharply. [38]

Taylor made still another innovation that startled his congregation. It had long been customary for the wealthier members of the parish to own or rent pews on the main floor of the church while tenant-farm families occupied the free but uncomfortable benches in the gallery. Ever since the original purchase of the pews in 1771, many had been handed down from one generation to the next. Some people had inherited two or more pews, in which case they either rented the extras or left them unused. Other pews were

---

[36] Graham Taylor, "The Heresy of Life," *The Christian Intelligencer*, XLIX (May 23, 1878), 1–2.

[37] Taylor, Diary, March 12, 1879; Taylor, Journal, March 12, 1879; Taylor, *Pioneering*, p. 359.

[38] Taylor, Diary, June 3, December 3, 1877.

habitually empty because the owners no longer lived in the area. The result, Taylor soon discovered, was a highly inefficient use of the space within the Hopewell church. His first approach to this touchy problem was to ask people who had moved out of the parish to relinquish ownership of their pews. Few complied, one man staunchly insisting that he would never part with his pew because it was the last piece of real estate he owned in Dutchess County. So Taylor asked the absentee pew holders to increase their financial contributions to the church to compensate for loss of rental income. Again most of them refused.[39]

Eventually Taylor concluded that "the only escape from this absentee landlordism" was to increase the seating capacity of the gallery. In the summer of 1879 the floor of the gallery was lowered, and the additional space partitioned into boxes and furnished with comfortable chairs. At the same time the walls of the church were repainted in a brighter, warmer color and a rear entrance was constructed. The new boxes looked so desirable that the pew holders quickly surrendered their inheritance on the main floor and took space in the gallery. "It soon came to pass," Taylor whimsically observed, "that more of my hearers were in the galleries than on the ground floor, giving our Sunday assemblies a somewhat top-heavy appearance."[40]

There was, of course, some opposition to Taylor's reforms and it came to a head in July, 1879, one month before the church closed for remodeling. On July 1, the sixth anniversary of his ordination, Taylor was grieved to learn from one of the church elders that there was "dissatisfaction . . . with my preaching, the cause of which he conceived to be my overestimate of the intellectual capacity of the congregation." Taylor felt that the trouble stemmed not from his preaching but from "that old malign spirit with which I have had to battle during my whole ministry among this people." Many of his parishioners were satisfied with one elaborate sermon a week and stood firmly

> opposed to the prayer meetings as means of grace to themselves or means of reaching others, to the pastoral visitation of "outsiders" and the poor, and to any effort to make provision for the large element in the church, who for a simple lack of room are kept out, and to any benevolent and missionary operations. This spirit I cannot submit to, cannot but withstand, as I am faithful to my Master and His Church.[41]

From the members of the consistory Taylor learned that the chief troublemaker was Theodorus Van Wyck Brinckerhoff, a retired banker and owner

[39] Henry E. Cobb, manuscript, no title, no date; Taylor, *Pioneering*, p. 355.
[40] Taylor, *Pioneering*, pp. 355, 356; Graham Taylor to the Classis of Poughkeepsie, April 15, 1880; Henry E. Cobb, manuscript.
[41] Taylor, Journal, July 1, 1879.

of a pew which had been purchased by his forefathers in 1771. Writing to his father and father-in-law, both of whom were experienced in church politics, Taylor sought advice. Dr. Demarest urged him to work through the consistory, making "every man show his hand and *commit himself*," but above all saying nothing "about resigning — the time has not come for that." Taylor's father preferred a direct confrontation with Brinckerhoff. That way "You will find either that he is a coward & will retreat: or a desperate rebel who must be put down or put out." Taylor lined up the members of the consistory first, and then on July 21, he and one of the church elders called upon Brinckerhoff. According to Taylor's diary, Brinckerhoff confessed to groundless criticism of the dominie in the hope of defeating his plan to remodel the church. Once the rebel had been isolated the affair quickly blew over. Taylor departed for his vacation still "hurt at heart," but he came back in October to the newly-renovated church with his "old spirit . . . quite restored."[42]

V

Just after he had consolidated his position in Hopewell, a new opportunity opened up for Graham Taylor. During the winter of 1879–80 the Fourth Congregational Church of Hartford was looking for a new pastor, and Dr. Hartranft, then a professor at the Theological Institute in Hartford, recommended his young friend. After repeated urging, Taylor consented to visit Hartford and preach at the church. He carefully inspected the surroundings of the Fourth Church and felt satisfied that there was "a *wide* & effectual door before it." Apparently the Fourth Church Society was contented too, for they offered him $1,800 a year, a suitable home in the parish, four weeks of vacation each year, and $50 for moving expenses. Before making up his mind Taylor wrote to Dr. Hartranft for more information. He was told that:

> Its membership on paper is over 400; in reality it is a little over 200. . . . It has had one or two unfortunate pastorates. The membership has fallen into a little fanaticism on temperance and church methods. . . . It would be hard work to build it up from the outside, but I believe it could be done. The inside, so far as I know, could be well moulded. . . . There is a debt of $8000 which I believe could be lifted, after the church has proven its right to live. . . . Let me add, the people, certainly the leading ones, *are* VERY *anxious* to have you accept.[43]

[42] Hasbrouck, *Dutchess County*, pp. 347, 294; Dr. D. D. Demarest to Graham Taylor, July 9, 1879; William J. R. Taylor to Graham Taylor, July 8, 1879; Taylor, Diary, July 21, October 5, 1879; Taylor, Journal, July 23, 1879.

[43] Taylor, Diary, February 28, 1880; J. B. Pierce to Graham Taylor, March 1, 1880; Chester D. Hartranft to Graham Taylor, March 5, 1880.

Taylor's decision was complicated by an unexpected offer in the middle of March from the Dutch Reformed Church of Somerville, New Jersey. They promised him $1,200 and a house, which Taylor considered a mere pittance, but he felt that his first duty was to his own denomination. Once again he sought advice from his father and got this shrewd reply: "As to climate, permanency, lack of pulpit competition, & comparative prominence it certainly has advantages." At Somerville, he continued, "you will also be in & of *your own church*, & surrounded by a homogenous population, & without the theological conflicts that have made Hartford famous of late years." On the other hand, Taylor's father felt that Hartford's climate was not bad, an urban parish would involve far less travel, and "would have all the other advantages of a live city which you have not at Hopewell & could not get at Somerville." The older man considered both salaries too low. The "Somerville people have very deliberately failed to offer you a proper support"; they are "abundantly able, but too mean to do better." In the Hartford negotiations he suggested that his son "consult Dr. Hartranft privately . . . & let him suggest an increase to the officials . . . before the meeting of the Congregation." [44]

Taylor followed his father's advice. As a result of the subtle hint, the Hartford committee increased the salary figure from $1,800 a year to $2,100. Finally, on March 25, Taylor received letters from his father and Dr. Demarest "which were so similar in tone & argument and so decidedly in favor of my going to Hartford . . . that I took this as the sign of the Lord's will for which I had anxiously prayed & looked. We thereupon decided to decline the Somerville & accept the Hartford call." The next morning he wrote his letters and hurried to the station to meet his brother Van who brought a final message from their father. Taylor persuaded the conductor to hold the Hartford-bound train until Van arrived, and then, after a quick consultation with his brother, he dispatched the letter of acceptance to the Fourth Congregational Church of Hartford. [45]

It was difficult for the Taylors to leave their pleasant Hopewell parsonage for an unknown city. But they had made a wise decision. Taylor's formal education at Rutgers and the seminary, it is true, had deprived him of "such academic studies as would have interpreted fellow-men and Mother Nature." Yet he had managed during his seven years at Hopewell to fill in some of the gaps. He had learned how to make religion relevant to the lives of his

[44] Graham Taylor to William J. R. Taylor, March 17, 1880; William J. R. Taylor to Graham Taylor, March 24, 25, 1880; William J. R. Taylor to Graham Taylor, March 5, 11, 15, 27, 1880, in the possession of Lea Taylor.

[45] E. L. Cooke to Graham Taylor, March 16, 1880; Taylor, Diary, March 25, 26, 1880; Taylor, *Pioneering*, p. 361.

country parishioners, and, almost without realizing it, he had begun his own transition "from a sense of individual responsibility to a community or civic consciousness."[46] By 1880 Taylor had completed his rural apprenticeship. He was ready for new contacts in an urban, industrial area and the Fourth Congregational Church of Hartford provided such an opportunity.

[46] Taylor, *Pioneering*, pp. 350, 360.

Two ⚔ *The Urban Apprenticeship*

Hartford was a pleasant, prosperous, self-satisfied town in the 1880's. Complacency, however, was not its heritage, for the town had been founded by John Steele and Thomas Hooker, religious rebels from Massachusetts, some two hundred and fifty years before. Even in the Gilded Age the city took considerable pride in its contribution to the Fundamental Orders and its protection of the colony's charter in Hartford's Charter Oak at the time Governor Andros sought to destroy it. Throughout the colonial period Hartford was a commercial center for a large and fertile hinterland, shipping down the Connecticut River crops of tobacco, oats, rye, corn, fruit, flax, and meat. In addition, gun-powder, glass, paper, and woolen textiles passed the city's piers. Until the War of 1812 stifled international trade, wealthy merchants sent their ships laden with these goods to English, Mediterranean, and West Indian ports.[1]

In the nineteenth century the industrialists usurped the power of the merchants. The decline of the port was offset by the growth of factories whose products were shipped over turnpikes and then by rail. Most of the industrial jobs went to people drawn from the New England countryside and to immigrants, particularly the Irish, who poured into Hartford during the decades just before and after the Civil War. By 1880 about half of the city's 42,000 people were foreign-born and about the same number were employed in industry. Pratt and Whitney, makers of precision tools and machinery, were Hartford's largest employers, though Samuel Colt's famous patent fire arms plant was the town's showplace of industrial efficiency. Hartford's national reputation rested upon its numerous and lucrative insurance companies. As early as the 1790's, Hartford bankers had invested in fire insurance

[1] J. Hammond Trumbull (ed.), *The Memorial History of Hartford County, Connecticut, 1633–1884* (2 vols.; Boston, 1886), I, 210–22, 322–37; *Connecticut, A Guide to Its Roads, Lore and People* ("American Guide Series," [Boston, 1938]), pp. 166–73; George L. Clark, *A History of Connecticut, Its People and Institutions* (New York, 1914), pp. 542–43.

companies and, finding it worthwhile, had tried marine insurance. During the nineteenth century continued profits plus favorable state laws facilitated development of life, accident, and liability insurance. The imposing head-quarters of these companies along Hartford's main thoroughfare contrasted sharply with the Irish slums around the old port area.[2]

Hartford was a predominantly Republican town in the 1880's. Some patriots claimed that its political conservatism stemmed directly from its historic posi-tion as the nursery of Federalism. Certainly its influential newspaper, the *Courant*, had done its best to keep Hartford sound by championing Federa-list, then Whig, and finally Republican political principles. Its editor in the 1880's was Charles Dudley Warner, co-author with Mark Twain of *The Gilded Age*, but the spokesman for Gilded Age orthodoxy in the editorial columns of the *Courant*. Hartford's loyalty was strengthened by its selection as the capital of a strongly Republican state and by the completion in January, 1880, of a spacious, new state house. Furthermore, one of the town's wealthiest and most powerful citizens, Marshall Jewell, three-time governor of the state and Grant's former Postmaster General, became chairman of the Republican National Committee in 1880.[3]

Hartford took great pride in its reputation as a philanthropic and educa-tional center. The Asylum for the Deaf and Dumb, established in 1817, was serving all of New England by the 1880's and training teachers and workers for other parts of the country. Almost as old was the Hartford Retreat for the Insane, a pioneer institution in the 1820's and still a model in the 1880's. The Orphan Asylum was one of Hartford's favorite charities, and it occupied impressive quarters of the latest design. The city's largest school was Trinity College, an Episcopalian enterprise dating back to 1824. After selling its land for the site of the state house, Trinity constructed a new campus which was finished in 1881. Not to be outdone, the Congregationalists maintained an im-portant seminary in Hartford, the Theological Institute. They too had just dedicated a new building to house their institute; in 1885 they changed the name of their school to the Hartford Theological Seminary.[4]

[2] Trumbull, *Memorial History*, I, 565–73, 499–522; Clark, *History of Connecticut*, pp. 362, 392–413; *Hartford, Conn., as a Manufacturing, Business and Commercial Cen-ter* (Hartford, 1889), pp. 153–55; Clive Day, *The Rise of Manufacturing in Connecticut, 1820–1850* ("Tercentenary Commission of the State of Connecticut Historical Publica-tions," Vol. XLIV [New Haven, 1935]), pp. 18–19; Kenneth R. Andrews, *Nook Farm, Mark Twain's Hartford Circle* (Cambridge, Mass., 1950), pp. 119–20.

[3] Trumbull, *Memorial History*, I, 605–9; Andrews, *Nook Farm*, pp. 101, 50.

[4] Trumbull, *Memorial History*, I, 525, 532–33, 425–30, 435–44; Clark, *History of Connecticut*, 472–73, 240–42, 244; William T. T. Squire, *Charities and Corrections in Connecticut* ("Tercentenary Commission of the State of Connecticut Historical Publi-cations," Vol. LVII [New Haven, 1936]), pp. 20–21, 24–26; Curtis M. Geer, *The Hartford Theological Seminary, 1834–1934* (Hartford, 1934), p. 136.

To the west of the city limits lay Nook Farm, a fashionable literary suburb enjoying its heyday in the 1870's and 1880's. Harriet Beecher Stowe had moved to Nook Farm in 1864 after her husband's retirement from Andover Seminary. Nearby lived her sister, Isabella, married to a prominent Hartford lawyer, John Hooker, a direct descendant of Thomas Hooker. Another resident was Charles Dudley Warner of the *Courant*, author of travel books, and successor to William Dean Howells as editor of *Harper's Magazine*. In 1871, Mark Twain joined them, eventually building a home there and spending the next two decades in his beloved "Heartford." The people of Nook Farm were well-to-do, but a distinct cut below such wealthy industrialists as the Jewells or the Colts. They built comfortable, rambling, Gothic houses adorned with a startling variety of gables, porches, balconies, and turrets. The architectural taste of Nook Farm sometimes caused raised eyebrows, but the literary achievement reminded the town's patriots of the glorious days of the Hartford Wits.[5]

Nor had the city forgotten that it was the battleground in the 1830's for a theological controversy which rocked all of Congregational New England. Professor Nathaniel W. Taylor of the Yale Divinity School started the trouble when he attempted to redefine the doctrine of election. He argued that a person once elected could lose his position of grace by a lapse from righteousness. Conservative theologians were horrified, for they insisted that election was irrevocable and unalterable. Bennet Tyler, a Yale graduate serving in a Congregational church in Portland, Maine, soon emerged as the leading defender of Calvinist doctrine, and he counted most of the Congregational pastors of Connecticut in his camp. In 1833 this group formed the Connecticut Pastoral Union and the next year established the Theological Institute in East Windsor to counter the insidious influence of Nathaniel Taylor in New Haven. Bennet Tyler was both president and Professor of Christian Theology in the new school, and from this vantage point he continued the quarrel until both he and Nathaniel Taylor died in 1858. Since the institute moved to Hartford in 1865, the town and its environs were naturally considered the center of Congregational conservatism.[6]

Meanwhile, Horace Bushnell, a recent graduate of the Yale Divinity School but unallied with either of the warring factions, had come to Hartford in 1833 as pastor of North Congregational Church. Although he occasionally considered leaving the ministry and was often bored by doctrinal disputes,

---

[5] Andrews, *Nook Farm*, pp. 3, 6, 8, 24, 100–1, 81, 145, 152, 155.

[6] Williston Walker, *A History of the Congregational Churches in the United States* ("American Church History," Vol. III [New York, 1916]), pp. 355–61; Geer, *Seminary*, pp. 43–50; Timothy L. Smith, *Revivalism and Social Reform in Mid-Nineteenth Century America* (New York, 1957), p. 89.

he continued to serve that church for twenty-six years. During this time, Bushnell played a leading role in the mid-nineteenth-century drive to loosen the sterner aspects of Calvinist theology. He never mastered the art of pulpit eloquence which was the goal of most of his colleagues, but his thoughtful, clearly-written sermons and books were widely read not only by Congrega-tionalists but other Protestants as well.[7]

Bushnell's revolutionary ideas unfolded slowly and logically as he con-templated the problems of his own congregation and those of upper-class Protestants in general. Concerned about the excessively emotional revivals of the 1830's, Bushnell came to the conclusion that everyday Christian con-duct in the home was a far better way to win people to Christ. So he prepared an article in 1836 in which he argued that revivals were the "most dishearten-ing impediment to the Christian minister." In 1847 he published *Views of Christian Nurture*, which developed his idea that the steady Christian nurture of children in the home and the Sunday School was preferable to sudden conversion when they reached maturity.[8]

Then Bushnell turned to a re-evaluation of the meaning of Christ's life and death. In the former he found a model that he and his contemporaries would do well to follow; in the latter, a symbol of God's love for mankind and promise that all men shared a part of God's divinity. Undaunted by the realization that this flatly contradicted Calvinist doctrine and that his "heresy" was certain to "make a little breeze," he spelled out his own views in *God in Christ* published in 1849, *Christ in Theology* in 1851, and *The Vicarious Sacrifice* in 1866. His generation's growing fascination with science and materialism threatened Christian belief of all kinds, and Bushnell met this challenge in 1858 with his *Nature and the Supernatural* in which he argued that geological evidence and technological progress supported the Christian pattern of history.[9]

Bushnell's ideas about Christian nurture, the significance of Christ's life, and the "moral influence" theory of the atonement eventually penetrated all Protestant ranks, undermining the harshest aspects of Calvinism and pointing the way to the social gospel developed by the next generation of theologians. Yet in his own day Bushnell was a prophet without honor. The Massachusetts Sunday School Society condemned *Views of Christian Nurture*, and the orthodox Calvinists viciously criticized his other publications. Be-

---

[7] Barbara M. Cross, *Horace Bushnell, Minister to a Changing America* (Chicago, 1958), pp. 29, 30; Walker, *History of Congregational Churches*, p. 365; Smith, *Revivalism and Social Reform*, pp. 28, 98, 106.

[8] Cross, *Bushnell*, p. 55, and chap. v; Theodore Munger, *Horace Bushnell, Preacher and Theologian* (Boston, 1900), chap. v.

[9] Cross, *Bushnell*, p. 94, and chaps. viii, ix; Munger, *Bushnell*, chap. xiii, xiv; Walker, *History of Congregational Churches*, pp. 365–68.

tween 1849 and 1854 there were several attempts to drive him from his pulpit, the conservatives at the Theological Institute stirring up much of this trouble. Deeply hurt, Bushnell struck back with the charge that the institute was not only behind the age, but behind all ages.[10]

Throughout his "martyrdom," however, his congregation remained loyal. When his health broke, they permitted him to travel in the South, then to Europe in 1852, Cuba in 1855, and California during 1856. While at the San Jose Mission Bushnell helped determine railroad routes and select the site for a college at Berkeley. That school became the University of California, the presidency of which he turned down in order to continue his writing. Bronchial trouble forced Bushnell's retirement from North Church in 1859, but he continued to publish until the end of his life. And he also maintained his lively interest in Hartford affairs, persuading the city to establish a thirty-five acre park in the 1850's and to locate the state house within the public park in the 1870's. Fortunately, Hartford had the grace to rename the area Bushnell Park just a few days before its creator died in 1876.[11]

Horace Bushnell left his mark upon the younger ministers of Hartford, especially upon the three Congregational preachers who dominated the scene in the 1870's, 1880's, and 1890's. Nathaniel J. Burton was the oldest of the triumvirate. He served the Fourth Congregational Church from 1857 until 1870 when he and a large number of parishioners moved to Park Congregational Church, a new structure on the edge of Bushnell Park. Edwin Pond Parker held forth for sixty years at South Congregational Church, while Joseph Twichell ministered to the Nook Farm colony from the elegant Asylum Hill Congregational Church. These three pastors were close friends of Horace Bushnell, pleased by the fatherly interest he took in their careers, and of course, sympathetic with his liberal theological views.[12]

There were other ties that held the triumvirate together. All were members of the Yale Corporation. All were intimates of Mark Twain and the Nook Farm circle, Burton and Twichell actually living in the tract. Each of them had a reputation for wit, eloquence, and geniality. They supported the conservative economic theories of their well-to-do parishioners, agreeing with Bushnell that wealth was "a reward and honor which God delights to bestow upon an upright people." Like their mentor they took a dim view of the "uncultivated and barbarous" immigrant stock pouring into the United

[10] Cross, *Bushnell*, pp. 112–17; Munger, *Bushnell*, pp. 142–52, 169–74, 183–86; Walker, *History of Congregational Churches*, pp. 368–69; Joseph H. Chandler, "Forward Movements in Theological Training. IV: The Educational Scheme at Hartford," *The Congregationalist*, LXXIX (May 10, 1894), 659.

[11] Munger, *Bushnell*, pp. 201–03, 206, 342, 350–51, 368–69; Cross, *Bushnell*, p. 135; Andrews, *Nook Farm*, pp. 26–28; Trumbull, *Memorial History*, I, 447.

[12] Trumbull, *Memorial History*, I, 389; Andrews, *Nook Farm*, pp. 4, 14, 42.

States. They had no interest in the lower classes of Hartford, for they agreed with Charles Dudley Warner that poverty was "the accompaniment of human weakness and crime." None of the three pastors ever indulged in evangelical appeals to his congregation. They preached to complacent, stolid business and professional people, "politically conservative, honest and cautious, content with a high return on their investments, and satisfied with conditions that made such returns possible." Twichell, Burton, and Parker "were of them, not above them." Their leadership in Hartford's Congregational affairs rested upon their personal and social position, not their theological acumen or spiritual fervor. They were pastors par excellence for the Gilded Age.[13]

II

Taylor was understandably apprehensive about moving to Hartford, "a city noted as a Theological battle ground and for the . . . independence and differences of its clergy." Moreover, he was worried about leaving the security of his family's Dutch Reformed Church for the more liberal, independent atmosphere of Congregationalism. Not until 1871 had the National Council of Congregational Churches been established and it took another twelve years before the Council agreed upon a statement of belief. Yet even after adopting the Creed of 1883, each congregation had complete freedom to govern itself and to decide matters of doctrine. Taylor knew about the noisy Congregational quarrels of past decades. He too had felt Bushnell's liberal influence, but not to the extent that it had moulded Twichell, Burton, and Parker. Their rejection of so many Calvinst doctrines seemed to Taylor to endanger the very foundations of faith. Consequently, the newcomer to Congregationalism was to find his closest ideological friends not among the triumvirate of fellow pastors, but rather at the conservative Theological Institute.[14]

Before Taylor could assume his responsibilities at the Fourth Church, his fitness had to be determined by the Congregational pastors of Hartford. It was with considerable anxiety that Taylor appeared before the Council on May 14, 1880. Much to his relief, however, "most of the questioning was done by those who thought as I did," and their inquiries "were all kind, considerate & respectful." That same day they installed Taylor as pastor of the Fourth Church in a ceremony which he felt was marked by a warm Christian spirit. Yet had he been more familiar with the terrain of Hartford's theological

[13] Cross, *Bushnell*, pp. 45, 40; Andrews, *Nook Farm*, 42–51, 128–29.
[14] Taylor, Journal, May 14, 1880, Taylor, *Pioneering*, 361; Walker, *History of Congregational Churches*, pp. 409–10, 413–14; Taylor, *Pioneering*, p. 379.

battle ground, he would have detected some un-Christian barbs in the address by Dr. William L. Gage of Pearl Street Congregational Church:

> We do not in Hartford much like the expressions "liberal religion" and "liberal Christianity," because we think that these are cant terms and have an ungracious flavor of denominationalism; but as far as the theory itself is concerned . . . you are to live in an atmosphere of perfect spiritual freedom. . . . You may expect to be heard with a pure and discriminating intelligence. Mere scholasticism, mere traditional phrases, are not much relished in this solid commercial capital; good hard practical sense and theology made plain is what most of our men and women crave.[15]

Knowing that it would require hard work to establish a reputation for eloquence in Hartford, Taylor labored over his first sermon. He was, of course, pleased to read in the *Evening Post* that his maiden effort had displayed "broad and solid scholarship" and "a gracefulness of composition that will be sure to command attention in a city where polished utterance is the rule rather than the exception in the pulpit." But Taylor was not content to rest upon these laurels. He intended to take advantage of Hartford's cultural opportunities to increase his own "intellectual equipment." Undoubtedly his good friend, Dr. Hartranft, Professor of Biblical and Ecclesiastical History at the institute, encouraged him in these plans. Almost immediately upon arrival Taylor arranged for private tutoring in German so that he could pursue more technical biblical studies. He wrote to his father, "I have the German mania bad! So that I am up & at it before breakfast daily and have Dr. Hartranft's German tutor to teach me twice a week." Moreover he registered for weekly elocution and voice lessons at the institute. Taylor was convinced that without this instruction, "piety of life and teaching" would count for little in the fierce clerical competition.[16]

He had no sooner launched his program of cultural improvement, however, than he realized that his church and parish must claim the "right of way." At first glance his church seemed to have more of a history than a future. Organized by Congregationalists as The Free Church in 1832, it had shocked public opinion by refusing to rent or sell its pews. Six years later it had taken the name Fourth Congregational Church, created the Ecclesiastical Society to handle its financial matters, and succumbed to the orthodox practice of selling and renting pews to support the work of the church. This was the

[15] Taylor, Journal, May 14, 1880; Taylor, Diary, May 14, 1880; *Evening Post* (Hartford), May 16, 1880.

[16] *Evening Post* (Hartford), May 16, 1880; Taylor, *Pioneering*, p. 362; Graham Taylor to William J. R. Taylor, September 14, 1883, in the possession of Lea Taylor; Taylor, Journal, July 11, 1880.

only surrender to orthodoxy, however, for the congregation in later years stirred many a controversy by its championship of the abolitionist cause, then the temperance movement, and eventually woman suffrage.[17]

There did not seem to be much of a future for the Fourth Church in the 1880's. Their edifice, built in 1850 and purposely located on Main Street near Trumbull to be near the center of the town, was described at the time of its dedication as "one of the principal ornaments of the city." Yet as Hartford expanded and the foreign-born swelled the population, the wealthier classes moved away from Main Street. In time the advent of trolleys and street-cars made possible a mass exodus of the middle classes to the outskirts of Hartford and facilitated the growth of suburbs such as Nook Farm. Most of the Congregational pastors, like those of other Protestant denominations, followed their flock. In 1870, for example, Nathaniel Burton and the wealthiest members of Fourth Church withdrew to join Bushnell's North Church, which in 1866 had migrated to the edge of town to become Park Congregational Church. At the same time, according to a Fourth Church historian, other "influential families were dismissed to join the newly organized Windsor Avenue Church. The dismissal . . . of so many, representing to a large degree the Church's social and financial strength, left the Fourth Church weak, but not discouraged."[18]

Hartford's Fourth Congregational Church was typical of Protestant churches left in the center of other industrial cities. They were little more than shells. For years they had ignored the new families moving into their neighborhoods, and quite naturally the immigrants and lower classes of native-born Americans scorned the disinterested churches. Taylor found the spire of the Fourth Church rising "above a district covering one-quarter of the city's area into which three-quarters of its poor and delinquent people were densely crowded." Yet he seldom drew more than 45 or 50 people for Sunday services in a church designed to hold 1,200. There even seemed to be some doubt about these faithful few. When Taylor was offered the Fourth Church position, he was told to reply immediately lest "members of the congregation may . . . be tempted to drift away from us because of uncertainty as to a pastor." Needless to say, the other Congregational ministers of Hartford considered the Fourth Church a hopeless cause.[19]

---

[17] Taylor, *Pioneering*, p. 362; *Memorial Manual of the Fourth Congregational Church* (Hartford, 1882), pp. 1–28; Fourth Congregational Church, *Seventy-Five Years and the Present Outlook 1832–1907* (Hartford, 1907), pp. 2–4; Graham Taylor, "The Fourth Congregational Church," in Trumbull, *Memorial History*, I, 391–94.

[18] *Memorial Manual of the Fourth Congregational Church*, pp. 22, 28–29; Chester D. Hartranft to Graham Taylor, March 5, 1880; Fourth Congregational Church, *Seventy-Five Years*, p. 4.

[19] Taylor, *Pioneering*, pp. 362–63; J. B. Pierce to Graham Taylor, March 1, 1880.

Taylor was undaunted by these hard facts. He took the church roll, a list of 542 names, and went in search of his members. Many of them were "the Lord's poor": firemen and policemen, mechanics and day laborers, small merchants, and families dwelling in the crowded tenements. Though Taylor and his wife spent many evenings sifting through the church rolls, they "could identify but 218, leaving 324 lost & straying."[20]

To hold the families they already had and to attract others back into the fold, Taylor promptly revived the Sunday school and organized adult Bible classes. Later he started a Saturday afternoon discussion group for children under fourteen, which he called the Young Disciples. After the regular Tuesday evening prayer meetings, Taylor conducted the Pastor's Normal Class for instruction in higher religious studies. And in time a Young Men's Meeting, the Ladies' Sewing Society, and the Young People's Union became vital parts of the Fourth Church.[21]

To increase church membership Taylor scheduled special prayer meetings. On one occasion he discussed "What becomes of God's preached word?" from Luke 8:18, and he followed this up with a sermon on "doing the truth." He also invited well-known evangelists to the Fourth Church, but the results were not always as fruitful as Taylor hoped. During a special week of prayer in January, 1881, he observed that "the meeting did not drag, neither did it have wings . . . the time seems not yet." Two years later an Ohio evangelist drew 150 people to an evening service but complained to Taylor of the "total lack of responsiveness and apparent coldness." Reporting this incident to his father, Taylor said the charge is "partly *so, mostly* 'New Eng.' and *some* Hartford with which places he is unfamiliar." Most of Hartford's other Congregational pastors looked askance at the Fourth Church's evangelical activity. One referred to it as "the 'Dry-Goods Store' policy or running the 'Church trade.'" At meetings of the Hartford Congregational Association they let Taylor know how they felt. "From the doleful yet sarcastic parodys [*sic*]" of prayer meetings, said Taylor, one would suppose that they fell "within the realms of purgatory." In his diary Taylor expressed his deep resentment at his colleagues' "light & trifling conception of this sacred & tender feature of our church service."[22]

[20] Taylor, Diary, July 14, 1880; Taylor, *Pioneering*, p. 374; Taylor, Diary, August 30, 1880.

[21] *Memorial Manual of the Fourth Congregational Church*, p. 48.

[22] Taylor, Journal, January, April, 1881; Graham Taylor to William J. R. Taylor, February 20, March 6, 1883, in the possession of Lea Taylor; Talyor, Diary, April 4, 1881. After Taylor moved to Hartford, he found it impossible to make daily or even weekly entries in his Journal. Sometimes he had to summarize the events of an entire month in one long entry.

Yet Taylor presevered. He told his father he was determined "to raise a voice in God's name in the densest and most neglected district . . . of the city." Within a few years he did increase both church attendance and membership. By 1883, he was drawing about 400 people to the Sunday morning services, some of whom came from outside the parish. In July, 1883 two families left Nathaniel J. Burton's Park Church to join the Fourth Congregational Church. "One brought a letter of dismissal," Taylor confided to his father, but "the other has had hard work to get it." Dr. Burton "very harshly demanded the reason" for the request, and when told that the person's "spiritual interests demanded the change" he put them off "until too late to be received by us."[23]

After reviving the social and spiritual life of the church, Taylor turned his attention to the $8,500 debt. In October, 1881, he took "*soundings* of the disposition of the church to raise its debt by its 50th Anniversary" which was coming in January, 1882. He met with "little encouragement" and "much doubt" from everyone "except . . . the two gentlemen who held the debt." Nonetheless, Taylor appointed a debt committee and he himself made the first pledge of $50. By December the committee had secured $4,000 from the Church members. The pastor then appealed to other Congregational churches in the community and collected an additional $2,825. On January 10, the day of the Jubilee Celebration, Taylor publicly announced that the long-standing debt had been lifted and privately noted that it was "*the* success of my ministry & of my life so far." The leaders of the congregation were so grateful for Taylor's courageous action "at a time when the Society was in the slough of despond," that they raised his salary to $2,500 a year.[24]

Two years later the pastor persuaded the Ecclesiastical Society to modernize the interior of the Fourth Church. They had the walls painted, new carpets laid, pews revarnished, and a "nicely carved & finished reading desk" installed in place of the "marble pulpit, which had served its day and generation." The energetic Taylor now hoped that "Being free from debt & having an attractive building," the church would "realize a benefit from it." He confidently expected "to gather many from the gospel-neglected part of the city in our vicinity . . . to travel with us on our journey Heavenward."[25]

[23] Graham Taylor to William J. R. Taylor, March 23, July 3, 1883, in the possession of Lea Taylor.

[24] Taylor, Journal, October 31, week of December 17–25, 1881, January 10, 1882; Taylor, Diary, January 10, 1882; Resolution passed by the Ecclesiastical Society, March 13, 1882, pasted in Journal, March, 1882; Ecclesiastical Society, Record Book (manuscript), March 13, 1882, Fourth Congregational Church, Hartford, Conn.

[25] Fourth Congregational Church, Records (manuscript), September 14, 1884, Connecticut State Library, Hartford, Conn.

III

It was appropriate that Taylor should seek to make the Fourth Church a center of missionary work, for it had played a prominent role in past revivals. Indeed, the Free Church had been brought into existence by a dedicated band of Congregationalists who asked themselves "whether it was not the duty of some to leave the well-filled houses of worship and form themselves into a New Church" to provide "the means of Grace for the neglected." The church had sponsored successful revivals in 1851 and 1852 when Charles G. Finney, president of Oberlin College, stirred all of Hartford, and again in 1877 and 1878 when Dwight L. Moody and Ira D. Sankey came to town. Though interest had tapered off by 1880, Taylor experimented with outdoor services on the church steps and in Bushnell Park, and he conducted lively prayer meetings at the Warburton Mission, a tenement-district chapel.[26]

He knew, however, that a more strenuous effort was necessary to spread the gospel in Hartford. Other cities by the 1880's were making imaginative approaches to the "unchurched masses." The Young Men's and Young Women's Christian Associations offered fully-developed social and religious programs to the people of the slums. For more than a decade city missions, especially in Boston and New York, had been providing for the material needs of the destitute, then guiding their physical and spiritual rehabilitation. This idea spread rapidly to other industrial cities where some of the missions were run by particular denominations or specific churches. But by 1880 at least thirty of these missions were non-sectarian. Still another development of the late 1870's was the Protestant "institutional church," which worked in a blighted area of a city to improve the economic status of parishioners, provide social outlets for them, and minister to their souls as well. A more recent experiment in spreading the gospel to industrial workers was the Salvation Army. Organized by Catherine and William Booth in England in 1878, its American branches led well-publicized, evangelistic crusades into the slums. Despite the sharp criticism of the American clergy, the Army awakened religious interest among the lower classes and drew the attention of more fortunate Americans to the ramifications of urban change.[27]

[26] Fourth Congregational Church, *Seventy-Five Years*, pp. 1, 3–5; *Memorial Manual of the Fourth Congregational Church*, pp. 17, 25, 31; Taylor, *Pioneering*, p. 363; First Congregational Church, *Manual of the First Church, 1884* (Hartford, 1885), 45; Taylor, "The Fourth Congregational Church," in Trumbull, *Memorial History*, I, 391–94.

[27] Henry F. May, *Protestant Churches and Industrial America* (New York, 1949), pp. 121–22; Aaron I. Abell, *The Urban Impact on American Protestantism, 1865–1900* (Cambridge, Mass., 1943), pp. 27–46, 118–21, 137–43; Robert H. Bremner, *From the Depths: The Discovery of Poverty in the United States* (New York, 1956), pp. 28–29, 57–59.

What spurred Taylor to action was a canvass of Hartford by the Connecticut Bible Society in 1883. This survey revealed no less than 674 families without any church affiliation, and it convinced the Fourth Church pastor that "the duty of the hour" was "democratic evangelism" on a systematic, citywide basis. Knowing that neither he nor his church could undertake this task alone, Taylor looked for support from a natural ally, the City Missionary Society. Established during the aftermath of the Finney revival, the Society made small loans to the poor, supplied the destitute with food and clothing, and kept open a small chapel on Morgan Street. It was, however, unwilling to engage in a large-scale evangelistic program. Neither the Y.M.C.A. nor the Y.W.C.A. in Hartford gave Taylor any encouragement. So in November, 1883, he spoke to a gathering of Protestant ministers on "The Religious Needs of Hartford" and proposed interdenominational support for city-wide mission work. They turned him down.[28]

Still resolute, Taylor approached the Congregational pastors. He laid his mission proposal before Edwin Pond Parker, but "failed to make him understand." In the privacy of his diary, the young minister castigated his colleague as "unsympathetic, suspicious, & unkind & unfair. The less we have to do with each other the better for us both." Fortunately, however, the others were willing to support Taylor's project. In February, 1884 the Congregational Pastors' Union formed a Pastors' Mission to supervise and finance the work. They appointed Taylor as superintendent, Joseph Twichell as treasurer, and promised to raised $1,000 to pay a full-time helper. The Fourth Church was designated as headquarters "because of its central location, the city missionary spirit which founded it and characterized its work for half a century, and because of its disposition to do much of the practical work involved, as well as to receive and care for all who preferred no other church." Greatly encouraged by this support, Taylor promptly hired Henry J. Gillette, the man who conducted the Connecticut Bible Society's canvass, as the permanent evangelist.[29]

Taylor and Gillette laid out an ambitious program of personal calls, concentrating at first on an area at the center of Hartford which covered less than one-tenth of the entire town, yet housed nearly half the total population. This same region, they quickly learned, sheltered 90 per cent of the brothels and 83 per cent of the saloons. Using as references the families and individuals who came to the Warburton and Morgan Street chapels, Gillette soon made

[28] Taylor, *Pioneering*, p. 363; Hartford City Missionary Society, *The Annual Report of the City Missionary to the City Missionary Society of Hartford, 1877–78* (Hartford, 1878); Trumbull, *Memorial History*, I, 537–39; Taylor, Diary, November 12, 1883.

[29] Taylor, Diary, January 30, 1884; *Five Years' Growth, A Sketch of Evangelistic Work Centering at the Fourth Church* (Hartford, 1889), pp. 7–8; Graham Taylor, "The Hartford Pastors' Mission," *The Congregationalist*, XXXIX (April 28, 1887), 2.

contact with hundreds of other tenement-dwellers whom he urged to come to chapel prayer meetings or attend regular church services. Later he called on men in the shops, at the hospitals, the police station, the jail, and even the state prison in nearby Wethersfield. He soon averaged three thousand calls a year, and these visits greatly increased church attendance in down-town Hartford, adding about three hundred members to the Fourth Church alone. In addition to the calls, both men kept regular office hours at the Fourth Church where the "poor and the troubled" could "bring their burdens to have them shared." Much of this time-consuming work was personal consultation, but frequently the superintendent and the evangelist were asked to locate new jobs, find better living quarters, help alcoholics, aid criminals at the city court, and even rescue young girls from procurers.[30]

Not satisfied with his own knowledge of missionary work or with what he had read of other experiments, Taylor wanted to travel and observe first-hand. In the spring of 1884 he conferred in New York with Henry Schauffler of the Congregational Home Missionary Society, attended a meeting of evangelists at Cooper Union, and examined the work of William S. Rainsford at St. George's Episcopal Church, soon to become the country's model institutional church. The next year a group of Taylor's friends helped finance a more extensive trip. In Cincinnati he attended the Inter-Denominational Congress arranged by Josiah Strong to discuss urbanism, socialism, alienation of working classes from the church, missionary efforts to win them back, and the need for religious censuses. Taylor noted in his diary that he liked the speeches of Strong, Richard T. Ely, Washington Gladden, and Lyman Abbott. Moving to Chicago, he studied the work of the Y.M.C.A. and the missionary activities of the Congregational churches, and he watched with some surprise the massive experiment of feeding destitute men on Sundays at the Adelphi Theater while an evangelist preached through a loudspeaker. The high point of the entire journey, however, was a tour of Dwight L. Moody's famous Chicago Avenue Tabernacle. Stopping in Detroit and Cleveland to study their Charity Organization Societies, Taylor reached home in late December, 1885, convinced that in his own work he was "on the right track, needing only to go on."[31]

[30] *Sketch of Evangelistic Work at the Fourth Church*, pp. 6, 8–12, 33; Taylor, *Pioneering*, pp. 367–74.

[31] Taylor, Diary, April 6, 7, 1884, December 6, 15, 22, 1885; Taylor, Journal, December 22, 1885. Strong's Cincinnati meeting led to the revitalization of the Evangelical Alliance, of which he became general secretary in 1886. Abell, *Urban Impact*, 90; Charles Howard Hopkins, *The Rise of the Social Gospel in American Protestantism, 1865–1915* ("Yale Studies in Religious Education," Vol. XIV [New Haven, 1940]), p. 113.

To expand the mission program in Hartford, Taylor and Gillette had to recruit and train more volunteers. They turned to the Seminary for these workers in the fall of 1886. Perhaps Taylor acted upon the suggestion of the Convention of Christian Workers that theological schools should provide such practical experience for their students. At any rate, the needs of city evangelism and theological training neatly coincided, and the Hartford seminarians volunteered in large numbers. Taylor and Gillette allowed them to choose the type of work which they preferred — prayer meetings, Bible classes, personal visitation, or consultation with the fallen. The arrangement proved satisfactory, was repeated in 1887, and was added to the curriculum when Taylor joined the seminary faculty in 1888.[32]

Members of the Fourth Church contributed a great deal to the success of the evangelistic work. Taylor had prepared them for their role in welcoming the new people to church fellowship, and regular members mixed freely with newcomers at the Sunday evening prayer meetings. About half the worshipers gathered afterwards in the chapel for Scripture readings, testimonials by the newcomers to the power of Christ to save, and an opportunity to confer with either Taylor or Gillette. As word spread of these highly successful Sunday evening meetings at the Fourth Church, the more fastidious Hartford citizens began calling it "the church for ex-convicts."[33]

Taylor and Gillette, however, were anxious to hold not only the ex-convicts, but also the ex-gamblers, reformed alcoholics, and others whom they had brought to the church. What they needed was some type of social organization for these men, most of whom lacked family ties. At Moody's Chicago Avenue Tabernacle, Taylor had studied closely a religious brotherhood known as the Yoke Fellows' Band, and he decided to use this as his model at the Fourth Church. In December, 1886, the pastor and eleven other men formed a Yoke Fellows' Band and pledged themselves to "serve our Saviour by helping each other to be Christians and bringing our fellow men to Him." Every Sunday morning Taylor spent an hour with the Band encouraging them to tell of "the week's experience in resisting temptation." At 10:45 A.M. the whole group entered the church in a body for the morning services. In addition, the Yoke Fellows took responsibility for greeting people at the evening

[32] Taylor, Journal, September 29, 1886; Abell, *Urban Impact*, pp. 95–96. Rev. A. F. Schauffler supervised the work of Union Theological Seminary students in New York's city missions beginning in 1887. These students, unlike Taylor's volunteers, were paid small sums for their services. In September, 1887, Taylor visited Union Seminary and observed "the new system adopted there." Taylor, Diary, September 23, 1887; Abell, *Urban Impact*, pp. 230–31.

[33] *Sketch of Evangelistic Work at the Fourth Church*, pp. 30, 31, 15; Taylor, *Pioneering*, p. 365; Abell, *Urban Impact*, p. 152.

prayer meetings, and they helped Gillette and Taylor follow up a number of cases.[34]

The organization increased so rapidly that it soon outgrew its cramped quarters in the Fourth Church. In the spring of 1887 the Ecclesiastical Society agreed to build a wing containing a clubroom for the Band plus a kitchen, conference room, and new office for the pastor. The first three $100 contributions to the construction fund came from an ex-gambler, a former alcoholic, and the "saintly widow" of Horace Bushnell. She had been watching Taylor's work with quiet approval and wanted now to help him "even up the odds against the Lord in saving a homeless man by building a place for him to go." Of the total cost of $8,000, more than one-quarter came from Fourth Church members. The remainder was contributed by other Congregational churches and the Hartford community, where Taylor admittedly used the Yoke Fellows' Band as a "lever . . . to raise the funds." The group proudly kept their new clubhouse open every evening. On holidays they planned special entertainments and the ladies of the Fourth Church always cooked Thanksgiving and Christmas dinners for them.[35]

If church members contributed nobly to the evangelistic work, so too did the Taylor family. The pastor was always on duty. He considered it routine while preparing a sermon to be "interrupted by only twelve calls & . . . a summons by mail to attempt a reconciliation of two sisters." Another manuscript had to be put aside in the early hours of the morning when Taylor received a note scrawled on the back of a torn envelope by a blackslider "at 55 Spruce St. — in the saloon — I have Fallen again & Want your help." Since Mrs. Taylor agreed that their home and family life ought to be shared with others, she never objected to feeding and clothing the strange assortment of people her husband brought home. She took an active part in the women's work at the church even though her family responsibilities increased with the birth of two more children. A second daughter, Lea, was born on June 24, 1883, and the last child, Katharine, arrived on the same date in 1888. Occasionally, but not often, Taylor and his wife found time for concerts and choral programs. The pastor's only exercise was walking with the Yoke Fellows, for he found that even a quick game of baseball or football at Sunday school picnics had the unhappy result of "staving me up in the joints."[36]

---

[34] *Sketch of Evangelistic Work at the Fourth Church*, pp. 17–18; Taylor, Diary, December 19, 1886; *Constitution of the Yoke Fellows' Band of the Fourth Church, Hartford, Conn.* (Hartford, 1890); *Hartford Pastors' Mission* (no date), p. 7.

[35] Taylor, *Pioneering*, pp. 363–64; Graham Taylor to Henry Gillette, November, 1911(?); Taylor, Journal, October 31, 1887; *Sketch of Evangelistic Work at the Fourth Church*, p. 23.

[36] Taylor, Diary, June 18, 1887; W. H. Crawford to Graham Taylor (no date); Taylor, *Pioneering*, p. 384; Taylor, Diary, June 30, 1886.

Despite their many new acquaintances in Hartford, both the Taylors detected a certain reserve on the part of most New Englanders. Taylor believed that living near the Fourth Church identified them so closely with the neighborhood that they were cut off from other social contacts. In time, however, they did become close friends of Mrs. Bushnell and her daughter, Mrs. Hillyer. Taylor found a kindred spirit in Charles E. Stowe, pastor of the Windsor Avenue Congregational Church and son of Harriet Beecher and Calvin Stowe. With three other younger ministers Taylor and Stowe formed the Pentagon, an informal social club including wives, which met in the members' homes to discuss topics ranging from the Decalogue to Henry George. Through Charles Stowe, Taylor was once invited to Nook Farm to meet "the old Prof" and "his celebrated wife," both "*genuine* people of sterling spiritual & intellectual qualities." [37]

A large part of the New England chill which the Taylors felt in Hartford came from the older Congregational ministers. The triumvirate never warmed up to the Taylors. In 1885, Leah wanted to entertain the members of the Pastors' Mission and their wives, and she had carefully written and addressed the invitations. But before mailing them Taylor discovered quite accidentally that his colleagues would have "none of our hospitality." This incident "showed me too roughly how little they really cared for us personally." Contrasting Hartford with Hopewell, Taylor was aware of "how hungry my heart feels here." [38]

He soon found that his colleagues cared even less for his evangelical work. At the first annual meeting of the Pastors' Mission Taylor and Gillette made a thorough report and three volunteers spoke briefly. "Then silence, unbroken except by a few strong expressions by Dr. Burton of the 'massiveness' of the work. . . . No word of appreciation or sympathy escaped the others. . . . My heart was overwhelmed by their coldness and lack of sympathy." The following year the superintendent and city evangelist "encountered trying treatment from Dr. P[arker]." Not until 1887, three years after the Pastors' Mission had been formed, did Taylor enjoy "the first pleasant and satisfactory meeting." [39]

Taylor was not successful in winning over the Hartford Liturgical Club, an organization composed of all the city's clergy. In January, 1883, Taylor addressed them on "The Evangelistic Mission of the Church" but failed to arouse any interest. Four years later he spoke again to the Hartford Liturgical Club. Describing this meeting for his father, Taylor wrote:

[37] Taylor, *Pioneering*, p. 374; Taylor, Journal, December 19, 1881, December 29, 1884; Taylor, Diary, June 4, 1883.

[38] Taylor, Diary, February 9, 1885.

[39] Taylor, Journal, February 11, 1885, February 16, 1886; Taylor, Diary, February 1, 1887.

I read an Essay on "The Evangelization of the World" in which I took the common ground of the missionary obligation of the Church and Ministry to the heathen abroad and at home, but carefully guarding 'Christian Nurture' vs. spiritual culture. I was amazed to hear every man but one openly disavow such obligation. . . . One man wished "all missionaries hauled in for 100 years until the church be united." Another would await the *Perfection* of ministries, ordinances, gifts, etc. before attempting more. Another deprecated the Church's "going down to the Slums." . . . Burton hedged shamefully — even declaring that our Lord was not of "the build of a 6th ward man" — referring to *the* mission ward of the city. . . . The trouble was that I struck him heavily in my essay by the declaration that we wanted ministers "who would make *men* the chief end of their culture and not culture the chief end of man." Such a discussion I never heard in that club. It was such an *earthly* subject as to disturb its heavenly-mindedness and arouse old Adam.

The only man who was man enough to stand by me was my good neighbor Nichols of Xt. P. C. [Christ's Episcopal Church]. . . . he said he was "ashamed of them all" and proceeded to lay the old codgers out very effectively and back me up in my work outside and *inside* my church, the latter they thought I must *neglect*. This emboldened me to use my right to reply to the same purpose — and such a sitting down as they got from us two youngest members seemed to amaze them. . . . Attempts at explanations followed and very cordial farewells and greetings since. But it makes one heart sick and *mad* too. *Don't let this get out.* It's in *"Club Confidence"* but none of these things move me.[40]

The Hartford clergy were not impressed, but Taylor's missionary work drew acclaim elsewhere. In 1884, he read a paper on the evangelical church before the Congregational Conference of Connecticut. He asserted that the church must grow "both from without and within, by accretion and expansion, through evangelization and nurture." Neither aspect of the work could be neglected, but he felt that emphasis at the moment should be placed on missionary work in the cities among the numerous non-churchgoers. Taylor joined the Convention of Christian Workers, an organization of city missionaries established in 1886, and he addressed them in 1887 in New York on the topic "Do We Need Churches or Missions, or Both, in City Evangelization?"[41]

[40] Taylor, Diary, January 29, 1883; Graham Taylor to William J. R. Taylor, January, 1887.

[41] Connecticut Congregational Churches, Minutes of the General Association, 1884; Taylor, Diary, November 12, 1884; Graham Taylor, "An Evangelical Church," *The Religious Herald*, December 25, 1884; Abell, *Urban Impact*, pp. 95, 176–77; Graham Taylor, "Do We Need Churches or Missions, or Both, in City Evangelization?" in Convention of Christian Workers, *Proceedings* (1887), 202; Taylor, Diary, September 26, 1887. Taylor claimed that the idea of establishing a national convention of Christian workers came from John C. Collins at a Warburton Chapel meeting in Hartford in

That same year Taylor described his own work in an article entitled "The Hartford Pastors' Mission" which was published in *The Congregationalist.* Shortly afterward he received a letter from Samuel Lane Loomis of Brooklyn. Loomis was preparing the manuscript of a book, *Modern Cities and Their Religious Problems,* and he found Taylor's article so valuable that he asked permission "to publish the whole of it as an appendix." Taylor assented, for he agreed with Loomis that although much had been written about urban religious problems, most of it was "afloat in papers, magazines, pamphlets" and should be collected in book form. During these same years Taylor worked with Rector William Nichols to establish a system of investigating alms applicants and secure a Charity Organization Society in Hartford. In addition, he was twice elected chaplain of the state Senate and he served in the same capacity at the state prison in Wethersfield.[42]

The young minister's energy and success in the Fourth Church pastorate attracted the attention of other churches. He turned down an offer from a church in Massachusetts in 1884 and was flattered to learn in 1886 that Josiah Strong, who was leaving a Congregational church in Cincinnati for a position with the Evangelical Alliance, had recommended Taylor as his replacement. The next year, while addressing an evangelistic conference in Philadelphia, Taylor saw John Wanamaker and the leaders of Bethany Church make a "dead set" for him. As he was considering their offer in February, 1888, Taylor learned that the Hartford Theological Seminary had elected him Professor of Practical Theology. He later claimed that this was the greatest surprise of his life, but considering his close relationship with the student volunteers, his position as a seminary trustee, and his friendship with Hartranft who had just been named president of the Seminary, Taylor's appointment was logical.[43]

What Taylor really wanted to do was to accept the position at the seminary yet retain his pastorate so that he could use the Fourth Church as a laboratory for his students. He would relinquish most of his salary, thereby enabling the Ecclesiastical Society to hire an associate pastor. The deacons of the Fourth Church warmly urged him to "remain in Hartford — in relation to both Seminary and Church if possible." Mrs. Bushnell paid him a "motherly call" and "Guardian-Angel-like" counseled him to join the seminary even though it had been her husband's bitter foe. She gave Taylor twelve copies of *Chris-*

1884. Graham Taylor, "The Christian Workers' Convention," *The Congregationalist,* LXXV (November 20, 1890), 412.

[42] Graham Taylor, "The Hartford Pastors' Mission," *The Congregationalist,* XXXIX (April 28, 1887), p. 2; Samuel Lane Loomis to Graham Taylor, June 20, 25, 1887, in the possession of Lea Taylor.

[43] Taylor, Diary, November 5, 1886, November 7, 1887; Taylor, *Pioneering,* p. 378.

tian Nurture which she wanted him to have for his classes but which she refused to present directly to the seminary library.[44]

The Congregational pastors, however, strongly objected to Taylor's proposed "dual relation" with the seminary and the Fourth Church. Parker warned Taylor that it was not in accord with New England custom. A few days later the annual meeting of the Pastors' Mission provided an ideal opportunity "for a combined attack," and "the painfullest scene" of Taylor's ministry "was enacted in a weary wearing hour." His careful explanations were "referred to as 'fixed up,' which language I felt bound to challenge." When his colleagues bluntly threatened to withhold financial support from his missionary work, Taylor "thanked them for what they had done" and showed them out of his study.[45]

Word spread quickly of this "rumpus" in the Pastors' Mission and Taylor's friends rushed to his defense. Daniel R. Howe, prominent stockbroker and financial supporter of the Warburton Mission, thanked "God that there are some ministers of His blessed Gospel who notwithstanding 'their culture & training,' *can* clasp hands with an ex-convict, & *can* lead men from the gutter to the throne." As for the members of the Pastors' Mission, he continued, "I abominate ministerial dudes." A woman volunteer told Taylor that his critics were trying to revive their old grudge against the seminary. They charged that Taylor's use of student volunteers was proof that he had been "aiming at a professorship." Thus when the offer actually came and Taylor proposed the dual relationship, his enemies could sit back and say, " 'There — that is what he has been driving at — control at both ends of the city.' "[46]

The opposition of the Pastors' Mission merely strengthened Taylor's resolve to hold both positions. The day after the rumpus he went to the seminary where he was "Royally received & trusted wholly & supported right loyally in my stand against the attempt to drive me from the Seminary or church." The faculty voted to accept Taylor's dual appointment, leaving up to him "the whole adjustment of time and toil between the two." They even offered to match the funds withdrawn by the Pastors' Mission. So the beleaguered minister "thanked G and took courage."[47]

[44] Taylor, Journal, February 6, 1888; Taylor, Diary, February 16, 1888; Taylor, *Pioneering*, pp. 379–80.

[45] Taylor, Journal, February 20, 22, 1888; Taylor, Diary, February 22, 1888.

[46] Daniel R. Howe to Graham Taylor, February 28, 1888; Elizabeth R. Hyde to Graham Taylor, February 23, 1888.

[47] Taylor, Diary, February 23, 1888; Taylor, Journal February 23, 1888. The Pastors' Mission disbanded when Taylor accepted the professorship. Some financial support continued to come from other Congregational churches, but after 1888 it was given to the Fourth Church Mission. Joseph H. Twichell to Graham Taylor, March 15, 1888.

IV

Taylor approached his new responsibilities with some trepidation. He fretted about his lack of preparation for the professorship and the fact that he had no technical training for teaching. It was true that his fifteen years in the ministry had been unusually busy ones, with very little time for scholarship. In the Hopewell parish his work with the neglected tenant-farmers had cut into his ambitious plans for reading and independent study. He went to Hartford, he later said, "to get a chance to be more scholarly. But I soon had to exchange my German tutor for 'the cave of Adullam' in which I have ever since lived." When forced to choose between the needs of his parishioners and preparation for an academic career, Taylor had always chosen action rather than scholarship. Heavy demands upon his time had forced him to abandon the German lessons and study of higher criticism. Yet he kept up with current periodicals, read some history, and sampled the works of the English Christian Socialists.[48]

At the same time Taylor knew that he was called to the Seminary because he had "done something" and was needed "to teach other men to do so." In the early 1880's, he said, no man with his academic background and active interest in missionary work "would have been thought of for this position." Moreover, President Hartranft was talking of overhauling the curriculum to make it more practical and introducing a new era of adjustment at the seminary. This helped to offset some of Taylor's misgivings.[49]

The professor-elect spent most of the summer reorganizing the department of practical theology, outlining courses, and drafting his inaugural address. He was relatively free of administrative work at the Fourth Church, for he had hired a recent seminary graduate, Henry Kelsey, as associate pastor. The day before school opened Taylor confessed "a sort of 'eve of battle' feeling — held between expectancy and uncertainty." The semester had barely started when Taylor contracted a severe case of typhoid fever. In what he thought was a death-bed statement, the patient told his wife that "this overwhelming disas-

---

[48] Taylor, *Pioneering*, pp. 378, 385; Graham Taylor to Lea and Katharine Taylor, September 6, 1911, in the possession of Lea Taylor. Before appointing Taylor to the faculty, the seminary trustees asked some of the alumni for their opinions. Henry Kelsey's reply was typical: "Mr. Taylor has some admirable qualifications" and "I should like exceedingly to see him with all his energy in the Faculty — But I question a little his qualification on the side of scholarship. He would certainly stir in his pupils a desire to preach the gospel to sinners, & send them out filled to do it." Henry H. Kelsey to A. C. Thompson, January 24, 1888, Archives, Case Memorial Library, Hartford Seminary Foundation, Hartford, Conn.

[49] Taylor, *Pioneering*, p. 378; Taylor, Diary, May 10, 1888; Chester D. Hartranft, *Some Thoughts on the Scope of Theology and Theological Education* (Hartford, 1888).

ter is due wholly to my own fault and is a swift execution against one who has never given himself the bodily rest fully demanded for him by his God." Taylor recovered, resumed his full teaching schedule at the seminary in January, 1889, and promptly forgot about his resolution not to overwork.[50]

As Professor of Practical Theology, Taylor came into contact with every student at the seminary. In the first year they took his introductory course and the following year his course on "Pastoral Functions." As seniors they spent four hours a week with him studying "Preaching, Evangelistics, Pastoral Care, Pastoral Superintendance, including Church Polity, Fellowship, Economics and Christian Sociology." In addition to this heavy teaching load, Taylor supervised the compulsory field work. He tried to give each man a taste of Sunday school instruction, evangelistic efforts and charity work.[51]

In his inaugural, "The Practical Training Needed for the Ministry of To-Day," Taylor proposed some bold innovations. Warning his listeners that he would "speak without reserve of the very definite convictions which I bring with me from the pastorate and the city-mission field," he went on to enumerate the changes he planned to make in the department of practical theology. First of all, there must be a closer relationship "between the Seminary and the life of the day" if the graduates were to minister "to the living." Biblical scholarship must be not only scholastic and scientific but practical as well. An academic knowledge of Christian doctrine must be accompanied by "a working knowledge of Christianity itself." Practice in applied Christianity was "the need of the hour." Taylor promised to train "men who *know* not only, but who know *how*" to use their knowledge.[52]

Then he pointedly told his audience that the pulpit was "no longer the only fulcrum of the Church's power." Other agencies — Sunday schools, the Christian Endeavor movement, the Evangelistic Missions, temperance societies, the Young Men's and Young Women's Christian Associations, and charity organizations — "these too are leverages" which demand trained leadership. Taylor considered it an obligation of his department to prepare students for responsible positions with all these Christian agencies.[53]

[50] Taylor, Diary, September 19, 1888; Statement dictated by Graham Taylor to Leah Taylor, November 7, 1888, in the possession of Lea Taylor. Taylor thought his speedy recovery from typhoid fever was due to the "doctor & nurse who *fed me* all through & did not 'starve it out.'" Graham Taylor to Mr. and Mrs. William J. R. Taylor, November 27, 1888, in the possession of Lea Taylor.

[51] Hartford Theological Seminary, *Catalogue, 1888–89*; Hartford Theological Seminary, *Annual Register, 1889–90*.

[52] Graham Taylor, *The Practical Training Needed for the Ministry of To-Day* ("Hartford Seminary Publications," No. 2, [Hartford, 1888]), pp. 6, 3–4, 9, 10.

[53] Taylor, *Practical Training*, p. 12.

Furthermore, he would try to interpret the tide of modern life that was moving "toward the interdependence of each with all."

> The channel through which life is now sweeping is less individualistic than sociological in its formation. All human life and interests, industrial and political, intellectual and spiritual . . . contribute toward the pull of this social gravity. Apart from these influences, not only is society not to be understood, but the individual may not be intelligently treated. . . .
>
> Heredity and environment are . . . prime factors in the problems of personal and social salvation. Without them, neither the cause nor the cure of pauperism, intemperance, and crime can be apprehended. Sanitary, social, and spiritual conditions are the moulds of personal and public character. However much we plead for repentance and the better choice, they condition the exercise and the issue of decision.

From these social phenomena Taylor saw emerging a new science of human relations. The "Church and her ministry and their training-schools must answer whether it is to be the science of godless or of Christian society." If the church wants the new science to be Christian, Taylor warned, "she must formulate a Christian Sociology, and train her leaders and people in it." This then was Taylor's ultimate goal as Professor of Practical Theology — to help formulate and teach the new science of Christian Sociology.[54]

Taylor and Francis G. Peabody of the Harvard Divinity School and William Jewett Tucker of Andover Seminary were the pioneer teachers of Christian sociology in America. Since 1880, Peabody had taught "The Ethics of the Social Question," a course popular with Harvard College students as well as theologians. He used case studies in an inductive approach to social ethics, and his scholars soon dubbed the novel course "Drainage, Drunkenness, and Divorce." Actually that title might better have been applied to Tucker's lectures at Andover, for he organized his material topically, discussing labor, crime, pauperism, and other problems. Professor of Sacred Rhetoric at Andover from 1879 until 1893, Tucker "smuggled his earliest lectures on social Christianity into his course on pastoral theology. In time, however, he added elective courses on "Social Economics," the outlines of which were published in *The Andover Review* during 1889 and 1890.[55]

Taylor was influenced, of course, by what he knew of Peabody's and Tucker's work, but during his first year of teaching all he heard were "faint

[54] Taylor, *Practical Training*, p. 15, 16, 17.

[55] Hopkins, *Social Gospel*, pp. 167–68; May, *Protestant Churches*, pp. 194–95; Taylor, *Pioneering*, p. 393; Abell, *Urban Impact*, pp. 232–34. For a fuller discussion of these early courses see: James Dombrowski, *The Early Days of Christian Socialism in America* (New York, 1936), chap. v; William Jewett Tucker, *My Generation, An Autobiographical Interpretation* (Boston, 1919), pp. 161, 169–77; Frank J. Bruno, *Trends in Social Work, 1874–1956* (New York, 1957), pp. 133–34.

echoes" from Andover and Harvard. He had no syllabi from these "or any other classrooms to guide me in the preparation of my own initial courses." There were no suitable textbooks either. Taylor had hoped to use Herbert Spencer's *The Study of Sociology* (1873), but he found it a disappointment, "more of a foil against which to strike . . . than a help to constructive procedure." As a result, Taylor drew upon a wide variety of books and articles for his instruction in Christian sociology.[56]

Fortunately, by the 1880's, there was a growing volume of literature that dealt with social and religious problems. Taylor was familiar with the work and the publications of Charles Loring Brace, especially his *Gesta Christi: or A History of Humane Progress under Christianity* (1882). Josiah Strong, who left a Congregational pulpit to head the Evangelical Alliance, wrote the influential *Our Country, its Possible Future and its Present Crisis* in 1885. Lyman Abbott's editorship of the *Christian Union* made that magazine a forum for social Christianity in the 1880's. Meantime Richard T. Ely, an economist at the University of Wisconsin, published *Social Aspects of Christianity and Other Essays* (1889), a volume which, along with his numerous articles, helped develop what Strong called "a Christian school of political economy." The many books by Washington Gladden were all rich in suggestions about how to apply Christianity to social problems. *Working People and their Employers* (1876) and *Applied Christianity: The Moral Aspects of Social Questions* (1886) were particularly useful in Taylor's early years of teaching.[57]

For expounding a liberal theological point of view Taylor found the sermons of Horace Bushnell, Henry Ward Beecher, and Phillips Brooks helpful. Richard S. Storrs's *The Divine Origin of Christianity Indicated by its Historical Results* (1884) was also of value. In addition, Taylor had his students read John R. Seeley's *Ecce Homo: A Survey of the Life and Work of Jesus Christ* (1866) because it "humanized the story of the gospels" and James B. Mosley's *Ruling Ideas in Early Ages* (1878). Most important of all was William H. Fremantle's *The World as the Subject of Redemption* (1882). These lectures by an English cleric exerted a powerful influence on many British

[56] Taylor, *Pioneering*, pp. 392, 393, 396. Taylor never mentioned, and hence apparently did not know, J. H. W. Stuckenberg's *Christian Sociology* (1880) or John Bascom's *Sociology* (1887). Stuckenberg's book foreshadowed the development of the social gospel, but it received only scant notice and most social gospel leaders in the late 1880's and 1890's were unaware of it. Hopkins, *Social Gospel*, p. 111.

[57] Taylor, Diary and Journal, *passim*; Taylor, *Pioneering*, pp. 389 n., 394; Sidney Fine, *Laissez Faire and the General-Welfare State* (Ann Arbor, 1956), p. 201; Ira V. Brown, *Lyman Abbott, Christian Evolutionist: A Study in Religious Liberalism* (Cambridge, Mass., 1953), pp. 100–12. In 1893 the *Christian Union* became the *Outlook* and its emphasis shifted from religion to public affairs and literary criticism. Brown, *Lyman Abbott*, pp. 77–78.

and American theologians, primarily because they broadened the scope of Christian obligation. Taylor was not the only one who discovered in Fremantle's book a new concept of salvation. It taught him that

> No less, but not only, is the one soul to be sought and saved, but the world itself. And the world as the divinely constituted order of human life and relationships is to be won back to what it was made and meant to be — the Kingdom of the Father. Never again was it to be misinterpreted as wholly evil, fitted for destruction. . . . Emancipated from that final fear, which had beclouded the horizon of hope, the shadow was lifted from my teaching. . . . Not to "leave the poor, old stranded wreck and pull for the shore" with one soul at a time, but to be world-savers, Kingdom-builders, I was to teach my students.[58]

Two other vitally important sources for Taylor's instruction in Christian sociology were the Bible and his own pastoral experiences. He was convinced that "the freshest, most original, most complete and living text-book on Practical Theology" was the Bible. And in showing students how to apply the social teachings of the Scriptures, he drew heavily upon his own efforts in rural Hopewell and "the hardpan of my city-center field" in Hartford. He once referred to his missionary experiences as "the *sources* of Practical Theology." There is no doubt that his classroom discussions of these sources left a vivid impression on the students. One remembered Taylor as

> the most irregular lecturer academically that I ever knew. . . . he was never on time. . . . he would come in with a rush, put down his papers . . . and then he would begin:
> "Now let's see, we had started in the concatenation of homilectic material. That makes me think, when I was shaving, Mike Sauer [member of the Yoke Fellows' Band] came over, bringing a drunk, and then I had to talk with him," and that was the last we ever heard about concatenation, and the coordinates that we must establish between just supposed sermon points, but we learned something that we never could have learned in any other way.[59]

Teaching was not Taylor's only interest during his years at the seminary. He had enthusiastically approved Hartranft's plan for a balanced diet of teaching, research, and publication for all members of the faculty. Thus, during 1889 and 1890, Taylor and Clark S. Beardslee produced a series of eight

[58] Taylor, Diary and Journal, *passim*; Taylor, *Pioneering*, pp. 389 n., 388–89; Shailer Mathews, "The Development of Social Christianity in America," in G. B. Smith (ed.), *Religious Thought in the Last Quarter-Century* (Chicago, 1927), pp. 230–33.

[59] Taylor, *Pioneering*, pp. 385, 389 n.; Taylor, *Practical Training*, p. 11; Graham Taylor to Chester D. Hartranft, June 11, 1890, Archives, Case Memorial Library, Hartford Seminary Foundation; Ozora S. Davis, in "Addresses at Dinner in Honor of Dr. Graham Taylor, May 27, 1930 (manuscript).

pamphlets entitled *Studies in the English Bible and Suggestions about Methods of Christian Work*.[60] Taylor wrote the latter part of each booklet, and he used that material for a series of public lectures at the seminary. Later he repeated these in Springfield, Massachusetts, at the School for Christian Workers, founded in 1885 by his friend David Allen Reed. In addition, Taylor contributed several articles and book reviews to *The Hartford Seminary Record*, a quarterly magazine launched in October of 1890.

Taylor's most significant publication, however, during his four years at the seminary was *A Religious Census of the City of Hartford*. The idea did not originate with him, for Y.M.C.A. secretaries since the 1860's had been making surveys of the communities in which they worked and a religious census had been taken in New Haven in 1880. But Taylor's census was more comprehensive than any of the earlier ones. The statistics were gathered in the summer of 1889 by six seminarians and three people from the Connecticut Bible Society. They covered the entire city, asking questions about nationality, religious denomination, church affiliation and attendance, and Sunday school participation. The published *Census* showed that more than half of the 48,000 people in Hartford were foreign-born. The Catholics with five churches claimed about 40 per cent of the population; the Congregationalists with ten churches ran a poor second with only 17 per cent. Fully one-tenth of the people questioned said they attended no church at all.[61]

The *Census* then listed the destructive forces in the city, such as saloons and houses of prostitution. Counteracting them were philanthropic and preventive agencies, like the Christian Endeavor Societies, Warburton Chapel and Morgan Street Mission, the Yoke Fellows' Band, the Good Will Club, temperance groups, and the Y.M.C.A. and Y.W.C.A. After describing the work of these organizations Taylor warned that his religious survey by no means exhausted the fact-finding that needed to be done in Hartford. He urged the churches to co-operate in more ambitious investigations of the causes of poverty, unemployment, illiteracy, intemperance, and vice. Indeed, "any facts that affect the social welfare of man should come within the scope" of church-supported surveys, for it was all part of the new "science of Christian society."

> Its field is the world, including all classes and conditions of men from all nationalities. Its work is to investigate the conditions of social and

[60] Clark S. Beardslee and Graham Taylor, *Studies in the English Bible and Suggestions about Methods of Christian Work* ("Hartford Seminary Publications," Nos. 1–8 [Hartford, December, 1889–July, 1890]).

[61] Bremner, *From the Depths*, pp. 42, 60; Hopkins, *Social Gospel*, p. 275; Charles Howard Hopkins, *The History of the Y.M.C.A. in North America* (New York, 1951), pp. 189–90; [Graham Taylor], *A Religious Census of the City of Hartford Made in the Year 1889* ("Hartford Seminary Publications," No. 10 [Hartford, 1890]), pp. 12, 13, 17.

personal life, discover the causes of suffering and the sources of inharmonious relations. When Christian sociology has done all this, it will be more possible to adjust differences, and harmonize the varying elements by applying the principles of Christianity.[62]

If Taylor had plans for other publications, he put them aside in the fall of 1890 when Dr. Hartranft fell seriously ill. For Taylor found himself acting as liaison between the ailing president and the Board of Trustees on the one hand, and the various faculty committees on the other. His anomalous position was clarified in the spring of 1891 when he was named Acting President, a post he held until September. During these months Taylor followed Hartranft's broad policies for modernizing the curriculum. In line with what was being done at other schools, Hartford Theological Seminary introduced the elective principle during 1890–91. Taylor sought to raise academic standards by dropping "all non-college-graduates" and "all disaffected men," and he felt satisfied that the class which he selected for admission in 1891 was the best the seminary had had in many years. With relief he surrendered his administrative responsibilities in the fall of that year. As he did so he resolved "to have as little to do with general institutional affairs as possible, to accept none but the most important outside appointments, and to devote myself to my department, its class-room work and general preparatory study, with so much church work as I could do in addition."[63]

Yet Taylor found it impossible to confine his interest and energy to the seminary and the Fourth Church. He became a trustee of Reed's School for Christian Workers in Springfield, he wrote Hartford dispatches under the name of "Delftshaven" for the *Christian Intelligencer* and the *Congregationalist*, and he was instrumental in organizing the Convention of Christian Workers' Hartford meeting in 1890. During 1889 and 1890 he was active in the local National Club which propagated the utopian socialism of Edward Bellamy. At one meeting he introduced Laurence Gronlund and at another he was quoted as saying that "in the broad meaning of the terms, Nationalism and Christianity are synonymous." Taylor spoke often to alumni of the seminary, to Y.M.C.A. audiences, and to colleges and theological schools in the east. In 1891 he delivered the commencement address at Rutgers, choosing as his subject "The Place of Sociology in Practical Education."[64]

---

[62] Taylor, *A Religious Census*, pp. 19, 20, 22, 31, 39, 40.

[63] *Hartford Seminary Record*, I (April, 1891), 173–74; Abell, *Urban Impact*, pp. 228–30; Taylor, Journal, September 17, 1891.

[64] *The Nationalist*, II (June, 1890), 276; *The Nationalist*, II (July, 1890), 343; *Hartford Seminary Record*, II (October, 1891), 36; Taylor, Diary and Journal, *passim*.

Moreover, Taylor participated in conventions of the American Missionary Association and the Evangelical Alliance. At the triennial meetings of the National Council of Congregational Churches, in 1886, 1889, and again in 1892, he served on the committee for city evangelization. By 1892, then, Taylor's achievements at the seminary and the Fourth Church in Hartford and his numerous public explanations of his work had won for him "an almost national reputation as an expert on Social Christianity."[65]

V

In April, 1892, the Chicago Theological Seminary, the leading Congregational school in the middle west, invited Taylor to address a distinguished gathering of its graduates. The trustees had recently been notified of a $100,000 bequest contingent upon raising $350,000 during the next two years. The chairman of the finance committee, Professor Samuel Ives Curtiss, claimed he could get the money if the seminary would establish a department of Christian sociology headed by Graham Taylor. Apparently the alumni liked Curtiss' strategy and Taylor's speech, for the whole matter was discussed informally with Taylor at the time. On the way back to Hartford he wrote in his diary: "Xtn Sociology is God's door to all that can make the remainder of my life most effectual. Henceforth I seek that Kingdom of God first . . . But whither? E[ast] or W[est]?" Three months later Taylor had to answer the question, for Chicago Theological Seminary offered him $3,000 a year as Professor of Christian Sociology and the English Bible and chairman of the first department of Christian sociology in any seminary in the United States.[66]

Once again Taylor found himself in a "painful dilemma." His Hartford Seminary colleagues, the members of the Fourth Church, and many individuals in the community — "from insurance company presidents to city firemen" — pleaded with him to stay. They stressed the loss to the seminary if he should depart, pointed out the need for further evangelistic work, and voiced their incredulity that anyone would voluntarily leave Hartford for the boisterous, crude city of Chicago. Professor Beardslee, with whom Taylor had

[65] National Council of Congregational Churches, *Minutes of the National Council of Congregational Churches, 1886, 1889, 1892* (Council, 1886, 1889, 1892); "Four Institutional Churches. II: The Fourth Church, Hartford," *The Congregationalist*, LXXVIII (April 20, 1893), 619.

[66] Ozora S. Davis, "History of Chicago Theological Seminary" (manuscript), Hammond Library, Chicago Theological Seminary, Chicago, Ill.; Chicago Theological Seminary, *Minutes of the Triennial Convention 1894* (Chicago, 1894), pp. 20–21; Taylor, Diary, April 20, 1892; Samuel Ives Curtiss to Graham Taylor, July 5, 1892; Hopkins, *Social Gospel*, p. 167; Abell, *Urban Impact*, pp. 236–37.

collaborated on publications, told him, "you are so *vitally* related to Dr. H[artranft] & to Hfd. and Hfd. Sem. as to put the question . . . beyond your reach. . . . *You*, of all men, *can* not leave Hfd. without bringing to H'f'd Sem. unmeasured disaster." Hartranft gently reminded Taylor that he had risen to his "present elevation, I will not say because of us, but while you were among us." And he cautioned his protégé that the "East is not exhausted, the West is as yet flabby & puffy. . . . You are moulding things here which you yourself started; there you will enter into other men's labors . . . you will only be an appendage to the Harper kite. . . . From your cathedra here, you can speak to the West & help it more than if you were a part of the seething & chaotic mess." [67]

Strong arguments in favor of the West came from Professor Curtiss, who bombarded Taylor with letters and telegrams throughout July. Feeling that his whole financial campaign would be jeopardized if Taylor refused, Curtiss came to Connecticut in August determined to stay until he got an acceptance. Finding that the Taylors had gone to Fishers Island, New York, for vacation, he followed them and camped across the bay. Calling daily, he read by instalments a one-hundred page manuscript explaining why Taylor should go west. "The compass of duty . . . points unerringly to Chicago," he insisted, "anyone who maintains the contrary has never been released from his shell." In addition, Curtiss thoughtfully drafted tentative letters of resignation for Taylor to send to the Hartford Seminary and the Fourth Church.[68]

By mid-August Taylor had resolved his dilemma. The Fourth Church, he knew, would continue its missionary work under Kelsey's able management. And he did not believe, he told the trustees, that he was essential to the vital interests of Hartford Seminary's future development. Their flattering counter-offer to raise his salary to $3,500 and rename his department Practical Theology and Christian Sociology failed to hold him. Chicago Theological Seminary had won its new professor with the promise of "unrestricted liberty" to "study, teach, and exemplify the application of our common Christianity to . . . social conditions." For six long weeks Taylor had carefully balanced

---

[67] Taylor, *Pioneering*, p. 381; Clark Beardslee to Graham Taylor, July 20, 1892; Chester D. Hartranft to Graham Taylor [1892]. Taylor had no fears that the West was "flabby & puffy" or a "seething & chaotic mess." In June of 1892 he lectured in Wyoming and wrote to his wife, "If it is the wild and wooly West, the fibre of the wool is almost as fine as any woven into our Eastern fabrics, and has less cold cotton in it. The West is all I thought it would be . . . and that you know is a great deal." Graham Taylor to Leah Taylor, June 27, 1892, in the possession of Lea Taylor.

[68] Davis, "History of Chicago Theological Seminary"; Taylor, *Pioneering*, p. 382; Samuel Ives Curtiss to Graham Taylor, July 27, 1892.

"future opportunities with present obligation, until at last they merged in my acceptance of the call of the West to pioneer on its social frontier." [69]

Taylor was ready for the new challenge. His twelve years in Hartford had closed the gaps in his formal education. He had traveled a long way theologically since his ordination in 1873. Just how far can be measured in a diary entry which he made on his fortieth birthday: "Renewedly . . . convinced that to see up toward God I must continue to look down into man — and to see down into men, I must look up to God." Learning from his pastoral experiences in Hopewell and Hartford and reflecting upon his wide reading during these years, Taylor had at last "grounded" his "faith and hope in the innate capacity of fellow-men to be restored to the likeness of their Creator." [70]

As Taylor became more interested in social Christianity, he grew critical of the laissez faire theory of government. He was "increasingly impressed with the fact that the way of making a living was often incompatible with the 'Way of Life.'" It had been true in Hopewell, where the "odds were stacked against the tenantry," and in Hartford too, where the vital connection between character and environment was brought to his attention almost every day. These experiences convinced him that "the evangelization of industrial and social conditions is necessary to the evangelization of the soul, still more of the world." Writing many years later, Taylor accurately summarized what he had learned from his rural and urban apprenticeships:

> As men came up from the pitfalls dug by themselves and by others, they taught me, on the one hand, that the fallen could rise, and on the other hand, that the conditions under which they fell could and should be changed so as to make it easier to live right and harder to go wrong in every community.[71]

So long as Taylor remained in Hartford his only weapon in the struggle would be missionary work with individuals and their families. Any "collective efforts by either the church or community to reduce or eliminate the odds" against Christian living were unthinkable. For Taylor knew that the "hard-boiled individualists . . . in control of city & Seminary" would never agree to "anything suspiciously challenging to laissez faire economic orthodoxy." Chicago, however, had promised him a free hand to experiment with family

[69] Graham Taylor to the Secretary of the Board of Trustees, Hartford Theological Seminary, August 16, 1892, Archives, Case Memorial Library, Hartford Seminary Foundation; Hartford Theological Seminary, Board of Trustees, Minutes, July 20, 1892, Case Memorial Library, Hartford Seminary Foundation; Taylor, *Pioneering*, pp. 381, 383.

[70] Taylor, Diary, May 2, 1891; Taylor, *Pioneering*, p. 366.

[71] Taylor, *Pioneering*, pp. 374, 358, 372, 109–10, 366.

and neighborhood rehabilitation. As head of a department of Christian sociology he could devote all of his time to the study, teaching, and application
of the principles of Christianity, to "the fulfillment of this purpose which
possessses my whole life." It was, he felt, "an opportunity . . . along exactly
the lines of work in which I am most interested and for which all my past
experience proves me to be best adapted." Thus, in the summer of 1892,
Graham Taylor responded to still another "new adventure of faith." [72]

[72] Taylor, *Pioneering*, p. 374; Graham Taylor to William R. Taylor, January 5, 1930;
Taylor, *Pioneering*, p. 381; Graham Taylor to Waldo S. Pratt, August 11, 1892, Archives,
Case Memorial Library, Hartford Seminary Foundation; Taylor, *Pioneering*, p. 384.

Three ❧ *The Challenge of Chicago*

The Taylors were only one of many thousands of families drawn to Chicago in the 1890's. The city was a "lodestone," said the English traveler George W. Steevens. It attracted the "enterprise and commercial talent of two hemispheres." By 1890 the midwestern metropolis was the country's second most important manufacturing center and the leading railroad center. Its population of more than a million people made it the second largest city in the United States and the fourth in the world.[1]

Chicago had always been ambitious. When it was scarcely three decades old and had only 100,000 residents, its numerous rail connections and hostelries helped it attract the Republican nominating convention of 1860. Ten years later the town had a population of 300,000. Its rail and water routes brought coal, iron, grain, and livestock, and provided access to markets throughout the country. Grain elevators, flour mills, stockyards, and meat-packing plants, warehouses, distilleries, and small manufacturing concerns pumped lifeblood into the rapidly growing city. Chicago's famous and infamous theaters, bars, gambling houses, and hotels catered to a steady flow of transients. Indeed so great was its fame that Bismarck told a visitor from the United States in 1870, "I wish I could go to America if only to see that Chicago."[2]

But the Great Fire of October, 1871, nearly dashed the city's hopes. That summer had been unusually hot and dry throughout the Middle West. Chicago ought to have been on guard, for most of its hurried construction in past decades had been of wood. Frame factories and houses were the rule, and the main streets had wooden paving blocks and plank sidewalks. Yet

[1] George W. Steevens, *The Land of the Dollar*, in Bessie Louise Pierce (ed.), *As Others See Chicago: Impressions of Visitors, 1673–1933* (Chicago, 1933), p. 400; Bessie Louise Pierce, *A History of Chicago*, Vol. III: *The Rise of a Modern City, 1871–1893* (New York, 1957), pp. 20, 64; Lloyd Lewis and Henry J. Smith, *Chicago: The History of Its Reputation* (New York, 1929), pp. 171, 173.

[2] Emmett Dedmon, *Fabulous Chicago* (New York, 1953), pp. 96, 122; Herman Kogan and Lloyd Wendt, *Chicago: A Pictorial History* (New York, 1958), pp. 102, 103, 106; Lewis and Smith, *Chicago*, p. 113.

Chicagoans paid little heed. They were confident that their efficient fire department with the aid of the new pumping equipment at the north side waterworks could control any blaze within the Garden City. On October 8 and 9, they found out differently.[3]

On Sunday evening, October 8, 1871, fire broke out in a barn behind the house of Patrick O'Leary on the west side. The fire department missed the O'Leary barn by more than a mile, and when it finally reached deKoven Street, its equipment broke down. With more than an hour's start, the flames spread through modest west side houses, stables, and factories. Spurred on by a southwesterly wind, the fire jumped the south branch of the Chicago River, and licked away at the downtown district. By Monday it had destroyed the heart of the city and crossed the north branch of the river to consume the waterworks and the north side residential area. Thousands of homeless, panic-stricken people made their way to the lake front. When sparks showered down on them even there, they waded out into Lake Michigan to watch their city burn. By Tuesday a slackening wind and brief periods of rain brought the holocaust to an end.[4]

The enormity of the disaster shocked the whole world. One hundred thousand people, one-third of the population, were homeless. Some 500 were dead or missing and scores of others injured. About three and one-half square miles had been destroyed, and few of the 18,000 buildings within the area were left standing. The property loss was estimated at $200 million, one-third of the wealth of Chicago. Competitors predicted that the cocky Queen of the Lakes would never rise from her ashes. "Chicago will never be the Carthage of old," said a New Orleans newspaper. Its hopes, "once so bright and cloudless, will be to the end marred and blackened by the smoke of its fiery fate."[5]

Quite different was Chicago's reaction. The embers were still hot when The Chicago *Tribune* announced that "the people of this once beautiful city have resolved that CHICAGO SHALL RISE AGAIN." Almost immediately the Relief and Aid Society took over distribution of food and clothing and the assignment of temporary shelter. Prompt and generous contributions, hauled free by the railroads from places as distant as New York, kept Chicago alive during the winter of 1871–72. Close to $5 million in relief funds from

[3] Lewis and Smith, *Chicago*, p. 124; Dedmon, *Fabulous Chicago*, p. 96; Kogan and Wendt, *Chicago*, p. 115; Pierce, *History of Chicago*, III, 3–4; Robert Cromie, *The Great Chicago Fire* (New York, 1958), chap. ii.

[4] Pierce, *History of Chicago*, III, 4–5; Dedmon, *Fabulous Chicago*, pp. 97–107; Lewis and Smith, *Chicago*, pp. 124–30; Kogan and Wendt, *Chicago*, pp. 115–24; Cromie, *Chicago Fire*, chaps. iii–xix.

[5] Pierce, *History of Chicago*, III, 5–6, 12–13; Dedmon, *Fabulous Chicago*, p. 107; Wayne Andrews, *Battle for Chicago* (New York, 1946), p. 58; Kogan and Wendt, *Chicago*, pp. 124–25; Lewis and Smith, *Chicago*, pp. 130–31, 136.

this country and abroad stimulated the enormous task of rebuilding. Within a week after the fire some 6,000 temporary structures were up. And the stock-yards and packing plants, some of the rolling-mills and grain elevators, and about 600 manufacturing concerns, all untouched by the fire, were back in full operation. On the first anniversary of the fire, Chicago's volume of trade actually exceeded that of October, 1871. On the second anniversary, the city ignored the panic of 1873 and held an Inter-State Industrial Exposition in its new glass and iron Crystal Palace on Michigan Avenue. A British journalist, contemplating Chicago's incredible recovery and incomparable bravado, decided that the city was the "concentrated essence of Americanism."[6]

Chicago's industrial and commercial potential, were, of course, only temporarily impeded by the catastrophe. That the Queen of the Lakes was able to recover her scepter surprised and disconcerted her rivals. But the city's industrial and commercial expansion in the next two decades provided an even greater shock. Chicago's well-known booster, Deacon Bross, touring the east in the winter of 1871 and 1872, had predicted this.

> Go to Chicago now. Young men, hurry there! Old men, send your sons! You will never again have such a chance to make money. . . . With few exceptions all can now start even in the race for fame and fortune. The fire has leveled nearly all distinctions. . . .
> I tell you within five years Chicago's business houses will be rebuilt, and by the year 1900 the new Chicago will boast a population of a million souls. You ask me why? Because I know the Northwest and the vast resources of its broad acres. I know that the location of Chicago makes her the center of this wealthy region and the market for all its products. What Chicago has been in the past, she must become in the future and a hundredfold more. She has only to wait a few short years for the sure development of her "manifest destiny."[7]

Though few people believed him at the time, Bross was correct. Fed by an influx of American migrants and European immigrants, the city claimed "a population of a million souls," not in 1900 as Bross had expected but in 1890. Moreover, Chicago became during the 1870's and 1880's "Hog Butcher for the World, Tool Maker, Stacker of Wheat, Player with Railroads and the Nation's Freight Handler."[8]

One of the few major industries untouched by the fire was meat-packing. In 1865, the mile-square Union Stock Yard had been laid out to the southwest of the city limits, and there a large portion of the country's livestock was slaughtered and prepared for market. Significant changes were introduced in

---

[6] Pierce, *History of Chicago*, III, 10, 8–9, 17, 19; Dedmon, *Fabulous Chicago*, p. 108; Lewis and Smith, *Chicago*, pp. 133–34; Kogan and Wendt, *Chicago*, pp. 131–32, 139.

[7] Quoted in Lewis and Smith, *Chicago*, pp. 137–38.

[8] Carl Sandburg, *Chicago Poems* (New York, 1916), p. 3.

the 1870's and 1880's by the "Big Three of the Yards," Nelson Morris, a German immigrant, and American-born Gustavus Swift and Philip Armour. They developed more efficient methods of dressing beef and pork, utilized the refrigerator car to carry fresh meat to distant markets, and found ways to turn packing plant waste into glue, fertilizer, and soap. In the 1880's, Chicago's packers built subsidiary plants in the Middle West to control the source of supply and they began selling their meat in the European market. Two decades after the fire, stock yard profits had jumped from $20 million a year to almost $200 million. By the 1890's Chicago was indeed "Hog Butcher for the world." [9]

The city's role as "Tool Maker" depended upon her access to iron ore and soft coal brought by rail and ship to the blast furnaces along the Calumet River and the south branch of the Chicago River. Chicago steel fed innumerable local manufacturers. Cyrus McCormick's reaper works, for example, mushroomed in size until by 1890 it was the giant American Harvester Company. Local industrialists produced railroad cars, locomotives, wheels, and the rails themselves. George Pullman's Palace Car Company was one of the most lucrative and widely-publicized of these concerns. Typical of Chicago's many foundries was the Crane Brothers' Manufacturing Company, which expanded from copper and brass in the 1860's to the production of valves, pipes, pumps, hydraulic elevators, and plumbing fixtures. By the end of the century Chicago was a leading "Tool Maker" for the American market, and her manufacturers were reaching out for a share of the European market as well. [10]

Instrumental in making Chicago a merchandising center for the Middle West was Marshall Field. Less than forty-eight hours after the fire he was selling salvaged bolts of cloth in a horse barn on the south side. In 1885, Henry Hobson Richardson built for Marshall Field and Company a seven-story granite structure covering an entire block of downtown Chicago. As his profits soared, Field invested in banking, real estate, railroads, and city traction. His influence in community affairs was extensive, and when he died in 1905 he left a fortune of $120 million. Chicago also had the first mail order house, Montgomery Ward. Established the year after the fire, it was widely patronized by the rural midwest. The largest mail order house was Sears, Roebuck and Company, founded in the 1890's by Julius Rosenwald, a native of Springfield, Illinois. Drawn to Chicago by the rich merchandising opportunities, he

[9] Pierce, *History of Chicago*, III, chap. iv; Lewis and Smith, *Chicago*, pp. 143–46.
[10] Pierce, *History of Chicago*, III, 154–64; Andrews, *Battle for Chicago*, pp. 162–63.

also amassed a sizable fortune and played an influential role in civic and philanthropic affairs.[11]

It was a varied labor force which performed Chicago's miracle of rebuilding and industrial expansion. The 300,000 residents at the time of the fire were augmented by thousands of Americans who left the countryside for the richer material and intellectual life that Chicago offered. Most of these people came from the old northwest, though some 14,000 Negroes were listed in the 1890 census. During the two decades after the fire some 250,000 immigrants poured into the city. By 1890, 40 per cent of the population were foreign-born and another 38 per cent were the offspring of foreign-born parents. Thus nearly four-fifths of Chicago's 1,100,000 people were of foreign parentage by 1890. Most numerous were the Germans, who found employment in breweries, distilleries, and factories. Next came the Irish, many of whom took construction jobs in the 1870's and helped rebuild Chicago. The lumberyards and stockyards absorbed hundreds of Gaelic newcomers, while the Democratic party in Chicago provided jobs for others. By 1890 the Scandinavians were almost as large a group as the Irish, and there were scatterings of Czechs, Bohemians, Poles, and Slovaks. During the 1890's Russian Jews sought refuge in Chicago, and that decade saw a sharp upsurge in the number of Italian immigrants. Though they constituted only 1 per cent of the foreign-born in 1890, they established both a "Little Sicily" and a "Little Italy."[12]

This population growth from 300,000 in 1870 to 1,700,000 by 1900 created huge problems for the municipal authorities.[13] The city council, composed of two aldermen from each ward and presided over by the mayor, exercised legislative power, but it generally delegated administration to boards and commissions. In the decades after the Civil War, Chicago's most difficult problems were garbage and sewage disposal, water supply, and public transportation.

Chicago did not master the municipal science of garbage disposal until well into the twentieth century. Her experiments in the 1880's and 1890's were uniformly unsuccessful. For a time garbage was hauled by the railroads out to the prairies. Later teamsters were hired to take both garbage and trash to vacant lots, or low-lying dumps, or uneven streets that needed filling. When the smell from these open pits became unbearable, the council built an in-

---

[11] Lewis and Smith, *Chicago*, pp. 175–76; Pierce, *History of Chicago*, III, 176–82; Andrews, *Battle for Chicago*, pp. 84, 120, 122, 123, 219; Ernest Poole, *Giants Gone: Men Who Made Chicago* (New York, 1943), chaps. viii and xv.

[12] Pierce, *History of Chicago*, III, 20–50; Lewis and Smith, *Chicago*, pp. 171–73, 229; *Eleventh Census of the United States: 1890* (Washington, 1892), I, clxix, 454.

[13] *Twelfth Census of the United States: 1900* (Washington, 1901), I, lxxiv.

efficient furnace in 1887 which consumed itself two years later. During the next decade the council studied the problem and kept employing teamsters to dump garbage in defenseless wards with the connivance of their aldermen. Collections were so irregular that a great deal of refuse was thrown into the Chicago River. While the World's Fair buildings were going up in 1892, the civic-minded *Daily News* kept calling attention to the disgraceful "surface sewer, which Chicagoans call the river. . . . Sewage and garbage of all kinds, animals more or less decomposed make it reek with stench. Standing on any of the bridges the odor is sickening."[14]

Sewage disposal and water supply problems were closely related, for Chicago both deposited its liquid wastes into and drew its drinking water from Lake Michigan. The city's sewers emptied into the north and south branches of the Chicago River, which in turn flowed slowly into the lake. Drinking water was so frequently polluted that the council built a powerful pumping station in 1867 with a crib far enough out to get clear water, free for the first time of sand and minnows. Though this installation was destroyed by the fire, it was soon rebuilt and other pumping stations were added in the 1880's and 1890's as the city grew.[15]

The council had decided, meantime, to utilize the Illinois and Michigan Canal for sewage disposal. This canal, opened in 1848 and connecting the Chicago with the Illinois and Mississippi Rivers, was almost immediately eclipsed as a commercial artery by the railroads. Starting in 1866, however, Chicago spent $3 million dredging and deepening the canal in the hope that gravity would make the sluggish Chicago River reverse its flow and carry the city's sewage down the Illinois Valley. For a brief time after its opening in 1871 the canal did serve this purpose. But Chicago's increasing population and growing volume of waste soon overstrained the gravity flow and not even an elaborate system of pumps could keep the water moving. Furthermore, heavy rains would send a "steady stream of sewage and filth . . . rushing with a velocity of fully five miles an hour into the lake," whence it was "brought back again in diluted form and used for drinking purposes." Finally, in 1892, Chicago began construction of a new Sanitary and Ship Canal, paralleling the old one, but deep and wide enough to accommodate commercial vessels and to provide drainage for a population of 3 million. Over the violent objections of St. Louis, the Drainage Canal went into operation in 1900 and Chicagoans hailed it as "one of the greatest engineering works of recent times."[16]

[14] *Daily News* (Chicago), May 7, 1892; Pierce, *History of Chicago*, III, 320–21.

[15] Pierce, *History of Chicago*, III, 309; Lewis and Smith, *Chicago*, pp. 96–97; Dedmon, *Fabulous Chicago*, pp. 96–97.

[16] *Daily News* (Chicago), May 6, 1892, January 2, 1900; Lewis and Smith, *Chicago*, pp. 114–15, 197–98, 267–72; Pierce, *History of Chicago*, III, 310–13.

Unlike New York City, Chicago had room to expand and it did so with a vengeance during the post-war decades. Transporting its burgeoning population over long distances presented still another challenge to municipal authorities. The familiar horse-drawn car was being replaced in the 1880's by the cable car. Chicago built her first one on State Street in 1882, and people noted with amazement that it could run twenty blocks in thirty-two minutes. At the end of that decade the council began granting franchises for railway companies to lay tracks on the city streets and operate electric trolleys. In Chicago, as elsewhere, this led to flagrant corruption, for men like Charles T. Yerkes soon learned that they could buy a council more cheaply than a franchise. By 1893 Chicago had more than 500 miles of railway tracks. Since the crossings were unguarded, there were frequent and gruesome crashes between cable cars and horse-drawn vehicles. Years of public protest finally forced the reluctant companies to elevate their tracks. The first such line in Chicago was the "Alley L" running south to Jackson Park and opened in 1892 in time to carry admiring throngs to the fair grounds.[17]

Not all of Chicago's visitors during these decades marveled at her achievement. Rudyard Kipling was typical of the sarcastic critics. When shown the reconstructed, fireproof, heavily decorated Palmer House, he dismissed it as "a gilded and mirrored rabbit-warren." Its spacious lobby was

> a huge hall of tesselated marble, crammed with people talking about money and spitting about everywhere. Other barbarians charged in and out of this inferno with letters and telegrams in their hands, and yet others shouted at each other. A man who had drunk quite as much as was good for him told me this was "the finest hotel in the finest city on God Almighty's earth."

Once having seen "the 'boss' town of America," Kipling urgently desired never to see it again.[18]

Very different, however, was the reaction of Carl Sandburg, an eighteen-year old Galesburg youth, visiting Chicago for the first time in 1896.

> I was seeing Chicago for three days on a dollar and a half. I went two nights to the Variety Show, vaudeville, in a top gallery at ten cents. . . . I walked through the big State Street department stores that I had heard about for years. . . .
> I walked miles and never got tired of the roar of the street, the trolley cars, the teamsters, the drays, buggies, surreys, and phaetons, the delivery wagons high with boxes, the brewery wagons piled with barrels, the one-horse and two-horse hacks, sometimes a buckboard, sometimes a barouche,

[17] *Daily News* (Chicago), May 27, 1892; Pierce, *History of Chicago*, III, 216–20; Kogan and Wendt, *Chicago*, pp. 142, 145.
[18] Rudyard Kipling, *From Sea to Sea: Letters of Travel* (New York, 1909), Part II, pp. 139–40.

with a coachman in livery, now and again a man in a saddle on horseback weaving his way through the traffic — horses, everywhere horses and here and there mules — and the cobblestone streets with layers of dust and horse droppings. I walked along Michigan Avenue and looked for hours to where for the first time in my life I saw shimmering water meet the sky. . . .

I walked around every block in the Loop, watched the frameworks of the Elevated lines shake and tremble and half expected a train to tumble down to the street. I dropped in at the Board of Trade and watched the grain gamblers throwing fingers and yelling prices. . . .

The afternoon of my third day in Chicago I stopped in at a saloon with a free-lunch sign. I helped myself to slices of rye bread and hunks of cheese and baloney, paid a nickel for a glass of beer, and sat down at a table by myself. . . . I had heard so much about Chicago saloons and their free lunches and funny doings that I wasn't going to leave Chicago without seeing the inside of a saloon.

Yet even on this first visit the city's poet laureate caught something of the paradox and ambiguity. At the time, he remembered, it wasn't "clear to me why the cartoonists drew Chicago as a tall robust woman with a big bosom and over her forehead a crown with the word, 'I WILL,' Chicago seemed to me many women saying, 'I will,' 'I won't,' 'I can't,' 'I wouldn't,' 'I couldn't.' "[19]

II

Nowhere were the contrast and paradox of Chicago better illustrated than in its types of housing. Her wealthy citizens, amassing huge fortunes from the city's phenomenal economic growth in the 1870's and 1880's, eagerly demonstrated their affluence by building enormous mansions. At the time of the fire Chicago's most fashionable residential area centered around Rush Street on the near north side. Cyrus Hall McCormick lived in regal splendor in a forty-five room French style structure, and so many other members of the clan built nearby that the area was irreverently dubbed "McCormickville." In the 1870's, however, a much more exclusive residential area developed on the south side. The Marshall Fields started the migration in 1873 when they moved into their new $100,000 house designed by Richard Morris Hunt. Soon the Philip Armours and the George Pullmans joined them on Prairie Avenue, making it "the street of the sifted few." Those who couldn't buy land there settled for "Millionaires' Row" along lower Michigan Avenue.[20]

The Prairie Avenue set was both startled and amused to learn in 1882 that

[19] Carl Sandburg, *Always the Young Strangers* (New York, 1952), pp. 379–81.
[20] Dedmon, *Fabulous Chicago*, pp. 114–15, 118–19, 132–33; Kogan and Wendt, *Chicago*, pp. 111, 153–54; Andrews, *Battle for Chicago*, pp. 80, 112; Pierce, *History of Chicago*, III, 59–60.

Potter Palmer planned to build the finest house in Chicago on the north side's neglected lake front. He purchased sand dunes and stagnant frog ponds, then filled in the site with more sands, disdaining the chance to use free Chicago garbage for fill. In 1885 he and his imperious wife took possession of their granite castle, designed by Henry Ives Cobb in the English battlement style with a pretentious porte-cochere and a multitude of turrets, balconies, and minarets. There were no exterior doorknobs, entrance being possible only when a servant was instructed to open a door. Once inside, the favored guest might inspect the French drawing room and Gobelin tapestries, or the Greek and Japanese parlors, the Spanish music room, and especially the sunken Turkish pool adjoining Mrs. Palmer's Louis XVI bedroom. Those who could afford it, rushed to build their own mansions near the Palmer Castle on Lake Shore Drive. North side frog-ponds suddenly skyrocketed in value until by 1892 land was selling for $800 a front-foot. Despite the scorn of Prairie Avenue residents, the Potter Palmers had touched off a new migration of Chicago's millionaires in the 1880's.[21]

The city's elite, regardless of whether they lived on the north or the south side, pursued a busy social schedule of personal calls, teas, receptions, dinners, balls, and attendance at concerts, operas, and the theater. A fairly large proportion of the women found time for some type of charitable activity, and a few followed "the Queen," Mrs. Potter Palmer, into the labyrinth of civic reform. During the 1870's Mrs. Palmer dominated the exclusive Fortnightly Club. In the 1880's she turned to the larger Chicago Woman's Club and in 1893 reached the apex of her career when she headed the Board of Lady Managers of the World's Fair. Not to be outdone by the females, Chicago's wealthy business leaders formed the Commercial Club dedicated to social and civic reform, and the younger men started a Mercantile Club. More exclusive socially was the Chicago Club, and more active politically was the Union League Club. Most of Chicago's two hundred millionaires in the 1890's belonged to the latter organization. Their handsome clubhouse, completed in 1886, was the scene of many a gala celebration during the World's Fair. The members' favorite drink that summer was champagne cooled in an iced watermelon, and their only cause for concern was a strong southwesterly wind which inevitably brought the smell of the stockyards into the otherwise genteel surroundings.[22]

That frightful odor came from the other side of town where the wage-

---

[21] Pierce, *History of Chicago*, III, 59–60; Andrews, *Battle for Chicago*, p. 111; Kogan and Wendt, *Chicago*, p. 154; Dedmon, *Fabulous Chicago*, pp. 128–29.

[22] Dedmon, *Fabulous Chicago*, pp. 121, 129; Pierce, *History of Chicago*, III, 190, 485; Bruce Grant, *Fight for a City, The Story of the Union League Club of Chicago and Its Times, 1880–1955* (Chicago, 1955), pp. 58, 88, 134–36.

earners lived. Clustered around the stockyards, they somehow became accustomed to the odor of manure, drying hides, and slaughter refuse. Packingtown was bounded on the east by the Union Stock Yard, on the south by railroad tracks and dusty prairie, on the west by a garbage dump, and on the north by a stagnant fork of the south branch of the Chicago River. Some 35,000 people lived in that square mile in the 1890's, most of them Germans and Irish, but the number of Bohemians, Slovaks, and Poles was increasing. There was no breathing space. Poorly-built frame houses sheltered three and four families, and shacks for others went up overnight on front and back lawns. Some four-story brick tenements could be found, but like the wooden shanties, they had little light or air, and no plumbing facilities of any sort. Enveloping Packingtown was the smoke from the railroads, the stench of the stockyards, the odor of an open garbage pit, and the nauseating fumes rising from Bubbly Creek, a refuse-clogged branch of the Chicago River. Life Back-of-the-Yards was unpleasant no matter which direction the wind blew.[23]

A mile to the north was Hull House, the home since 1889 of a remarkable woman from Cedarville, Illinois — Jane Addams. Like some of her middle-class contemporaries, she was deeply troubled by the paradox of poverty amidst material progress. Finding no answers at Rockford College but inspired by what she had seen at Toynbee Hall in East London, she deliberately chose to make her home on Halsted Street in Chicago. Charles Hull's spacious house, built in the suburbs in 1856, was by the 1890's the center of a teeming, immigrant, working-class neighborhood. Jane Addams soon learned that the more properous German and Irish settlers were moving out, while Italians, Poles, Russian Jews, and Bohemians scrambled to take their places. She was struck immediately by the overcrowded, shabby, frame tenements surrounding Hull House and the appallingly dirty streets and alleys. "Little ideas can be given," said an 1895 Hull House report,

> of the filthy and rotten tenements, the dingy courts and tumble-down sheds, the foul stables and dilapidated outhouses, the broken sewer-pipes, the piles of garbage fairly alive with diseased odors, and of the numbers of children filling every nook, working and playing in every room, eating and sleeping on every window-sill, pouring in and out of every door, and seeming literally to pave every scrap of "yard."

And Jane Addams added:

> The streets are inexpressibly dirty, the number of schools inadequate, sanitary legislation unenforced, the street lighting bad, the paving misera-

[23] Howard E. Wilson, *Mary McDowell, Neighbor* (Chicago, 1928), pp. 25–31.

ble and altogether lacking in the alleys and smaller streets, and the stables foul beyond description.[24]

Chicago had almost three thousand miles of streets in the early 1890's. Fewer than one-third were paved, and those were located in the heart of the city and the better residential districts. Even there paving was not uniform, some of it was done with cedar blocks, with cobblestones or asphalt or macadam or just loose cinders. The majority of Chicago's streets, however, were unsurfaced and became beds of dust in summer and bogs of mud in fall, winter, and spring. They trapped horses and wagons and were hazardous for children to cross. When the Belgian crown prince visited Hull House, he exclaimed, "such a street — no, not one" exists in all Belgium. Only the most important thoroughfares in Chicago had stone sidewalks. The others were bordered by "rickety and worm-eaten planks." One foreign visitor warned that the city's sidewalks, "irregularly laid, dropping now a foot or six inches without notice," played "havoc with the toes and the temper of the unwary pedestrian." George W. Steevens, an English correspondent who toured Chicago's bleak west side in 1896, accurately but grimly depicted it as "the home of labour," a "vast wilderness of shabby houses . . . mostly wooden, begrimed with soot, rotting, falling to pieces. . . . The streets are quagmires of black mud, and no attempt is made to repair them." [25]

The intolerable physical conditions on the west side convinced at least one visitor that Chicago was "the *cloaca maxima* of the world." But in the opinion of Jane Addams and others it was the economic exploitation of women and children that constituted Chicago's worst crime. In the 1890's, some 25,000 people worked in the "sweating system" of the garment industry. The wholesaler gave cut garments to a sweater, who in turn hired immigrant women at the lowest possible piece rate to finish the clothing. Sometimes the finishing was done in the sweater's hot crowded loft or dank basement room. More often, however, the women took the garments back to their own miserable quarters where their young children could baste, sew buttons, and perform other chores. Epidemic diseases like scarlet fever and smallpox were

[24] Residents of Hull-House, *Hull-House Maps and Papers* (New York, 1895), p. 5; Jane Addams, *Twenty Years at Hull-House* (New York, 1911), pp. 93–98; Pierce, *History of Chicago*, III, 465. Jane Addams and the early residents used a hyphen in Hull-House. Since the 1930's, however, it has generally been called Hull House.

[25] F. H. Stead, "The Civic Life of Chicago," *Review of Reviews* [New York], VIII (August, 1893), 179; George W. Steevens, *The Land of the Dollar*, in Pierce (ed.), *As Others See Chicago*, pp. 399, 400; Dedmon, *Fabulous Chicago*, pp. 189, 247; Lewis and Smith, *Chicago*, p. 190; Ray Ginger, *Altgeld's America, The Lincoln Ideal Versus Changing Realities* (New York, 1958), p. 24; William T. Stead, *If Christ Came to Chicago!* (Chicago, 1894), p. 425 n.

spread across Chicago on these garments, and many of the women contracted tuberculosis. They were forced to work, however, to hold a family together or to augment their husbands' meager wages. A large number of children, nobody knows exactly how many, found employment in factories, or as messengers and cash carriers in stores, or on the streets as bootblacks, newsboys, musicians, and vendors. Few of these youngsters attended school. Their "dwarfed and ill-fed" bodies were a constant reminder to Jane Addams of the plight of her less fortunate west side neighbors.[26]

The sharp contrast between the lives of Chicago's two hundred millionaires and her many thousands of wage-earners was not lost upon the latter. A socialist labor leader described the situation in these words: "Upon the one side we find the propertied classes. . . . They are in possession of the earth. Upon the other side we find a large army of workmen who have nothing on earth except their labor."[27] Driven by the hard economic facts of their existence and encouraged by a variety of labor organizations, the workingmen of Chicago tried intermittently during the 1870's, 1880's, and 1890's to sell their labor at a better price. Their attempts to improve working conditions and wages led to the bloody railroad riots in 1877, the trouble in Haymarket Square in 1886, and the climactic Pullman strike in 1894. If Chicago was a city of contrast in the postwar decades, it was also one of conflict.

The railroad strike grew out of the wage cuts enforced in July, 1877. Chicago railroad workers, bitter about previous reductions in pay, walked off their jobs. The city's industrialists were worried about the transport crisis and frightened by the efforts of socialist Albert Parsons to rally the striking railroad employees. Businessmen armed with Civil War rifles patrolled their own residential areas and volunteered to help crush "the ragged Commune wretches." A week of sporadic fighting at the McCormick plant, in several railroad shops, and around a viaduct on Halsted Street ended abruptly when two companies of the United States Army marched into Chicago from Fort Laramie. The businessmen were further reassured when Pinkerton's Detective Agency agreed to help them keep order. Parsons and August Spies, editor of the fiery *Arbeiter Zeitung*, were nonetheless determined to organize Chicago's vast working-class population.[28]

The socialists made little headway until widespread unemployment hit the city again in 1884. Then they drew large crowds to lake-front meetings, launched an English counterpart to the *Arbeiter Zeitung, The Alarm*, and

---

[26] Stead, *If Christ Came to Chicago!* p. 19; *Hull-House Maps and Papers*, pp. 6, 27–45, 49–76; Ginger, *Altgeld's America*, pp. 23–24; Pierce, *History of Chicago*, III, 237–39.
[27] Quoted in Pierce, *History of Chicago*, III, 299.
[28] Ginger, *Altgeld's America*, pp. 35–42; Dedmon, *Fabulous Chicago*, pp. 148–53; Lewis and Smith, *Chicago*, pp. 150–57; Pierce, *History of Chicago*, III, 242–68.

began preaching anarchism and the use of the bomb. By May 1, 1886, some 58,000 people were on strike in Chicago, most of them asking for an eight-hour day and having no connection with any socialist organization. When Pinkerton's detectives and company guards fired into a crowd of strikers in front of the McCormick plant, August Spies called a mass protest meeting in Haymarket Square for the night of May 4, 1886. Despite rainy weather, about 1,000 people came to hear Parsons, Spies, and other socialists. The crowd was orderly, as Mayor Carter Harrison, watching from the fringes, was later to testify. Yet an irresponsible police inspector sent 176 men to disband it. Just as the officer presented his order and one of the speakers protested, someone threw a bomb. The explosion killed seven policemen and wounded sixty others. Their outraged companions fired into the crowd injuring an untold number of workers. In five minutes the violence was over, but the repercussions of America's first anarchist bomb were heard for years.[29]

Hysteria swept Chicago. Scores of socialists, anarchists, and labor leaders spent weeks in jail. Parsons, Spies, and six others stood trial in June for the murder of one of the policemen. Their case was argued before Judge Joseph Gary, who agreed with the prosecution that "Anarchy is on trial." The eight defendants admitted their anarchist beliefs but denied any connection with the Haymarket bomb. All were found guilty; seven were sentenced to death. Chicago newspapers hailed the verdict and many people throughout America felt that justice had been done. In Hartford, Connecticut, Graham Taylor "shared the country-wide indorsement of their conviction and penalty." However, Chicago banker Lyman J. Gage called a meeting of fifty leading businessmen to sign a petition asking for clemency. When Marshall Field expressed approval of the death sentence, Gage lost his case. "Afterwards," he said.

> Many of the men present came around to me singly, and said they had agreed with me in my views, and would have been glad to join me in such an appeal, but that in face of the opposition of powerful men like Marshall Field, they did not like to do so, as it might injure them in business, or socially.

In the end, four of the men including Parsons and Spies were executed, another took his own life, and three were condemned to life imprisonment.[30]

There were other repercussions. Field told the Commercial Club that he wanted a regiment of soldiers to be stationed just outside Chicago "instead

---

[29] Ginger, *Altgeld's America*, pp. 42–48; Dedmon, *Fabulous Chicago*, pp. 153–60; Lewis and Smith, *Chicago*, pp. 159–61; Pierce, *History of Chicago*, III, 269–80.

[30] Taylor, *Pioneering*, p. 136 and chap. x; quoted in Andrews, *Battle for Chicago*, p. 137; Ginger, *Altgeld's America*, pp. 49–55; Dedmon, *Fabulous Chicago*, pp. 160–62; Pierce, *History of Chicago*, III, 205, 281–87; Lewis and Smith, *Chicago*, pp. 161–65. In June, 1893, Governor Altgeld pardoned the three men serving life sentences.

of a thousand miles away, like Fort Laramie." So the club purchased and presented to the government 632 acres north of the city for an army base, Fort Sheridan. Taking the cue, the Merchants' Club gave the government more land to establish the Great Lakes Naval Training Station. Members of the Union League Club sponsored an annual Washington's Birthday celebration to impress upon workingmen "the ideals of loyalty . . . personified in Washington." More realistic was Lyman J. Gage's reaction to the Haymarket tragedy. He started an Economic Club whose membership was open to all and whose purpose was to hear from Democrats, Republicans, single-taxers, capitalists, labor organizers, socialists, and even anarchists. Attending the Economic Club meetings was a cross-section of Chicagoans — with one exception. "The well-to-do were feebly represented," observed Gage, and "the more the pity. From these meetings they might have learned much to which, in their superior wisdom, they remained blind." [31]

<h1 style="text-align:center">III</h1>

Nothing in the early 1890's could shake the conviction of well-to-do Chicagoans that their city was "a delightful abiding place, a center of the fine arts." They were proud of the new university rising on the south side, and they helped collect paintings for the Art Institute. They flocked to the Chicago Orchestra concerts and operatic performances in the handsome Auditorium. Their civic chauvinism knew no bounds when Chicago captured the prize of the Columbian Exposition. Not until Mayor Harrison was assassinated during the closing days of the World's Fair, and thousands of hungry, unemployed Chicagoans prowled the streets, and ugly class warfare broke out in Pullman — not until these grim events took place — did Chicago's upper classes see another dimension to life in the metropolis. Meanwhile, they were busily making their city "a self-conscious center of culture." [32]

One of their most important contributions was the University of Chicago. The first such institution had been a small Baptist school, but its debts and administrative quarrels forced it to close and sell its land in 1886. Thereupon the country's foremost Baptist layman, John D. Rockefeller, offered $600,000 toward the construction of a new university if the Baptist Educational Society could raise $400,000 by 1890. When his terms were met, Rockefeller gave $2

[31] Quoted in Grant, *Fight for a City*, pp. 102, 103; Dedmon, *Fabulous Chicago*, p. 162; Ginger, *Altgeld's America*, p. 42; Pierce, History of Chicago, III, 285–86; Lewis and Smith, *Chicago*, p. 166; Lyman J. Gage, *Memoirs of Lyman J. Gage* (New York, 1937), pp. 70–71.

[32] Lewis and Smith, *Chicago*, p. 231; Bernard Duffy, "Two Literary Movements: Chicago, 1890–1925," *Newberry Library Bulletin*, III (October, 1952), 1.

million more. Chicago businessmen pledged another $1 million and Marshall Field donated a ten-acre site on the south side. The board of trustees selected as president William Rainey Harper, former teacher of Old Testament literature at Yale and a leader in the Chautauqua movement. By offering attractive salaries, Harper gathered a distinguished faculty to greet his students in the fall of 1892.[33]

Always responsive to the newest ideas in higher education, Harper established the first department of sociology in any school in the world. It was headed by Albion W. Small, former professor of political economy and president of Colby College. In addition, Harper brought to the Divinity School Charles Richmond Henderson, a Baptist pastor and labor mediator in Detroit. Until his untimely death in 1905, Harper promoted adult education through extension courses, enlarged the scientific offerings of the University, and still found time to cheer the football team.[34]

The Chicago Orchestra was as much Theodore Thomas' creation as the University was Harper's. After numerous visits to the city to conduct concerts in the 1870's and 1880's, Thomas decided that "the excitement and nervous strain" of living in Chicago necessitated "a permanent musical institution in such a community." Fifty of Chicago's leading businessmen, including Field, Armour, McCormick, and Pullman, formed the Orchestral Association and gave the German-born conductor his permanent Chicago Orchestra in 1891. Its artistic triumphs were a source of great pride to the city's many music-lovers.[35]

President of the Art Institute from 1882 until his death in 1924 was Charles L. Hutchinson a civic-minded banker. His right-hand man was Martin Ryerson, lawyer, student of the arts, and heir to a lumber fortune. Combining their complimentary talents at money raising and ferreting out valuable works of art, particularly the French impressionists, the two stimulated widespread public interest in the museum. In 1893, the Art Institute took possession of the marble Renaissance-style structure on Michigan Avenue built by the city as an assembly hall for the World's Fair congresses. No doubt the *Daily News*

[33] Pierce, *History of Chicago*, III, 390–91; Lewis and Smith, *Chicago*, pp. 198–99; Thomas W. Goodspeed, *A History of the University of Chicago* (Chicago, 1916), pp. 45–272.

[34] Fine, *Laissez Faire*, p. 264; Mathews, "The Development of Social Christianity in America," in Smith (ed.), *Religious Thought*, pp. 232–33; Abell, *Urban Impact*, p. 240; Poole, *Giants Gone*, chap. xix.

[35] Theodore Thomas, *Theodore Thomas: A Musical Autobiography*, ed. George P. Upton (2 vols., Chicago, 1905), I, chap. xi; quoted in Dedmon, *Fabulous Chicago*, p. 196; Pierce, *History of Chicago*, III, 493–94; Poole, *Giants Gone*, chap. xvii.

expressed the view of many when it praised the Art Institute for furthering "the intimacy of Chicago with all that is glorious and revered."[36]

Across Michigan Avenue from the museum an impressive Public Library was completed in 1897. Meantime the Chicago Historical Society occupied a new building in Lincoln Park and the Crerar and Newberry libraries were established with funds bequeathed by prominent Chicagoans. Not to be outdone by other philanthropists, Philip D. Armour provided the money for the Armour Institute, a technical training school opened in 1893 with more than one thousand students. It later became the Illinois Institute of Technology.[37]

A literary renaissance was still another of Chicago's cultural achievements in the 1890's. Eugene Field was writing his lively "Sharps and Flats" column in the *Daily News,* and Finley Peter Dunne allowed Mr. Dooley to entertain readers of the *Times-Herald.* Budding novelists such as Hamlin Garland, Henry Blake Fuller, Frank Norris, and Theodore Dreiser were either writing or working in Chicago during the 1890's. Fuller thought Chicago's highly-vaunted culture a thin veneer. It is, he said "the only great city in the world to which all its citizens have come for the avowed purpose of making money. There you have its genesis; its growth, its object; and there are but few of us who are not attending to that object very strictly." More charitable was *The Dial,* the outstanding magazine of the Chicago literary renaissance. Citing as evidence of "Chicago's Higher Evolution" the establishment of the University, the Orchestra, the new Art Institute building, the Crerar and Newberry Libraries, it concluded that the city was "passing to a higher and maturer stage of civic existence."[38]

The skyscraper was another Chicago contribution in the 1880's and 1890's. The fire, by wiping out the heart of the downtown district, and the enormous economic expansion in the decades which followed, acted as stimulants to the builders. But there were technical problems to be mastered, the first of which was Chicago's swampy base. John W. Root and Daniel H. Burnham solved this by building on a "spread foundation" of criss-crossed steel rails held together with concrete. On such a base they erected Chicago's first "tall building," the ten-story Montauk Block, in 1880. Hydraulic elevators

[36] Chicago *Daily News,* May 12, 1893; Andrews, *Battle for Chicago,* pp. 155–157; Dedmon, *Fabulous Chicago,* pp. 129, 200–201; Pierce, *History of Chicago,* III, 494–96; Poole, *Giants Gone,* chap. xvi; Aline B. Saarinen, *The Proud Possessors* (New York, 1958), pp. 6, 20–21, 23.

[37] Pierce, *History of Chicago,* III, 420–22, 394–95; Dedmon, *Fabulous Chicago,* pp. 186–87; Lewis and Smith, *Chicago,* pp. 136, 173–74.

[38] Dedmon, *Fabulous Chicago,* pp. 186, 201–9; Duffy, "Two Literary Movements," pp. 1–24; Kogan and Wendt, *Chicago,* pp. 160–62; "Chicago's Higher Evolution," *The Dial,* XIII (October 1, 1892), 206.

made it possible for them to go even higher in the sixteen-story Monadnock Building. Like the Montauk Block it was modified Romanesque in style with traditional masonry-bearing walls. Meantime, two other pioneers, William Le Baron Jenney and William Holabird, conceived the idea of using a steel skeleton with only a thin outer skin of masonry or brick. Jenney's ten-story Home Insurance Company Building, completed in 1885, is generally considered to be the first skyscraper. Burnham and Root capped this achievement in 1892 by applying the steel skeleton principle to their twenty-one-story Masonic Temple, finished just in time for the Exposition crowds to marvel at the world's tallest building.[39]

Less spectacular, but eventually just as important, was the work of Dankmar Adler and his moody, philosophical partner, Louis Henri Sullivan. Their most highly-praised building in Chicago was the huge Auditorium, a combination hotel, office structure, and theater-auditorium, capable of seating four thousand. When it was dedicated in 1889 all of Chicago's high society turned out to hear President Harrison, the governor, the mayor, and Adelina Patti who sang the "Swiss Echo Song" and "Home, Sweet Home." "In half a century," marveled the governor, Chicago had passed "from the war whoop of the savage to the ravishing strains of a Patti." Perhaps the greatest service that Adler and Sullivan performed for Chicago was their decision to hire Frank Lloyd Wright as a draftsman in 1887. This audacious young man was already something of a rebel when he hit Chicago. The "only beauty" he could find anywhere was the "gray, soiled river with its mist of steam and smoke," and it "smelled to heaven."[40]

Unfortunately, Chicago's architects missed an opportunity to demonstrate their wares at the World's Columbian Exposition scheduled for 1892. Daniel H. Burnham, chief of construction, could have encouraged the innovators. But, unnerved by the sudden death of his collaborator Root and overly anxious to secure as many well-known eastern architects as possible, Burnham agreed to a classical motif for the main buildings. He persuaded Richard Morris Hunt to design the Administration Building and procured the services of McKim, Mead, and White, sculptors Augustus Saint-Gaudens and Lorado

[39] John Burchard and Albert Bush-Brown, *The Architecture of America* (Boston, 1961), pp. 153–54, 250–51; Wayne Andrews, *Architecture, Ambition and Americans* (New York, 1955), 207–13; Carl Condit, *The Rise of The Skyscrapers* (Chicago, 1952), chaps. iii, iv, v; Pierce, *History of Chicago*, III, 499–500; Dedmon, *Fabulous Chicago*, pp. 187–89; Andrews, *Battle for Chicago*, pp. 123–24.

[40] Condit, *Rise of the Skyscrapers*, pp. 103–11 and chap. viii; Hugh Morrision, *Louis Sullivan, Prophet of Modern Architecture* (New York, 1935), chap. iii; Kogan and Wendt, *Chicago*, pp. 152–54; Andrews, *Architecture, Ambition and Americans*, pp. 213–20; Andrews, *Battle for Chicago*, pp. 124–27, 150–51; Dedmon, *Fabulous Chicago*, pp. 174–77, 187; Frank Lloyd Wright, *Autobiography* (New York, 1943), p. 66.

Taft, and landscape architect Frederick Law Olmsted. Gazing on the assembled talent at one planning session, Saint-Gaudens described it as "the greatest meeting of artists since the fifteenth century." Less impressed was Louis Sullivan, whose Transportation Building was the only modern structure in the entire White City. He acidly observed: "Thus architecture died in the land of the free and the home of the brave. . . . The damage wrought by the World's Fair will last for half a century . . . if not longer."[41]

The opening of the fair was advanced to 1893 because of construction difficulties. But even so, workmen were pressed for time to transform six hundred acres of south side sand dunes into lagoons and wooded parks, build the enormous exhibition halls, lay out the Midway, apply countless gallons of white paint to stucco walls, and instal the five thousand electric arc-lights which illuminated the White City at night. In October, 1892, 150,000 Chicagoans including the newly-arrived Taylor family streamed out to the muddy fair grounds to hear the Vice-President of the United States "dedicate these buildings to humanity." Not until May 1, 1893, was the Exposition officially opened. That ceremony drew more than 600,000 people, once again including the Taylors who got there in time to see "Pres. Cleveland, Gov. Altgeld, & Mayor Carter Harrison escorted to the grounds." So great was the excitement and so dense the crowd that women fainted and children were lost in the crush. A pickpocket tried to snatch Jane Addams' purse but was frustrated by an alert guard.[42]

All during the summer and fall of 1893 throngs of people made their way to the great White City. They gazed across the Court of Honor at Hunt's Administration Building and admired the many statues and fountains. Some studied the exhibits in the Agriculture and Manufacturing Buildings, the Fine Arts Palace, the Halls of Transportation, Mining, and Machinery, and the Woman's Building. The fair's playground was the Midway Plaisance, a stretch of sideshows and replicas of foreign villages, cafes, bazaars, and streets. Two of its most popular attractions were the enormous ferris wheel, an innovation at the Paris Exposition four years before, and a bewitching Ar-

---

[41] Burchard and Bush-Brown, *The Architecture of America*, pp. 253–55; Andrews, *Architecture, Ambitions and Americans*, pp. 220–23; Ginger, *Altgeld's America*, pp. 15–18; 22; Pierce, *History of Chicago*, III, 501–4; Lewis and Smith, *Chicago*, pp. 177–78, 184–86; Dedmon, *Fabulous Chicago*, pp. 200–1; Charles Moore, *Daniel H. Burnham, Architect, Planner of Cities* (2 vols.; Boston, 1921), I, chap. iv.

Henry Adams was another who deplored the imposition of "classical standards on plastic Chicago." But, he added, "All traders' taste smelt of bric-a-brac; Chicago tried at least to give her taste a look of unity." Henry Adams, *The Education of Henry Adams* (New York, 1931), p. 340.

[42] Lewis and Smith, *Chicago*, pp. 187–88, 199–208; Ginger, *Altgeld's America*, pp. 18–19; Taylor, Diary, October 21, 1892, May 1, 1893.

menian dancer, Little Egypt, who performed the hootchy-kootchy on the streets of Cairo.[43]

Very different from the carefree atmosphere of the Midway were the scholarly conferences held in the new Art Institute under the auspices of the World's Congress Auxiliary. The first of these meetings was devoted to Women's Progress. Others dealt with education, prohibition, city government, and suffrage reform. The Labor Congress drew 25,000 to hear Samuel Gompers of the American Federation of Labor, single-taxer Henry George, and Chicago attorney Clarence Darrow. A much smaller audience, the American Historical Association, listened to Frederick Jackson Turner read a paper on "The Significance of the Frontier in American History." Graham Taylor participated in three of the conferences held that summer. The International Congress of Charities, Corrections and Philanthropy devoted one of its June sessions to a discussion of "Sociology as a Special Topic of Investigation and Instruction in Institutions of Learning." They asked Taylor, the new Professor of Christian Sociology at Chicago Theological Seminary, to describe "Sociological Work in Theological Seminaries." In September he attended, but did not address, the Parliament of Religions. This was the largest and most widely-publicized of all the congresses, and its general secretary was Jenkin Lloyd Jones, a prominent Chicago Unitarian minister. During the last month of the fair the Evangelical Alliance heard Taylor discuss "The Sociological Training of the Ministry."[44]

The World's Columbian Exposition was a great success, unless judged by architectural standards. More than 20 million people visited it between May 1 and October 30, 1893, and stockholders were pleased by their 10 per cent dividends. The fair made a deep and lasting impression upon all who saw it. Hamlin Garland wrote to his aged parents in Dakota, "Sell the cook stove if necessary and come. You *must* see this fair." They came and were moved "to tears of joy" by "the wonder and the beauty of it all." Journalist Murat Halstead agreed that it was "grand and glorious beyond description and beautiful in its parts and as a whole." Graham Taylor and his wife felt that "the great city & wondrous Exposition were potent educators in our lives and those of our children." Chicagoans, of course, were immensely proud

[43] Dedmon, *Fabulous Chicago*, pp. 226–35; Lewis and Smith, *Chicago*, pp. 208–13; Pierce, *History of Chicago*, III, pp. 504–8.

[44] Pierce, *History of Chicago*, III, 508–11; Ginger, *Altgeld's America*, p. 21; Taylor, Diary, June 8–18, September, 1893; Graham Taylor, "Sociological Work in Theological Seminaries," in *International Congress of Charities, Corrections and Philanthropy, Chicago, 1893* (Baltimore, 1894), pp. 64–79; Graham Taylor, "The Sociological Training of the Ministry," in Evangelical Alliance, *Christianity Practically Applied* (New York, 1894), I, 396–413.

of their achievement in Jackson Park. Perhaps Carter Harrison best expressed their mood when he told a large crowd on Mayor's Day at the fair: "Genius is but audacity, and the audacity of . . . Chicago has chosen a star, and has looked upward to it, and knows nothing that it cannot accomplish."[45]

IV

The "White City . . . constructed only for a season and finished to the minutest detail, must disappear forever, while the black city, which will endure forever, is only at its commencement." So wrote departing journalist Paul Bourget in December, 1893. Many Exposition visitors had already made the acquaintance of the Black City, for Chicago was wide-open and its saloons, gambling dens, and brothels did a brisk business in 1893. Drinking establishments were liberally scattered throughout the city, and some tourists were surprised to learn that there was a bar for every two hundred people and that they outnumbered churches by ten to one. The vice district centered around the Levee on the near south side. One of its showplaces was "King Mike" McDonald's four-story gambling house from whence he dispensed Democratic patronage and controlled a chain of Illinois and Indiana race tracks. He operated on the premise that "There's a sucker born every minute." The Levee's fanciest brothel was run by Carrie Watson. To meet the demand in 1893 she doubled her supply of girls, redecorated the brownstone mansion throughout, and trained a parrot stationed at the door to say, "Carrie Watson. Come in, gentlemen." There were so many saloons, gaming parlors, and bordellos that an enterprising publisher put out a *Sporting and Club House Directory* to help the unknowing make their choice.[46]

It can hardly be denied that Carter Harrison's long mayoralty fostered the growth of Chicago's sporting life. A voluble, aristocratic, Kentucky Democrat who arrived in 1855, Harrison promptly claimed the city as his "bride." Though he himself lived handsomely and associated with the elite, he was genuinely sympathetic with the economic and social problems of the vast immigrant population. He supported their labor unions, kept their saloons open on Sunday, spoke acceptable French, German, and Italian, and could repeat at least a few lines of poetry in the native tongue of Poles, Bohemians, and Swedes. Honestly believing that no legislation could prevent gambling

[45] Pierce, *History of Chicago*, III, 508; Hamlin Garland, *A Son of the Middle Border* (New York, 1918), pp. 358, 360; *Daily News* (Chicago), June 1, 1893; Taylor, Diary, October, 1893; Lewis and Smith, *Chicago*, p. 214.

[46] Paul Bourget, "A Farewell to the White City," *Cosmopolitan*, XVI (December, 1893), 135; Lewis and Smith, *Chicago*, pp. 233, 236–37; Dedmon, *Fabulous Chicago*, pp. 136–37, 139–147; Ginger, *Altgeld's America*, pp. 22–23; Herbert Asbury, *Gem of the Prairie, An Informal History of the Chicago Underworld* (New York, 1940), chap. v.

and prostitution, he favored a wide-open policy for Chicago. As a result, Harrison was able to build a powerful political machine on the invincible combination of working-class votes and financial support from the Levee. He served two terms in Congress in the 1870's, four consecutive terms as mayor from 1879 to 1887, and then confounded his opponents by seeking an unprecedented fifth term in 1893 so that he and his "bride" could preside over the Exposition.[47]

There were, of course, civic reformers in the 1870's and 1880's, people who wanted to redeem the "Gomorrah of the West" by purging the city council, driving out prostitutes and gamblers, and closing saloons on Sunday or permanently. But the Committee of Seventy, the Committee of Twenty-five, the Committee of One Hundred, the Citizens' Law and Order League, and even the dedicated Women's Christian Temperance Union failed to break the Democrats' tight hold on city hall. In the words of one firm believer in Harrison's wide-open policy: "This is a frontier town and its got to go through its red-blooded youth. A church and a WCTU never growed a big town yet." "Our Carter" was Chicago's overwhelming choice to lead it through its red-blooded youth. He was at the peak of his political power in 1893, when, just a few days before the fair was scheduled to close, a deranged office-seeker knocked on the mayor's door and fired three fatal shots.[48]

Following close upon the assassination of Mayor Harrison came the depression of 1893. Chicago had weathered the financial crisis of early spring. Two national banks and several private ones had closed, but in June the *Daily News* announced that the temporary panic of small-savings depositors had been stemmed. There was an unusually large number of unemployed during the summer of 1893, many of them former construction workers at the fair grounds, but they were allowed to sleep in the parks and the newspapers studiously ignored them as long as the White City was on display. Though Chicago escaped the worst of the panic, she was hard-hit by the depression of "that terrible winter after the World's Fair." Desperate men and women — homeless, jobless, hungry, and numb from the bitter winds blowing off Lake Michigan — staged "huge demonstrations" which reminded Jane Addams of "the London gatherings in Trafalgar Square." Many jammed the county poorhouse. Others tried to pawn or peddle their meager belongings. Some fought for space on the hard floors of police stations and the city hall where

---

[47] Dedmon, *Fabulous Chicago*, pp. 135–36; Poole, *Giants Gone*, chap. x; Lewis and Smith, *Chicago*, pp. 73–74, 158–59; Claudius O. Johnson, *Carter Henry Harrison I, Political Leader* (Chicago, 1928), chaps. v, x, xi; Willis J. Abbot, *Carter Henry Harrison, A Memoir* (New York, 1895), chaps. iv, vi, viii, ix.

[48] Lewis and Smith, *Chicago*, pp. 213–14, 263; Dedmon, *Fabulous Chicago*, pp. 136, 138–39.

they made a "pavement of human bodies . . . pigged together literally like herrings in a barrel."[49]

Like many other Chicagoans, Graham Taylor was shocked by "the sudden fall from the World's Fair piping times of peace and plenty to the . . . dire poverty and public emergency immediately following the close of the Exposition." He walked the streets seeking an answer to the nagging question of "where and how the hungry, shelterless, homeless man kept soul and body together."

> I found them sleeping on the bare floors of miserable lodging-houses and barrel-house saloons, in the corridors of police-station cell rooms, on the stone floors and stairways of the old City Hall, as well as wandering about the streets begging for a dime, as the last chance to get under shelter for the night. Then for the first time I imagined what an inconceivable experience it must be not to have, or know how to find, a place to sleep through the night already darkening down upon one.

For the Professor of Christian Sociology those hundreds of "upturned faces and calloused hands" were a "transforming experience" and "an ineffaceable memory."[50]

Accompanying Taylor on some of these expeditions was William T. Stead, British journalist, reformer, and editor of the London *Review of Reviews*.[51] After dispatching his articles on the White City, Stead began prowling the Black City, often posing as an unemployed laborer so that he could talk more freely. Sometimes he stopped at Hull House "between eleven and twelve o'clock at night . . . wet and hungry from an investigation of the levee district," eager to compare notes with Jane Addams and drink "hot chocolate before an open fire." But this curious Englishman understood the paradox of Chicago, the "mixed goodness," as Jane Addams described it, "the lack of rectitude in many high places, the simple kindness of the most wretched to each other." Stead analyzed the alliance of vice lords and Democratic chieftains and asserted that Chicago was unique in "the way in which gaming is utilized as an engine of party finance." The machine was built on "Bribery, intimidation, bull-dozing of every kind, knifing, shooting, and the whole swimming in whiskey!" Yet after talking with individual saloon-keepers

[49] *Daily News* (Chicago), June 7, 1893; Pierce, *History of Chicago*, III, 197, 509; Addams, *Twenty Years*, pp. 159–60; Lewis and Smith, *Chicago*, pp. 216–18; Stead, *If Christ Came to Chicago!* p. 21.

[50] Taylor, *Pioneering*, p. 110.

[51] William T. Stead was the son of an English Congregational minister. Before establishing *Review of Reviews* in 1890 he had edited the *Pall Mall Gazette*. His younger brother, F. Herbert Stead, was also a writer and a prominent theologian. His *Kingdom of God* was a volume which Taylor often assigned to students.

and gamblers who, at their own expense, fed and sheltered hundreds during those grim months, Stead realized that

> here, even in this nethermost depth, was the principle of human service, there was the recognition of human obligation, set in motion, no doubt, for party reasons, and from a desire to control votes rather than to save souls. But whatever might be the motive, the result was unmistakable. . . . In its own imperfect manner this rough, vulgar, faulty substitute for religion is at least compelling the heeler and the bartender and the tough, whom none of the churches can reach, to recognize that fundamental principle of human brotherhood which Christ came to teach.[52]

Though his plea for civic reform failed to rouse the Chicago clergy, Stead did get strong support from organized labor. With their backing he called a mass meeting for Sunday evening, November 12, 1893, in Central Music Hall. An enormous crowd packed the auditorium. On the podium was an incongruous group of Chicagoans:

> Side by side sat leading business men and labor leaders, representatives of the city government and of its exclusive clubs, preachers and saloon-keepers, gamblers and theological professors, matrons of distinguished families and notorious "madames" from houses of ill fame, judges of the courts and one of the men convicted in the Haymarket Riot trial who had recently been pardoned from the state prison by Governor Altgeld.

Stead's eloquent speech sought to answer the question, "If Christ came to Chicago today, what would he think of it?" The English reformer hit hardest at the unnecessary industrial crisis, which, he argued, was "due to the lack, the irregularity, the low pay and excessive hours of work." He condemned the connivance among aldermen, police, and vice lords, and he deplored the voters' toleration of such inept municipal government. The "disreputable" classes in Chicago, insisted Stead, were not the unemployed but the "rich, cultured" men and women who were "dowered with endless opportunity for serving the city" yet "did nothing and cared nothing for its welfare." This, he concluded, "is the plague spot in Chicago which eats far more deeply into the vitals of the community than fifty sporting houses or one thousand saloons." Taylor, listening intently from the stage, felt that Stead "at white heat denouncing preventable evils . . . seemed to rise to the stature of one of the Hebrew prophets."[53]

When Stead finished, labor leader Thomas J. Morgan took the platform. He too was an Englishman who had emigrated to Chicago in 1869, worked

---

[52] Taylor, *Pioneering*, p. 28; Addams, *Twenty Years*, p. 160; Stead, *If Christ Came to Chicago!* pp. 233, 67–68.

[53] Taylor, *Pioneering*, pp. 29, 30, 31; Stead, *If Christ Came to Chicago!* p. 113.

as a machinist for the Illinois Central Railroad, and was a member of the Socialist Labor Party and their candidate for mayor in 1891. In 1886, however, Morgan had headed a socialist faction which declared itself opposed to Spies and Parsons and "emphatically opposed to anarchy." Morgan rose in Central Music Hall to praise Stead's plea for a united effort at civic reform. But he startled the audience when he continued:

> Now the veil has been torn aside and you members of the G.A.R., the Y.M.C.A., of your temperance societies, of your Sons of America and Daughters of America have been able to see the skeletons in your closet. . . . If you well-to-do people do not listen, will not wake up, you do not know that in your midst, there may be . . . a desperate man who feeling himself all the injustice that is inflicted on his fellows, will kill, will destroy. . . . And if the pleadings of editor Stead, in the name of Christ and for justice, cannot shake you out, may someone blow you out with dynamite.

At this the audience rose in tumult, some cheering, others shaking their fists, a few walking out. Morgan tried to explain, but Stead led him to his seat and introduced the next speaker, Graham Taylor. Seeing that it was impossible to deliver his own remarks, Taylor brought Morgan back to the platform and shouted, "Who is afraid of little Tommy Morgan! He has been misunderstood." The mention of dynamite, however, had riled this incongruous Chicago gathering and nothing could calm them. The meeting adjourned after approving a resolution to form a Civic Confederation of Chicago.[54]

Two things grew out of this unusual mass meeting. One was Stead's vitriolic book, *If Christ Came to Chicago!* Unable to get a verbatim report of what had been said that evening, Stead returned to the city, augmented his earlier findings, and wrote this angry volume. It was, he said, "an attempt to illustrate how a living faith in the Citizen Christ would lead directly to the civic and social regeneration of Chicago." By the time his book came off the press in 1894 Chicago had established a Civic Federation "to discover and correct abuses in municipal affairs and to increase the interest of the citizens in such affairs." Lyman J. Gage was president, Mrs. Potter Palmer and a labor official were vice-presidents, and Jane Addams was one of the trustees. The work of the Civic Federation was carried on by councils in each of Chicago's thirty-four wards and by six major committees to handle political, municipal, industrial, moral, educational and social, and philanthropic

---

[54] John Laslett, "Socialism and the American Federation of Labor: 1886–1903" (Ph.D. thesis, Oxford University, 1962), p. 38; Pierce, *History of Chicago*, III, 267, 370–71; Taylor, *Pioneering*, pp. 31–32, 33; Albion W. Small, "The Civic Federation of Chicago, A Study in Social Dynamics," *American Journal of Sociology*, I (July, 1895), 88–89.

matters. Mrs. Lucy Flower, member of the school board and advocate of industrial training schools, was appointed head of the Philanthropic Department, and Graham Taylor was a committee member.[55]

Under Mrs. Flower's guidance the Civic Federation established a Central Relief Association to help meet the crisis of Chicago's grim winter of 1893 and 1894. During a five month period the association raised and disbursed $135,000, distributed quantities of food and coal, and processed nearly 28,000 applications for relief. Though insignificant when compared to the 60,000 people fed each day by Chicago saloon-keepers, it was nevertheless a creditable beginning for the new Civic Federation. Furthermore, the Philanthropic Department tried to operate according to the newest theories of scientific charity. To keep the recipients of relief funds busy, it organized sewing rooms for women and a brigade of male street sweepers. It kept careful records to prevent overlapping with other agencies, and it made every effort to place unemployed workers in jobs for which they were qualified.[56]

Taylor helped process the applications that poured into the Central Relief Association, and he investigated the plight of families living in miserable tenements. When the emergency was over the association disbanded and presented its records to the newly-created Bureau of Charities. It was hoped by Mrs. Flower, Taylor, and others that the bureau would function like Charity Organization Societies elsewhere, as a clearing-house for all the city's philanthropic activities. The jealousy of the older Relief and Aid Society, however, prevented this until 1909 when the two rivals finally merged to form the United Charities of Chicago.[57]

There was little that the Civic Federation could do about the trouble brewing in the town of Pullman, twelve miles to the south on the shore of Lake Calumet. Established in the early 1880's, it was a self-contained industrial city, free, according to its creator George M. Pullman, of "all that was ugly, discordant and demoralizing." In addition to the manufacturing plant there were substantial brick cottages for the workers, macadam streets, a theater, library, bank, schools, church, beautifully-landscaped park, and an arcade for the stores and shops which sold everything except "demoralizing" liquor. Pullman City represented a sizable investment, but thanks to the Pullman Land Association, sufficient revenue was collected to repay the

---

[55] Stead, *If Christ Came to Chicago!* pp. 11–16, 465–71; Douglas Sutherland, *Fifty Years on the Civic Front* (Chicago, 1943), pp. 6–9; Small, "The Civic Federation of Chicago," pp. 80–81.

[56] Sutherland, *Fifty Years*, 8–10; Small, "The Civic Federation of Chicago," p. 86; Addams, *Twenty Years*, 160–62; Stead, *If Christ Came to Chicago!* pp. 139–43; Bremner, *From the Depths*, pp. 50–53.

[57] Taylor, *Pioneering*, pp. 41–42, 111–12.

parent Pullman Palace Car Company. Rent, gas, water, and groceries were 10 to 15 per cent higher than comparable prices in Chicago.[58]

Understandably the model city attracted hundreds of visitors in the 1880's and 1890's. Richard T. Ely thought it "un-American," a "benevolent, well-wishing feudalism." So too did William T. Stead who investigated George Pullman's "business experiment" in 1893. During his first trip west in 1885, Taylor visited the town of Pullman and talked with many residents. He found "much to interest, much to admire & much to criticize in this gigantic monopoly." After Taylor moved to Chicago, he chanced to meet George Pullman in an elevator and "asked him what means the Company took to ally its employees and other residents of the town with its policies. His terse remark . . . fairly startled me . . . 'A clause in every lease enables us on short notice to be rid of undesirable tenants.' " It was not surprising that some people in the model town felt resentment rather than gratitude. Said one: "We are born in a Pullman house, fed from the Pullman shop, taught in the Pullman school, catechized in the Pullman church, and when we die we shall be buried in the Pullman cemetery and go to the Pullman hell." [59]

A free pamphlet distributed by the Pullman Company during the World's Fair described the community as a "radiant little island in the midst of the great tumultuous sea of Chicago's population." Yet only a few months later George Pullman's "restful oasis" was a bloody battleground. When wages were repeatedly cut in the spring of 1894 without any reduction in rent, a delegation of workers asked to see Pullman. He refused and fired them, whereupon the Pullman local of Eugene Debs' American Railway Union walked out on strike May 11. Pullman steadfastly refused to negotiate with his employees, for he insisted that wages and working conditions must be determined by management alone. The Civic Federation appointed Jane Addams to its conciliation board, but its strenuous efforts to arbitrate the strike were futile.[60]

In June, the national American Railway Union voted to support the strike, and after June 26 workers boycotted all trains with Pullman cars attached. The twenty-four railroads running out of Chicago, acting through their General Managers' Association, welcomed the opportunity to break Debs'

[58] Almont Lindsey, *The Pullman Strike: The Story of a Unique Experiment and of a Greater Labor Upheaval* (Chicago, 1942), chaps. iii, iv; Ginger, *Altgeld's America*, pp. 145–48; Andrews, *Battle for Chicago*, pp. 168–72; Pierce, *History of Chicago*, III, 53; Dedmon, *Fabulous Chicago*, pp. 238–41.

[59] Richard T. Ely, "Pullman: A Social Study," *Harper's New Monthly Magazine*, LXX (February, 1885), 465; Stead, *If Christ Came to Chicago!* pp. 88; Taylor, Diary, December 15, 1885; Taylor, *Pioneering*, p. 115; Ginger, *Altgeld's America*, p. 149.

[60] Taylor, *Pioneering*, p. 112; Lindsey, *Pullman Strike*, pp. 230–31; Addams, *Twenty Years*, pp. 214–15.

union. On July 2, they secured federal intervention. Attorney General Richard Olney ordered court injunctions forbidding interference with interstate commerce and delivery of United States mail. When the railroads attached mail cars to all trains entering or leaving Chicago, rioting and violence broke out. Olney thereupon persuaded President Cleveland to order federal troops down from Fort Sheridan, despite the protests of Mayor Hopkins and Governor Altgeld that city police and state militia had control of the situation. On July 10, Debs was arrested for conspiracy and contempt, and within a week the American Railway Union, unsupported by organized labor and unable to carry on alone, allowed the strike to peter out. Gradually the 14,000 armed men in Chicago — private guards, police, militia, and soldiers — dispersed. Pullman reopened his plant in August with one-fourth of his labor force replaced and all employees pledged not to join a union.[61]

The scars of the Pullman strike were permanent. Eugene Debs spent six months in jail and converted himself to socialism. Governor Altgeld, his own political aspirations cut short by the Haymarket pardons of 1893, determined to even the score with President Cleveland and proceeded to do so at the Democratic national convention in 1896. The Civic Federation, smarting under Pullman's contemptuous treatment, secured state legislation in 1895 establishing a Board of Conciliation and Arbitration. Jane Addams learned that settlement houses must maintain "avenues of intercourse with both sides" to prevent "the growth of class bitterness" and the "cleavage of society." In a speech before the Chicago Woman's Club she described George Pullman as "The Modern King Lear," a man who

> cultivated the great and noble impulses of the benefactor until the power of attaining a simple human relationship with his employees, that of frank equality with them, was gone. . . . In so far as philanthropists are cut off from the influence of the *Zeit-Geist* . . . from the great moral life springing from our common experiences, so long as they are "good to people" rather than "with them," they are bound to accomplish a large amount of harm. . . . We are all practically agreed that the social passion of the age is directed toward the emancipation of the wage-worker; . . . that nothing will satisfy the aroused conscience of men short of the complete participation of the working classes in the spiritual, intellectual and material inheritance of the human race.[62]

[61] Harvey Wish, "The Pullman Strike: A Study in Industrial Warfare," *Journal of the Illinois State Historical Society*, XXXII (September, 1939), 288–312; Lindsey, *Pullman Strike*, chaps. v–xi; Ginger, *Altgeld's America*, chap. vi; Dedmon, *Fabulous Chicago*, pp. 238–46; Andrews, *Battle for Chicago*, pp. 172–76.

[62] Lindsey, *Pullman Strike*, chaps. xii–xiv; Ginger, *Altgeld's America*, pp. 164–167; Sutherland, *Fifty Years*, p. 11; Addams, *Twenty Years*, pp. 214, 217; Jane Addams, "A Modern Lear," in Graham Romeyn Taylor, *Satellite Cities: A Study of Industrial Suburbs* (New York, 1915), pp. 76, 84–85, 86.

For Graham Taylor the Pullman strike provided insights into the field of industrial relations which came like "the glare of a bursting bomb." He considered it "a trumpet call to refuse to be classified and to stand in between," so that he could be in contact with both sides and help mediate future disputes. For George Pullman the strike was such "black ingratitude" that he found little satisfaction in its outcome. In time he saw his model town annexed by Chicago and heard the courts forbid the Pullman Company to hold property not needed in the manufacture of Pullman cars. When he died in 1897 he left $17 million and instructions that he be buried secretly at dusk in an asphalt-coated casket, lowered into a cement-walled tomb that in turn was covered with steel rails, more concrete, then sod, and finally myrtle.[63]

In the year of Pullman's demise an observant Englishman published a book entitled *The Land of the Dollar*. George W. Steevens visited Chicago in 1896, just twenty-five years after the fire, and he found that "everybody is fighting to be rich, is then straining to be refined, and nobody can attend to making the city fit to live in." Yet the many faces of Chicago, the contrasting poses and attitudes that impressed young Sandburg that same year, were clear to Steevens.

> Chicago, queen and guttersnipe of cities, cynosure and cesspool of the world! Not if I had a hundred tongues, everyone shouting a different language in a different key, could I do justice to her splendid chaos. The most beautiful and the most squalid, girdled with a twofold zone of parks and slums; where the keen air from lake and prairie is ever in the nostrils and the stench of foul smoke is never out of the throat; the great port of a thousand miles from the sea; the great mart which gathers up with one hand the corn and cattle of the West and deals out with the other the merchandise of the East; . . . the chosen seat of public spirit and municipal boodle, of cut-throat commerce and munificent patronage of art; the most American of American cities and yet the most mongrel; the second American city of the globe, the fifth German city, the third Swedish, the second Polish, the first and only veritable Babel of the age; all of which twenty-five years ago next Friday was a heap of smoking ashes. Where in all the world can words be found for this miracle of paradox and incongruity?[64]

V

Throughout the year of the World's Columbian Exposition the Chicago Theological Seminary was deeply engrossed in its own financial campaign. The trustees had secured Graham Taylor's acceptance as head of the new

[63] Taylor, *Pioneering*, pp. 111, 116; Addams, *Twenty Years*, p. 217; Dedmon, *Fabulous Chicago*, p. 246; Andrews, *Battle for Chicago*, p. 176; Poole, *Giants Gone*, chap. xii.

[64] George W. Steevens, *The Land of the Dollar*, in Pierce (ed.), *As Others See Chicago*, pp. 400, 395–96.

Department of Christian Sociology in August of 1892, but they still had to raise the matching $350,000 to collect the gift of $100,000. It was agreed that Taylor was the logical spokesman to explain the new discipline and to impress upon potential contributors the importance of training students for city missionary work. Almost immediately Taylor set out on a tour of the state associations beginning at Great Bend, Kansas, where he spoke at the Opera House and two hundred people stayed until nearly midnight to question him. By the end of October, 1893, he had presented the "Seminary cause 52 times in 25 cities or towns in 7 states, in 36 churches, in 7 associations & 4 colleges." The seminary's benefactor was so pleased with the successful campaign that he promised another $50,000 if the trustees could match that. When the deadline came on November 1, 1893, the finance committee had collected $350,000 plus the additional $50,000. They even had $3.76 to spare. The donor gave still another $30,000, which meant that the Chicago Theological Seminary, with Taylor's indispensable help, added a total of $580,003.76 to its endowment.[65]

Taylor's speeches for the seminary, his inaugural address in the spring of 1893, and the papers he read before the International Congress of Charities, Corrections and Philanthropy and the Evangelical Alliance all developed the same theme. Only when theological students are trained in Christian sociology, will the modern church be able to perform "its world-work for the Kingdom." Small though the beginnings of Christian sociology may be, he told his audiences, "they indicate the rise of a mighty social movement within the churches, which, while quiet, unrecognized, and hardly conscious of its own existence as yet, is deep, pervasive, intensely practical, eager to learn, and destined to prevail." He promised that the first textbooks of his students would be "the street, the shop, the school, the mission." He expected to establish a seminary settlement house where his students could live among the working classes and observe social and industrial conditions. The goal of his Christian sociological teaching was "to develop the life of the individual out of a mere self-conscious existence into a personality that shares the life of the whole brotherhood of man and the Fatherhood of God."[66]

Taylor's first introduction to the settlement house movement came from references to Toynbee Hall and Hull House in magazine articles of the

[65] Chicago Theological Seminary, *Minutes of the Triennial Convention, 1894* (Chicago, 1891–1904), pp. 21, 22; Taylor, Diary, May 5, October, 1893; Davis, "The Great Financial Campaign of 1893," in Davis, "History of the Chicago Theological Seminary."

[66] Graham Taylor, *The Sociological Training of the Ministry, Address Delivered before The Evangelical Alliance Congress, At Chicago, October 13, 1893* (Chicago, 1893), pp. 16, 8; Graham Taylor, "Addresss When Inaugurated Prof. of Christian Sociology in C.T.S.," April 18, 1893, Typewritten manuscript, p. 9; Graham Taylor, "Our New Professorship," *The Advance*, XXV (September 8, 1892), 698.

1880's and 1890's. Toynbee Hall in London, the earliest social settlement, was the creation of an Anglican cleric, Samuel A. Barnett. As a student at Oxford he was influenced by the lectures of John Ruskin and philosopher Thomas Hill Green and also by Christian Socialist literature. After five years as vicar under Canon Fremantle, Barnett, in 1872, deliberately chose a slum parish in Whitechapel, East London. Urging young men from Oxford and Cambridge to spend vacations and if possible establish residence in the parish, Barnett argued that such "a settlement of University men will do a little to remove the inequalities of life, as the settlers share their best with the poor and learn through feeling how they live." One of those who responded to the call was Arnold Toynbee, a promising tutor at Oxford and lecturer on the industrial revolution. Toynbee's untimely death in 1883 moved a group of his friends to erect a building in Whitechapel that would provide permanent quarters for University "settlers." This was the origin of Toynbee Hall, which, with Canon Barnett as warden, opened its doors on Christmas eve, 1884. Its fourteen residents and numerous associates dedicated themselves to serve the parish as "teachers, citizens, and hosts." [67]

Toynbee Hall was the inspiration and model for most of the American settlement houses. During the winter of 1886 Stanton Coit lived at Toynbee Hall, and upon his return to the United States he began searching for a place in New York City to establish residence. Finding quarters on the lower east side, he opened Neighborhood Guild in the summer of 1886, America's first social settlement. Two years later Jane Addams made a pilgrimage to Toynbee Hall, and after talking with the Barnetts, came back to Chicago to open Hull House in September, 1889. There is no evidence that Graham Taylor visited, or even knew about, the New York experiment while he was in Hartford in the 1880's. But he did read Coit's book, *Neighbourhood Guilds; An Instrument of Social Reform*, shortly after it was published in 1891. And he later claimed that Coit's volume "encouraged me to include as a condition of my acceptance of the professorship [at Chicago Theological Seminary] the liberty to establish and live in a settlement." [68]

Taylor mulled over the settlement idea during his first two years in Chicago. The poverty and unemployment he had observed in Hartford seemed to be due to "individual faults or personal misfortune." But as an

[67] Graham Taylor to Albert J. Kennedy, September 20, 1912; Taylor, *Pioneering*, p. 6; Robert A. Woods and Albert J. Kennedy, *The Settlement Horizon, A National Estimate* (New York, 1922), p. 27, and chap. ii; J. A. R. Pimlott, *Toynbee Hall, Fifty Years of Social Progress 1884–1934* (London, 1935), p. 48, and chaps. i–iii; Kathleen Woodroofe, *From Charity to Social Work* (Toronto, 1962), pp. 64–74.

[68] Woods and Kennedy, *Settlement Horizon*, pp. 41–42, 46, and chap. iv; Addams, *Twenty Years*, pp. 87–88; Taylor, *Pioneering*, p. 6; Graham Taylor, manuscript, no title, no date.

agent of the Central Relief Association in Chicago, Taylor quickly learned that hundreds of people were "willing and able to work yet forced to be idle and dependent." While his Hartford contacts had been "too individualistic to include . . . sympathy with organized labor," his observation of the Pullman strike remedied that. As a troubled newcomer to Chicago, Taylor went frequently to Hull House "to listen and to learn." He agreed with William T. Stead that Jane Addams had created "the ideal settlement . . . enthusiastic without being intolerant, and broad without losing the fervour of its humanitarian zeal." What Chicago needed, he decided, was "a multiplication of Hull House all over the city." Already Charles Zueblin had secured the backing of Northwestern University for a settlement on the west side in the midst of Germans, Scandinavians, and Poles. And Taylor knew that Albion Small's sociology department at the University of Chicago was preparing in 1894 to establish a settlement in Packingtown with a former Hull House resident, Mary McDowell, in charge. He talked at great length with Percy Alden, warden of Mansfield House, a Congregational settlement in East London. By the spring of 1894 Taylor was pressing the seminary trustees for funds. None were forthcoming, but he felt he could wait no longer. Determined to teach Christian sociology "from the ground up and not from the clouds down," he began searching for the best location in Chicago for Christian settlement work.[69]

Taylor finally settled on the seventeenth ward, a working-class district crowded with German, Scandinavian, and Irish immigrants. Four of Taylor's students spent the summer of 1894 scouting the neighborhood for a house large enough to accommodate both the residents and neighborhood gatherings. Eventually they spotted a run-down brick structure at the corner of Union Street and Milwaukee Avenue. It was surrounded by boarding houses, small factories, and shops. Taylor promptly signed a five-year lease on the property, and in October he and his wife and four children plus the four students took possession. At the time they had no name for their enterprise. "We were just a household. We knew what we were there for, but how to let others know this and what to call . . . [ourselves] perplexed us." Publishers of a seminary brochure wanted a name for the sociological laboratory. At the last minute Taylor appealed to one of his business acquaintances who sug-

[69] Graham Taylor, "The Commons — The Chicago Seminary Settlement," *The Advance*, XXIX (October 11, 1894), 60; Taylor, *Pioneering*, pp. 108, 111, 7; G. S. F. Savage to Graham Taylor, September 7, 1892; Taylor, "The Commons — The Chicago Seminary Settlement," p. 60; Stead, *If Christ Came to Chicago!* pp. 412, 413; Woods and Kennedy, *Settlement Horizon*, pp. 48, 50; Taylor, Diary, May, 1893; Graham Taylor, "Response of Graham Taylor," *Chicago Theological Seminary Register*, XVII (January, 1927), 8.

gested The Commons. Samuel Ives Curtiss observed, "Any movement to be great must have Chicago in it." So the settlement was christened Chicago Commons.[70]

In 1894, Taylor thought of the settlement primarily as a "social observatory" and "statistical laboratory" for his students. In time it became much more than that. All of Taylor's later ventures — the training school for social workers, editorial columns, books, and articles, labor arbitration, and participation in civic reform — stemmed from experience and insight acquired at the settlement. Toward the end of his life Taylor declared, "Upon what I have seen, heard, and felt at Chicago Commons . . . my whole life proves to have been pivoted. Chicago Commons is part of me and I am part of it." In the long run, then, Graham Taylor's 1894 decision to establish his own settlement was an effective response to the challange of Chicago.[71]

[70] Graham Taylor, *Chicago Commons Through Forty Years* (Chicago, 1936), p. 9; *Chicago Theological Seminary, Department of Christian Sociology* (Chicago, 1895), p. 9; Taylor, *Pioneering*, p. 7; Herman F. Hegner to Graham Taylor, April 26, 1934, in the possession of Lea Taylor.

[71] *Chicago Theological Seminary, Department of Christian Sociology*, p. 9; Taylor, *Pioneering*, p. 9.

Four ⚜ *Religion and Social Action*

All of the large, industrial, urban centers had "Black Cities" within their midsts. Like Chicago, they too experienced rapid growth, an influx of immigrants, and great disparity between poverty and wealth. Thy struggled with festering slums, inadequate municipal facilities, and political corruption. Though many city dwellers paid little attention to these problems, there were reformers who ardently advocated a variety of solutions. Some thought Henry George's single tax was the answer. Nationalists insisted that Edward Bellamy's views were correct. A few people argued for socialism, while many others joined civic reform movements to drive the corrupt bosses and aldermen out of politics. Advocates of city parks and playgrounds and the leaders of charity organization societies often joined hands with the settlement house residents and institutional church workers to build a better city according to their blueprints.

Among the most persistent reformers were the liberal religious leaders of the late nineteenth century. Catholic efforts to aid the urban poor were spearheaded by Cardinal Gibbons of Baltimore and Archbishop Ireland of St. Paul, Minnesota. Their concern for the laboring man was given official sanction by the papal encyclical *Rerum Novarum* in 1891 which defended the dignity of labor and called for the application of religious ethics to solve class conflict. Jews could turn to the Society for Ethical Culture, founded by Dr. Felix Adler in 1876. It provided a practical way for established Jewish families to help less fortunate people stranded in the slums.[1]

Reaching many more people in the 1880's and 1890's, however, were the Protestant advocates of the social gospel. This movement was an attempt to apply the social teachings of Jesus to an urban, industrial society. It was influenced by British Christian Socialism as well as by pre-Civil War developments in American theology. But the growing tension between employers

---

[1] Arthur M. Schlesinger, *The Rise of the City, 1878–1898* ("A History of American Life, Vol. X, [New York, 1933]), pp. 343–44; Blake McKelvey, *The Urbanization of America, 1860–1915* (New Brunswick, 1963), pp. 158–59.

and employees and the obvious failures of American city government brought the social gospel movement to a climax in the late 1890's and the early years of the twentieth century. Supporters of the movement were convinced that social Christianity was the only way to secure justice for both employers and employees and the only way to achieve permanently effective municipal reform.[2]

In the 1870's only a handful of Protestant ministers dared call for the application of the social teachings of Jesus, and their voices were lost in the chorus of clerical praise for the Gilded Age. But social Christianity gained many middle-class converts in the 1880's, made a deep impression upon Protestant churches and seminaries in the 1890's, and became an important element in the twentieth century reform movement. In these decades the leaders of the social gospel formulated their own progressive theology and promoted a wide variety of social and economic reforms. Graham Taylor's thirty-six years as a professor of theology — from his appointment at Hartford in 1888 until his retirement from Chicago Theological Seminary in 1924 — coincided with the rise of the social gospel. He was one of the spokesmen for the movement, contributing to its success through his teachings, his advocacy of social Christianity before theological and lay audiences, and his ardent pleas for reform in numerous magazine articles and in his book, *Religion in Social Action*.

Among the precursors of the social gospel were Horace Bushnell and the revivalist preachers of the pre-Civil War years. The latter had insisted as early as the 1840's that men could sin as a group as well as individually and that only a "general revival of religion" could purify society. Meantime, Bushnell's concept of Christian nurture was breaking down the extreme individualism in Calvinist thought and focusing attention on God's mercy rather than His stern justice. In addition, Bushnell helped to narrow the gap between nature and the supernatural and to restore Christ to the center of the Christian system. Once theologians viewed man's nature as divinely inspired and conceived of Jesus's life and teaching as a model for mankind, the way was open for man to work toward his own redemption. He no longer had to sit back and wait for salvation at the whim of an inscrutable God.[3]

---

[2] Shailer Mathews defined the social gospel as "the application of the teaching of Jesus and the total message of the Christian salvation to society, the economic life, and social institutions . . . as well as to individuals." Shailer Mathews and G. B. Smith, *A Dictionary of Religion and Ethics* (New York, 1921), pp. 416–17.

[3] Smith, *Revivalism and Social Reform*, p. 152, and chaps. x, xi; Charles C. Cole, Jr., *The Social Ideas of the Northern Evangelists, 1826–1860* (New York, 1954), pp. 96, 98–104; W. A. Visser 'T Hooft, *The Background of the Social Gospel in America* (Haarlem, 1928), chap. v; Hopkins, *Social Gospel*, p. 5; Arthur C. McGiffert, *The Rise of Modern Religious Ideas* (New York, 1915), p. 277; John W. Buckham, *Progressive Reli-*

Bushnell's ideas found acceptance at Andover Seminary, a leading Congregational school in Massachusetts. In the 1880's, Andover became a center of "progressive orthodoxy" which sought to adjust Calvinism to the liberating influence of Bushnell as well as to scientific criticism of the Scriptures and the doctrine of evolution. The *Andover Review,* founded in 1884, was the chief organ for expressing these new ideas. Among those who wrote for it were Professor William Jewett Tucker of Andover Seminary, Samuel Lane Loomis, a Brooklyn pastor, John Bascom, president of the University of Wisconsin, and Theodore Munger, a New Haven pastor, author of *The Freedom of Faith* (1883), and future biographer of Horace Bushnell. These men made it clear that they did "not reject the specific doctrines of the church of the past." Rather, the progressives asked for acceptance of the theory of evolution "as the probable method of creation." They called for a study of the Scriptures as literature and asked the church to promote "the solidarity of the race" and "ally itself with all movements for bettering the condition of mankind."[4]

In *Progressive Orthodoxy* (1886), a compilation of articles from the *Andover Review,* the reformers touched on the idea of a whole society sinning. Tucker, for example, said, "It is difficult to maintain the personal sense of sin under the knowledge of what society has done and is doing to make the individual a sinner." By 1891 he was writing, "if we would analyze the poor man's poverty, we must stop and analyze the rich man's wealth." Many years later when William Jewett Tucker looked back on progressive orthodoxy, he decided that its "distinctive characteristic" was

> its humanistic impulse. . . . It took account of the individual in his human environment. It viewed him more definitely as a social being, a part of a vast but closely fitting social organization. . . . It refused to obey the mandate of the old political economy, and leave the individual to the fortune of the market-place.[5]

The Protestant social conscience was also affected by English Christian Socialism. After careful investigation of mid-nineteenth-century industrial England, the Christian Socialists appealed to the Church of England to emphasize God's love of mankind rather than the theme of eternal damna-

---

gious Thought in America (Boston, 1919), chap. i; Frank H. Foster, *The Modern Movement in American Theology* (New York, 1939), chap. iv; Cross, *Bushnell,* chap. x; Munger, *Bushnell,* chap. xix; May, *Protestant Churches,* p. 85.

[4] Hopkins, *Social Gospel,* pp. 61–63; Theodore T. Munger, "The New Theology," prefatory essay in *The Freedom of Faith* (Boston, 1883), pp. 9, 25.

[5] Quoted in Daniel Day Williams, *The Andover Liberals* (New York, 1941), pp. 122, 123; Tucker, *My Generation,* pp. 96–97; Buckham, *Progressive Religious Thought,* chaps. ii–iv.

tion. They wanted to substitute the Christian idea of co-operation for competition in the economic sphere. And they hoped that the church would seek a union of "labour and learning" by establishing contacts between the upper and the lower classes. Among the leading Christian Socialist spokesmen were Frederick Denison Maurice and Charles Kingsley. In the 1850's, 1860's, and 1870's, Maurice and Kingsley turned out Christian Socialist tracts, edited a weekly paper, lectured in the universities, and helped establish a Working Men's College in London. Kingsley also wrote popular novels of social protest. Christian Socialism left its mark on John Ruskin and John R. Seeley at Oxford and Cambridge, Canons Fremantle and Barnett, Arnold Toynbee, the Stead brothers, and scores of others. In the United States Kingsley's novels sold well, and Phillips Brooks edited an important collection of Maurice's writings in 1886 under the title *Faith and Action*.[6]

Still other intellectual influences were at work in this period. The tendency to picture Jesus as a man whose advice and example could be taken literally was greatly strengthened by John R. Seeley's *Ecce Homo: A Survey of the Life and Work of Jesus Christ* (1886). In this seminal book, Seeley stated that the religious significance of Christ's life lay in his social ethics and that Christian morality necessitated an active "enthusiasm for humanity." He concluded that each Christian was obligated "to do as much good as possible to every other." Seeley felt that this would help make the Kingdom of God realizable on earth. Another man who identified Christianity with social progress was Charles Loring Brace. His *Gesta Christi: or a History of Humane Progress under Christianity* (1882) contained the persuasive argument that Jesus' teachings provided the "moral force" to make Christianity "the *greatest* element in modern progress." The marriage of social Christianity and the idea of progress spawned a powerful religious optimism that permeated the social gospel movement.[7]

Yet it was the bitter industrial conflict in the United States which did more than anything else to jolt middle-class Protestants from a conservative outlook in the 1870's to the liberal social gospel point of view by the 1890's. The recurrent strikes and depressions forced complacent clergymen to re-evaluate laissez faire government. The fierce economic competition and exploitation of labor encouraged many to study the role of labor unions, and some to weigh the attractions of socialism. Social gospel spokesmen were soon defending organized labor as necessary for the "mutual protection and defense" of the working class. They described the political and economic philos-

[6] D. C. Somervell, *English Thought in the Nineteenth Century* (New York, 1929), pp. 111–12, 116–18; Pimlott, *Toynbee Hall*, pp. 4, 17, 40; Hopkins, *Social Gospel*, p. 7.
[7] Somervell, *English Thought*, p. 120; Hopkins, *Social Gospel*, pp. 22–23, 19–20, 63–65; May, *Protestant Churches*, p. 150 and n.

ophy of the Gilded Age as "selfish," "inhumane," "unchristian," "unethical," "immoral," and "barbaric." "Is it not evident," asked one advocate of social Christianity,

> that our economic system is diametrically opposed to Christian teaching? Christianity is the religion of peace, but industrial classes are avowedly in a state of warfare. . . . Christianity means co-operation and the uplifting of the lowliest; business means competition and the survival of the strongest.[8]

If industrial warfare provided "the drastic, sudden shocks" needed "to shatter Protestant complacency," another jolt came from the country's burgeoning cities. The clergy of the 1860's and 1870's had been able to cater to urban upper classes, to praise their scientific, industrial, and financial progress, and to commend their patronage of the arts. Some of these ministers in the 1880's moved off to the better residential areas with their parishioners and managed to ignore the rot and decay at the heart of the city. But others scrutinized "the 'putrefying sores' of the city." They found that immigrants pouring into already crowded quarters bred slums, disease, violence, and misery. Furthermore, their religious censuses showed that many families had no church affiliation and wanted none with the "gilded pulpit." [9]

Social Christianity made a genuine effort to reach the unchurched masses in American cities. These ministers were distressed by Samuel Gompers' charge that the working men had "come to look upon the church and the ministry as the apologists and defenders of the wrongs committed against the interest of the people." The "real God" of Protestantism, said Gompers, was "the almighty dollar." Social gospel leaders tried to convince the embittered union members that not all churches were financed by "tainted money" and not all pastors were worshipers of mammon. In addition, they found that many of the immigrants coming in the 1880's and 1890's had no "Christian culture . . . behind them" and no understanding of the concepts "with which all the Americans, whether of pious parentage or not, have been familiar from childhood." Rather than limit or cut off the flow of immigrants, as some Americans were demanding, most social gospel leaders wanted the Protestant churches to adapt their services and programs to meet the needs of the newcomers. City missions, institutional churches, and religious settle-

---

[8] May, *Protestant Churches*, p. 111 and Part III, chap. i; quoted in Hopkins, *Social Gospel*, p. 81; quoted in Fine, *Laissez Faire*, pp. 172–73; Charles Worcester Clark, "Applied Christianity: Who Shall Apply It First?" *Andover Review*, XIX (January, 1893), 23–24.

[9] May, *Protestant Churches*, p. 112 and Part III, chap. ii; Josiah Strong, *The New Era, or the Coming Kingdom* (New York, 1893), p. 332; Abell, *Urban Impact*, chap. i and pp. 61–62; Hopkins, *Social Gospel*, p. 83.

ments were the most successful ways in which social Christianity ministered to classes dwelling in the heart of American cities.[10]

Social gospel spokesmen tackled these baffling, complex problems with confidence and optimism because they were certain that "the Christian law covers every relation of life." They demanded more Christianity, just as political reformers at the turn of the century urged more democracy as the solution for political corruption. The religious reformers and their largely middle-class followers were confident that Jesus' social gospel was "the key to all industrial problems, the solvent for all class distinctions, the law for all righteous elevation, the remedy for all remediable social evils and the method of adjustment for all conflicting interests."[11]

Convinced of the efficacy of their healing balm, they naturally rejected political socialism as a remedy, and most of them disliked the concept of a general welfare state too. "Only a small portion of the Kingdom of Heaven cometh through legislation," explained one. It was far better to Christianize individuals and let them Christianize capitalist society and ultimately usher in the kingdom of God on earth. At the core of the social gospel movement was the facile belief that

> When the Golden Rule of Christ shall measure the relations of men in all their duties towards their fellows, in factory and workshop, in the mine, in the field, in commerce . . . the promise of the prophet and the poet shall be fulfilled . . . and peace on earth shall prevail.[12]

II

By the end of the 1890's a large number of ministers, teachers, and laymen, and a variety of organizations were advocating social Christianity. One of the earliest voices from the pulpit was that of Washington Gladden, "the father of the social gospel." Studying under John Bascom at Williams College and influenced by Horace Bushnell, Gladden tried his hand at teaching and journalism before he took a Congregational church in Springfield, Massachusetts, in 1875. Observing the warfare between employers and employees within his own organization, Gladden determined "to grapple with it, and to try and get at the rights of it." By the time he published *Applied Christianity* in 1886, he was a strong defender of labor unions and a critic of "the wage-system when it rests on competition as its sole basis. . . . it has been bringing hell to earth in large installments for a good many years." In 1882,

[10] Quoted in Abell, *Urban Impact,* p. 63; Samuel L. Loomis, *Modern Cities and Their Religious Problems* (New York, 1887), p. 91.

[11] Washington Gladden, *Recollections* (Boston, 1909), p. 252; quoted in Hopkins, *Social Gospel,* p. 88.

[12] Quoted in Fine, *Laissez Faire,* p. 179.

Gladden moved to the First Congregational Church in Columbus, Ohio, where he remained until his death in 1918. Throughout these years he took an active interest in industrial relations and civic reform, even serving on the Columbus city council from 1900 to 1902.[13]

If Gladden's own life was an inspiration to the religious reformers, so too were his writings. In *Ruling Ideas of the Present Age* (1895), he distinguished three basic concepts at the heart of the social gospel: the "immanence of Christ," the "vital unity of the race," and the "presence of the kingdom." For Gladden, as for other believers in social Christianity, God's immanence in nature and human society broke down the long-standing barrier between the material and the spiritual realms. The "vital unity of the race" led them to emphasize the brotherhood of man, a concept which most of them considered fully as important as the fatherhood of God. Gladden, for example, felt that one's "deepest religious experiences" should come from identification with one's fellow-men. But he added that it was necessary to strike a balance between "the independence of the individual" and "the solidarity of society." Neither laissez faire government nor socialism were capable of achieving the balance, said Gladden in *Ruling Ideas*. The only way to protect the interests of the one and the many was to apply Christian principles to capitalist society. For the "chief end of man is not the upbuilding of one at the cost of many . . . but the perfection of one in the blessedness of the many."[14]

Gladden also maintained that the Kingdom of God was immanent. "The reality is here," he said, "its completion is yet to come."

> Few lives are yet wholly under its influence; few homes are completely ruled by its pure precept; few institutions perfectly obey its royal law: yet its benign sway is felt. . . . The thought of the world is gradually being freed from superstition and prejudice; the social sentiments are being purified; the customs are slowly changing for the better; the laws are gradually shaped by finer conceptions of justice. There are reactions and disasters, but taking the ages together the progress is sure.[15]

Gladden's buoyant optimism brought cheer to thousands of troubled Americans. His clear prose and straight-forward theology did a great deal to disseminate the new ideas. And the example he set by seeking to promote industrial understanding and civic reform encouraged countless advocates of the social gospel.

[13] McKelvey, *Urbanization of America*, p. 161; Hopkins, *Social Gospel*, pp. 25–26; Gladden, *Recollections*, p. 294; Washington Gladden, *Applied Christianity, The Moral Aspects of Social Questions* (Boston, 1893), p. 33, 135–36; May, *Protestant Churches*, pp. 171–74; Fine, *Laissez Faire*, pp. 184–85.

[14] Washington Gladden, *Ruling Ideas of the Present Age* (Boston, 1895), pp. 294, 92, 63, 96.

[15] Gladden, *Ruling Ideas*, pp. 289–90.

Another influential exponent of the social gospel was Richard T. Ely. He taught at Johns Hopkins in the 1880's and in 1892 went to the University of Wisconsin to head the school of economics, political science, and history. Ely considered the state "religious in its essence" and the primary function of government the creation of "the good life" for all its citizens. He steered a middle course between Gladden's "two opposing errors," rigid conservatism and socialism. The golden mean lay in effecting reforms within the framework of existing society. In *Social Aspects of Christianity* (1889) Ely urged the church to utilize the state as a means of securing necessary reform.

> It is as truly a religious work to pass good laws, as it is to preach sermons; as holy a work to lead a crusade against filth, vice, and disease in slums of cities, and to seek the abolition of the disgraceful tenement-houses of American cities, as it is to send missionaries to the heathen.

All of Ely's speeches, articles, and books, as well as his teaching career and work with the American Economic Association, helped to promote an interest in the social side of the church's mission.[16]

The Congregational pastor and editor, Lyman Abbott, also spread the appeal of social Christianity. Protégé of Henry Ward Beecher, Abbott edited a religious journal, *Christian Union*, during the 1880's, making it an important forum for social Christianity. After 1893 when the magazine became the *Outlook*, Abbott shifted its emphasis from religious to political and literary affairs. But he continued to dwell on aspects of the social gospel as Beecher's successor at Plymouth Congregational Church in Brooklyn and as a prominent lecturer and author. Though he felt that individual regeneration must precede far-reaching social reforms, he was willing to make use of the state as an instrument of change. In *Christianity and Social Problems* (1896) he argued that the functions of government ought to be enlarged. Abbott was keenly interested in the doctrine of evolution and thought that it offered invincible proof of man's "spiritual evolution" and of the ultimate triumph of good in an earthly kingdom of God. Among his many contributions to the social gospel movement was a succinct answer to the question, "What is Christianity?" "The object of Christianity is human welfare; its method is character-building; its process is evolution; and the secret of its power is God."[17]

[16] Richard T. Ely, *Socialism: An Examination of its Nature, its Strength, and its Weakness, with Suggestions for Social Reform* (New York, 1894), pp. 253–61; Richard T. Ely, *Social Aspects of Christianity, and Other Essays* (New York, 1889), p. 73; Fine, *Laissez Faire*, pp. 180–81, 229–41; Hopkins, *Social Gospel*, pp. 106–9; Abell, *Urban Impact*, pp. 68–69; May, *Protestant Churches*, pp. 140–42.

[17] Ira V. Brown, *Lyman Abbott, Christian Evolutionist: A Study in Religious Liberalism* (Cambridge, Mass., 1953), pp. 77–78, 104–7; Lyman Abbott, *Christianity and Social*

Urbanism as a challenge to social Christianity was the primary interest of the energetic Josiah Strong. He filled several pulpits and was secretary of the Congregational Home Missionary Society before publishing his first important book, *Our Country, Its Possible Future and its Present Crisis* (1885). The sensational reception of this book encouraged him to leave the pulpit for the Evangelical Alliance, a moribund organization which he took over in 1886 and promptly revitalized. Strong organized three national conferences to discuss social Christianity, in 1887, 1889, and the one in Chicago during the 1893 Exposition. When the Alliance failed to support his ambitious program for mass education in social issues, Strong resigned and established first the League and then the American Institute of Social Service. In addition to scores of tracts published by these various organizations, Josiah Strong found time to write among other volumes *The New Era, or the Coming Kingdom* (1893), *The Twentieth Century City* (1898), and *The Challenge of the City* (1911). Like other social gospel advocates, Strong argued that urban problems, political problems, and industrial problems could all be reconciled if the church took up her proper mission and became "the controlling conscience of the social organism."[18]

The drive to enlist the church in social and political reform affected Unitarians as well as other Protestants. One of their leaders was Jenkin Lloyd Jones, general secretary of the World's Parliament of Religions and pastor of All Souls Church in Chicago from 1882 until his death in 1918. In addition, Jones edited the magazine *Unity* in which he discussed controversial topics of the day and stressed the common bonds of all religions. Worried by the bitter industrial conflict of the 1890's, particularly the Pullman strike, he warned of the "forked lightning" that threatened all Americans. He hoped that employers would someday share his view of labor organizations as "the morning star of the new day, the latest and finest product of social evolution." Municipal corruption also concerned him. Chicago, he said in 1894, "has had prosperity thrust upon it. It remains to be seen whether it can convert this prosperity into greatness."

> Chicago has outrun the moral development of its citizens. . . . That is what is the matter with the politics of our city, the destinies of which are shaped in the saloons instead of in our churches and the council chambers of the wise. . . . Six thousand saloons thrive in this city, every one of which is a political headquarters, and a score or more of the keepers of these saloons are in our city council.

Problems (Boston, 1896), pp. 115–17; Lyman Abbott, *The Evolution of Christianity* (Boston, 1893), pp. 254–58; Lyman Abbott, "What is Christianity?", *Arena*, III (1891), 46; Fine, *Laissez Faire*, pp. 174, 182–83.

[18] Strong, *New Era*, p. 313; Hopkins, *Social Gospel*, pp. 259–62.

Jones urged respectable citizens to unite and present a solid front against these corrupt influences. Under his guidance, All Souls Church by the 1890's was sponsoring a kindergarten, many classes, public lectures and discussions, a library and reading room, and a settlement house near the stockyards. Early in the twentieth century he got Frank Lloyd Wright to design Abraham Lincoln Center, which housed church, settlement, and community hall.[19]

The social gospel movement found its theologian in Walter Rauschenbusch. Minister of a German Baptist church near Hell's Kitchen in New York City from 1886 until 1897, he knew at first-hand the social and religious ramifications of urban decay and economic exploitation of immigrants. During the depression of 1893 the sound of "human virtue cracking and crumbling all around" made him question the validity of his orthodox theological views. He read widely during these years, including the works of English Christian Socialists, the American reformers such as Henry George, Edward Bellamy, and Jacob Riis, the mounting social gospel literature, as well as the books of Ruskin, Tolstoi, and Marx. With a small group of clerical friends he formed the Brotherhood of the Kingdom in 1892 to "re-establish" the concept of an earthly kingdom of God "in the thought of the church, and to assist in its practical realization in the world." New recruits flocked to this lively religious organization, making its discussions and annual summer conferences, its publication of tracts and a quarterly periodical, effective propaganda for social Christianity.[20]

Increasing deafness forced Rauschenbusch to leave his church in 1897 and accept a professorship at the Rochester Theological Seminary. Long before his death in 1918 his teaching and writing made him the intellectual leader of the social gospel movement. In *Christianity and the Social Crisis* (1907) he described the social aspects of religion in historical perspective, sketched the present crisis, and briefly suggested "What to Do." Further analysis of current problems and their solution was the theme of *Christianizing the Social Order* (1912). Here Rauschenbusch developed the concept of an entire society sinning or winning salvation.

[19] Jenkin Lloyd Jones, *The Word of the Spirit of the Nation, Church, City, Home and Individual* (Chicago, 1894), pp. 12, 14, 33, 36, 37–38; Louise C. Wade, "Chicago Settlement Papers," *Social Service Review*, XXXVII (December, 1963), 462; William Kent, "Jenkin Lloyd Jones," *American Magazine*, LXX (July, 1910), 320–22.

[20] Ray Stannard Baker, "The Spiritual Unrest: A Vision of the New Christianity," *American Magazine*, LXIX (December, 1909), p. 179; Dores R. Sharpe, *Walter Rauschenbusch* (New York, 1942), chap. v, vii; Charles H. Hopkins, "Rauschenbusch and the Brotherhood of the Kingdom," *Church History*, VII (1938), 138–56; Hopkins, *Social Gospel*, pp. 131–33, 216–17.

> Sin is a social force. It runs from man to man along the lines of social contact. . . . Salvation, too, is a social force. It is exerted by groups that are charged with divine will and love.

Complete salvation, wrote Rauschenbusch, was an impossibility until man created "a Christian social order which will serve as the spiritual environment of the individual." [21]

Aware that "righteous life and action" must precede the reign of God on earth, Rauschenbusch called for the immediate application of the social teachings of Jesus. In 1916 he prepared a study manual, *The Social Principles of Jesus*, and the following year published his most important book, *A Theology for the Social Gospel*. In this volume he categorically stated that "Since the Kingdom is the supreme end of God, it must be the purpose for which the Church exists." Therefore, the "institutions of the Church, its activities, its worship, and its theology must in the long run be tested by its effectiveness in creating the Kingdom of God." [22]

On the left wing of the social gospel movement were the Christian Socialists William D. P. Bliss and George D. Herron. These non-Marxian reformers would win the kingdom of God by socializing all productive property. Influenced by Henry George, Edward Bellamy, and the English Christian Socialists, Bliss formed in Boston a Society of Christian Socialists and later worked with the Christian Social Union. In addition, he edited *The Dawn* to prove that "the teachings of Jesus lead directly to some form of socialism." Though Bliss was content to establish socialism gradually, George Herron was not. He dismissed capitalist competition as "social imbecility," and his answer to the Gilded Age's Gospel of Wealth was an angry dissertation on "The Message of Jesus to Men of Wealth." From 1893 until 1901, Herron occupied a chair in applied Christianity at Iowa (later Grinnell) College where he was financed by a well-to-do parishioner and shielded from public criticism by the president. Herron's divorce in 1901 and subsequent marriage to his benefactress' daughter ruined his theological career and drove him into exile in Italy. Prior to his departure, however, he launched in 1894 and edited until 1899 the social gospel's most widely circulated journal, *The Kingdom*. Moreover, Herron's agitation in the 1890's inspired the establishment of a unique Christian Commonwealth Colony in Georgia where some 350 people tried to "obey the teachings of Jesus Christ in all matters of life, and labor, and

[21] Hopkins, *Social Gospel*, pp. 218–20; Walter Rauschenbusch, *Christianizing the Social Order* (New York, 1912), p. 116.

[22] Hopkins, *Social Gospel*, pp. 228–32; Walter Rauschenbusch, *A Theology for the Social Gospel* (New York, 1917), p. 143.

in the use of property." They too had a magazine, *The Social Gospel*, and though it folded with the colony in 1900, it is generally credited with popularizing the term "social gospel." [23]

A spate of novels in the 1880's and 1890's helped to propagandize the principles of social Christianity. One of the earliest was Washington Gladden's *The Christian League of Connecticut* (1883), a brisk account of an interdenominational union of churches that reformed a factory town. The most successful social gospel novel, however, was Charles M. Sheldon's *In His Steps: What Would Jesus Do?* (1896). Trained for the ministry at Andover, Sheldon took a church in 1889 in Topeka, Kansas, and promptly investigated social, political, and economic questions in the community. He wrote a series of realistic sermon stories for a Congregational paper in the 1890's but never attracted national attention until the publication of *In His Steps*. The plot of this best seller revolves around the experiment of fifty volunteers who promise to take no action of any kind until they asked themselves, "What would Jesus do?" Needless to say, their application of the social teachings of Jesus revolutionizes the life of their city and promises to start a national revival of social Christianity. By June, 1897, more than 100,000 copies had been sold, and Sheldon estimated in 1933 that a total of 23 million copies had been purchased in the English-speaking world.[24]

The blossoming of social Christianity in the late 1890's was hastened by the influential Chautauqua movement. Among the favorite lecturers at Lake Chautauqua and on the local circuits were Richard T. Ely, Washington Gladden, Lyman Abbott, Josiah Strong, Francis G. Peabody, Jacob Riis, Charles Henderson, Jane Addams, Charles Zueblin, and Graham Taylor. Educational aspects of the movement were developed by two organizations modeled after their English counterparts — The Church Association for the Advancement of the Interests of Labor, C.A.I.L., founded in 1887, and the Christian Social Union established in 1891 to encourage "scientific study and analysis of social problems." Two years later Richard T. Ely created the American Institute of Christian Sociology for the purpose of studying "how to apply the principles of Christianity to the social and economic difficulties of the present time . . . by publications, by lectures, and addresses, by the establishment of libraries, professorships, etc." The professorships, however, were unnecessary, for social Christianity was already penetrating many theological seminaries.

[23] Quoted in Abell, *Urban Impact*, p. 76; Fine, *Laissez Faire*, p. 174; Hopkins, *Social Gospel*, 196, chaps. x, xi; Dombrowski, *Christian Socialism*, chaps. ix, x, xii, xiii; May, *Protestant Churches*, Part IV, chap. v.

[24] Hopkins, *Social Gospel*, pp. 140–48. In London William T. Stead immediately recognized the similarity between Sheldon's book and *If Christ Came to Chicago!* He labeled the 1899 edition of his volume, "The precursor of *In His Steps*."

The appearance of numerous institutional churches and religious settlements and the formation of a national federation of Protestant churches which endorsed many social gospel concepts in the early twentieth century were further proof that the movement toward social Christianity was coming of age.[25]

III

Graham Taylor was an avid reader of this social gospel literature. He had already assigned some of it to his classes in Hartford and would use much more during his years of teaching at the Chicago Theological Seminary. He felt that his own growing comprehension of social Christianity was reflected in his inaugural address delivered in the spring of 1893. In his first inaugural in 1888 he had "coveted for the church" the sole responsibility of redeeming the community. By 1893, Taylor had learned that "other groups and agencies were essentially religious and constituted along with the church the kingdom of God on earth." Moreover, he knew that "the church did not always prove to be the best executor of its own ideals." Thus "family, neighborly, industrial, civic, cultural, and other groupings and agencies" must be considered "tributary to the whole endeavor to realize the ideals of religion."[26]

Taylor went on to discuss the problems of communicating the social gospel point of view to students. He would not insist upon memorization of facts, theories, or history. Rather, he would teach them to observe social and industrial conditions, classify facts, and draw conclusions for themselves. Above all, he wanted his students to comprehend the interdependence of family, business, state, social and recreational activities and the church. This was the ambitious goal which Taylor set himself in his 1893 inaugural. But the testimony of Chicago Theological Seminary graduates over the next three decades suggests that the Professor of Christian Sociology fulfilled it.[27]

Taylor had contact with every student at the seminary for he taught three required courses and directed the compulsory field work. In the 1890's first-year men took "Biblical Sociology" with him, second-year students the "Economics of the Kingdom," and seniors a course in sociology. After the turn of the century, Taylor broadened the scope of these courses and in 1905 changed the name of the department to Social Economics. The freshman course was called a "Survey of the Field and Functions of Religious and Social Work." Second year students studied the "Social Teachings of the Scriptures," while

[25] Hopkins, *Social Gospel*, pp. 163–67, 150–52; Abell, *Urban Impact*, pp. 106–13, 236–43; May, *Protestant Churches*, pp. 184–85; Fine, *Laissez Faire*, pp. 171–72, 239.

[26] Taylor, *Pioneering*, p. 398.

[27] Graham Taylor, "Address When Inaugurated Prof. of Christian Sociology in C.T.S.," April 18, 1893 (typed manuscript); Graham Taylor, "Our New Professorship," *The Advance*, XXV (September 8, 1892), 698.

the seniors took "Social Theory and Practice as Related to Christian Faith and Forces." In addition to these required courses Taylor offered a wide variety of electives over the years. Among these were "Social Institutions," "Causes and Treatment of Dependency," "Ethical and Religious Aspects of Industry," "Municipal Economics and Reform," and "Delinquency, Vice and Crime." Of course, the Chicago Commons settlement remained the center for seminary field work throughout these decades.[28]

By 1900, Taylor felt that he had worked up a well-rounded survey of Christian sociology, and he published the outline of his course in a thirty-page pamphlet entitled *Syllabus in Biblical Sociology*. Distributing this to his students saved time in the class-room, and he could mail it to the "many correspondents, who are inquiring for guidance and bibliography." Taylor divided the *Syllabus* into five parts. Section one defined the subject and discussed methodology, while section two traced the historical origin of the idea of kingdom in the Old Testament and the social structure and institutions of the Hebrews. Taylor's next division, "Christian Social Order as Disclosed in the Life and Teachings of Christ," treated the social ideals personified by Jesus and expressed in His ministry. Section four outlined the Christian social ideals of the early churches, and the final section summarized "The Principal Social Concepts of Scripture." Here Taylor maintained that "the concept of the Kingdom is . . . the progressive realization in human experience and history of the divine ideal of relationship between man and God and man and man" within the five life-spheres — the family, neighborhood, economic sphere, political sphere, and religious sphere of the churches.[29]

Taylor assigned his *Syllabus in Biblical Sociology* to his own students for many years and mailed out hundred of copies. Since this pamphlet was widely used in other seminaries and appeared in most libraries, it may well have been his best-known publication. To help the layman who was interested in social Christianity, Taylor compiled a fourteen-page bibliography, *Books for Beginners in the Study of Christian Sociology and Social Economics*. He referred the reader to books by Herbert Spencer, John Ruskin, Jacob Riis, Edward Bellamy, Henry George, John Fiske, Lester Ward, John R. Commons, Woodrow Wilson, and William Dean Howells. In the social gospel literature he called attention to the work of Kingsley and Maurice, as well as Gladden, Ely, Strong, Brace, Fremantle, and F. Herbert Stead. He also listed periodicals such as *Charities Review, Social Science Journal, Annals of*

[28] Chicago Theological Seminary, *Year-Books*, 1892–93 through 1914–15; "Social Economics — Prescribed and Elective Courses," 1906 (typed manuscript).

[29] Graham Taylor, *Syllabus in Biblical Sociology* (Chicago, 1900), Apologia, 14, 23, 26–27.

the American Academy of Political and Social Science, and the proceedings of the American Economic Association and the Evangelical Alliance.[30]

Books for Beginners and Taylor's reading suggestions in the *Syllabus* reflect the rapid growth of Christian sociological literature in the 1890's. He still assigned some of the books he had used in Hartford: Fremantle's *The World as the Subject of Redemption,* Seeley's *Ecce Homo,* Bushnell's *Nature and the Supernatural,* and Brace's *Gesta Christi.* But he was able to add F. Herbert Stead's *Kingdom of God* (1894), a "remarkably compact and suggestive little volume . . . used wherever possible . . . as a reference text-book." And after 1897 he could refer his students to William D. P. Bliss's monumental *Encyclopedia of Social Reform,* the first scholarly compilation of sociological data in America. In addition, Taylor made frequent use of Gladden's *Ruling Ideas,* Strong's *The New Era,* Francis G. Peabody's *Jesus Christ and the Social Question* (1900), Henry S. Nash's *The Genesis of the Social Conscience* (1897), Shailer Mathews' *The Social Teachings of Jesus* (1897), and several volumes by George Herron who was at the peak of his career in 1900.[31]

Taylor knew that much valuable material in his field could be found only in pamphlets, periodicals, or government documents. Fortunately the chairman of the board of directors of the seminary, E. W. Blatchford, was also connected with the Newberry Library and was willing to order $75 worth of periodicals and reports. Taylor requested the *Charity Review, Proceedings of the National Conference of Charities and Correction,* and *The Johns Hopkins University Studies in History and Political Science.* He also wanted the publications of the Knights of Labor, the Brotherhood of Locomotive Engineers, the Farmers' Alliance, the *New Nation* put out by Bellamy's followers, and the Christian Socialist *The Dawn.* Furthermore, Blatchford secured the journals of the American Economics Association, the American Academy of Political and Social Science, the American Statistical Association, the American Social Science Association, the National Prison Association, and the Christian Workers' Association.[32]

Taylor's method of teaching was inductive. A visitor to his classroom in 1894 observed that his lectures moved from "a study of the conditions of the day" to "principles and general rules of action." The students claimed that they always knew how the class period would start and end, for their

---

[30] Graham Taylor, *Books for Beginners in the Study of Christian Sociology and Social Economics* (Boston and Chicago, 1895?).

[31] Taylor, *Pioneering,* 399; Hopkins, *Social Gospel,* 163, 258; Taylor, *Syllabus,* Apologia, *passim.*

[32] E. W. Blatchford to Graham Taylor, September 15, 1892; Graham Taylor to E. W. Blatchford, November, 1892, E. W. Blatchford Collection, Newberry Library, Chicago, Ill.

professor invariably "began with the last incident which captured his attention on the way from the Commons to the Seminary" and "ended with some discussion of the social or cosmic system." Taylor himself described his pedagogical technique this way: "I tried to start each course on some common ground shared by my students. Usually it was the Christian 'burden of the soul'. . . . Gradually we worked back into the antecedents and out into the social conditions." [33]

He was always ready to admit that two things were more useful for his students than lectures or reading assignments. One was careful contemplation of the Scriptures, and the other was field work. Taylor often said that his success as a teacher was due in large part to his rich experience at Chicago Commons. Without it, "my classroom would have been more academic than practical, more theoretical than exemplary, more in second-hand touch with literary sources than in direct contacts with life, . . . more stereotyped than original or progressive." [34]

Taylor's students admired his catholicity of spirit, his ability to sympathize and encourage, his enthusiasm, and his sense of humor. Much of their respect stemmed from the knowledge that he was a man "who *lived what he taught*." Many of them arrived at the Seminary with the same outlook as James Mullenbach, a self-styled "rugged individualist" with no conception of the church's social mission. Yet Mullenbach was so impressed by Taylor that he took all Taylor's electives, lived for a time at the settlement, and went on to a distinguished career in charity administration and labor mediation. The classroom impact of the "Doc" was expressed by one student in these words:

> He starts like a Ford on a cold morning — on one cylinder — he halts and feels around for words, but after about ten minutes he is hitting on all four and runs like a Packard Twelve with intellect, will, emotion, and body in action. He is a torrent and a whirlwind, a great soul always driving on to a big destiny.

Whenever his busy schedule permitted, Taylor joined the students at their favorite eating spots along West Madison Street to swap jokes, give advice, and talk. "We surely had some great arguments with him over social questions at those oil-cloth covered tables at Hoffman's," recalled one seminarian. Another concluded that the jovial Doc Taylor was a powerful influence upon

[33] Joseph H. Chandler, "Forward Movements in Theological Training. III: Sociology and Field Work at Chicago Seminary," *Congregationalist*, LXXIX (May 3, 1894), 628; Arthur E. Holt, "Graham Taylor, 1851–1938," *Chicago Theological Seminary Register*, XXVIII (November, 1938), 1–2; Taylor, *Pioneering*, p. 398.

[34] Taylor, "Our New Professorship," p. 698; Taylor, *Pioneering*, p. 400; Taylor, "Response," *Chicago Theological Seminary Register*, XVIII (November, 1928), 26.

the seminary men because "his intense understanding and sympathy broke through the formalities of teacher into companionable friend which is the highest art of teaching." [35]

Taylor's success at the Chicago Theological Seminary did not escape the sharp eye of President William Rainey Harper, who was eager to attract talented teachers to his own rapidly expanding University of Chicago. In December, 1896 he wrote to Taylor, enclosing "a clipping which refers to you as a member of the University of Chicago. This is as it should be and I wonder sometimes whether, with all your other work, you might not do some for us down here. Can we not talk about it sometime?" Nothing came of this overture until December, 1902. At that time Harper asked Taylor to join the faculty of the sociology department as a full-time lecturer and he held out the promise of a professorship within two years. Taylor's seminary colleagues were distressed at the thought of losing him to the "business men" on the Midway, and they warned that the unique religious complexion of his "settlement work would soon become secularized at the University." [36]

Taylor would accept Harper's offer only if he could lecture part-time at the University and still keep his position at the Chicago Theological Seminary. Harper agreed to these terms, and so did the seminary. So from 1903 until 1906 Taylor taught a reduced load at the seminary and lectured in the University's department of sociology and anthropology with such men as Albion Small, Charles Henderson, and Charles Zueblin. Taylor offered courses in "Documentary and Biographical Sources of the History of Modern Philanthropy," the "Labor Movement Historically and Critically Considered," and "Humanitarian Progress in Local Institutions." At the end of the 1906 term he severed his connection with the department for reasons that are not entirely clear. It may have been due to administrative changes after Harper's death in January, 1906. Or it may have been Taylor's own decision. He was deeply involved in executive responsibilities at the seminary by 1906, and in addition he had his hands full with settlement work, editorial duties for

[35] J. W. F. Davies, "Graham Taylor: A Tribute From the Alumni," *Chicago Theological Seminary Register*, XVIII (November, 1928), 14, 15, 16; Letter from Class of 1894 to Graham Taylor, May 3, 1894; Robert W. Gammon, "Twenty-five Years of Chicago Commons: How Graham Taylor's Dreams Came True," *Congregationalist and Advance*, CIV (May 15, 1919), 621; Jane Mullenbach, "James Mullenbach: A Study in Social Leadership" (Master's thesis, University of Chicago, 1931), p. 33; quoted in Graham Taylor, "Seer and Saver," *Social Action*, I (May 1, 1935), 4; W. A. Whitcomb, "The Seminary 1893–96," *Chicago Theological Seminary Register*, XLI (March, 1951), 14; Robert W. Gammon, "Graham Taylor: An Intimate Portrait," *Advance*, CXXXI (January 1, 1939), 17.

[36] William R. Harper to Graham Taylor, December 5, 1896; Samuel Ives Curtiss to Graham Taylor, December 13, 16, 1902.

Charities and The Commons and The Chicago *Daily News*, and the training school for social workers which he had launched in 1903. Whatever the reasons, Taylor was dropped from the regular university faculty in 1906, though he continued to teach in the extension division until 1912. There his courses included "Human Partnerships," the "Ethics of Industry," "Studies in Social Biography," "Social Tendencies of Modern Industrialism," and "Philanthropic and Social Service." [37]

Taylor's pioneer teaching of Christian sociology and settlement work at Chicago Commons were staunchly supported by his seminary colleagues and the board of directors. Occasionally the aging president, Franklin W. Fisk, rose in chapel to ask God's special "protection and guidance" for the Professor of Christian Sociology. But when the University of Chicago sounded Taylor out in 1902, the directors of the seminary strongly urged him to remain and even granted a leave of absence from March until November of 1903 so that the Taylors could make their first trip to Europe.[38]

The seminary's faith in Taylor's work was tested shortly after his return to Chicago. Two city newspapers stepped up their running attack on Christian sociology, social settlements, and Graham Taylor. The *Chronicle*, a conservative financial journal, had first opened fire on Taylor and the seminary in 1893. The paper was soon joined by the *Inter-Ocean*, a right-wing Republican organ purchased by Yerkes during the traction fight. Through a series of sharply worded editorials, the *Chronicle* and *Inter-Ocean* tried to smear the seminary and Chicago Commons with socialism and thereby scare away their financial backers.[39]

At the time of President McKinley's assassination in Buffalo in 1901 a wave of hysteria swept bomb-conscious Chicago and scores of suspected anarchists were summarily thrown into jail. When Jane Addams and Raymond Robins of Chicago Commons sought the release of one Russian immigrant whom they knew personally, the newspapers charged the settlements with "abetting anarchy." A west side robbery and murder in November, 1903, enabled the editors to revive the charge that settlement workers, sociologists, and socialists "in their respective ways" were undermining "the moral fiber of society." Taylor's settlement was singled out as one "dedicated to the propo-

[37] Graham Taylor to William R. Harper, December 15, 1902; Chicago Theological Seminary, Sub-Committee Recommendation to Executive Committee of Board of Directors, February 6, 1903; University of Chicago, *Annual Register*, 1903–4 through 1912–13.

[38] Taylor, *Pioneering*, p. 403; Chicago Theological Seminary, Faculty Resolution sent to Board of Directors, December 17, 1902, and adopted by the Board on December 18, 1902; Sub-Committee Recommendation to Executive Committee of Board of Directors, February 6, 1903.

[39] Taylor, *Pioneering*, pp. 401–2.

sition of Christian socialism," that is, "state socialism advocated and prompted by Christian people from Christian motives."

> Now the Chicago Commons has demonstrated that when Christianity embarks on socialism it is the blind leading the blind and both of them fall into the ditch together. . . . Though dedicated to the destruction of private property, this institution is supported almost entirely by the rich . . . none of whom seems to perceive that they are throwing down the ladder by which they climbed, and to change the figure, cutting off the limb on which they are sitting.[40]

Taylor knew, of course, that this publicity not only disturbed his colleagues' peace of mind, but complicated the board of directors' efforts to raise funds. Fortunately, however, both Taylor and the seminary had the backing of Victor F. Lawson, editor and publisher of the influential Chicago *Daily News*. Son of a Norwegian immigrant and reared on the west side, Lawson was impressed with the work of the social settlements and he had a high regard for Graham Taylor. He had contributed generously to the financial campaign that created the department of Christian sociology at the seminary in 1892. Furthermore, the *Daily News* reported clearly and accurately the work of Chicago's social settlements. And in 1902 Lawson began printing a weekly column by Graham Taylor, in which Taylor interpreted "current events from the settlement point of view." [41]

The next year Victor Lawson demonstrated his support in another fashion. Without saying a word to the Professor of Christian Sociology, he sent a $3,000 check to the president of the seminary to pay Taylor's salary for 1903, and he promised to do the same for 1904 and 1905. In an accompanying letter, Lawson wrote:

> I have been moved to make this contribution not merely on the general ground of aiding the seminary but more particularly on the ground . . . that I should be thus able to make it possible for you to say to others, who do not take the same view of Prof. Taylor's sociological work that I do, that their contributions would not need to be applied in any degree whatever to a line of work concerning which they did not feel any personal responsibility.

[40] Taylor, *Chicago Commons*, pp. 133–34; Taylor, *Pioneering*, chap. xvi; Addams, *Twenty Years*, pp. 402–11; Allen F. Davis, "Raymond Robins: The Settlement Worker as Municipal Reformer," *Social Service Review*, XXXIII (June, 1959), 134–35; "Socialism, Sociology and Crime," *Chronicle* (Chicago), November 30, 1903; newspaper clipping, no title, 1903[?].

[41] Taylor, *Pioneering*, pp. 403, 430, 330; Charles Dennis, *Victor Lawson, His Time and His Work* (Chicago, 1935), pp. 429–30; Graham Taylor to Albert W. Palmer, January 4, 1937.

Editorially the *Daily News* and the *Evening Post* defended the settlements, and neither Taylor nor the Seminary made any public statements. During this and subsequent periods of "annoying notoriety" Taylor was pleased that his colleagues stood by him, "both privately and in public." Years later he testified that there was never "any interference with my freedom of teaching or action" and no one ever "expressed to me a doubt or fear, or suggested any caution upon my part."[42]

IV

The faculty and board of directors not only supported Taylor in 1903, but frequently looked to him for administrative leadership and tried repeatedly during 1906, 1907, and 1908 to make him president of the seminary. The sizable endowment of the 1890's had steadily dwindled until by the spring of 1906 the seminary's finances were so precarious that the president resigned in despair. The faculty then asked Taylor to become dean of the faculty or acting president. He was extremely reluctant to undertake either assignment, for he knew that it would steal time from his settlement and social work training school at just the moment he felt himself "crossing the threshold of my real influence and constructive effort in the city and beyond." But he was caught in a difficult dilemma. He needed the $3,000 salary from the professorship because the only supplements to his income were $500 from the University of Chicago and a small fee for his *Daily News* column. Yet if he remained "under full professorial obligations" at the seminary, he knew that "whether I consent . . . or not" the "laboring oar" of administration "will fall to me."[43]

Trustees of Chicago Commons and the training school, eager to prevent the seminary from monopolizing Taylor's time and services, arranged for him to draw a small salary from both the settlement and the school. Thus he was financially able to resign his professorship in March, 1906, and offer to serve the seminary as a "professorial lecturer in Social Economics" at $1,500 a year but free of all administrative and financial responsibilities. The board of directors refused to act on Taylor's proposal in the spring of 1906. Meantime Taylor's colleagues recommended him for the presidency and in June elected him permanent chairman of the faculty. Taylor accepted the latter post for the summer months only and in the fall of 1906 once again submitted his resignation. The faculty, however, were unwilling to let him escape so easily. In

[42] Victor F. Lawson to J. H. George, March 13, April 7, 1903; Taylor, *Chicago Commons*, pp. 143–44, 147; Taylor, *Pioneering*, p. 403; Taylor, "Response to Graham Taylor," p. 7.

[43] Graham Taylor to Victor F. Lawson, March 13, 1906.

November they recommended for the second time that the board of directors elect Taylor president.

> He has all the requisites necessary for the place. . . . He has the large acquaintance with men, the executive ability, the confidence of the churches over the whole country, the practical knowledge of educational matters, the touch with the State Universities in all the states of our constituency, in fact all the qualifications fitting one to grip at once the Seminary situation and carry out the policy we all believe in.

The board agreed. When it met in December it ignored Taylor's letter of resignation and voted thirteen to two to name him president of the seminary.[44]

Taylor was sorely torn between loyalty to the seminary and obligation to his other endeavors. After long consultation with the board he finally agreed "to accept the Acting Presidency as the utmost I can now do." He laid down certain conditions. As acting president he must have "all the authority and prerogatives with which the presidency is invested" but no responsibility "to solicit funds for the Seminary or to travel in its behalf." This awkward compromise put Taylor in an untenable position as he later found out. But he thought at the time that he had taken "good care to forefend" himself and that without sacrificing his other interests he would be able "to turn the present acute stage of the Seminary's crisis." Glad to have Taylor even under these conditions, the board unanimously reduced his teaching load and salary to $1,500 a year and named him acting president at an additional $2,500 a year.[45]

For a year and a half Taylor headed the Chicago Theological Seminary. His selection was in accord with a trend among all Protestant theological schools in the early years of the twentieth century to choose as executives men prominently associated with social Christianity. Many of the changes introduced by Taylor had already been instituted in other seminaries with marked success. For example, admission to the three year course at the seminary was restricted to college graduates only. Hebrew and Greek were made "almost entirely elective." Revision of the curriculum placed new emphasis on evolution, Biblical criticism, comparative religion, and psychology.[46]

[44] Graham Taylor to Executive Committee of Board of Directors, March 27, 1906; Chicago Theological Seminary, Faculty Minutes, 1859–1913 (manuscripts in Hammond Library, Chicago Theological Seminary, Chicago, Ill.), May 4, June 6, 1906; Graham Taylor to Victor F. Lawson, March 13, 1906; Faculty to Executive Committee of Board of Directors, November 5, 1906.

[45] Graham Taylor to Board of Directors, December 19, 1906; Graham Taylor to Victor F. Lawson, January 2, 1907; Board of Directors, Excerpts from Minutes of Special Meeting, December 19, 1906.

[46] Abell, *Urban Impact*, pp. 236, 229; "Revised Course of Study," *Chicago Seminary Quarterly*, VI (February, 1907), 3–5.

Meantime the seminary's financial plight grew worse. Receipts in 1906 amounted to $91,067 but fell to $82,795 by 1908. The deficit increased yearly, and Taylor estimated that the seminary would have a debt of $26,466 by the end of 1909. Student enrollment had fallen from an all-time high of 202 scholars in 1893–94 to 38 during the 1907–8 term. Of course the *Chronicle* and *Inter-Ocean* gleefully capitalized on, and to some extent aggravated, the seminary's difficulties during Taylor's tenure of office. An editorial on "Sociology and Theology" gloated:

> As Professor Taylor is a prominent socialist, best known from his connection with Chicago Commons, the condition of the Seminary suggests the question whether there is any connection between its socialism and its financial condition. . . . if the Seminary is stranded it is necessary to look further than the denominational finances to find the cause of it. For this result Professor Taylor and his seminary, which has always backed him, are largely responsible. . . . and now he does not consider the presidency of his own seminary as worth taking.
>
> That is exactly what might have been expected from a substitute of socialism for Christianity, and politics for preaching. . . . The Christian socialist falls between two stools. He sacrifices Christianity without winning the socialists. That is what ails the Chicago Theological Seminary.[47]

The barrage of newspaper criticism did not disturb Taylor. But the fact that he was diverted from his own work did. "Not only am I unable to improve my fine opportunity to develop the settlement and training school," he complained, "but I am equally prevented from keeping up the reading, editorial work and even the correspondence of my department." By the spring of 1908 he was "nearly worn out with the prolonged struggle." In a sharp letter to the board of directors he declared his intention to resign as acting president at the end of the academic year. The faculty and directors made one last attempt to persuade Taylor to accept the presidency, but he flatly refused. During the summer of 1908 he helped select the new president, Ozora S. Davis, a former student of his in Hartford. Taylor spoke frankly to the younger man of the "eagerness to detract" from the seminary, the "disloyalty of some of its own alumni in this time of stress and storm," and the disruptions caused by several faculty deaths. But he predicted, "you will be caught

[47] Chicago Theological Seminary, Faculty Minutes, March 6, 1908; Samuel Ives Curtiss, "Twenty-Five Years as a Seminary Professor 1878–1903," *Chicago Seminary Quarterly,* III (July, 1903), 13; Ralph H. Ferris to Graham Taylor, March 23, 1908; Quoted in Taylor, *Pioneering,* pp. 402–3. Taylor identified this editorial as "Sociology and Theology" in *Chronicle* (Chicago), December 26, 1908. The *Chronicle,* however, ceased publication in 1907, and the author was unable to locate this editorial in either the *Inter-Ocean* or the *Record-Herald.*

up as all the rest of us have been by the inspiration of the field, which will soon make you forget its obstacles."[48]

At the time Taylor ended his second and final stint of seminary administration, he was fifty-seven and inclined to believe that his "working years" were numbered. Yet he served the seminary for another sixteen years. In the summer of 1921, when he had reached the age of seventy, he wrote to President Davis, "I deem it only fair . . . to leave in your hands my offer to retire," but "I never felt so able to do my part or happier in teaching than this very year." Davis would hear nothing of retirement, though Taylor's teaching schedule was lightened. In the spring of 1922 he made a long trip to the Far East, and the next two winters he spent in California. In October, 1924, Arthur E. Holt was named as Taylor's successor at the seminary.[49]

The school found several ways to honor its distinguished professor emeritus during his fourteen years of retirement. The decision to affiliate with the University of Chicago was made in 1914, but for almost a decade after moving to the Midway the seminary shared quarters with the Divinity School. By 1919 architectural plans had been approved for a $50,000 structure to be named "GRAHAM TAYLOR HALL, in honor of a man whom a generation of Seminary men love and admire." The alumni contributed generously to the building fund, but Victor Lawson's unexpected $100,000 bequest turned their dreams into reality.[50]

The cornerstone of Graham Taylor Assembly Hall was laid in November, 1926, in a ceremony complete with academic regalia. Taylor's son noticed that the guest of honor was so engrossed in conversation that he forgot his hood and was the only one "without any of the fancy trimmings." But he thought the omission was characteristic of his father's "simplicity of life and his impatience with titles and embellishments." James Mullenbach presided over the June, 1928, dedication ceremony in which both Jane Addams and Professor Holt participated. Taylor's two brothers joined other members of the proud family on this occasion, Will later protesting, "you need not feel so grateful to Livie & me for coming to see you crowned. We would not have

[48] Graham Taylor to Charles Crane, March 24, 1908; Graham Taylor to Executive Committee of Board of Directors, March 17, 1908; Hugh M. Scott to Graham Taylor, March 21, 1908; Grace T. Davis, *Ozora Stearns Davis, His Life and Poems* (Boston, 1932), 90; Grace T. Davis to Lea D. Taylor, October 8, 1938; Graham Taylor to Ozora S. Davis, November 27, 1908.

[49] Graham Taylor to Ozora S. Davis, July 28, 1921.

[50] John R. Montgomery, "Historical Statement," *Chicago Theological Seminary Register*, VIII (November, 1914), 3–6; Goodspeed, *History of the University of Chicago*, p. 363; *The Chicago Theological Seminary Register*, IX (April, 1919), n.p.; "Victor Fremont Lawson," *Chicago Theological Seminary Register*, XV (November, 1925), 3; Dennis, *Lawson*, p. 454.

missed it for the world." Seven years later the seminary paid its final tribute by granting Graham Taylor an honorary degree.[51]

Taylor's long association with the Chicago Theological Seminary was fruitful both for the school and for him. As a popular and influential lecturer he molded the outlook of scores of young ministers. Moreover, his prominence in social and civic reform movements enhanced the stature of the seminary, a fact which President Davis acknowledged when he jocularly described his friend as "the big mogul and the Grand Chief of Makiak in this very joint." At the same time, the seminary connection gave Taylor a certain prestige that was essential for the success of his various Chicago projects. For no matter how loudly his critics railed about socialism they always had to reckon with the solid support that Taylor had at the seminary. In addition, the income from his teaching enabled him to tide both the settlement and the training school over numerous financial crises. Professor Curtiss, who was instrumental in getting Taylor to Chicago, summed up the role of the seminary in his colleague's life: it has "sustained you here. . . . Your salary and the moral support you have had from the Seminary has given you the point of vantage so that you could develop and build the Commons." Perhaps most important of all, the classroom experience kept Taylor constantly re-evaluating and explaining his own religious convictions. In the process he became an articulate spokesman for social Christianity, an effective propagandist for the social gospel.[52]

V

Graham Taylor's first book, *Religion in Social Action*, was a vigorous plea for social Christianity, for "a religion of right-relationship to fellow men and Father God." During 1911 and 1912 he wrote twelve articles on this theme for *The Survey*. The response to his series was so enthusiastic that the editorial board urged him to publish the articles in a small book which they could offer to new subscribers. Taylor himself was a contributing editor of *The Survey* and eager to promote circulation, but he was reluctant to "disgrace" himself by putting the articles "in permanent form." To Jane Addams he confided that he had "very little ambition for authorship of anything more permanent than current comment which may serve in scattering about some waymarks of progress." However, continued pressure from *The Survey* editors, plus the willingness of Dodd, Mead & Co. to publish the book, and the

[51] *Daily News* (Chicago), November 18, 1926, June 7, 1928; Graham Romeyn Taylor to Paul Kellogg, November 30, 1926, Survey Associates Editorial Research Files, Columbia University School of Social Work Library, New York; William R. Taylor to Graham Taylor, June 11, 1928.

[52] Ozora S. Davis to Graham Taylor, September 15, 1910; Samuel Ives Curtiss to Graham Taylor, December 16, 1902.

offer of Jane Addams to write an introduction finally forced Taylor to change his mind. *Religion in Social Action* appeared late in 1913 and was a Christmas bonus for new *Survey* subscribers.[53]

The burden of Taylor's argument was that religion implied not only man's individual responsibility to God but also man's collective responsibility to his fellowmen. It was spelled out in the first two commandments, " 'Thou shalt love the Lord thy God . . . Thou shalt love thy neighbour as thyself.' On these two together, not on either one of them apart, all religion hangs." The "ethical tragedy of the age," according to Taylor, was the vain effort of his contemporaries "to be religious on one of these lines alone." Far too many people, he thought, were

> trying to be religious individually while collectively we are pagans; trying to live an individual Christian life, while our own and others' relationships in business and pleasure, in society and politics, ignore Christian exactions and ideals, wholly or in such large part that our collective life is essentially heathen.

Taylor sought to convince his readers that in the urban, industrial era of the twentieth century the "burden of the soul" had become "the burden for the whole self, in all its relationships." It was therefore incumbent upon every Christian "to care for the life and limb, the livelihood and standard of living, the health, and well-being, the growth and the happiness of our fellows."[54]

Religion in Social Action was also an urgent plea to the churches to readjust their faith to the changing conditions of life. Taylor saw in the need to change and adapt to new conditions an "inexorable law of all life," and he knew that the spiritual life was no exception. The church was facing its greatest challenge in the twentieth century, for it must deal simultaneously with

> the transition from an agricultural to a commercial age; from rural to urban conditions of life; from working for a living alone or with a few, to working together with large groups in complicated processes of producton; from sharing a national life with people of our own language and race to living and working in great international and cosmopolitan populations.

The ability to "manifest and transmit the life of God through the lives of men" in this new era was a crucial test for the Christian church.[55]

Like other optimistic advocates of the social gospel, Taylor found more to reassure than to disturb him in this religious challenge. If men realized that

[53] Graham Taylor, *Religion in Social Action* (New York, 1913), p. 81; Graham Taylor to William R. Taylor, April 19, 1912; Graham Taylor to Jane Addams, September 13, 1913.

[54] Taylor, *Religion in Social Action*, pp. 81, 82, 94.

[55] Taylor, *Religion in Social Action*, pp. 95, 98–99, 94.

sin and salvation could no longer be considered an individual matter, they would see that "regeneration is as necessary for the community as for the soul, if either or both are to be fully saved." Once the collective nature of sin and salvation was understood, the challenge of the urban, industrial age could be met and mastered. All it required was obedience to Christ's "marching orders . . . to apply the Gospel's age-long, time-tested, saving truths so much further as to bring the whole of human life under their sway and the whole world into the Kingdom." According to Taylor's analysis, the world which the kingdom of God was destined to win was "nothing more or less than those primary, elemental, essential relationships which we call the family, the neighbourhood, industrial associations, fellow citizenship, and religious affiliations." [56]

Taylor went on to analyze the obligations of the church in the life-spheres — family, neighborhood, industrial relations, and community service. He found it impossible to conceive of religion apart from the family unit and felt that "preservation and development of the family is our primary religious duty." He would have the church concern itself with birth control and sex education, "delicate, difficult, and dangerous" though it may be. He would also have the church co-operate with family and school to guard "the health, intelligence, recreation, and morals of the children." In developing this avenue of responsibility Taylor drew heavily upon Bushnell's concepts of Christian nurture. Finally, the church must actively preserve the "sanctity of marriage . . . upon which the existence of the home depends." This meant legal protection for women and children "from wanton divorce and desertion." It also meant investigation of housing problems, for the home "not only shelters but shapes the family life for better or for worse.[57]

The second life-sphere was the neighborhood, an extension of the home and the Church and closely identified with both. According to Taylor, neighborship was "our most ancient treasure, the heritage of the race, the one thing common to all who share the same origin, and to all of different origins who live near each other." But it was endangered in the twentieth century by tidal waves of immigration and by seasonal employment and economic depressions which pulled "settled families up by the roots" and seldom left them "long enough in one place to take root again." Furthermore, neighborhood ties were hard to establish in areas where mothers worked, fathers were often absent on distant jobs, and racial tensions existed. These were only a few of the forces that corroded the neighborhood and family unit and made people "lose their sense of belonging to anything or anybody, to the neighbourhood, the craft

[56] Taylor, *Religion in Social Action*, pp. 100, 99, 110; cf. *ibid.*, chaps. v, vi.

[57] Taylor, *Religion in Social Action*, pp. 114, 115, 121, 138, 130, 134, 136; cf. *ibid.*. chap. vii.

fellowship, the church membership, to citizenship, and at last to the family circle itself."[58]

As usual, however, Taylor saw a brighter side of the picture. He believed that new neighborhood ties were being forged. Fraternal orders, insurance societies, and trade unions were a natural substitute for the loyalty of the old craft guilds. Public schools, playgrounds, libraries, institutional churches, and social settlements, were all seeking to re-establish neighborhood ties. But a revitalized community, Taylor cautioned, should never lose sight of the fact that it is only one small part of an entire city. A detached or isolated neighborhood would be fatal. He called upon the churches to work closely with the new neighborhood organizations in order to usher in the kingdom of God. For,

> All three, home, neighbourhood, and church, share a common religious origin, sanction, aim, and spirit. No one of them can fulfill its function without the cooperation of the others.[59]

The church had an integral connection with still another life-sphere, that of industry. Taylor singled out three common denominators which should enable religion and industry to work together: the value which each places upon human life, upon the standard of living, and upon "union through sacrifice as essential to progress." The value of every individual life was a basic tenet of Christianity, yet Taylor pointed to the "shameless inconsistency" of the churches which condoned long hours and low wages for women, child labor, and the high rate of industrial accidents. The churches must support laws controlling working conditions, hours, and wages and must insist upon their enforcement. In addition, Taylor argued that the church should cooperate with industry to establish a standard of living for wage-earners that was "compatible with the value of life." He advocated a minimum wage and wanted the church to help "keep it rising, above a mere living wage, as far as the conditions of the trade or craft will allow." For unless the church translates it "religious love of souls into . . . economic care for selves, religion will mean very little to those who are in the struggle for life and livelihood in an industrial age."[60]

Still a third common ground for industry and religion was that "both have taught men to sacrifice in order to unite for the common good." Taylor felt that this justified the existence of labor unions as well as corporations, for a trade union "cannot differ, *per se*, morally and as an economic necessity from a combination of capitalists or the communion of members of the same reli-

[58] Taylor, *Religion in Social Action*, pp. 166, 141, 144, 148.
[59] Taylor, *Religion in Social Action*, p. 166, cf. *ibid.*, chap. viii.
[60] Taylor, *Religion in Social Action*, pp. 178, 180, 181, 184, 186.

gious faith." It was both unfair and unrealistic for employers to make their "profits under the modern method of combining all available resources," yet insist upon their workers dealing with them "under the old outworn and discarded system of individual industry." The church, therefore, must support the right of labor to organize. But no minister should join either a labor union or a manufacturers' association, thought Taylor. The "minister should refuse to be classified, should be a mass-man not a class-man." And the church should display "judicial impartiality" between capital and labor. "The Church stands for all, if for any. Its ministry is mediatorial." [61]

In addition to its responsibilities to the family, the neighborhood, and to industry, the church had an obligation to the city. Any church will fail to accomplish its full mission, Taylor warned, unless it seeks to uphold the highest civic ideals. In the long run, Taylor asserted,

> The efficiency of the Church will be tested by the extent to which social conditions and town government make it easier to be good and harder to be bad. The claim of being a community of Christians will not be conceded to those who do not constitute a Christian community.

The church must be the executor of these high ideals without, however, duplicating the work of charitable agencies or usurping the functions of government. Taylor saw no reason for the pulpit to be turned "into a lectureship on economics and politics," but he felt that the church must "take the social point of view" and apply the gospel of Christ to all areas of community life.[62]

Religion in Social Action was favorably reviewed by two of the leading spokesmen for the social gospel, Washington Gladden and Walter Rauschenbusch. The former referred to the book as Taylor's " '*Apologia pro vita Sua*' . . . though by no means so intended." He felt that few people "have thought out the social problem more patiently or with profounder insight." Rauschenbusch discovered in it guidelines for Christian action that were "as trustworthy as a pick and shovel." The margins of his copy, he said, were heavily marked because he came across "many sentences and passages so full of marrow and good sense that it is hard to pass them by without some physical act of approbation." Emil Hirsch, editor of *The Reform Advocate*, thought that Taylor's emphasis upon religion as "rooted in the consciousness of the 'all-togetherness' . . . may well lead Jewish and Christian students alike to endeavor each to make his own particular religion effective as the dominating force of social action." Much to Taylor's surprise his old Hartford foe, Edwin Pond Parker, confessed that he found "little to criticise, much to admire and commend. Taken entire it is certainly a timely, sane, sound, wise

---

[61] Taylor, *Religion in Social Action*, pp. 186–87, 188, 201–2. cf. *ibid.*, chaps. ix, x.
[62] Taylor, *Religion in Social Action*, pp. 227, 244, cf. *ibid.*, chap. xi and chap. xii.

and honest book, highly creditable to its author." The author of *Religion in Social Action* was gratified by these reviews, but he let another decade pass before starting work on a second book.[63]

VI

Though *Religion in Social Action* was Taylor's only book on social Christianity, he delivered hundreds of speeches on the subject and was active in many organizations that supported the social gospel. Taylor had long urged the churches to educate their own members, and he practiced what he preached in the ranks of Congregationalism. The National Council had ap‧ pointed a five-man committee in 1892 to report on the relations between capital and labor. Reappointed at the triennial conventions in 1895 and 1898, the committee took no action beyond recommending that the "Christian rule, as applied to industrial relations is not a quixotic rule; it is a thoroughly practical rule; it is the only rule that will work." [64]

But the next year the International Congregational Council meeting in Boston heard a challenging address by Taylor on "The Church in Social Reforms." [65] He asserted that

> The formative social functions of the church are three: first, the recognition of the divine ideal of human life, individual and social for itself and all men; second, the initiation of movements and agencies for its realization in the world; third, the transmission of the Spirit's power for the social regeneration.

In developing his third point, the sacrificial spirit necessary for the regeneration of society, Taylor strongly criticized the prevailing political and economic system of the 1890's.

> *Laissez faire* was the lisping of the infancy of economic science. Civilization repudiated it, much more Christianity. For even civilization means

[63] Washington Gladden, review of *Religion in Social Action* in *Congregationalist and Christian World*, XCIX (March 19, 1914), "Literary Section," n.p.; Walter Rauschenbusch, review of *Religion in Social Action* in *The Survey*, XXXI (January 31, 1914), 527; Emil Hirsch, "Religion in Social Action," *Reform Advocate*, XLVI (January 17, 1914), 738; Edwin Pond Parker, "The Optimist — Religion in Social Action," *Courant* (Hartford), February 8, 1914.

[64] Taylor, *Religion in Social Action*, p. 209; *Minutes, National Council of Congregational Churches, 1895* (Boston, 1896), p. 157.

[65] Graham Taylor, *The Church in Social Reform, An Addresss Delivered in Boston, Mass., September 23, 1899, Before the International Congregational Council* (n.p., n.d.). This speech was also printed in *Proceedings of the Second International Congregational Council . . . Boston, 1899* (Boston, 1900), pp. 143–50. Under the title, "The Social Function of the Church," it appeared in the *American Journal of Sociology*, V (November, 1899), 305–21.

human interference in the cosmic struggle for existence. The "let alone theory" of society bears the mark of Cain. Its theological definition is hell. . . . Will we, dare we as a body, bear that cross of economic sacrifice and social self-denial. . . ? This is the church's social question. Will we reform ourselves in order to conform the world to Christ?

In the discussion period Washington Gladden referred to Taylor's speech as "magnificent. . . . Every word of it I believe." [66]

Responding to the constant prodding of the social gospel advocates, the National Council finally appointed a permanent Labor Committee in 1901, including among its members Washington Gladden and William Jewett Tucker. At the next triennial convention in Des Moines this committee urged the churches to establish state councils to stimulate local interest, make contact with labor and employers, and publish and distribute literature on social questions. One of the major addresses at the 1904 convention was Graham Taylor's analysis of "The Principles of Christianity Applied to Industrial Problems." Industry and religion, he said, were the two most important factors in modern life. He urged his listeners to apply Christian principles to industrial problems. Those principles must be extended "from the personal relationship of one man to the one God to all the relations which this same man sustains to every other man." Taylor and six others were added to the Labor Committee, reorganized as the Industrial Committee in 1904, and authorized to investigate child labor, immigration, socialism, organized labor, and employers' unions.[67]

From 1907 until 1913 Taylor was chairman of the Industrial Committee, working closely with the state organizations, co-operating with the newly established Federal Council of Churches of Christ in America, and utilizing Congregational brotherhoods for social services. At the 1910 convention Taylor repeated the Committee's request for a paid secretary: "It is time that we take up or give up the function for which this committee was created." His plea jolted the National Council into action, and Taylor was authorized to hire the first industrial secretary. By 1913 the Industrial Committee was convinced that its powers and scope were no longer broad enough to cover the wide field of social action. So in that year the National Council approved a nineteen-man Commission on Social Service with an annual budget of

---

[66] Taylor, *The Church in Social Reforms*, pp. 1, 6, 10.

[67] *Minutes, National Council of Congregational Churches, 1904* (Boston, 1904), p. 419; Graham Taylor, "The Principles of Christianity Applied to Industrial Problems," *Minutes, National Council of Congregational Churches, 1904*, pp. 87, 96; *Minutes, National Council of Congregational Churches, 1907* (Boston, 1907), pp. 310–20; Hopkins, *Social Gospel*, 288; Graham Taylor, "The Labor Question in the Church," *Daily News* (Chicago), October 19, 1907.

$6,000. The chairmanship passed to Fred B. Hill, but Taylor was a commission member from 1913 to 1915 and again from 1919 to 1923. This body remained the official social action branch of the Congregational churches until 1934 when it was reconstituted as the Council for Social Action to meet the peculiar problems of the depression.[68]

In addition to the work with the National Council, Taylor lectured on social Christianity to Chautauqua audiences and academic gatherings, he participated in numerous conferences, and wrote articles for social gospel publications. The parent Chautauqua organization first recognized social Christianity when, in the summer of 1889, it invited Richard T. Ely, Washington Gladden, and Lyman Abbott to discuss social and religious problems. Taylor spoke at Chautauqua in 1894 on "The Church and Problems of Modern Society," and again in 1897, 1900, and 1908 on programs concerned with social Christianity. He was a popular speaker on the western Chautauqua circuits, visiting Bay View, Michigan, or Crete, Nebraska, or Des Moines, Iowa, almost every year. In 1896 he reported that the size and enthusiasm of the audiences were "simply astonishing."

> So great was the demand for teaching on social topics at the Chautauqua Assembly that the writer's eighteen appointments grew to thirty during the ten days of his visit, special conferences being requested by the young women college graduates and under-graduates, by public school teachers and superintendants, by pastors . . . a question hour was held every evening and drew nearly as many people as the lecture.

Taylor was also interested in the short-lived American Institute of Christian Sociology, a study organization founded by Richard T. Ely and later headed by Josiah Strong and George D. Herron. He spoke at the latter's conferences at Iowa College in the early 1890's and at many university forums. Furthermore, he contributed articles to Herron's journal, *The Kingdom*, of which Jane Addams was an associate editor, and to *The Social Gospel*, the publication of the Christian Commonwealth Colony in Georgia.[69]

During the 1890's Taylor made a persistent effort to enlist the Y.M.C.A. in the cause of social betterment. In powerful speeches before Y.M.C.A. conventions and student groups and in articles in the *Young Men's Era* he expounded the doctrines of the social gospel and pleaded for their acceptance.

---

[68] *Minutes, National Council of Congregational Churches, 1910* (Boston, 1910), p. 230; *Minutes, National Council of Congregational Churches, 1913* (Boston, 1913), pp. 276–78.

[69] Hopkins, *Social Gospel*, 163–65, 196, 264; *Chautauqua Assembly Herald*, August 7, 1897, July 22–28, 1900; *Chautauqua Daily*, July 29–August 3, 1908; Graham Taylor, "The Social Propaganda: Field Notes of the Western Summer Schools and Chautauquas," *Chicago Commons*, I (July, 1896), 2–3; Dombrowski, *Christian Socialism*, pp. 111, 138, 170; May, *Protestant Churches*, p. 227.

He urged the International Convention meeting in Springfield, Massachusetts, in 1895,

> To make of ourselves and our buildings centers for the social unification of the mixed and disunited hosts of young men, especially in the downtown wards of our cities; to make of our meetings and educational classes schools in which the young men of the nation may study and learn their social and civic rights and duties as a part of their citizenship and religion; to raise up an intelligent body of young men who will be too loyal to the commonwealth both of our country and of the kingdom of God to engage in the fratricidal strife of class warfare; to push the Association movement into the lodging houses and labor unions, and street life and recreative rendezvous of young men . . . so only can we fulfill our supreme duty and opportunity in the "present crisis" to become "peace makers" and leaders of our common Christianity in saving the souls and the social relations of America's young manhood.

Yet the Y.M.C.A. failed to take a stand on the major social or economic issues of the 1890's, and its magazine followed the same non-committal policy. After 1900 the *Young Men's Era* became *Association Men* with headquarters in New York rather than Chicago, and Taylor ceased to be a member of the editorial board though he still contributed occasional articles. The Y.M.C.A. never really warmed up to the social gospel movement.[70]

Realizing the value of co-operation among the churches in fulfilling their social obligation, Taylor worked tirelessly with several interdenominational organizations. One was the Men and Religion Forward Movement, established in 1910 to draw men into active church membership. Taylor helped formulate the social service aspects of the program and spoke to many audiences about the relationship between the kingdom of God and social and economic problems. An earlier venture was the Open and Institutional Church League, designed to promote Christian unity and bring

> the denominations into federative relations through which they can work out the problems of Christian service in city, country and abroad without the present waste of forces.

Taylor was a vice-president of the League and his frend Elias B. Sanford was executive secretary. The latter was responsible for the creation in 1900 of the National Federation of Churches and Christian Workers. Taylor, who had long been interested in the Christian Workers' Convention, became a vice-president of the larger organization. It was this Federation which actively

---

[70] Graham Taylor, "The Relation of the Y.M.C.A. to the Social-Economic Questions of the Day," *Proceedings of the 31st International Convention of the Y.M.C.A.* (New York, 1895), pp. 125–26; Charles H. Hopkins, *History of the Y.M.C.A. in North America* (New York, 1951), p. 402.

promoted Protestant church unity, arranged a preliminary conference in New York City in 1905, and thus helped create the Federal Council of the Churches of Christ in America in 1908.[71]

The Federal Council was a friend of the social gospel movement. One of its objectives was "to secure a larger combined influence for the Churches of Christ in all matters affecting the moral and social conditions of the people, so as to promote the application of the law of Christ in every relation of human life." The Council's Social Creed called upon all Christians to concern themselves with industrial problems. To implement the Social Creed the Federal Council established a Commission on the Church and Social Service. Taylor became a member of this Commission in 1913, and four years later the Federal Council asked him to serve as its executive secretary. The opportunity, he wrote, "is in line with my life work and offers an open way to extend it to the very limits of my capacity." But, he continued,

> I do not see how I can possibly add any thing, much less this big thing, to the obligations which have prior claim upon me and exact all there is of me.
>
> I am carrying full teaching work at the Seminary, with large classes four days each week, teach and administer at the Chicago School of Civics and Philanthropy, head up the work of Chicago Commons, raise over $40,000 a year to support both of these agencies, and am holden for *Survey* copy all the while and an editorial in the Chicago *Daily News* once a week.

Reluctantly he turned down the offer of the Federal Council.[72]

Taylor was sixty-six years old at the time, and in his life-span he had seen the Protestant churches federate and a national program for social Christianity come into being. He could rejoice with Rauschenbusch in 1917 that the social gospel had at long last "become orthodox." That movement had enabled Taylor and others like him to find meaning and order in the chaos of industrial America, and it had sustained their strenuous efforts to establish the kingdom of God on earth. Taylor's Hopewell and Hartford ministries and his experiences as teacher and social reformer in Chicago had revealed to him the basic truth of social Christianity — that "to apply the simple

---

[71] Taylor, *Religion in Social Action*, p. 250; Fayette L. Thompson and others, *Men and Religion* (New York, 1911), pp. v–vii; Samuel W. Wiley, *History of Y.M.C.A.-Church Relations in the United States* (New York, 1944), pp. 42–43; Hopkins, *Social Gospel*, pp. 296–98, 303–4; Elias B. Sanford, *Origin and History of the Federal Council of the Churches of Christ in America* (Hartford, 1916), p. 55; Charles S. Macfarland, *Christian Unity in the Making: The First Twenty-five Years of the Federal Council of the Churches of Christ in America, 1905–1930* (New York, 1948), pp. 15–37.

[72] Macfarland, *Christian Unity in the Making*, pp. 50, 45; Graham Taylor to Charles Macfarland, January 27, 1917.

Gospel to the saving of the soul was to extend and apply the common faith to the social conditions of the common life." The pursuit of this goal led Taylor out of the pulpit and the classroom into the wider fields of settlement and social service work, civic reform, industrial mediation, and journalism. The social gospel was the mainspring of his life. It compelled him to put religion into social action.[73]

[73] Rauschenbusch, *A Theology for the Social Gospel*, p. 2; Taylor, *Religion in Social Action*, p. vii.

Five ❡ *Chicago Commons*

After Taylor decided in the spring of 1894 to establish his own settlement without waiting for the financial backing of the seminary's board of directors, he and four students searched the west side of Chicago for an appropriate location. They soon settled on the seventeenth ward. It was approximately one mile square, bounded on the east by the Chicago River, on the south and north by railroad tracks and freight yards, and on the west by another crowded working-class district. A proud residential section in the days before the Civil War, the ward was badly over-crowded by the 1890's. Conversion of single family residences into apartments and rooming houses, plus the appearance of small manufacturing concerns, furniture and woodworking factories, and numerous saloons, had completely altered the character of the neighborhood.[1]

Of the 28,000 people living in the seventeenth ward in the early years of the decade, less than half were native-born. Among the newcomers, German, Scandinavian, and Irish immigrants were most numerous. The majority of the residents, however, spoke English. It was the predominantly lower middle-class, Protestant character of the area and the absence of a language barrier that convinced Taylor it would make an ideal base for the type of settlement he hoped to establish. Its "family population," he explained, "was well adapted to settlement methods" and "the prevalence of the English language among the people of British, Irish, German and Scandinavian origins rendered them more readily approachable."[2]

During the summer of 1894 Taylor's scouts lived in a small room on West Erie Street, learning as much as they could about the ward and looking for a suitable settlement base. One student examined the churches and religious life of the neighborhood, another health and sanitary conditions, while the

---

[1] Taylor, *Chicago Commons*, pp. 8–9.
[2] *The Daily News Almanac and Political Register for 1891* (Chicago, 1891), p. 338; *Eleventh Census of the United States: 1890* (Washington, 1892), I, 674; Taylor, *Chicago Commons*, p. 8; Taylor, "Initiatives and Motives" (typed manuscript).

other two investigated the political structure and the relationship between public schools and immigrant families. Meantime they searched for a house large enough to accommodate the Taylor family and themselves and still have "space to share with neighborhood gatherings." In time they did locate a satisfactory place, and Taylor tried at once to get a long-term lease. The owners, somewhat perplexed, finally decided to let him have it if he promised not to use the building as a hospital or a dance hall. Taylor readily agreed to their terms and thus was able to secure a five-year lease on the property.[3]

The house at 140 North Union Street had been built shortly before the Civil War by a prosperous German-American family who deserted it when less pretentious buildings obstructed their fine view of the Chicago River. After the fire of 1871 the Northwestern Railway, burned out of its downtown offices, leased the property for temporary headquarters and constructed a wooden addition to house the large, three-story, fire-proof vault. When the railroad officials departed the house fell rapidly into disrepair, keeping pace with the neighborhood's deterioration. By 1894 the original building was a sailors' boarding house and the ugly structure behind was a crowded Italian tenement.[4]

In October, 1894, Taylor, his wife, four children, and the four students moved into the brick house. When the Italian families departed from the annex, Taylor secured possession of that too. For weeks they scrubbed, painted, and repaired. And they waged a relentless battle against unwelcome inhabitants: "Great gray rats, fearless and impudent, stalked the halls by day as well as by night; small brown creatures sidled up and down the walls and along the floors, and monster roaches helped dispute inch by inch the territory which the new-comers gained." Eventually, however, the two buildings became "habitable though never comfortable." Lack of closet space, the sparse supply of running water, and the eighteen coal stoves required to heat the upper floors constituted housekeeping problems which the residents never solved.[5]

---

[3] Taylor, *Chicago Commons*, 9–10; Taylor, *Pioneering*, p. 283. The students occupied their rented room on May 1, 1894, and that date subsequently was taken as the founding of Chicago Commons. All settlement anniversary celebrations, for example, were held the first week in May. Robert A. Woods and A. J. Kennedy, *Handbook of Settlements* (New York, 1911), p. 40.

[4] Taylor, *Chicago Commons*, pp. 10–11; *Chicago Commons: A Social Settlement . . . An Account of the Work* (Chicago, 1899), pp. 6–7.

[5] *Chicago Commons: A Social Settlement*, pp. 7–8; Taylor, *Chicago Commons*, p. 11. Prior to taking up residence in the settlement house the Taylors had lived at 397 West Monroe Street near Ashland Avenue where the Chicago Theological Seminary was located. A fashionable area in the 1880's, Ashland Avenue was changing rapidly in the 1890's, and the Taylors found it a "non-descript district" in which "neighborship had

Yet Taylor and the others considered themselves fortunate to find such a house. The second and third floors were used as living quarters for the settlement residents. Parlors, dining room, and kitchen were on the first floor. The basement of the main building and all of the annex were used for clubs and class rooms. And the basement of the annex, which had been a stable at one time, was renovated and turned into an assembly hall. "There," reported Taylor, "beneath octopus-like furnace pipes attached to the low ceiling, our neighbors and guests from near and far met on equal terms." [6]

The newcomers soon discovered that "all the dangers and discomforts were not within doors." North Union Street was unpaved and "clouds of dust drove in at the doors and windows and up to the roof whenever the wind blew or the big freight trucks plowed through." Furthermore, the "street grade had been raised five feet above the front steps so that we had to go down and up again from our spacious veranda to reach the sidewalk. Between the two levels the wind deposited all the dust and paper refuse from near and far." On one side of their house was a furniture factory whose buzz-saw rasped all day long, and on the other side a saloon with a sausage factory in the rear. Out in front of the tavern was a large horse trough which bore the sign, "Water your horses and don't forget yourself." Alexander Johnson, who visited the settlement during its early months, found it situated "in an old and dilapidated part of Chicago's west side, which had escaped the cleaning-up of the great fire." It was "all tenements, shabby little stores and saloons . . . a mere slum." He was convinced that "missionaries in the heart of Africa could hardly present a greater contrast with their surroundings than did these cultured refined people in such a neighborhood." [7]

But the seventeenth ward "missionaries" were undaunted by the physical handicaps. They considered their building "a twin to the old Hull-House" which lay just one mile to the south. And they were proud of the name Chicago Commons. For, as Taylor later expressed it, the words captured "the

---

faded away at the incoming of a transient population." Taylor, Diary, October 19, 1892; Pierce, *History of Chicago*, III, 60–61; Taylor, *Pioneering*, pp. 295.

[6] Taylor, *Chicago Commons*, pp. 13, 11; Johnson, *Adventures in Social Welfare*, p. 380.

[7] Taylor, *Chicago Commons*, p. 12; Johnson, *Adventures in Social Welfare*, p. 380. When Taylor pressed Johnson for his opinion of the venture, the latter told him that "it reminded me of a story of a convivial party of Scotchmen, one of whom got his jag earlier than the rest and started for home; another followed him shortly after and found number one sitting in the mud holding on to a lamp-post; number two tried to get his friend up on his feet but could not manage it so he said, 'Old fellow, I can't lift you up but I can sit down alongside you,' and did so in the mud. I said 'Graham, I don't know whether you can lift up your neighbors, but Heaven knows you have sat down in the mud with them.' " Johnson, *Adventures in Social Welfare*, p. 380.

idea of sharing what each can be to all and what all can be to each," and that was "the essence of the social settlement motive and movement." By the end of October they had prepared a statement of their goals and of the purpose of Chicago Commons. We are, declared the residents,

> a group of Christian people, who choose to live where they seem to be needed, for the purpose of *being* all they can to the people with whom they identify themselves. . . . It is as little of an organization and as much of a personal relationship as it can be made. It seeks to unify and help all other organizations and people in the neighborhood that will make for righteousness and brotherhood. It is not a church, but hopes to be a helper of all churches. It is not a charity, but expects to aid in the organization and cooperation of all existing charities. It is not an exclusive social circle, but aspires to be a center of the best social life and interests of the people. It is not a school, but proposes to be a source and agency of educational effort and general culture. It is non-political, yet has begun to be a rallying point and moral force for civic patriotism. It is non-sectarian, but avowedly Christian, and openly cooperative with the churches.[8]

II

Implementing these lofty goals proved more difficult. The first problem the settlement had to overcome was the suspicion and curiosity of the neighbors. None of them could understand why the residents had moved voluntarily to North Union Street or why such an odd collection of people shared one house. Furthermore, the saloon keepers and politicians regarded the newcomers "as competitors and dangerously observant critics." The Italians living in the annex stared in amazement through the glass partition as the Taylor family settled their household possessions. And the woman who helped run the saloon next door gave the Taylors a cheery welcome but could never comprehend why they refused to patronize her husband's place of business. In time, however, the residents' genuine interest in the ward, their friendly greeting to all who knocked on the door, and the presence of the entire Taylor family at the settlement won a measure of acceptance. Speaking in 1896, a Scots woman explained:

> When Chicago Commons opened its doors and invited us to visit there, we hardly knew what it meant. But we called, and to our surprise found ourselves among friends — friends who were interested in us and in

[8] Taylor, *Chicago Commons*, p. 10; Johnson, *Adventures in Social Welfare*, p. 379; Taylor, *Pioneering*, p. 8; "Chicago Commons: Social Settlement of the Chicago Theological Seminary, 140 North Union Street, October 21, 1894," in "Chicago Commons Scrapbook," Vol. I.

our daily lives. Its doors were opened to us at any and all times. . . .
Very soon we began to wonder how we ever managed to exist without
the Commons.[9]

Like other American settlements the Commons soon found that work
with neighborhood children and young people provided an effective opening wedge. As soon as the residents had settled their personal quarters, they
established a kindergarten. The director was Bertha Hofer, a recent graduate
of the Pestalozzi-Froebel Kindergarten Training School in Berlin and a
convert to the belief that children's play should be constructive and educational. She cleared the backyard of broken glass and rubbish, planted a tiny
garden, and taught her young charges how to raise vegetables and flowers.
In addition, they washed and ironed clothes, dusted, made beds, and helped
prepare food for the settlement table. In good weather she took them to
the public parks where, seeing stretches of grass for the first time in their
lives, they "stooped down and gently smoothed the tips of the blades, as if
they were the fur of some great kitten." Realizing that the success of the
kindergarten depended in part upon the co-operation of the parents, Miss
Hofer tried to organize a mothers' club. It took time. Despite written invitations and personal calls, made in her best clothes and in her worst, she
had to wait almost a year before the mothers were willing to come to the
settlement on Friday evenings to discuss the care of their children and the
aims of the kindergarten.[10]

The Commons sponsored a day nursery, run by a group of sympathetic
Chicago women who formed the Matheon Club. In the spring of 1897 they
rented a house two doors from the Commons and furnished it with the
necessary cribs and play equipment. For a fee of five cents a day the babies
and young children of working mothers were tended from 6:30 A.M. until
6:30 P.M. — "washed, fed, given a nap and made to know, as nearly as possible,

[9] Taylor, *Pioneering*, pp. 284, 296; *Chicago Commons*, I (November, 1896), 3–4. Two
more families soon joined the settlement, the Bollers with three young boys and the
Gavits whose son was born at Chicago Commons. Other settlements had the same problem of overcoming neighborhood distrust. Taylor, in addition, had to allay the fears
of his mother and brothers about the safety of the Taylor children. In 1895 he informed
his mother that "Lill's management of the big house makes it run smoothly and well.
We have efficient help so that she can supervise and be hostess to the large number of
visitors who come from all parts of the city and the land to see the place and the
work. . . . Our family life does not suffer. We are very happy — all of us. . . . We
keep well too" and "exercise great sanitary precaution." Graham Taylor to Mrs. William
J. R. Taylor, September 29, 1895, in the possession of Lea Taylor.
[10] Woods and Kennedy, *Settlement Horizon*, pp. 73, 131–32; *Chicago Commons*, I
(April, 1896), 2; Taylor, *Chicago Commons*, p. 52; *Chicago Commons: A Social Settlement*, p. 17; *The Commons*, I (May, 1897), 15; *The Commons*, I (July, 1897), 8–9.

'all the comforts of home.'" Starting with five youngsters during its first week of operation, the day nursery averaged thirty to forty children by 1904, even though its fee had risen to ten cents. When a new settlement house was completed at Grand Avenue and Morgan Street in 1901, the Matheon Day Nursery moved there and continued its vital service of caring for neighborhood children of working mothers.[11]

Clubs and social groups took shape as local interest in the Commons increased. The settlement program, wrote Taylor, "just grew up out of the people's wants and aspirations, good will and co-operation." The first of these was the Chicago Commons Woman's Club, which scheduled speeches of civic interest and held regular social gatherings. The Girls' Progressive Club united the "working girls of our neighborhood . . . for mutual helpfulness, culture, and social fellowship." Starting with only six members, it soon grew to nearly one hundred, including several young college graduates from the northern suburbs who regularly attended the club meetings. Younger girls were welcomed into the Little Women, which met on Thursday evenings for social events, games, songs, and stories. The unruly gangs of boys who roamed the streets were eventually urged to use the Commons as their headquarters. In time they too were organized into clubs and study groups with special interests in electricity, wood working, athletics, and even a boys' cooking class. The "miracle of the Chess Club," wrote one of the residents, was "made up of boys who once were irrepressible embodiments of perpetual motion and sleepless mischief; but who now spend often an hour or more at a time in silent study over a game of chess." [12]

Summer heat brought a special kind of misery to the crowded seventeenth ward. The residents soon learned what their neighbors already knew, that with the "thermometer at 98° . . . for a week of intolerable days and less tolerable nights, life becomes all but unbearable." A rich variety of smells drifted through the streets, vegetables and meat rotted in the stores, milk was sour when delivered, "sickness besets the children with unerring certainty, and little white crepe is a common sight upon the doors." Taylor felt that "no ministry of the settlement" was more rewarding than helping people escape "from the desperate imprisonment of summer in the city." The Commons arranged daily picnics in the city parks and along the lake front, while some financial backers of the settlement opened their suburban estates for all-day

[11] *The Commons*, I (May, 1897), 13; *Chicago Commons: A Social Center for Civic Co-operation* (Chicago, 1904), pp. 12, 18.

[12] Graham Taylor, "Social Aspects of Life and Labor," *Daily News* (Chicago), December 27, 1902; *Chicago Commons: A Social Settlement*, 18, 19, 20; Herman F. Hegner, "Education at Chicago Commons," *The Outlook*, LII (August 31, 1895), 343–44; Woods and Kennedy, *Settlement Horizon*, chaps. vii, viii.

outings. After 1901 two vacant lots across from the new Commons building were equipped as a playground and supervised at settlement expense, while residents occasionally organized games on the less traveled streets. Throughout the 1890's the "only breathing space" for adults was run-down Bickerdike Square, an acre of land "containing a few trees and weedy grass." Taylor's dogged lobbying and his service on the Special Park Commission from 1903 until 1906 finally forced the city to establish Eckhart Park, the first public park and playground in the crowded ward.[13]

The Commons, like other American settlements, experimented with coun try camps for its neighborhood children. In 1897, a farmer donated a large tract of land on the Fox River, just north of Elgin, Illinois, about thirty-five miles from Chicago, and this became Camp Commons. The youngsters lived in tents, and in addition to swimming and playing games, they helped with the farming. About three hundred boys and girls had a chance each summer to spend a few weeks at the camp. It closed during World War I, and not until 1923 did the settlement acquire another site. This was a 200-acre farm near New Buffalo, Michigan, which in time was equipped with cabins and able to accommodate 450 children during the summer. Taylor was a frequent visitor at the camp, but through most of these years his family vacationed at Macatawa, Michigan. During the 1890's they rented a minister's ramshackle cottage which Taylor thought as unsound as the owner's theology. In 1900 he built his own place and thereafter joined the family for weekends as often as his busy schedule permitted.[14]

While summer aggravated the physical hardships of life on Chicago's west side, there were the year-round problems of unsanitary streets and alleys, dilapidated tenement buildings and a deplorably low standard of community hygiene. Like other settlement workers across the country, the Commons residents rose to this challenge. Following the example of Jane Addams at Hull House, one of them became a city garbage inspector and checked the removal and disposal of debris. Five others served as tenement-house inspectors, forcing landlords to repair property if it failed to meet city regulations.

[13] *Chicago Commons: A Social Settlement*, pp. 23, 24; Taylor, *Chicago Commons*, p. 58; "Report Submitted by Special Park Commission to West Chicago Park Commissioners, May 24, 1902," p. 3, Raymond Robins Papers, State Historical Society, Madison, Wis.; Graham Taylor, "A Day in the City Playgrounds," *Daily News* (Chicago), June 10, 1905; Graham Taylor, "Vote for the West Parks — New and Old," *Daily News* (Chicago), October 14, 1905; Woods and Kennedy, *Settlement Horizon*, chap. x.

[14] *The Commons*, III (June, 1898), 3–4; *The Commons*, III (September, 1898), 12–13; Taylor, *Chicago Commons*, pp. 38, 58–59, 230–31; *Chicago Commons: Twenty-Fifth Year, 1894–1919* (Chicago, 1919), p. 21; Chicago Commons Association, *Thirty Years and After* (Chicago, 1924), pp. 28–29; Woods and Kennedy, *Settlement Horizon*, chap. xi.

In addition, the residents offered neighborhood women instruction in techniques of tenement housekeeping, problems of marketing and meal-planning, care of young babies, and advice about medical facilities. In co-operation with public health officials and the Infant Welfare Society they established clinics for children and expectant mothers. During the summer the Commons sold sterilized milk at cost, disposing of 250 bottles daily by 1911.[15]

The newcomers to North Union Street were shocked to find men, women, and children drinking with horses from the water trough next door to the settlement. For three years they vainly pleaded with city officials to condemn the trough. Finally in 1897 the settlement built a drinking fountain around the corner on busy Milwaukee Avenue, forcing even "the greatest sceptic concerning the usefulness of public drinking fountains" to admit its superiority.[16]

Another victory was the gradual improvement in neighborhood health standards. Rosa Cassettare provided one illustration of how this was accomplished. She recalled the early days when she and her friends "used to sit down in the yard and drink beer, like the men. . . . When the kids come home from school the mothers were a little 'dippy' and they start to cuss and scold those kids and swear at them, and they don't know what to do, those poor kids." But then "Dr. Taylor talk to these ladies, so nice and so kind! . . . We thought we was in another world, those nice, good talks, makes us feel so good!" After a while the women "didn't sit in the yard and drink beer like the men; they know it was wrong." This, added Mrs. Cassettare, was only one instance in which "many mothers and many children learned so much from Chicago Commons."[17]

Adult education had been one of the main goals of Canon Barnett and the Toynbee Hall settlers and it soon became an integral part of the English settlement house program. In the 1890's, American settlements tried to emulate this English pattern. The Commons' residents, for example, felt obligated to offer classes for "the working people of their neighborhood, who deprived of the opportunities of school and reading by the necessity of going early to work, aspire to improve themselves in the evening hours." In conjunction with the Plymouth Congregational Church, Chicago Commons sponsored an adult education program called the Plymouth Winter Night College. More than forty courses were offered at the settlement. During the

---

[15] Taylor, *Chicago Commons*, pp. 54, 65–66; *Chicago Commons*, I (April, 1896), 2; Taylor, *Pioneering*, pp. 291–92; *Chicago Commons: A Social Center for Civic Co-operation*, p. 12; *Chicago Commons, 1894–1911*, p. 33.

[16] *Chicago Commons*, I (May, 1896), 5; *The Commons*, II (August, 1897), 10–11.

[17] Rosa Cassettare, speech delivered at fortieth anniversary of Chicago Commons, May 4, 1934 (manuscript); Woods and Kennedy, *Settlement Horizon*, chap. xxiii.

first year four hundred students studied English, American history and literature, book-keeping, home nursing, mechanical drawing, German, Latin, physical culture, and other subjects.[18]

Within a few years, however, the initial interest tapered off. In the fall of 1898 the Commons suspended the college because neighborhood people were "unable, for various reasons, to respond to offers of formal educational classes." Other American settlements had the same experience during the 1890's. The trouble was due in part to language, for few of the immigrants arriving in that decade were prepared to pursue advanced studies in English. Furthermore, the degree-candidates were drawn off by public evening high schools and university extension work, both of which became available in these years. Nonetheless, the Commons did continue its popular language and citizenship classes for immigrants. And it placed new emphasis upon social clubs that were "only incidentally educational." Those in cooking, home making, child care, sewing, rug weaving, and manual training always had large enrollments. In addition, Taylor worked closely with the public schools, persuading neighborhood ones to offer a variety of evening courses for adults, and he himself taught for many years in the University of Chicago extension program.[19]

Following the lead of Toynbee Hall and Hull House, Chicago Commons promoted a wide variety of cultural activities — a library, picture collection, music lessons, concerts, dramatic performances, and pageants. Its first loan library started with the personal collections of the residents. Friends of the settlement contributed other volumes, while Henry Demarest Lloyd, Richard T. Ely, and William T. Stead sent complete sets of their publications. In exchange for subscriptions to its magazine, *The Commons*, the settlement received more than sixty periodicals. After Taylor became a director of the Chicago Public Library in 1906 he arranged for the establishment of a branch library in the basement of the settlement. The neighborhood children could avail themselves of musical instruction at a small cost, and the guitar and mandolin club was one of the settlement's most lively organizations. A choral club for adults and another for children were perennially popular and their concerts drew city-wide acclaim. The settlement loaned pictures to neighborhood families, but the Commons' collection never rivaled the outstanding one of Ellen Gates Starr at Hull House. For almost three decades Taylor conducted a Pleasant Sunday Afternoon program which attracted

[18] Pimlott, *Toynbee Hall*, chaps. iv, ix; Woods and Kennedy, *Settlement Horizon*, p. 134; *Chicago Commons: A Social Settlement*, p. 24; *Chicago Commons* (Chicago, 1895), p. 3; Hegner, "Education at Chicago Commons," pp. 343–44.

[19] Woods and Kennedy, *Settlement Horizon*, pp. 135–36; *The Commons*, III (November, 1898), 6; Taylor, *Chicago Commons*, pp. 81–84.

several hundred people to the settlement parlors to hear musical selections, view picture slides, or listen to a short, informal talk before partaking of refreshments.[20]

The broad, non-sectarian approach of the Pleasant Sunday Afternoon gatherings characterized the entire settlement program. Taylor felt that the settlement movement was "essentially religious in motive," but he knew that "church and settlement has each its distinctive sphere and neither can take the place of the other without losing its own place." Hence he insisted that even in areas "where the churches are conspicuous for their absence or their feebleness," the settlement must disavow "being in any sense a substitute or a rival of the church or the mission." He wanted Chicago Commons to express "the broadly religious spirit, which seems to actuate Protestant, Roman Catholic, Jew and Ethical Culturist alike." And he hoped that it would be able to unite these and other groups within "the all-embracing framework of neighborship and fellow-citizenship."[21]

The same religious tolerance prevailed within the Commons household, where throughout the years the majority of its residents were Protestants. In the 1890's many joined the nearby Tabernacle Congregational Church. Built in 1866, it had suffered a sharp decline in membership as waves of Scandinavian Lutherans and Irish and German Catholics moved into the area. By 1894 it was the only English-speaking, Protestant church in the seventeenth ward (though there was a Presbyterian Mission), and the Commons residents were anxious to preserve it. Taylor served without pay as pastor, another resident was assistant pastor, and several women from the Commons taught Sunday school classes. Under their guidance the old church took on new life, sometimes boasting a congregation of 400 or 500 people. Yet it remained desperately poor and could do nothing about the deterioration of its building. A solution was reached at the end of the 1890's when Chicago Commons secured the Tabernacle Congregational Church land at Grand Avenue and Morgan Street, built a new settlement house, and provided permanent quarters for the congregation in the spacious auditorium.[22]

---

[20] Woods and Kennedy, *Settlement Horizon*, p. 146; *Chicago Commons*, I (October, 1896), 6; *Chicago Commons*, I (January, 1897), 16; Taylor, *Chicago Commons*, p. 153; Chicago Commons Association, Board of Trustees, Minutes of Meetings, Warden's Report for 1908; *Chicago Commons: A Social Settlement*, p. 21; *The Commons*, III (October, 1898), 13.

[21] *Chicago Commons*, I (October, 1896), 9; Graham Taylor, "The Soul of the Settlement," National Federation of Settlements, *Eighth Conference, 1918*, p. 12; Graham Taylor, "Social Settlement, Religion, and the Church," in Jerome Davis (ed.), *Christianity and Social Adventuring* (New York, 1927), p. 167; Graham Taylor to F. Herbert Stead, March 8, 1918; Taylor, *Pioneering*, p. 332.

[22] Taylor, *Chicago Commons*, pp. 39–40; Graham Taylor, "The Frontier in Our Rear," *The Advance*, XXXV (May 12, 1898), 636–37.

Another vital part of the settlement program was the Tuesday evening Free Floor meeting, a forum, said Taylor, where "extremes meet, clash, knock off their sharp edges, modify or counteract each other and settle most of the auditors down upon the golden mean." The idea did not originate with him, for Lyman Gage had pioneered such gatherings in Chicago in the late 1880's, and both Hull House and Toynbee Hall sponsored public discussions of current economic and social problems. Taylor's forums, however, were more exciting. Held weekly from October until June, they were based upon the proposition that "all classes of men, all shades of thought, all degrees of prosperity and of culture, shall for once come face to face and 'have it out.'" The speaker of the evening delivered a twenty-minute address and then answered questions and comments from the floor. There were no restrictions on freedom of speech, with the exception of a three-minute time limit and the understanding "that advocacy of violence would be out of order." The Chicago *Daily News* helped publicize the assemblies by printing a weekly invitation. Attendance in the basement assembly hall on Union Street averaged a hundred people, but in the new settlement auditorium the audience was two to three times that size. The majority were from the seventeenth ward, but there were also seminary and college students, professors, businessmen, lawyers, and doctors from distant parts of the city.[23]

A sample of the topics for discussion, always proposed from the floor, will indicate the controversial nature of these forums: "The Social Boiling Point," "Ethics and Competition," "The Single Tax," "Socialism," "Municipal Ownership," "Child Labor," "Trusts and Monopolies," or "Tolstoy and the Russian Peasant." The speakers included social gospel leaders Lyman Abbott and Washington Gladden, Chicago attorney Clarence Darrow, Mayor "Golden Rule" Jones of Toledo, anarchist Emma Goldman, Chicago's socialist labor leader Thomas J. Morgan, and Mrs. Lucy Parsons, widow of the Haymarket martyr Albert Parsons. Taylor was understandably nervous the night Mrs. Parsons spoke, but she calmly related the events preceding the riot and refused to be goaded into bitter recriminations by questions from the floor. One early Commons resident had a vivid recollection of Taylor presiding over these meetings, "courteously, cautiously on watch lest the potential explosives . . . be touched with a sudden flare. . . . I remember several occasions when the match came perilously close to the powder." An *Arena* reporter, who visited Chicago in 1902 to cover these forums, explained that the

[23] Graham Taylor, "Social Aspects of Life and Labor," *Daily News* (Chicago), December 6, 1902; *The Commons*, VI (March, 1902), 15, 16; Taylor, *Chicago Commons*, pp. 124, 125, 126; *Chicago Commons: A Social Settlement*, p. 26.

questions come thick and fast, many of them keen and searching, finding
the vulnerable places in the speaker's logic, and he must have quick wits
and a ready tongue to meet them all promptly and squarely. . . . In
such a crowd there are always would-be orators eager to air their theories
and notions, and they spring to their feet gesticulating wildly to catch
the chairman's eye. . . . The one who gets the floor evidently feels that
remorseless three-minute ruling hanging over him like a Damocles'
sword . . . but he does not know how to select and condense, so he is
usually in full career when the pitiless gavel falls, and he must sit down
swelling with unspoken speeches. . . .

   As a rule the audience is in good humor, but sometimes there is wild
commotion; faces scowl, fists clench, voices clash, and a riot seems immi-
nent. Then the chairman rises and pounds for order, and as soon as he
can make himself heard he smoothes the boisterous waves with the oil
of a little humor, and the incident passes off with a laugh all around.[24]

The reporter concluded that Taylor's forum was a safety-valve for the discontented people in the neighborhood. Undoubtedly it was during the 1890's.
But in the early years of the twentieth century the character of the meetings
began to change. Trade unionists, college students, and professional people,
who were once the most vocal participants, now came only "to look on and
listen in," refusing to challenge the most absurd claims of radical speakers.
The Chicago *Inter-Ocean* and the *Chronicle* accused the settlement of
radical political activity every time a socialist or anarchist spoke at the forum.
Still another factor that militated against the success of the Free Floor was
the arrival in the ward of large numbers of immigrants from southern and
eastern Europe who could neither speak nor understand English. Unable
to participate in the Free Floor discussions, they formed cheering sections,
often supporting the most extreme anarchists. By 1902, the seventh year of
the meetings, Taylor concluded that the play to the galleries by "extreme
radical spokesmen and their retainers from other parts of the city" had at
last "impeached the sincerity" of the meetings. Reluctantly the Commons
canceled its Tuesday evening forum.[25]

III

   At Chicago Commons, as at other American settlements, the need to
co-operate with city government on such matters as schools, sanitation, and

---

[24] *The Commons*, III (January–April, 1889), 21; *Chicago Commons: A Social Settle-
ment*, 26; John Palmer Gavit, "Chicago Commons Free Floor Labor Discussions," *The
Commons*, V (October, 1900), 9–11; Taylor, *Chicago Commons*, 131–33; Helen Gavit
Swan to Graham Taylor, April 28, 1934, in the possession of Lea Taylor; R. Warren
Conant, "Anarchism at Close Quarters," *Arena*, XXVIII (October, 1902), 340–41.

[25] Conant, "Anarchism at Close Quarters," p. 341; Taylor, *Chicago Commons*, pp. 138,
140; Taylor, *Pioneering*, chap. xxiii.

public playgrounds soon became apparent to the residents. But there was disagreement among settlement leaders on how to achieve their political goals. Robert Woods of South End House in Boston and Mary Simkhovitch of Greenwich House in New York urged settlement workers to stay out of partisan politics on the grounds that they had little to gain and much to lose by embroiling their houses in party affairs. In Chicago, however, both Jane Addams and Graham Taylor did take an active part in local politics as independents. The nineteenth ward in which Hull House was located was the domain of alderman John Powers, chairman of the city council's finance committee and a leader in the Democratic party. In 1896, Jane Addams, settlement residents, and members of the Hull House Men's Club backed an independent Irish bricklayer against Johnny Powers. The reformers went down to defeat that year, but they vowed to try again in 1898. The second Hull House campaign against alderman Powers attracted wide publicity, but it also ended in failure for the reformers. One Hull House resident, Florence Kelley, wanted to keep up the battle for "municipal honesty," but Jane Addams felt that any further efforts to unseat Powers would be futile. After 1898 she retired from nineteenth ward politics and concentrated upon persuading city hall or the state legislature to do the right thing.[26]

Graham Taylor was more successful in the seventeenth ward, which had two active parties and a number of independent voters. Settlement residents soon found that the Scandinavians tended to be Republicans, the Irish Democrats, while the party bosses fought over the uncommitted German, Italian, and Polish votes. The political leaders controlled primaries and caucuses, neglected to print or circulate campaign literature, and refused to mention the issues. "The candidates for alderman," observed Taylor, "attempted little more than a 'saloon canvass.' Laying down from $5 to $50 on a saloon bar, the would-be alderman asked the saloon-keeper and the bartender to see that 'the boys' voted for him on election day." Both sides hired floating voters and altered election results "in accordance with deals made by the party machines." Taylor and members of Chicago Commons decided to challenge the bosses by rallying the independent vote in the seventeenth ward. At a meeting in Chicago Commons, a local branch of the Civic Fed-

---

[26] Woods and Kennedy, *Settlement Horizon*, p. 224, chap. xxi; Jane Addams, "Why the Ward Boss Rules," *Outlook*, LVIII (April 2, 1898), 879–82; Florence Kelley, "Hull House," *New England Magazine*, XVIII (July, 1898), 565–66; Ray Stannard Baker, "Hull House and the Ward Boss," *Outlook*, LVIII (March 26, 1898), 769–71; Allen F. Davis, "Jane Addams vs. the Ward Boss," Illinois State Historical Society, *Journal*, LIII (1960), 247–65; Allen F. Davis, "Spearheads for Reform: The Social Settlements and the Progressive Movement, 1870–1914" (Ph. D. diss., University of Wisconsin, 1959), 96–130; Anne Firor Scott, "Saint Jane and the Ward Boss," *American Heritage*, XII (December, 1960), 12–17, 94–99.

eration was formed in December, 1894. Like the parent organization, the Seventeenth Ward Council of the Civic Federation was non-partisan, pledged only to elect capable, honest city councilmen.[27]

The council's Political Action Committee began immediate preparations for the spring election of 1895. It promised that judges and clerks of election would not be "tools of political bosses" in the seventeenth ward. A few weeks later Herman Hegner, a settlement resident, reported to the council that ten of the judges and clerks should be disqualified and that some of them were actually political office holders. One judge lived in a small two-story house from which thirty-nine voters had registered in the last election. The Political Action Committee got eight of the ten offenders dismissed from their election posts.[28]

Next the council approved five Republicans and five Democrats as acceptable candidates for alderman, and they planned to submit these names to the Democractic and Republican bosses of the ward. The Republican leader, James H. Burke, told the reformers "that none of the names offered could be considered for a moment by the party as they were not in good and regular standing in the party." Their crime, continued Burke, was voting split tickets at the last election. He also threatened to disfranchise those voters who continued to split their ballots. The Democratic boss, Maurice O'Connor, evaded the Political Action Committee by refusing to keep two appointments. So the council endorsed an independent candidate, Thomas Johnson. In the election of 1895 this "Citizens & Taxpayers candidate" was beaten.[29]

In 1896, the Seventeenth Ward Civic Federation worked within the two parties to secure the nomination of good candidates. The Republican candidate, Magnus Knudson, appeared before the council, declared himself in favor of civil service reform and against municipal corruption, and asked for their support. The council endorsed him, and the reformers campaigned for him. Knudson won the election, but almost immediately began voting in the city council with the corrupt faction.[30]

Chastened by these experiences, the seventeenth warders fought and won

[27] Each ward had two aldermen serving two-year terms, but only one alderman was elected each year. Graham Taylor, "The Pending Independent Vote," *Daily News* (Chicago), March 31, 1906; Minutes of the Seventeenth Ward Council of the Civic Federation, p. 1.

[28] Minutes of the Seventeenth Ward Council of the Civic Federation, p. 6.

[29] Minutes of the Seventeenth Ward Council of the Civic Federation, February 15, March 1, March 15, March 29, 1895. Johnson ran as an independent and lost in 1894 also. The Seventeenth Ward vote in 1895 was 1,531 for Johnson, 1,055 for the Democratic candidate, and 1,705 for the Republican candidate, Stephen Revere. *Daily News Almanac, 1895*, p. 360; *Daily News Almanac, 1896*, p. 386.

[30] Minutes of the Seventeenth Ward Council of the Civic Federation, March 14, 1896.

an important battle in 1897. The Political Action Committee visited both party headquarters and asked "for honest clerks and judges of election, and for candidates for whom the citizens could vote without loss of their self-respect." The party bosses laughed, and the reformers decided to run one of their own members, James Walsh, on an independent ticket. They covered as many polling places as they could on election day to guard against fraud. When the ballots were counted, Walsh led by eighty votes. But the following morning the returns from a few precincts which had been held overnight showed that the Republican candidate had won by a small margin. Taylor called a mass meeting to protest these irregularities, and he invited the Municipal Voters' League (which had taken over the political action work of the Chicago Civic Federation) to enter the case. By mandamus proceedings the League secured a recount of the ballots and the fraud was uncovered. Two Democratic judges and a Republican clerk of elections were brought to trial; eventually the clerk and one of the judges went to prison for three years. Meantime, Walsh took his seat in the city council. This victory, claimed Taylor, "did much to redeem the ward from the most flagrant violations of the election laws."[31]

The following year the reformers again tried to influence the selection of good candidates by both the Republican and Democratic caucuses. They visited Boss Burke first. He told them that he didn't need either their advice or their support because the Italians holding city jobs through his patronage would guarantee a Republican victory. That year some of the reformers helped an outstanding Republican candidate in the adjacent sixteenth ward, a Polish lawyer named John F. Smulski. He won a seat on the council the following year and was re-elected in 1899. After the ward boundaries were redrawn in 1901, part of the former sixteenth ward was included in the new seventeenth ward. So the reformers asked the Republicans to nominate Smulski. Burke was extremely reluctant, but at the last minute the Republican caucus did nominate Smulski and he won the election handily. He served on the city council until 1903, then went on to a distinguished career as corporation counsel, state treasurer, chairman of Chicago's West Park Commission, and a Polish-American leader of national stature. Meantime Burke asked Taylor how long he intended to stay in the seventeenth ward. The settlement warden replied that he held a ninety-

[31] Minutes of the Seventeenth Ward Council of the Civic Federation, April, 1897; Graham Taylor, "Ward Politics Good and Bad — Challenge," *Daily News* (Chicago), March 5, 1910; *Daily News* (Chicago), April 5, 7, December 11, 18, 1897; *The Commons,* II (December, 1897), 6; Taylor, *Chicago Commons,* p. 69. The final count in the 1897 election was 1,484 for Revere, the Republican alderman, 1,112 for the Democrat, and 1,629 for Walsh. *Daily News Almanac, 1898,* p. 350.

nine year lease on the property at Grand and Morgan where Chicago Commons was building a permanent home. Burke exclaimed, "My God, I might as well begin to tell you things." Talyor listened, but was unimpressed. When the Republican leader tried to join the Seventeenth Ward Civic Federation, his application was rejected. And his persistent efforts to contribute to the settlement likewise came in naught.[32]

The Civic Federation's successor was the Seventeenth Ward Community Club. It was allied with the Municipal Voters' League and, like the Seventeenth Ward Civic Federation, was independent of Chicago Commons although it maintained headquarters in the settlement building. All male residents of the ward were eligible for membership, and the club rooms were open during the day and in the evening for social purposes as well as for reading and study. The Community Club, like its predecessor, was strictly non-partisan and encouraged both parties to nominate honest and capable men for office. Club members helped select candidates, urged eligible voters to register, scrutinized candidates' records, and analyzed issues at stake in each election. Graham Taylor was the leading figure behind the Civic Federation and the Community Club, but he was aided by a dedicated group of men at the settlement. John Palmer Gavit headed the Municipal Committee of the Civic Federation, and Herman Hegner became so interested in sanitary problems of the ward that he followed the Hull House example and became a Sanitary Inspector. Others who were active in politics were James Mullenbach, pastor of the Tabernacle Church and later director of the city's Municipal Lodging House, and Allen T. Burns. The most effective reformer was Raymond Robins, who joined the Commons household in February, 1901, after a colorful career as a lawyer in California and a gold-miner in Alaska. Vitally interested in civic reform, he soon proved to Taylor that he was "a past master in ward politics."[33]

It was Raymond Robins who drew William E. Dever into politics. A promising young man working in a tannery by day and attending law school at night, Dever had run unsuccessfully in the aldermanic election of 1900. Robins persuaded him to run again on the Democratic ticket in 1902, and with the help of the Community Club Dever won that election and four

[32] *Chicago Commons, 1894–1911*, 18; Taylor, *Chicago Commons*, pp. 67–69; *Daily News Almanac, 1899*, p. 419; *Daily News Almanac, 1900*, p. 383; *Daily News Almanac, 1902*, pp. 395, 293.

[33] Minutes of the Seventeenth Ward Council of the Civic Federation, January, 1898; *Chicago Commons, 1894–1911*, pp. 17–18; Taylor, *Chicago Commons*, pp. 259–60; Allen F. Davis, "Raymond Robins: The Settlement Worker as Municipal Reformer," *Social Service Review*, XXXIII (June, 1959), 133, 134; Graham Taylor to Raymond Robins, September 1, 1902, August 14, 1903, Raymond Robins Papers.

subsequent ones. After leaving the city council, he became judge of Cook County Superior Court and eventually mayor of Chicago. In 1903 Robins and the reformers elected a German-American, Lewis D. Sitts, on the Republican ticket. That same year Robins became head resident of Northwestern University Settlement, which was located about one mile away but still in the seventeenth ward. There he organized a Civic Club which worked closely with the Community Club to control ward elections for another fourteen years. From 1901 until 1917 the reformers were able to elect a Republican one year and a Democrat the next. In fact, Dever was so popular that the Republicans did not put up a candidate against him in 1904 or 1908. Dever was succeeded by a Democrat named Walkowiak in 1911. Sitts was the seventeenth ward Republican on the city council from 1903 until 1917, when he was finally beaten by a Democrat. The reformers were less successful in their occasional efforts to elect representatives or senators to the state legislature, though they did win one contest in 1902. The real contribution of Taylor and Robins was proving that settlement residents and independent voters could beat the party bosses at their own game. Few other American settlement houses rivaled Chicago Commons' long record of political success.[34]

Through all the political battles fought by the Seventeenth Ward Civic Federation and the Community Club, Taylor and the Commons residents adhered to their non-partisan creed. Taylor was certain that this position was most advantageous for the settlement. Writing to a friend in 1924 he explained that "our policy at Chicago Commons has been to keep out of party politics and devote what influence we could gather and wield toward swinging the balance of power for the better candidate in *local elections.*" This decision, the Chicago Commons warden continued, "has deprived me personally from engaging in national campaigns for party candidates," for such partisan activity "would surely compromise my position" in the seventeenth ward as "an independent between the lines."[35]

Taylor had no regrets about his life-long policy to eschew all political affiliations. Never a party man at heart, he preferred to use his personal influence and his newspaper column to support the most worthy candidates for city, state, and federal offices regardless of their party labels. To the end of

[34] Taylor, *Chicago Commons*, pp. 70–71; Graham Taylor to Raymond Robins, August 14, 1903, Raymond Robins Papers; Davis, "Spearheads of Reform," pp. 142–46; *Daily News Almanac, 1905*, p. 357; *Daily News Almanac, 1909*, p. 384.

[35] Graham Taylor to Newton Jenkins, January 28, 1924. In a letter to Raymond Robins in 1902 Taylor insisted upon staying out of a mayoralty campaign in order to "stick close to the aldermanic struggle and the permanently larger issues involved therein." Graham Taylor to Raymond Robins, December 20, 1902, Raymond Robins Papers.

life he maintained that the settlements had nothing to gain "by having their head residents identified with party movements." Such ties could only obstruct their main function which was "to afford common ground on which people of different parties, classes and sects can meet to understand each other" and "cooperate for the common good." [36]

Taylor's stand as an independent did not prevent him from taking forthright political action when the occasion demanded. Immediately after McKinley's assassination by an anarchist in Buffalo the Chicago police arrested hundreds of suspected radicals, most of them immigrants living on the west side. One of the victims was Abraham Isaaks, a Russian immigrant who was a philosophical anarchist and editor of a small newspaper called *Free Society*. Jane Addams knew him well, and so did Graham Taylor and Raymond Robins, for he was an enthusiastic participant in the Free Floor forums. Learning that the police had arrested Isaaks and his family, destroyed his printing presses, and confiscated his books, the two settlements decided to take action. Jane Addams and Raymond Robins, who was acting for Chicago Commons in Taylor's absence, protested to Mayor Carter Harrison, Jr., and were allowed to secure legal counsel for Isaaks and another prisoner whom they knew. Within a short time the two men were released and the other radical suspects soon afterwards. Isaaks' property was replaced at city expense, but not the windows broken at Hull House and Chicago Commons by those who disagreed with the settlements' bold stand.[37]

Naturally, the Chicago *Chronicle* and *Inter-Ocean* used this opportunity to accuse the two settlements of aiding and abetting radicalism. Two years later Taylor and Jane Addams again roused their ire by criticizing Chicago's chief of police for shooting down an unemployed Russian immigrant without provocation. Furthermore, in 1908 they joined with many others in protesting against the Russian government's demand that an obscure Chicago carpenter named Christian Rudowitz be deported. Eventually the man was granted political asylum in the United States, but the *Inter-Ocean* branded Rudowitz's backers as "precisely those who are always expressing 'sympathy' for the

[36] Graham Taylor to Newton Jenkins, January 28, 1924.

[37] *Chronicle* (Chicago), September 7, 11, 12, 13, 1901; *Record-Herald* (Chicago), September 7, 8, 9, 1901; Taylor, *Chicago Commons*, pp. 133–34; Taylor, *Pioneering*, pp. 314–17, 136–37; Davis, "Raymond Robins: The Settlement Worker as Municipal Reformer," pp. 134–35; Addams, *Twenty Years*, pp. 403–8. Shortly afterwards Isaaks moved to New York City where he continued to publish *Free Society* until 1905. Later he went to California and spent the remainder of his life farming. In 1919 he wrote to Taylor: "It is almost 18 years since I left Chicago, but I still have often occasion to refer to you as the only & true democrat I have met in America." Abraham Isaaks to Graham Taylor, November 25, 1919.

murderers and would-be murderers, who call themselves 'anarchists.'" The *Chronicle* charged that

> the social settlements in this city have been made identical with opposition to the constitution of the United States and hostile to the laws of Illinois. . . .
>
> Anarchists, as Professor Taylor correctly says, believe the world against them. But when he says "These people must be taught that the law is not against them," he embarks upon a hopeless task and exposes his own error. To attempt to teach them by ordinary means is as useless as to read the Riot act to a pack of wolves. There is no middle way of dealing successfully with the anarchist. He must be wiped out or allowed to wrap the world in flame. He himself has decreed it, and Professor Taylor and Miss Addams are in poor business when they try to conceal this fact, and thus become the apologists of such a hideous creature. . . .
>
> Thus the immigrants and the children they bring or bear after arrival are trained by the "social settlements" in hostility to the lawful institutions of the country in which they seek liberty and the pursuit of happiness. . . . It is a cruel fate which guides the ignorant immigrant into the socialist precincts of Hull House and Chicago Commons. It is a sad misuse of Chicago money which maintains these alluring pitfalls for the trustful and helpless.[38]

Neither Chicago Commons nor Hull House made any public rejoinder to these editorial attacks, but both the Chicago *Daily News* and the Chicago *Evening Post* came to their support. They ran illustrated articles depicting the work of the settlements and condemned editorially the "ignorant or designing abuse which has recently been wantonly heaped upon these little groups of citizens in settlements." The

> settlements of Chicago need no defense in this community. But when the chief of police declares that settlements are first cousins to the anarchists, it is time that the official intelligence be brought to the realization of the nature of our institutions for social amelioration, their functions, their rights and the places they hold in the respect of the intelligent class of the community.
>
> Because the settlements deal with conditions as they find them, and therefore are often associated necessarily with extremists, it is assumed that they encourage extreme views and support extreme acts. But the conditions are not created by the settlements. They are being studied and bettered by them. It is preposterous that any apology or any explanation should be called for in a community like Chicago on behalf of an institution like the social settlement.[39]

[38] Taylor, *Pioneering*, pp. 205–9; "Some Reflections on Rudowitz's Case," *Inter-Ocean* (Chicago), December 29, 1908; editorial from *Chronicle* (Chicago), quoted by Taylor in *Pioneering*, pp. 325–26, and *Chicago Commons*, pp. 142–43.

[39] Taylor, *Chicago Commons*, pp. 144–45; quoted in Taylor, *Pioneering*, 208.

IV

American settlements did indeed deal with conditions as they found them. And this meant constant readjustment of their program to meet the needs of a rapidly changing population. Taylor deliberately located the Commons in the seventeenth ward in 1894 "because the people's heritage, traits, speech, and faith . . . were kindred to our own." Yet during the next quarter century the neighborhood experienced many racial changes. The Irish, Scandinavians, and Germans of the 1890's gave way to Italians and Poles, and they in turn were joined by Hungarians, Russians, Armenians, Turks, and Greeks. By 1917 there were twenty-two different nationalities represented in the area.[40]

The census figures reveal the scope of this change. In 1900 the ward's native-born and foreign-born inhabitants were almost equal in number. Close to four-fifths of those born in the United States were second generation immigrants. By 1910, however, the foreign-born constituted 57 per cent of the population, and second generation immigrants accounted for nine-tenths of the native-born people in the ward. While the vast majority of the newcomers to the seventeenth ward in the 1880's had been Germans, Irish, and Scandinavians, these three nationalities supplied only 13, 1, and 8 per cent respectively of those arriving in the first decade of the twentieth century. The bulk of the newcomers, 63 per cent, were from the Austro-Hungarian Empire, while another 12 per cent came from Italy, and 10 per cent from Russia.[41]

World War I made such sharp inroads on the flow of immigrants that the 1920 census showed native-born once again outnumbering foreign-born in the seventeenth ward. Yet the proportion of second generation immigrants among the native-born had risen to 93 per cent. Of these, the Poles accounted for 62 per cent, and the Italians came next with 19 per cent. Germans, Scandinavians, and Irish immigrants combined constituted only 6 per cent by 1920.[42]

The size of the ward population increased during these years as well. There were approximately 28,000 people when Taylor settled on North Union Street in 1894. But the ward boundaries were redrawn after the 1900 census,

---

[40] Taylor, *Pioneering*, p. 187; Graham Taylor, "How Neighborly Citizenship Counts," *Daily News* (Chicago), May 3, 1913; R. C. Tibbetts, "History, Neighborhood, and Work of Chicago Commons" (manuscript), 1925; Helen R. Jeter, *Trends of Population in the Region of Chicago* (Chicago, 1927), pp. 59–61.

[41] *Twelfth Census of the United States: 1900* (Washington, 1902), I, 651; *Thirteenth Census of the United States: 1910* (Washington, 1913), II, 513.

[42] *Fourteenth Census of the United States: 1920* (Washington, 1922), III, 275.

and the seventeenth almost doubled its territory. In 1901 the ward had a population of 58,000. This jumped to 70,000 by 1910, though it dropped back to less than 60,000 by the time the 1920 census was taken. Congestion in the seventeenth ward was at its worst in the years just before World War I when there were only 4,289 dwellings for more than 14,000 families. In a *Daily News* editorial in 1913 Taylor touched upon the qualitative and quantitative changes in the neighborhood. "Houses which used to hold one or two Norwegian or German families are now occupied by three or four families from southern Italy and Sicily, from the Polish and Hungarian parts of Austria and Russia and by men from Turkey and Greece without their families." [43]

This constant human flux posed a number of problems for the settlement workers, who now had to overcome barriers of language, custom, and religious background before they could establish contact with their new neighbors. In time, however, they found that each national group had its own distinctive characteristics. The Italians were much gayer, more exuberant, and demonstrative than the reserved Scandinavians. Their colorful religious life, with the frequent *fiestas* for patron saints, involved more ritual and ceremony than that of the Irish Catholics. The Poles were "difficult to approach and far slower to respond" than the friendly Italians. Temperamentally they seemed more phlegmatic to the residents, but with the help of a Polish-speaking worker they were able to draw a portion of these people into settlement activities. The ward also had its share of migrant workers, largely Greek and Turkish men who labored on railroad construction during the spring, summer, and fall, and spent the winters in west side rooming houses.[44]

The Commons residents mediated numerous ethnic conflicts over the years. One of the earliest was a neighborhood row in the 1890's which started when an Irish washerwoman's clothesline broke and fell onto boards of tomato paste carefully laid out in the sun by an Italian housewife. The Scandinavians

---

[43] Ward Maps, 1888, 1890, 1901, 1912, 1921, Chicago Historical Society; *Eleventh Census of the United States: 1890*, I, 674; *Twelfth Census of the United States: 1900*, I, 651; *Thirteenth Census of the United States: 1910*, II, 513; *Fourteenth Census of the United States: 1920*, III, 275; Taylor, "How Neighborly Citizenship Counts," *Daily News* (Chicago), May 3, 1913. In the 1890's the seventeenth ward boundaries were Lake Street on the south, the North Branch of the Chicago River on the east and north, and May Street, Chicago Avenue, and Carpenter Street forming the western boundary. After the wards were redrawn in 1901 the seventeenth was bounded by West Kinzie Street on the south, the Chicago River on the east, West Division Street on the north, and Ashland Avenue on the west. It became the thirty-first ward in 1921 but retained the same boundaries.

[44] Taylor, *Pioneering*, chap. xv; Taylor, *Chicago Commons*, pp. 98, 99, 101, chap. viii; Board of Trustees, Minutes of Meetings, Warden's Report for year ending September 30, 1917; Woods and Kennedy, *Settlement Horizon*, chap. xxx.

also had trouble with the Italians. One Sunday they threatened to call the police when Italians exploded firecrackers all day long. Taylor's explanation that this was the Sicilian way of celebrating the presentation of a gift to the church only partially satisfied the older residents. Most of the Scandinavians, Irish, and many of the Germans preferred to move out of the area rather than tolerate the "merrier and noisier ways" of the Latins. One of Taylor's Irish friends lamented, "The longer I stay here, the more of a stranger I am." In addition, there were ill feelings between Poles and Russians, Armenians and Turks. Moreover, each group had its own contesting factions, such as the Armenian adherents of the Gregorian church and the Armenian Protestants, or the Greek Orthodox and Greek Protestant groups.[45]

Time and time again the residents came across examples of the "heartbreaking breach" between immigrant parents, clinging tenaciously to the language and customs of their homeland, and impatient children, already Americanized and looking with contempt upon cultural vestiges of the Old Country. "Immigration," thought Taylor,

> is for at least two generations so meanacing a tragedy in the family life that the sympathetic observer of the struggle wonders how so many families survive it. There is no more pathetic figure in America today than the immigrant working mother, fearingly, often frantically, clasping a babe to her bosom while desperately struggling, yet always failing, to keep pace with the older children's progress in the language and strange ways of the new world.

Fortunately, the settlement was able to offer educational and social opportunities to both generations. This, plus "patient, tactful, skillful guidance," restored in many cases "the peace and order of family life."[46]

Over the years Taylor became an eloquent spokesman on behalf of American immigrants. Though he had had few personal contacts with them during his youth, he felt that his own Dutch "hyphen" enabled him to understand something of their pride in ancestry and cultural heritage. And his travels in Europe, together with the trans-Atlantic trips of other settlement workers, bound the Commons residents closely with neighborhood families from all parts of the world. Taylor frequently used his *Daily News* column to praise the melting-pot contribution to American society. In the 1920's when Chicago was plagued with Sicilian racketeers, he reminded his readers that

[45] Lea D. Taylor, "The Social Settlement and Civic Responsibility — The Life Work of Mary McDowell and Graham Taylor," *Social Service Review*, XXVIII (March, 1954), 36; Taylor, *Pioneering*, p. 192; Taylor, *Chicago Commons*, pp. 102–3.
[46] Taylor, *Chicago Commons*, pp. 85, 86; Graham Taylor, manuscript, no title, n.d.; Woods and Kennedy, *Settlement Horizon*, pp. 312–14.

the great majority of our good American citizens of Sicilian birth justly protest against being suspected of having any part or lot with these parasites of their race, from whose lawlessness they themselves have suffered most. . . . we must not forget how long we have tolerated similar forms of American lawlessness.[47]

Taylor wanted a national immigration policy, but not one that would restrict the number of people eligible for entrance. Speaking before the National Conference of Charities and Correction in 1913 he called for a "domestic or internal immigration policy" that would seek "To receive, distribute and locate immigrants; To protect their persons and property; To inform and train them for citizenship." Taylor felt it important to establish "a consistent and effective national policy for naturalizing, educating and assimilating the strangers within our gates who seek the right to live and labor with us." But he warned against forceful, indiscriminate Americanization.

> It will be a great loss and very little gain to American to have its adopted citizens throw away their great heritage of language, national experience, folklore and song, custom and tradition, instead of adding them to our American inheritance.

In short, argued Taylor, "In this country we want to eliminate the hyphen, but not what lies at the end of the hyphen."[48]

Taylor's sympathetic understanding of American immigrants was tested during the war years. When the fighting broke out in Europe he found that many of the Commons' neighbors sided openly with their former homelands. Like most other settlement leaders, however, he supported President Wilson's neutrality policy, while at the same time urging some type of negotiated peace upon the belligerents. During the uneasy summer of 1914 he accepted an invitation from the Carnegie Church Peace Union to attend an international peace conference in Constance, Germany. Before his ship landed at Cherburg, Austria had declared war on Serbia, and by the time he reached Paris, both Russia and Germany had joined the conflict. This turn of events,

---

[47] Taylor, *Pioneering*, p. 188; Taylor, *Chicago Commons*, pp. 88, 100; Graham Taylor, "The Foreign Born as American Assets," *Daily News* (Chicago), June 1, 1918; Graham Taylor, "Worthy Italian-American Neighbors," *Daily News* (Chicago), March 13, 1926.

[48] Graham Taylor, "Report of Committee on Distribution and Assimilation of Immigrants," National Conference of Charities and Correction, *Proceedings, 1913*, p. 32; Graham Taylor "Foreign Born Citizens as Political Assets," National Conference of Social Work, *Proceedings, 1918*, p. 459; Graham Taylor, "Race Lines and the Main Line in America," *Daily News* (Chicago), March 19, 1910; Graham Taylor, "Our International Neighborhoods and the New America — Assimilation," National Federation of Settlements, *Seventh Conference, 1917*, p. 49.

noted Taylor in his diary, "tragically emphasizes & embarresses [sic] our peace conference." He was lucky to secure steerage passage back to the United States and quick to see the humor as well as the irony in his dilemma.[49]

In November, 1915, Henry Ford sent a telegram to Taylor asking him to accompany one hundred representative Americans, including Jane Addams, Thomas Edison, and John Wanamaker, to an international conference at the Hague. Ford wanted the Americans to join with delegates from six other neutral nations to "frame terms of peace, based on justice for all, regardless of the military situation." He flatly predicted that "when the pilgrims reach The Hague, the moral power of the peace movement will be irresistible." Taylor declined on the grounds of his wife's illness, but in a subsequent letter he took issue with Ford's "weird judgment" of the European situation.

> I feel obliged to inform you that were I free to consider your generous invitation, I would be constrained to decline it by my loyalty to the peace cause. . . .
> Thus far I have found no dissent from the judgment prevalent here that both the Pacifist cause and American intervention have been discredited seriously by this ill-advised project. . . .
> While appreciating your sincere desire to do anything you can toward ending this fratricidal strife, I would not be true if I did not tell you how sincerely I deplore the words and acts which are so seriously embarrassing those who are truly the friends of peace.

Ford's peace crusade departed in December, but without either Wanamaker or Jane Addams, who was incapacitated by illness. Its objective, continuous mediation by the neutral countries, was never achieved.[50]

When the United States finally declared war on Germany in April, 1917, Taylor like most of the American settlement leaders promptly backed the Wilson administration. Only a handful followed Jane Addams, who remained an outspoken pacifist throughout the entire conflict. At its 1917 meeting, the National Federation of Settlements held a long discussion before announcing its support of the government's war effort. The Federation's statement read:

> We conceive it to be our peculiar task to oppose in our neighborhoods every attempt to sow the seeds of disloyal and illegal action; and at the same time to uphold the right of honest discussion of questions of public

---

[49] Graham Taylor, "Log of a Peace Errand Ending in War," *Daily News* (Chicago), September 5, 1914; Taylor, Diary, July 31, 1914; Taylor, *Pioneering*, p. 222.

[50] Telegram from Henry Ford to Graham Taylor, November 25, 1915; Henry Ford to Graham Taylor, November 27, 1915; Taylor, *Pioneering*, p. 235; Graham Taylor to Henry Ford, December 1, 1915, quoted in Taylor, *Pioneering*, p. 236; Allan Nevins and Frank E. Hill, *Ford: Expansion and Challenge, 1915–1933* (New York, 1957), pp. 35–39, chap. ii.

policy, to the end that we may not lose the very soul of democracy in undertaking its defense.[51]

Chicago Commons abided by this resolution. Taylor agreed to serve as chairman of Draft Board 39, for he knew that many of the bewildered seventeenth ward inhabitants would come "to the Commons to meet the requirements of the draft with far more confidence and less suspicion than they might have had in going anywhere else for this strange and more or less tragic experience." The auditorium of the settlement became draft board headquarters; Lea Taylor was assistant secretary and organized the office staff; numerous residents helped with the immense job of interpreting the long questionnaires and tabulating the results. The draft cut "like a great cleaver" through the community, disclosing many facts which even the settlement residents had never uncovered. Draft Board 39 registered over 12,000 men between the ages of 18 and 45, four-fifths of whom were born abroad and were still alien non-declarants. Only 17 per cent of the men called by that board ever entered service. Compared to the national average of 35 per cent this figure was low, but it was due in large part to dependency, physical defects, and the unusual number of aliens.[52]

In still other ways the settlement was able to ease the strain of war on an immigrant neighborhood. The Draft Board doubled as an information center, helping hundreds of puzzled men who did not understand the official notices or could not untangle problems of allotments. The residents tried to look after families and dependents of men at war; they co-operated with the Red Cross in first-aid and home-care courses and instruction in food conservation and war cookery. In addition, Chicago Commons supported the Liberty Loan Drives and acted as neighborhood fuel administrator during the coal famine. As the war neared an end, Taylor joined other settlement spokesmen in urging the government to release servicemen through their home draft boards. Taylor told Secretary of War Newton D. Baker that the boards could help veterans find jobs. But this was never tested because the government disbanded the draft boards. Taylor did, however, persuade the city of Chicago to set up a Bureau for Returning Soldiers, Sailors and Marines. As chairman he supervised the counseling of more than 50,000 men before the Bureau closed in March, 1920. Taylor's war-time services — added to his already crowded schedule of teaching at the seminary and the Chicago School of

[51] Graham Taylor, "Settlements Loyal to Democracy and War," *Daily News* (Chicago), June 9, 1917; Woods and Kennedy, *Settlement Horizon*, chap. xxvii.

[52] Board of Trustees, Minutes of Meetings, October 23, 1917, Warden's Report for year ending September 30, 1917; Taylor, *Pioneering*, 210–11; Graham Taylor, "Searchlight of the Draft Exemption," *Daily News* (Chicago), August 11, 1917; *Chicago Commons, 1894–1919*, pp. 23–25.

Civics and Philanthropy, writing editorials and articles, and administering the settlement — was "an inspiring though strenuous experience." In retrospect he considered it the "greatest opportunity we have ever had to serve our neighbors, our city and our country during twenty-five years of residence."[53]

V

Settlement finances were one of Taylor's many responsibilities throughout these years. He personally signed the lease on the brick house at North Union Street in 1894, agreeing to pay $40 a month rent. This jumped to $160 when he got possession of the frame building at the rear of the property. The cost of renovation was cheerfully assumed by the warden who expected "the sole financial responsibility" to be his "during the period of initiation." The residents paid for their own living expenses and contributed about half the rent. This money, plus small fees collected from neighborhood people in the clubs and classes, and the help of friends, carried the Commons through its first years. Two families soon joined the Taylors, as did a number of other young men and women. By 1899 there were twenty-five people at the settlement, each sharing a portion of the cost and serving without salary.[54]

The budget kept pace with the expansion of the settlement program. During 1898 it required $6,271 to run Chicago Commons — $291 for the kindergarten, $461 for the Tabernacle Church, $225 for relief, $62 for manual training equipment and materials, and $353 for the summer camp. By 1901, the year the settlement occupied its new building, the operating budget was well over $8,000. Taylor knew that financial support from outside the household and the neighborhood was indispensable. To attract this support it was necessary to incorporate the Commons as a non-profit charitable institution. In 1895 the Illinois legislature authorized the Chicago Commons Association

> To provide for a higher civic and social life, to initiate and maintain religious, educational and philanthropic enterprises, and to investigate and improve conditions in the industrial districts of Chicago.

The first board of trustees consisted of eleven people: a faculty member and a member of the board of directors of Chicago Theological Seminary; Thomas Ballard of the publishing firm, Ginn and Company; Charles Hulburd, presi-

[53] *Chicago Commons, 1894–1919,* p. 26; Graham Taylor, "Demobilization Needs a Human Touch," *Daily News* (Chicago), November 23, 1918; Graham Taylor, "Demobilization and Re-employment," *The Survey,* XLI (December 14, 1918), 342–343; Graham Taylor to Graham Romeyn Taylor, December 28, 1918, February 2, 1919, in the possession of Lea Taylor; Graham Taylor, "Tiding Men Over From War to Peace," *Daily News* (Chicago), April 3, 1920; Graham Taylor to George M. Basford, January 25, 1919.
[54] Taylor, *Chicago Commons,* p. 13; Graham Taylor, "A Personal Statement," *The Commons,* I (December, 1897), 5–6; *Chicago Commons: A Social Settlement,* pp. 1, 2.

dent of the Elgin Watch Company; three other Chicago business men; Jane Addams of Hull House; Taylor, and another Commons resident, John Palmer Gavit.[55]

The lease on the property at North Union Street was due to expire in 1899, and the Chicago Commons Association had to decide whether to purchase and repair the two buildings at an estimated cost of $50,000 or find another site and build new quarters. Early in the year the board began negotiating with the City Missionary Society, owner of a lot 76 feet by 117 feet on which the Tabernacle Congregational Church was located. This was at Grand Avenue and Morgan Street a few blocks west of the Union Street house. The Society was willing to let the settlement have a ninety-nine year lease on the property, rent-free, if Chicago Commons would provide space for church activities and an auditorium suitable for Sunday services. The board of trustees agreed to these terms. It then hired the firm of Pond and Pond, architects for the Hull House additions, to design a modern settlement building to be constructed on the southeast corner of Grand Avenue and Morgan Street.[56]

The choice of Allen B. Pond as architect was fortunate. His varied experiences at Hull House, where for many years he had been a trustee, enabled him "to understand the settlement from within" and to design the new Chicago Commons building "in conformity with its purpose." By June, 1899, he presented tentative sketches for a structure that could be erected in "progressive sections as funds were secured." The plans as finally approved by the board of trustees called for a five-story, L-shaped building. The residence wing facing Grand Avenue would have kindergarten rooms in the basement, parlor and reception rooms on the first floor, women's and girls' club rooms on the second, kitchen and dining quarters for the residents on the third, and residence rooms and an apartment for the warden and his family on the fourth and fifth stories. The other wing fronting on Morgan Street would have basement rooms for manual training, cooking classes, and boys' clubs and an auditorium on the ground floor that could be used for neighborhood gatherings during the week and the services of the Tabernacle Church on Sunday. There would be class rooms on the second floor, men's club rooms on the third, and a gymnasium on the fourth and fifth floors.[57]

[55] *Chicago Commons: A Social Settlement*, p. 16; Board of Trustees, Minutes of Meetings, December 7, 1901; Taylor, *Chicago Commons*, pp. 27–28, 29, 31.

[56] *Chicago Commons: A Social Settlement*, 15, "Our Building Project," *The Commons*, IV (May, 1899), 7.

[57] Taylor, *Chicago Commons*, pp. 40, 41; Board of Trustees, Minutes of Meetings, June 27, 1899; *The Commons*, Supplement, IV (June, 1899), n.p.; Allen B. Pond, "The Settlement House, II," *The Brickbuilder*, XI (August, 1902), 160–62; *The Commons*, IV (November, 1899), 7–9; "Concerning the Building," *The Commons*, IV (November, 1899), 9–11.

With characteristic vigor Taylor devoted the summer of 1899 to raising funds for the new building. Not all the people he approached were willing to help. One neighborhood businessman refused to contribute to Chicago Commons

> for the reason that just after we made the last subscription we were forced into trouble with our workmen. . . . It was a strike without principle or equity, cost us upwards of $50,000.00, and my company therefore feel that it is useless to subscribe either for charity or organizations that help labor when labor turns upon them as viciously as they did upon us in connection with our last troubles. I merely mention this to show you how foolish some people connected with labor movements are. They fail to recognize the fact that the manufacturer wants to see their condition bettered, and they seem to keep constantly before them the idea that capital is antagonistic to them, when quite the contrary is, and should be the case.

Despite occasional rebuffs, Taylor had the necessary $16,000 by July to let contracts and begin work on the Morgan Street wing. When he resumed his seminary teaching in October he admitted feeling "a little jaded" from the "weeks of incessant work, morning, noon and night," but at least he had enough money to complete the walls and roof of the wing before winter set in. Unfortunately, however, a bitter strike paralyzed the Chicago construction industry before the building was enclosed. Much to Taylor's disappointment, his half-finished structure stood exposed to snow and rain from February until August of 1900.[58]

He did his utmost to settle the strike between the Building Contractors' Association and the newly-formed Building Trades' Council of construction unions. The employers refused to recognize or to deal with the union council, and they insisted upon the right to purchase non-union materials, hire non-union apprentices, determine hours of labor and other working conditions. The ensuing deadlock eventually idled 75,000 men in the Chicago area, and Taylor predicted a long, bitter conflict. He felt that he was in a "rare position . . . to stand in between and try to make peace on the basis of justice." Undaunted by Mayor Harrison's recent failure to get the two sides to negotiate, Taylor decided to try his hand at mediation.[59]

---

[58] W. J. Chalmers to Graham Taylor, November 7, 1898; *The Commons*, IV (October, 1899), 4, 5; Graham Taylor to John Marshall Williams, June 24, 1899; "Progress of the Building," *The Commons*, IV (November 30, 1899), 11; Graham Taylor, "Building Progress Stopped," *The Commons*, IV (January 31, 1900), 8; "Our New Building," *The Commons*, V (September, 1900), 24.

[59] Graham Taylor, "Building Progress Stopped," 8; Lewis and Smith, *Chicago*, p. 265; Royal E. Montgomery, *Industrial Relations in the Chicago Building Trades* (Chicago, 1927), p. 25; Taylor, *Pioneering*, p. 117; Graham Taylor, "Between the Lines in Chicago's

He arranged to speak before the Building Trades' Council and got assurances from both the *Daily News* and the *Record-Herald* that his remarks would be printed in full. Armed with this guarantee of fair publicity, Taylor "spoke straight from the shoulder," attacking "the unions as impartially as he did the contractors." He began by expressing his sympathy with the fundamental principles of organized labor, but warned that the "cause of human brotherhood . . . is more sacred than any labor organization. That sacred cause is at stake in Chicago today. Its appeal must at last be made to the public." Taylor condemned the Contractors' Association for

> insisting upon disbanding the council while resolutely maintaining its own association; in demanding the cessation of the sympathetic strike while busily organizing a sympathetic lockout; . . . in avowedly waging their warfare for industrial liberty and free labor while curtailing the small contractors' freedom to compete, if they refused to join the association, by cutting off their supply of material and labor.

On the other hand, labor organizations were unwise to accept political patronage which "keeps even the best and most incorruptible union officers under a cloud of suspicion" and "destroys the confidence not only of the public but of the rank and file." He concluded with the suggestion that an independent investigating commission should be appointed.[60]

Though the labor delegates were willing to support an impartial commission, Taylor's efforts came to naught. A spokesman for the contractors promptly branded him an

> avowed, unqualified champion of unionism. A man of Prof. Taylor's intelligence should be able to recognize the fact that there is no greater menace to our modern civilization than so-called organized labor. . . . If he so carefully studied the "cause of human brotherhood," he as an American citizen, ought certainly to recognize that any and every man has the privilege to exercise the God-given right to work for a living, even if he does not carry a Chicago Building Trades Council card.

So the strike dragged on through the summer. In August several unions voted to withdraw from the Council and make their peace with the contractors. Others followed during the fall and winter, and by April, 1901 the shattered Building Trades' Council agreed to disband.[61]

Industrial Civil War," *The Commons*, V (April 30, 1900), 1–4; Graham Taylor to John Marshall Williams, August 2, 1900.

[60] Taylor, *Pioneering*, p. 117; *Daily News* (Chicago), May 14, 1900; *Times Herald* (Chicago), May 14, 1900.

[61] *Daily News* (Chicago), May 14, 19, August 7, 15, 1900; Montgomery, *Industrial Relations in the Chicago Building Trades*, pp. 30–31; Virgil W. Peterson, *Barbarians in Our Midst: A History of Chicago Crime and Politics* (Boston, 1952), p. 79; *Daily News* (Chicago), December 31, 1901.

Meantime, construction work on Chicago Commons recommenced in August, 1900, and a few months later the first three floors of the Morgan Street wing were being used for settlement activities. In May, 1901, the residents moved into temporary living quarters on the fourth and fifth floors of the building. Just two months after they had evacuated the old house on North Union Street, a fire broke out in the furniture factory next door to it and both sides of the entire block were completely destroyed. One other stroke of luck for the settlement in 1901 was a generous gift totaling $20,000 for construction of the residence wing. Thanks to this bequest the John Marshall Williams Residence Hall was finished in December, 1901. Chicago Commons residents held a joyful Christmas celebration that year, grateful that $45,000 of the total $64,021 construction costs had already been paid, and pleasantly aware that their modern quarters were the envy of settlement workers throughout the country.[62]

Expansion of the program after 1901 was limited only by the number of workers available and the size of the operating budget. The latter increased each year, rising from about $12,000 in 1904, to $19,000 in 1910, and $24,000 by 1915. When the settlement reached its twenty-fifth anniversary, the annual expenditures exceeded $30,000, and in 1924, the thirtieth year, the budget was $44,000. In addition to meeting its operating costs, Chicago Commons Association was able to acquire additional property. In 1910 they purchased two adjoining tenement houses and remodeled them to provide club rooms for boys' and men's groups, a model apartment for the housekeeping class, and dormitory space for students in the School of Civics and Philanthropy.[63]

The Association approached the City Missionary Society in 1914 about purchasing the land on which the settlement stood. It was rent-free as long as the Commons maintained the Tabernacle Church, but by 1914 most of the members of the congregation had moved away and continued support of a sparsely-attended Protestant church in an overwhelmingly Catholic neighborhood was "embarrassing." But the Society wanted $10,000 for the land, a figure which the Association considered too high. Five years later the settlement was able to purchase the land for $5,000. Thus, when Chicago Commons celebrated its twenty-fifth anniversary in May, 1919, its main building and

[62] "Opening The New Building," *The Commons*, V (December, 1900), 3; Taylor, *Chicago Commons*, p. 43; Board of Trustees, Minutes of Meetings, April 17, December, 1901.

[63] Graham Taylor, "A Social Center for Civic Co-operation: Chicago Commons," *The Commons*, IX (December, 1904), 594; Board of Trustees, Minutes of Meetings, Warden's Report of Work ending September 30, 1919; Chicago Commons Association, *Thirty Years and After*, p. 31.

annex were free of debt and it owned the land at the corner of Grand and Morgan — a total property valuation of $100,000.[64]

The burden of fund-raising during this quarter-century fell upon Taylor and the Chicago Commons Association. There were changes in board membership, but several of the trustees served for many years. Allen B. Pond was a trustee not only of Chicago Commons but of Hull House and Gads Hill Center as well. Edwin Burritt Smith, attorney and professor of law and active in the Municipal Voters' League, handled legal affairs for the Commons and defended it and other settlements against the assaults of the *Chronicle* and *Inter-Ocean*. Edward L. Ryerson, son of iron and steel magnate, Joseph T. Ryerson, was a Commons trustee for many years, and his son, Edward L. Ryerson, Jr., followed him on the board. The head of Crane Brothers Manufacturing Company, Charles R. Crane, served for fourteen years and resigned only because diplomatic appointments kept him out of the country. Jane Addams, who like Taylor was a charter member of the Association, remained on the board from 1895 until her death in 1935. And lawyer Frank H. McCulloch, who lived in Evanston, was a member of Chicago Commons Association for forty-seven years.[65]

Though the trustees made generous contributions themselves, they were not always able to interest others in giving on a similar scale. Time and again Taylor had to meet financial crises with his own funds or by underwriting loans. To William Kent he confessed in 1913, "I am in such a deep hole that I have already advanced $1,400 from my own slender savings account"; or to Julius Rosenwald, "I have personally loaned all I dare, but am not catching up fast enough to tide me over the next three or four months' ends." During the building program of 1900–1 Taylor personally held $5,542 of the debt, a fact which prompted John Marshall Williams to express his surprise "that your large board of trustees don't materialize better and come to your rescue, and not leave you alone to labor." Taylor disliked the solitary labor of raising money. "Often I turned away from office threshholds until I could gather more confidence and courage to cross them with my appeal." Taylor never repeated a request for funds after a person declined to contribute. And he took pride in the fact that Chicago Commons "never overburdened or presumed upon any one's goodwill."[66]

[64] Graham Taylor to Julius Rosenwald, December 29, 1910; Board of Trustees, Minutes of Meetings, February 4, 1914; Graham Taylor to William Kent, January 18, 1919; Graham Taylor to Roger Williams, January 14, 1919.

[65] Taylor, *Chicago Commons*, pp. 28–29, 36–37, 294–96; Graham Taylor, "Allen B. Pond — Patriot and Architect," *Neighborhood*, II (April, 1929), 109–11; Mrs. Mary Lee Edwards to Louise C. Wade, January 26, 1960.

[66] Graham Taylor to William Kent, December 1, 1913; Graham Taylor to Julius Rosenwald, December 11, 1913, Rosenwald Papers, University of Chicago Library;

Taylor kept from overburdening the friends of the settlement by a system of annual pledges and by starting an endowment fund. The perennial donors were reminded by personal letter from the warden. Stanley McCormick gave $1,000 annually from 1902 on, Edward L. Ryerson gave $500, as did Frank McCulloch, while Victor Lawson sent $300 and William Kent contributed $250. Julius Rosenwald, as was his custom, agreed to aid Chicago Commons only after Taylor assured him that other financial support was forthcoming. Satisfied that the project had a wide base of support, Rosenwald agreed to give $200 a year and from 1912 through 1918 sent $500. The first large gift to the endowment fund came from a Chicago merchant, G. E. P. Dodge, in 1905. Angered by the newspaper attacks on the settlements and encouraged by his clergyman, Dr. Frank Gunsaulus, to include both Chicago Commons and Hull House in his will, Dodge left $25,000 to Taylor's endowment fund. Hobart W. Williams, a wealthy Chicagoan living in seclusion in Cheshire, Connecticut, surprised the settlement and nine other institutions by naming them as beneficiaries of his large fortune. In 1921, the Ryersons gave $25,000 to the endowment, and upon Victor Lawson's death it was discovered that he left $100,000 to the settlement. By 1925 Chicago Commons had an endowment of $390,000, yielding $20,000 annually.[67]

The week-long celebration of the twenty-fifth anniversary in the spring of 1919 brought trustees and donors to the settlement to mingle with residents and neighbors. Many former workers as well as seventeenth warders who had moved to other parts of the city returned for the festivities. Letters and telegrams of congratulation poured into the settlement from all over the country. Victor Lawson, who for many years had been a staunch friend of Chicago Commons but strangely enough had never visited it, decided to surprise Taylor with a "25-year deferred call." The distinguished newspaperman arrived at the settlement in a dress suit and was startled to find the neighborhood people in working clothes. His companion, Charles Dennis, reported that "despite his sartorial splendor, Lawson mixed genially with the somewhat overawed throngs from the back streets that jostled him amid the extremely populous scenes of celebration." When Lawson rose to speak, however, he expressed the feelings of other trustees and financial supporters and, no

---

Board of Trustees, Minutes of Meetings, December, 1901; John Marshall Williams to Graham Taylor, May 1, 1900; Taylor, *Chicago Commons*, p. 45; Taylor, Diary, June 3, 1902; Graham Taylor to Roger Williams, June 23, 1921.

[67] Graham Taylor to Julius Rosenwald, June 10, 26, 1907, Rosenwald Papers; Julius Rosenwald to Graham Taylor, June 11, October 11, 15, 1907; Morris P. Werner, *Julius Rosenwald: The Life of a Practical Humanitarian* (New York, 1939), pp. 105–6; Taylor, *Chicago Commons*, pp. 33–35; Thomas W. Goodspeed, *The University of Chicago Biographical Sketches* (2 vols.; Chicago, 1925), I, 285; Graham Taylor to Mabel Hawkins, August 4, 26, 1925.

Aerial photograph taken in 1939 looking southwest toward Chicago's Loop and lakefront. Chicago Commons was at Grand Avenue and Morgan Street in a triangle bounded by railroad tracks on the south, tracks and the Chicago River on the east, and Ogden Boulevard on the northwest.

House at 140 North Union Street, in which Chicago Commons was founded in 1894.

New building for Chicago Commons, constructed between 1899 and 1901 on the southeast corner of Grand Avenue and Morgan Street.

Typical views of congested housing and dirty, unpaved alleys in the
seventeenth ward in the 1890's.

Seventeenth ward garbage box and dirt sidewalk, characteristic of those found on Chicago's west side.

Neighborhood children at play.

Settlement house residents introducing a group of children to Grant Park and to green grass, a novelty which some of them saw for the first time.

The Chicago Commons kindergarten and classes for children were among its most rewarding activities.

The Seventeenth Ward Community Club waging a vigorous campaign to elect Lewis D. Sitts as alderman.

The lively Free Floor forum, which began in the basement of the North Union Street building.

Conference of settlement house workers at White Plains, New York, in May, 1908. *Top row* (*left to right*): Helen Green of Hartley House, New York; Helena Dudley of Denison House, Boston; John Elliot of Hudson Guild, New York; Meyer Bloomfield of Civic Service House, Boston; Mary Simkhovitch of Greenwich House, New York; and Ellen Coolidge of the Boston Social Union. *Middle row*: Cornelia Bradford of Whittier House in Jersey City, New Jersey; Jane Addams of Hull House; Lillian Wald of Henry Street Settlement, New York (*seated*); Elizabeth Williams of College Settlement, New York; and Dr. James Hamilton of University Settlement, New York. *Bottom row*: Graham Taylor; Mary McDowell of the University of Chicago Settlement (*seated*); and Robert Woods of South End House, Boston.

Photograph of Graham Taylor taken in the 1930's by Helen Balfour
Morrison.

doubt, of many neighbors as well. The Chicago Commons' "adventure for spiritual and civic good citizenship," he said, "is really the finest thing in these twenty-five years of Chicago's history." [68]

VI

At the time of the anniversary celebration Robert Woods, head of South End House in Boston, commended Taylor upon his achievement. "Uniquely named, Chicago Commons has always lived up to its suggestion of a hospitable out-reach to the whole fabric of humanity. . . . Its spirit and atmosphere, in its breadth and depth, has reached every settlement house in the United States." To a large extent Graham Taylor and his wife were responsible for molding the spirit of Chicago Commons. The warden, Taylor realized, "must be the unifying personality at the center of the settlement family." He must be able to command the loyalty of his fellow-workers but at the same time avoid "autocratic supervision." Taylor knew that "spontaneous development and activity is the charm of settlement service, if it be not the secret of its power, and any exercise of authority or surveillance beyond what is absolutely essential to the corporate life and co-operative work of the household, robs it of its distinctive spirit and strength." [69]

In the final analysis, Taylor believed, it would be the internal life of the settlement that determined its contribution to the community. The spirit of the household

> may not be foisted upon any, but can be fostered in all. Its atmosphere and ideality must exert their pressure unconsciously upon all, if the tone of the inner relationship and the standard of outward service are to be maintained. Upon this essentially religious spirit the settlement group depends for its unity and spiritual dynamic.

One of the Commons' frequent visitors, Alexander Johnson, watched Taylor integrating the new residents "with an art that conceals the art." The warden relied upon the gathering of his large family for the evening meal and short services in the parlor immediately afterwards as a way of developing the "corporate personality" of the settlement. Almost all the residents stayed to hear a musical selection or sing a hymn, read a Scripture passage, or listen to the warden, another resident, or guest comment briefly upon the social significance of a recent event or new publication. Johnson found these sessions

[68] Victor F. Lawson to Graham Taylor, April 17, 1919, Victor F. Lawson Collection, Newberry Library, Chicago, Ill.; Dennis, *Lawson*, p. 431; Victor F. Lawson to Charles H. Dennis, April 17, 1919.

[69] Robert Woods to Graham Taylor, April 22, 1919; "The Settlement 'Head Worker,' " *The Commons*, III (May, 1898), 5; Taylor, *Chicago Commons*, p. 24; *Chicago Commons: A Social Center for Civic Co-operation*, p. 49.

Simple, informal, sincere with no least slant towards sectarianism; but with a warm pervasive religious spirit thruout; these vesper services lent a tone to the settlement which was felt by everyone privileged to share them. Heterodox, almost agnostic, tho I was, I loved the Common vespers and never missed them unless some imperative call took me away.[70]

Taylor was the director of the settlement, assuming the title "warden" as in the British houses and designating a "head resident" as his deputy. In the early years he was aided by two committees, an executive and a household committee, each consisting of six members elected annually by the residents. Taylor was an ex-officio member of both groups. The house committee was responsible for appointing a housekeeper, assigning rooms, supervising the janitor service, and seeing that residents took care of their personal quarters. The executive committee had jurisdiction over applications for residence, the actual work of the settlement, and the apportionment of duties among resident and non-resident workers. Applicants accepted by the executive committee were allowed thirty days of trial residence; at the end of this time the entire house voted on whether to accept the person for permanent residence, two dissenting votes being enough to prevent it. Later on the warden assumed responsibility for accepting new residents.[71]

Things usually ran smoothly at Chicago Commons, but not always. Years later the early residents could still remember "those difficult days on Union Street" with "the invincible rats" which the male residents tried to catch in barrels in the basement. John Palmer Gavit's sister recalled one vesper service when Taylor was interrupted "by a large rat . . . slowly ascending the stairs with great dignity and arrogance." Moreover, the janitor was "a periodical drinker" and residents "would awaken in the grip of Chicago's winter morning to find the house stone cold." In 1899, the household committee decided that the hired help were being treated inconsiderately and it issued a plea to the residents to include all workers in "the life and privileges of the Settlement." During the summer of 1902 Raymond Robins was contemplating taking rooms elsewhere because the Commons was so noisy and the executive committee so inefficient. Taylor begged for "a little tolerant patience" and predicted that the committee would soon "straighten out the mix." He added, "I clearly ought to leave decisions affecting the personal convenience and household management to the Committee appointed by the Residents. Democracy

[70] *Chicago Commons: A Social Center for Civic Co-operation*, p. 49; Taylor, *Chicago Commons*, pp. 24, 25; Johnson, *Adventures in Social Welfare*, pp. 381, 382.

[71] *Chicago Commons: A Social Settlement*, pp. 4, 37, 38. Later on Taylor took the customary American title of "Head Resident," while his deputy became "Assistant Head Resident."

costs confusion, but I have no taste to assume autocracy. It will come out right." [72]

Much of the credit for establishing a successful settlement spirit belongs to Leah Demarest Taylor. Still the quiet, retiring companion of Hopewell and Hartford days, she gave strong support to her husband's decision to abandon their own house and take up residence in the seventeenth ward. Though friends insisted that it was physically dangerous, the Taylors nevertheless took with them to North Union Street their four children, ranging in age from six to eighteen. They were the first family to make their home in an American settlement, and this was always one of the unique features of Chicago Commons. Few people outside the settlement realized the extent of Mrs. Taylor's personal sacrifice in building "so splendid and real a home in so public an atmosphere." Within the Commons, however, most of the residents sooner or later felt the influence of her strong character. Raymond Robins said she was "an anchor cast to windward through all the changing turbulent currents of our Commons' life." One girl credited Mrs. Taylor with creating the feeling "we residents had that we were part of a large family group." Assessing the long-range achievement of the Commons, Robert Woods declared:

> All settlement workers think . . . of the happy and noble family life which has been the vital nucleus about which everything of the Commons has grown. . . . a quite unmatched achievement in the history of the settlements on either side of the water. For many this fact seemed to make the Commons the central fireside for the whole settlement fellowship.[73]

Settlement experience left its mark upon each of the four Taylor children. The eldest, Helen, attended Vassar, and completed Bertha Hofer Hegner's course in kindergarten training, and helped with the secretarial work at the Commons. She married a Chicago architect, George Wallace Carr, who was associated with the firm of Pond and Pond and who had lived for a few years at Chicago Commons. Graham Romeyn Taylor graduated from Harvard

[72] Helen Gavit Swan to Graham Taylor, April 28, 1934, and Lydia Wellman to Graham Taylor, April 4, 1934, in the possession of Lea Taylor; Report of Committee of Residents, February, 1899 (manuscript); Graham Taylor to Raymond Robins, August 26 [1902], Raymond Robins Papers.

[73] Taylor, *Pioneering*, pp. 281, 282; "Children in Settlements," *The Commons*, II (August, 1897), 3; George W. Overton to Graham Taylor, September 8, 1918; Evelina Belden to Graham Taylor [1918]; Raymond Robins to Leah Taylor, May 13, 1903, copy in the possession of Lea Taylor; Elsie E. Atkins to Graham Taylor, August 11, 1918; Robert A. Woods to Graham Taylor, August 28, 1918, April 22, 1919; Woods and Kennedy, *Settlement Horizon*, pp. 431–32.

and returned to the settlement to write for *The Commons, Charities and The Commons,* and *The Survey.* During World War I he went to Moscow as special assistant to the American ambassador. Thereafter young Taylor joined the Chicago Commission on Race Relations and helped edit their report, *The Negro in Chicago.* From 1922 until his death two decades later he was with the Commonwealth Fund in New York City. Lea Demarest Taylor, a Vassar graduate, headed the settlement work for girls and served as secretary to her father and then for Draft Board 39. In 1917 she became Assistant Head Resident and five years later Head Resident, a position which she held until her retirement in 1953. Katharine Taylor, the youngest, taught at Vassar, then at the Francis W. Parker School in Chicago, and in 1922 became director of the Shady Hill School in Cambridge, Massachusetts. None of the six Taylors regretted their 1894 decision to move to the seventeenth ward. They never desired to "reclaim an hour of the life, a dollar of the money or any part of the energy we have invested in settlement service so human has it all been and so rich has been its return withal." [74]

Most of the other residents at Chicago Commons agreed that no matter how long their stay "all our contacts since we left have been richer because of our settlement background." John Palmer Gavit, who with his wife and infant son were among the "aborigines" of the 1890's, could think of "no university course on earth for which I would exchange the experience of those five years." It "has had profound and ineradicable effects, not only in point of view and specific ideas and opinions, but in the whole attitude toward and atmosphere of life." Gavit's later connections with the Y.M.C.A., the Associated Press, the New York *Evening Post, The Survey,* and his study of immigration, *Americans by Choice,* gave him ample opportunity to continue his work of settlement interpretation which he had so ably started in 1896 with the little magazine, *The Commons.* [75]

Raymond Robins also helped with *The Commons* and in addition moderated some of the Free Floor meetings and guided the seventeenth ward political reform movement. He drew on this experience in his subsequent positions as superintendent of the Municipal Lodging House, head resident of Northwestern University Settlement, and political reformer in Chicago. Later on he worked with the Y.M.C.A., the Red Cross, and in state and national Republican politics. James Mullenbach, a student of Taylor's at Chicago Theo-

---

[74] Taylor, *Chicago Commons,* pp. 250–53; Board of Trustees, Minutes of Meetings, October 23, 1917, December 29, 1921; "Chicago Honors Lea Taylor," *Social Service Review,* XXIV (March, 1955), 75; Graham Taylor, "The Soul of the Settlement," National Federation of Settlements, *Eighth Conference, 1918,* 13.

[75] Quoted in Taylor, *Chicago Commons,* p. 255; John Palmer Gavit to Graham Taylor, April 13, 1919; Taylor, *Chicago Commons,* pp. 256–58.

logical Seminary, worked at the Tabernacle Church, the settlement, and with Robins at the Municipal Lodging House. He moved on to an outstanding career in charity administration and industrial arbitration. Many of the former residents, totaling six hundred by the late 1920's, took positions with charitable or social agencies, teaching jobs, government posts, or entered the professions. Most of them carried forth from Chicago Commons social ideals which found expression in many communities throughout the country.[76]

Even temporary residents caught the settlement spirit. Charles M. Sheldon, popular minister-novelist of the 1890's, spent a week at the Commons and was deeply impressed with the way Taylor and his staff were "daily rescuing from some sort of human hell" the "flotsam and jetsam of poor humanity" in the seventeenth ward. Sheldon added, "I may also truthfully say that my first thought of the character of the 'Bishop' in *In His Steps* was suggested to me there." Frances Perkins, Secretary of Labor in Franklin Roosevelt's administration, lived at the Commons for three weeks during the summer of 1906. Arriving with "almost no knowledge or experience in the field," she learned a great deal about living and working conditions and family problems by accompanying the visiting nurses, helping with the milk depot, attending the Pleasant Sunday Afternoon programs and many of the clubs and classes. Her three week stay "really clinched my decision to become a professional social worker. . . . The insights and direction gained through the contact with Dr. Taylor and his co-wokers have stood by me all my life."[77]

In a sense Taylor was speaking for all the residents, whether temporary or permanent, when he said,

> By maintaining within the walls of our settlement house common ground upon which all can meet, mingle, exchange values, and learn to live and work together for the common good . . . we settlement residents have found . . . the enlargement and enrichment of our own lives in attaining a larger share of the race life ourselves. The settlement spirit has been "A Way of Life" to us.[78]

VII

Given Taylor's rich and varied experience and his deep conviction about the importance of his work, it was only natural that he should interpret the

[76] Taylor, *Chicago Commons*, pp. 259–67; Davis, "Raymond Robins: The Settlement Worker as Municipal Reformer," pp. 131–41; quoted in Taylor, *Chicago Commons*, p. 269.

[77] Charles M. Sheldon, "Four People I Knew," *Christian Herald*, October, 1936, p. 32; Charles M. Sheldon, "Work With Humanity at First Hand — Impressions of Chicago Commons," *The Commons*, V (December, 1900), 6–7; Frances Perkins to Louise C. Wade, February 24, 1954.

[78] Graham Taylor, "The Social Settlement As a Way of Life," manuscript.

settlement movement to American laymen. Already in 1894 he realized that "public presentation of the cause for which Chicago Commons stands . . . is a primary part of its work." Hence he spoke frequently in the Chicago area for church groups, women's clubs, gatherings of business men, schools and colleges, indeed, wherever he could secure a hearing. In time he traveled farther afield. At Chautauqua, New York, he participated in a discussion with Percy Alden of Mansfield House, East London, in 1897. Five years later he and Jane Addams and three other settlement workers presented another symposium. In addition, the western Chautauqua circuits used Taylor almost every year at Bay View, Michigan, Crete, Nebraska, and Des Moines, Iowa. Taylor's effectiveness can be measured by the fact that approximately half the contributors to Chicago Commons lived outside the Chicago area, representing twenty-three different states by 1914.[79]

Another method of communicating with settlement workers and the public at large was through the pages of *The Commons: A Monthly Record Devoted to Aspects of Life and Labor from the Social Settlement Point of View.* First published in April, 1896, this magazine promised to explain "the motive and the progress of social settlements in general, and of Chicago Commons in particular" and to give "a view of work for the humanizing and uplifting of social conditions in the 'river wards' and other industrial sections of Chicago." The first editor was John Palmer Gavit, a former Hartford newspaper reporter and member of the Fourth Congregational Church, whom Taylor persuaded to come to Chicago and join the settlement venture. A skilful writer with a lively sense of humor and a passionate hatred of social injustice, Gavit made an excellent editor of *The Commons.* He sent copies to all the settlements in existence, asking in return for their reports and brochures. He carried a monthly resume of this material, plus reviews of recent books, editorial comment by Taylor, evaluations of the labor movement, and special articles by settlement workers, social gospel leaders, university professors, and social and political reformers.[80]

Though *The Commons* increased steadily in size and circulation under Gavit's guidance, there were always financial problems. The first three issues were only eight pages, but they received so much praise that Taylor and

[79] *Chicago Commons,* I (April, 1896), 3; "Settlement Rally at Chautauqua," *The Commons,* I (August, 1897), 6–7; *Chautauqua Assembly Herald,* July 8–12, 1902; Jane Robbins, "Chautauqua's Social Settlement Week," *The Commons,* VII (August, 1902), 5; Board of Trustees, Minutes of Meetings, November 1, 1911; Report of Warden for year September 30, 1913–September 30, 1914.

[80] *Chicago Commons,* I (April, 1896), 6, 7; John Palmer Gavit, "At Home With Graham Taylor," *The Survey,* LXIV (June 1, 1930), 236. During the first year of publication the title was *Chicago Commons: A Monthly Record of Social Settlement Life and Work.*

Gavit decided to enlarge the magazine to sixteen pages. By January, 1897, circulation reached 3,000 and a few years later when *The Commons* took over the unfulfilled subscriptions of the expiring social gospel journal, *The Kingdom*, circulation jumped to 7,000. "With no little embarrassment," the editors raised the price to fifty cents for twelve issues. Even so, there was usually a deficit which had to be met from settlement funds. Gavit tried to get advertisements in the magazine, promising that they would be "READ with attention by a large, increasing, and yet selected constituency of the keenest minds and most intelligent observers of the affairs of the world." Nonetheless, as Gavit reminisced years later with Taylor,

> Insofar as my services and energies belonged to the settlement, including any cash in hand, they went into that paper. . . . time and time again my own "salary" check bounced without appreciable pause from-you-to-me-to-the-bank-to-the-printers, like a triple play in a baseball game. God knows what a book-keeping audit would have shown.[81]

After Gavit departed in 1900 for a Y.M.C.A. position, some of his editorial duties were taken over by Raymond Robins and later by Edwin Balmer and Graham Romeyn Taylor. They broadened the scope of the magazine and in January of 1904 added a new masthead: *The Commons—For Industrial Justice, Efficient Philanthropy, Educational Freedom and the People's Control of Public Utilities*. Contributing authors included Richard T. Ely, John R. Commons, Washington Gladden, Jane Addams, Julia Lathrop, and from England, Ramsay MacDonald and F. Herbert Stead. Circulation remained at about 4,000, only 3,000 of which were paid subscriptions. Though the size of the magazine was again doubled to thirty-two pages, the price remained stationary and annual deficits increased. The influence of Taylor's magazine, however, was spreading. In 1904 the National Council of Congregational Churches recommended *The Commons* as an "invaluable . . . monthly journal of social betterment." Speaking for British settlement house workers, Percy Alden pronounced it "the recognized organ of American Settlements." [82]

In the fall of 1905 Taylor agreed to merge *The Commons* with *Charities*, the journal of the New York Charity Organization Society edited by Edward T. Devine. The new publication, *Charities and The Commons*, covered news

---

[81] *Chicago Commons*, I (July, 1896), 8; *Chicago Commons*, I (January, 1897), 6; Dombrowski, *Christian Socialism*, p. 120; "A Financial Statement," *The Commons*, IV (November 30, 1899), 12; *The Commons*, II (January, 1898), 14; John Palmer Gavit to Graham Taylor, November 28, 1934, Survey Associates Editorial Research Files.

[82] *The Commons*, IX (January, 1904), 3–5; National Council of Congregational Churches, *Minutes of the National Council of Congregational Churches, 1904* (Boston, 1904), p. 420; Percy Alden, "American Settlements," in Will Reason (ed.), *University and Social Settlements* (London, 1898), p. 150; Taylor, *Chicago Commons*, pp. 162–67.

of the settlements as well as "progressive charitable and reformatory effort both public and private." Headquarters were in New York and Devine was the editor, but Graham Taylor was an associate editor and his son a frequent contributor. In April, 1909, the magazine underwent another shake-up. It became *The Survey*, a weekly publication treating "industrial conditions and relationships and the social, moral and civic interests and efforts of our times." From 1909 until 1919, Taylor was an associate editor of *The Survey* and head of its Chicago office. He contributed numerous articles and editorials, and conducted a column entitled "The Industrial Survey of the Month" from 1909 until 1911 and "Church and Community" from 1912 until the outbreak of the war. In addition, he sought new subscribers and raised funds in the midwest, securing, for example, annual contributions from Mrs. Cyrus McCormick and Victor Lawson.[83]

Friction developed between the New York and Chicago offices during the war years. Editor Paul Kellogg had helped plan Ford's 1915 peace crusade which Taylor refused to join. Whenever Kellogg allowed Jane Addams to air her pacifist views in *The Survey*, Victor Lawson would complain to Taylor:

> Every now and then I find myself forced into a feeling of lack of confidence in the sanity of some good people who, once they have attained a measure of success in some good line of social uplift, apparently lose their heads and imagine themselves directors in general to the American people. Did I mention Jane Addams' name? No, I think not.

Taylor had grievances of his own. In 1919 he wrote to Paul Kellogg:

> I have felt myself to be in an increasingly anomalous position as outside member of the staff. While I am supposed hereabouts at least to know of the changes in the policy and the staff, I have been embarrassed in being unaware of decisions and appointments until after they are made and announced. Though due to inadvertance or the pressure of time . . . yet it is none the less trying to me to be considered partly accountable for decisions in which I have no chance to give ear or voice. . . . The very fact that I am not needed to share such responsibilities makes my service far less relevant than it used to be and its continuance less justifiable upon your part or mine.

Furthermore, Kellogg was pressing him to raise funds and increase the *Survey*'s circulation in the midwest. Taylor no longer had time to search for new subscribers, and he was hampered in soliciting funds because *The Survey*

[83] Taylor, *Chicago Commons*, p. 166, 167; Graham Taylor, "Industrial Basis for Social Interpretation," *The Survey*, XXII (April 3, 1909), 10; Graham Taylor to Mrs. Cyrus H. McCormick, November 11, 1912; Graham Taylor to Edward T. Devine, January 27, 1912.

depended upon many of the same people who supported Chicago Commons and the Chicago School of Civics and Philanthropy. For all these reasons Taylor finally resigned as associate editor in 1919.[84]

A few months later, however, he agreed to become a contributing editor of *The Survey* "on the understanding that this relationship involves no obligation to furnish any specified amount of copy," that "what I write shall be printed as written, or returned to me," and that he should have "the prerogative of offering friendly, constructive criticism . . . without fear of being considered hyper-critical, much less obstructive." Despite the hard feelings in 1919, Taylor remained a contributing editor until his death. His articles and book reviews appeared with regularity; he was consulted on the 1922 decision to divide *The Survey* into two magazines, a *Midmonthly Survey* of technical information for social workers and a *Survey Graphic* for wider circulation among general readers; and he was delighted when his old friend John Palmer Gavit joined the editorial staff in 1928. Never one to bear a grudge, Taylor referred in his autobiography to his long associations with *The Survey* as a "cherished privilege."[85]

Insofar as *The Survey* grew out of Taylor's little magazine of the 1890's, he had every reason to be satisfied with its achievement. Lillian Wald expressed her obligation in a letter to editor Paul Kellogg in which she praised *The Survey* for voicing

> the fundamental principle that give life and purpose to the Settlement. What most of us can only do locally the Survey does nationally, as reporter and interpreter. . . . Without such a publication as yours, I believe that the Settlement and other Social efforts and many Social workers would tend to be parochial.

Understandably John Palmer Gavit shared Taylor's pride in their brain-child:

> in a way and degree peculiar (I know of no competing agency) "The Commons" was and The Survey continues to be, *the* expression of the "social settlement idea" in all its bearings and implications. . . . The Survey, whose chief if not sole purpose is to awaken, inspire, inform and lead that social spirit without which none of these enterprises would exist.

[84] Nevins and Hill, *Ford: Expansion and Challenge*, p. 28; Victor F. Lawson to Graham Taylor, November 30, 1915; Graham Taylor to Paul Kellogg, September 26, 1919; Graham Taylor to Mabel Hawkins, June 11, 1919, Hawkins Papers, in the possession of Lea Taylor. Unfortunately Taylor's letters to the New York office during these years cannot be located in the Survey Associates Editorial Research Files. Copies of a few of the letters are in the Taylor Collection, and a frank discussion of the differences can be found in Taylor's letters to Graham Romeyn Taylor, June 24, July 12, August 25, 1919, in the possession of Lea Taylor.

[85] Graham Taylor to Paul Kellogg, November 10, 1919; Paul Kellogg to Graham Taylor, December 30, 1937; Taylor, *Pioneering*, pp. 423, 424.

Chicago Commons as such started it, and it has been loyal to that spirit from that day to this.[86]

In addition to interpreting the settlement movement by speaking and writing, Taylor had a hand in molding its development through his participation in the National Federation of Settlements and the National Conference of Social Work. During the fall of 1894 Chicago Commons joined with Hull House and four other Chicago houses to establish the Chicago Federation of Settlements. It was the first such city-wide organization, and leadership came largely from Jane Addams, the first president, and Graham Taylor, the secretary. At their quarterly meetings the members discussed common problems like guidance of clubs and classes, fees to be asked of the neighbors, relationship between the settlements and the politicians, enforcement of city ordinances, and labor disturbances. Other cities followed Chicago's example, and in June, 1911, a National Federation of Settlements came into existence. Taylor was elected president of this organization in June, 1917. At the time there was a strong difference of opinion between the settlement people who followed Jane Addams' pacificism and those who supported President Wilson. Taylor reported to his son that he was chosen to head the federation "despite my somewhat decided stand against ultra pacifists."[87]

In 1897, Taylor and a small contingent of settlement workers joined the National Conference of Charities and Correction, then under the presidency of Alexander Johnson. It was an important occasion, for many of the charity organization people believed that their own scientific casework approach to poverty was far superior to that of settlement residents who tried to teach the underprivileged to help themselves. Mary Richmond of the Baltimore Charity Organization Society was wise enough to see the need for a joint attack upon the problem, and she warmly welcomed the newcomers. "Heretofore we have been like an arm with a cord tied tightly round the middle, preventing free circulation. This meeting has cut the cord. . . . We need all the light that settlement workers can bring." Jane Addams graciously responded for the settlement workers:

> I feel a little apologetic at being here at all. The settlements are accused of doing their charity work very badly. They pretend not to do it at all; and then they become overwhelmed with the poor and the needy, and

[86] Lillian D. Wald to Paul Kellogg, March 20, 1917, Lillian Wald Papers, New York Public Library; John Palmer Gavit to Graham Taylor, November 28, 1934, Survey Associates Editorial Research Files.

[87] Woods and Kennedy, *Settlement Horizon*, pp. 376–77, 399, chap. xxxiv; Ruth Austin, "The Old Records Speak," *Survey Midmonthly*, LXXXI (December, 1945), 326–28; Graham Taylor to Graham Romeyn Taylor, June 24, 1917, in the possession of Lea Taylor.

they do it, not as trained people should do it, but as neighbors do it one for the other, which is not scientifically. In spite of that, however, settlements are, I believe, valuable to charities.[88]

The settlement workers brought new blood and new ideas into the National Conference of Charities and Correction. Taylor, like Jane Addams, Florence Kelley, Julia Lathrop, Robert Woods, and others, served on many committees, drew up reports, and delivered major addresses at the annual conventions. Most of the settlement people aligned themselves with the action wing of the Conference, arguing that state and national social legislation and strict enforcement of government regulations were essential steps toward eradicating poverty and dependency. In 1914, Taylor was elected president of the National Conference, "a recognition," according to Jane Addams, "both of his personal achievements and of his sympathy with the newer developments in philanthropy."[89]

Once again Taylor performed the useful function of interpreting to the general public the "significant change" within the National Conference. In a 1913 Chicago *Daily News* column he explained why social workers throughout the country were actively participating in "lawmaking and public administration."

> The spirit and aim, the demands and the methods of all their constituent agencies are broadening their charity in the direction of justice. While they well know that the best efforts to secure justice will never do away with the need of charity, yet they realize that injustice creates poverty and the demoralization which must grow out of dependency.
>
> They feel that it is the rankest injustice to offer charitable help to anyone as a substitute for the right or the chance to help himself. So, with common consent, they are discussing and promoting legislation and public measures to prevent industrial accidents and occupational diseases and to compensate those who thus suffer from the loss of their health or their breadwinners.

The next year, 1914, while Taylor was president of the Conference, he optimistically reported: "There is now no cleavage between the ranks of those who are applying the old experience and attested methods" and those who are "demanding the advance movement toward social democracy. A few years ago a cleft was threatened, but surely and swiftly each side approached the other's point of view," and they are now marching "in the middle of the

---

[88] Johnson, *Adventures in Social Welfare*, pp. 277–78; National Conference of Charities and Correction, *Proceedings, 1897*, pp. 474, 338; Frank J. Bruno, *Trends in Social Work, 1874–1956, A History Based on the Proceedings of the National Conference of Social Work* (New York, 1957), chaps. x, xi.

[89] Woods and Kennedy, *Settlement Horizon*, p. 387; Jane Addams, "Introduction," in Taylor, *Religion in Social Action*, p. xxix.

way toward the one great goal of the common welfare." The meeting of minds was not quite this smooth, but the action wing did gain the upper hand and did succeed in 1917 in changing the name of the organization to the National Conference of Social Work.[90]

Thus Graham Taylor had been honored with the presidency of both the National Federation of Settlements and the National Conference of Charities and Correction by the time his settlement celebrated its twenty-fifth anniversary. On that occasion a Chicago social worker described him as "Big Brother to many of us youngsters in social work, cheering us, leading us and setting the pace." [91]

Taylor was able to set the pace in part because of his influential position in the settlement movement. But it was due also to the impact of his training school for social workers. Graham Taylor was not content merely to teach social Christianity at the seminary, to direct the many activities at Chicago Commons, or to interpret the settlement impulse for the American public. He was determined to train young men and women for the broader field of social welfare. Thus he made time in his crowded calendar to establish and run the unusual Chicago School of Civics and Philanthropy.

---

[90] Graham Taylor, "Public Welfare Work and Its Enemies," *Daily News* (Chicago), August 16, 1913; Graham Taylor, "Clearing House for Community Work," *Daily News* (Chicago), May 16, 1914; Edward T. Devine, *Social Work* (New York, 1922), pp. 15–16; Bruno, *Trends in Social Work*, p. 353. Taylor told his son, "The Conference weathered its change of name . . . safely and well. There were some signs of cleavage between conservatives and radicals, but the conciliating spirit prevailed." Graham Taylor to Graham Romeyn Taylor, June 24, 1917, in the possession of Lea Taylor.

[91] Eugene T. Lies to Frank McCulloch, April 22, 1919.

Six ⚓ *Chicago School of Civics and Philanthropy*

Throughout his long career Taylor cared deeply about communicating his experiences and ideas to others. He did this from the pulpit for two decades, in the classroom for over thirty years, from public platforms as a lifelong spokesman for a wide variety of causes, and in a weekly newspaper column that he began in his early fifties and continued until well into his eighty-seventh year. Lea Taylor once referred to this trait as her father's "innate educational concern." She said he had a rare ability to "share experience vividly" and to interpret complex problems in language easily understood by all. Even at Chicago Commons, where the warden might well have buried himself in detailed neighborhood work, Taylor found time to evaluate what was being done and communicate the essential meaning of that activity to people outside the seventeenth ward.[1]

One of the earliest such ventures at the settlement was the Chicago Commons School of Social Economics, a series of informal conferences for residents, ministers, teachers, and others interested in social and economic questions. In April, 1895, Percy Alden of Mansfield House in England addressed the first conference on "Movements of Labor and Life in East London." A second one in the summer of 1895 drew large crowds to hear George Herron, Jane Addams, Josiah Strong, and Robert Woods. In 1896 the social function of education was the theme of the spring session, while the December conference on "Social Reconstruction" heard religious leaders like Washington Gladden and John Graham Brooks, political reformers such as Ernest Crosby and Henry Demarest Lloyd, Jane Addams and Taylor from the settlement movement, and Charles Henderson and John Dewey from the University of Chicago. The audiences were so large and enthusiastic

[1] Lea D. Taylor, "The Social Settlement and Civic Responsibility — The Life Work of Mary McDowell and Graham Taylor," p. 37.

that some of the sessions had to be moved to the more spacious auditorium at Hull House. In the words of one participant the School of Social Economics exerted an "uplifting influence . . . upon us all. We go forth with . . . the lightening consciousness that many share . . . in the bond of a common purpose applied to the solution of a common problem." [2]

Still another outgrowth of the Commons' educational work was the Pestalozzi-Froebel Kindergarten Training School established by the settlement's kindergartner, Bertha Hofer Hegner. Encouraged by the success of an 1897 summer institute, she opened her own school that fall in the basement of the settlement with twenty students. In time it developed into a two-year course with instruction in psychology, Froebel's theory, history of education, mother play, music, games, arts and crafts. The graduates of this Kindergarten Training School invariably did well on Chicago Board of Education examinations and found good jobs in whatever part of the country they chose. By 1913, however, the growing number of students and amount of equipment needed in the kindergarten itself forced the school to move from the settlement to larger quarters on Michigan Avenue.[3]

Aware of the valuable interchange of information between the colleges and universities of the country and the settlement, Taylor experimented with various fellowships at Chicago Commons. He arranged with Professor Charles Cooley, head of the sociology department at the University of Michigan, to have one student each year spend six months at the settlement investigating and writing reports on special topics. During the eight years that this program was in operation the young sociologists studied saloon life in the seventeenth ward, juvenile delinquency and dependency, earnings and spendings of school children, recreation for working girls, and the problem of truancy in tenement districts. Three of these reports Taylor considered worthy of publication in *The Commons*. From 1906 until 1915, Auburn Theological Seminary in Auburn, New York, sent one person each summer to live at Chicago Commons, and in 1921 the McCullochs, long-time friends and trustees of the settlement, established a Rockford College Fellowship

---

[2] *Chicago Commons*, p. 4; Max West, "Chicago Commons and its Summer School," *Altruistic Review*, III (October, 1895), 167–70; *Chicago Commons*, I (December, 1896), 2–7; A. H. Fish, "The Summer School of Social Economics at Chicago Commons," *The Kingdom*, VIII (September 6, 1895), 326–27.

[3] Bertha Hofer Hegner, "Historical Sketch — Twenty-Five Years," in *Pestalozzi–Froebel Teachers College News–Letter, Silver Anniversary Number 1896–1921* (Chicago 1921), pp. 2–3; "Pestalozzi–Froebel Kindergarten Training School at Chicago Commons, 1903–4," "Chicago Commons Scrapbook"; *The Commons*, IV (January 1, 1900), 10–11; *Chicago Commons: A Social Center for Civic Co-operation*, p. 12.

which enabled one girl from each graduating class to spend an entire year in residence.[4]

Moreover, Taylor was concerned about the development of the permanent residents at Chicago Commons. He helped interpret and analyze their neighborhood experiences in staff meetings, household conferences, and personal interviews. Some of the newcomers were advised to take additional courses at the University of Chicago, others were given special topics of investigation, and all were encouraged to read widely in current economic and social literature. Taylor considered this guidance "more or less incidental and occasional," but it produced results. Year after year the Commons attracted bright young men and women eager to learn about settlement life. After a few years' apprenticeship they usually moved on to paid positions with social agencies or public institutions. When the valuable John Palmer Gavit announced his decision to leave, Taylor wrote resignedly, "I suppose the Commons must get used to sending its best workers to other fields, as it claims to be more of a training school for social service than perhaps anything else."[5]

Yet Taylor soon found that the growing demand for social workers made it impossible for him to keep an adequately trained staff at the Commons and at the same time furnish recruits for other fields. It was this constant turnover which impressed upon him "the increasingly urgent need for more thorough, consecutive preparation for social work."[6]

Others had already reached the same conclusion. At the International Congress of Charities, Corrections and Philanthropy which met in Chicago in 1893 Anna L. Dawes called attention to "The Need of Training Schools for a New Profession."

> What is needed, it seems to me, is some course of study where an intelligent young person can add to an ordinary education . . . those special studies in political and social science which are most closely connected with the problem of poverty; and where both he and his associate, already learned in the study of books, can be taught what is now the alphabet of charitable science — some knowledge of its underlying ideas, its tried and trusted methods, and some acquaintance with the various devices employed for the upholding of the needy, so that

[4] Charles H. Cooley, "Settlement Fellowships and The University," *The Commons*, V (October, 1900), 2; Taylor, *Chicago Commons*, pp. 150–52; Susan E. Foote, "The Settlement as a Sociological Laboratory," *Ethical Record*, IV (March, 1903), 85.

[5] Taylor, *Chicago Commons*, p. 154; Graham Taylor to B. C. Baumgardner, March 30, 1900.

[6] Taylor, *Pioneering*, p. 306; Taylor, *Chicago Commons*, p. 155.

no philanthropic undertaking, from a model tenement-house to a kindergarten or a sand heap, will be altogether strange to his mind. Some more immediately practical experience of the work likely to be required should also be given, some laboratory practice in the science of charity, if we may so speak.

Four years later Mary Richmond reiterated this demand before the 1897 convention of the National Conference of Charities and Correction. Asking for the prompt establishment of a two-year School of Applied Philanthropy, she insisted that training for professional charity work should be as systematic and rigorous as training for medical practice.[7]

The first response to these pleas came from the New York Charity Organization Society. Its Committee on Philanthropic Education sponsored a six-week course in the summer of 1898. The program included "talks and discussions, visits to public and private institutions, special investigations, and as much practice in district visiting and office work as will be useful in showing the practical application of the principles which underlie charitable administration." The course was repeated the following summers, and in the fall of 1903 the Society offered a three-month course during the late afternoons. Finally during the winter of 1903-4 they ventured a six-month full-time program of social work training. Its warm reception plus the donation of $250,000 to the New York Charity Organization Society for support of a permanent training school led to the establishment of the New York School of Philanthropy in the fall of 1904. Edward T. Devine was the director of this first full-time school of social work in the United States.[8]

Similar steps were taken in other cities at about the same time. The St. Louis Conference of Charity Workers sponsored a series of lectures during the winter of 1901, but not until 1908 was the St. Louis School of Philanthropy established in connection with Washington University. In Boston the School for Social Workers, affiliated with Harvard University and Simmons College

---

[7] Anna L. Dawes, "The Need of Training Schools for a New Profession," *International Congress of Charities, Corrections and Philanthropy, Chicago, 1893*, p. 19; Mary Richmond, "The Need of a Training School in Applied Philanthropy," in National Conference of Charities and Correction, *Proceedings, 1897*, pp. 181–86.

[8] Elizabeth G. Meier, *A History of The New York School of Social Work* (New York, 1954), chaps. ii, iii; "Summer Plans," *Charities*, I (March, 1898), p. 2; "Training School in Practical Charity," *Charities*, I (March, 1898), 5; "The New York School of Philanthropy," *Charities*, XIII (October 8, 1904), 48, 49; "The Endowment of the New York School of Philanthropy," *Charities*, XIII (November 26, 1904), 177–78; Ernest V. Hollis and Alice L. Taylor, *Social Work Education in the United States* (New York, 1951), p. 9; Frank J. Bruno, "Twenty-Five Years of Schools of Social Work," *Social Service Review*, XVIII (June, 1944), 152.

and under the direction of Jeffrey R. Brackett, opened its doors in October, 1904. Six years later Philadelphia secured its first full-time institution, the Pennsylvania School of Social Service.[9]

Taylor knew, of course, about the lectures in New York and St. Louis and the plans in 1904 to create the New York School of Philanthropy and the Boston School for Social Workers. He also was aware that the Charity Organization Society in London had sponsored a training program since 1895 and that it was planning to launch a School of Sociology in 1903. That summer Taylor and his wife visited Europe on their first long vacation in eleven years. They spent six weeks in England, touring the industrial cities, stopping at the settlement houses, and investigating methods of training settlement residents and social workers. Taylor consulted with Helen Gladstone, daughter of the late prime minister and director of social work courses for the London Charity Organization Society and the Women's University Settlement. In Birmingham he attended a conference of settlement workers and heard economic historian William James Ashley and philosopher John Henry Muirhead call for new methods of training. Taylor was stirred by the latter's observation, "to succeed we must dare to fail, for they who make no mistakes make nothing else." When he returned to the United States in the fall of 1903, Taylor had made up his mind to accept the challenge. He would "dare to fail" in establishing a training program for social workers in Chicago.[10]

[9] "Profession Schools in Philanthropy," *Charities*, XII (March 5, 1904), 229; *Charities*, VIII (February 1, 1902), 94; Graham Taylor, "Training for Social Workers," *The Commons*, X (September, 1905), 513–17; Sophonisba P. Breckinridge, "Report of the Committee on Securing and Training Social Workers," National Conference of Charities and Correction, *Proceedings, 1911*, pp. 365–69; "Encouraging Opening of the Boston School for Social Workers," *Charities*, XIII (November 5, 1904), 112–13; Bruno, "Twenty-Five Years of Schools of Social Work," pp. 152–53; James E. Hagerty, *The Training of Social Workers* (New York, 1931), pp. 42–43; Alice Channing, "The Early Years of a Pioneer School," *Social Service Review*, XXVIII (December, 1954), 430; Earle E. Eubank, "The Schools of Social Work of the United States and Canada: Some Recent Findings," *Social Service Review*, II (June, 1928), 263–64. Eubank and Channing credit the School for Social Workers in Boston with being the first full-time training school.

[10] Kathleen Woodroofe, "C. S. Loch," *Social Service Review*, XXXII (December, 1958), 410; Elizabeth Macadam, *The Social Servant in the Making* (London, 1945), pp. 22, 23; Graham Taylor, "Report of the Committee on Training for Social Workers," National Conference of Charities and Correction, *Proceedings, 1905*, pp. 436–44; Taylor, Diary, June 20, 1903; Graham Taylor to Helen Taylor, June 30, September 14, 17, October 10, 1903, in the possession of Lea Taylor; Graham Taylor, "Some Eddies in London's Life," *Daily News* (Chicago), July 11, 1903; Graham Taylor, "English Settlements Federating," *The Commons*, VIII (September, 1903), 15; Taylor, *Pioneering*, p. 307.

II

Taylor first broached the idea to a gathering of seminary professors whom he hoped would be interested in sponsoring lectures on social work. But the only reaction "came silently in the form of a visiting card, bearing the name of William R. Harper, on which were penciled the words: 'When you want to talk business about this, call upon me.'" Almost immediately Taylor presented his plans to the receptive president of the University of Chicago, who agreed to include the lectures in the downtown extension courses. Thus the instruction commenced in October, 1903, under the ponderous title, "Social Science Center for Practical Training in Philanthropic and Social Work." Taylor and Charles R. Henderson taught the only course, "Dependency and Preventive Agencies." It met weekly for three months and attracted twelve students, all of whom were social workers.[11]

During the winter and spring terms of 1903–4 two more courses were offered.[12] The teaching staff was expanded to include as occasional lecturers Alexander Johnson, soon to become associate director of the New York School of Philanthropy and secretary of the National Conference of Charities and Correction, Dr. Hastings Hart of the Illinois Children's Home and Aid Society, Ernest Bicknell of the Chicago Bureau of Charities, Judge Julian Mack of Cook County Circuit Court, Dr. William Evans, Chicago health commissioner, George Perkins, head of the Cigar Makers International Union, and Jane Addams, Julia Lathrop, Mary McDowell, Charles Zueblin, and Raymond Robins from the settlement field. During the second year of its existence, 1904–5, the school increased its enrollment to an average of forty students each term. Furthermore, the curriculum comprised seven courses: "Introduction to the Study of Social and Philanthropic Work," "Child Helping Agencies," "Dependency and Charities," "Care of Dependent, Delinquent and Defective Children," "Industrial Relationships," "Correctional and Reformatory Measures," and "Public Charities."[13]

President Harper assumed financial responsibility for the Social Science Center. Throughout the first year all lecturers served without pay. However,

[11] Taylor, *Pioneering*, p. 307; University of Chicago, *Annual Register, 1903–4*, pp. 245–46. Classes were held in the Fine Arts Building on Michigan Avenue.

[12] The two courses were "Personal, Institutional, and Public Effort for Dependents" and "Preoccupying and Preventive Policy, Agencies, and Methods." University of Chicago, *Annual Register, 1903–4*, pp. 245–46.

[13] Graham Taylor, "Historical Sketch of Dv. of Course of Instruction in the Chicago School of Civics and Philanthropy 1903–13," (manuscript); Meier, *History of The New York School of Social Work*, pp. 23, 30; Taylor, *Pioneering*, pp. 307–08; Taylor, *Chicago Commons*, pp. 156–57; "The Institute of Social Science, Chicago," *Charities*, XIII (January 28, 1905), 393–94.

Taylor soon found, as he wrote to Harper, that the "administrative initiative upon which success depends . . . involves a tax upon my time and personal attention which you will not underestimate or expect to be given entirely gratuitously this first and hardest season." The following year Taylor received $500 for his services as director, and each staff member was paid $10 per lecture. In spite of the $30 tuition fee for six courses, the program ran at a loss during 1904–5. But the deficit of almost $1,000 was quietly taken care of by Harper.[14]

In the fall of 1905 Taylor sent a cheerful report to Harper about the success of the Institute of Social Science and Arts, as it had been renamed. The community response, he thought, warranted a summer session and future support on a permanent basis by the University of Chicago. Just one month later, however, he learned from Professors Albion Small and Charles Henderson that the ailing president had no intention of making the institute an integral part of the University. No reasons were given for this decision, but Taylor knew that as of December 31, 1905, he would have to take financial responsibility for the program. Shortly after Harper died in January, 1906, Taylor discovered that the institute had never been a part of the University of Chicago budget and that Harper's contributions had come from private funds.[15]

Immediately the Chicago Commons trustees voted to assume responsibility for the school, giving it still another name, the Chicago Institute of Social Science. They appointed Edward L. Ryerson treasurer, and Victor Lawson provided him with $1,500 for administrative expenses in 1906, promising an additional $2,000 a year for the next two years. The Relief and Aid Society donated the use of class rooms on the second floor of its LaSalle Street building, and the new sponsors were able to pay Taylor and the staff lecturers the same salaries they had received before. "We launched our training school on the first of January," reported Taylor to Lawson, "and it sailed right away as soon as it struck the water. The practical experts from the University as well as from the city philanthropies all stand by it." "Personally," he added, "I estimated the opportunity thus offered for real and desperately needed

[14] Graham Taylor to William R. Harper, January 6, July 31, 1904, Harper Correspondence, University of Chicago Library; William R. Harper to Graham Taylor, August 3, 1904, Harper Correspondence; Graham Taylor, "Training Center for Social Workers," *The Commons*, IX (January, 1904), 19; Taylor, "Historical Sketch of Dv. of Course of Instruction."

[15] Graham Taylor to William R. Harper, November 6, 1905; "The Status of the Institute Social Science . . ." (manuscript). The Harper Correspondence does not reveal the reasons for Harper's decision or the source of the money he contributed from 1903 through 1905.

service so highly, that I would rather devote myself to its development than to anything else." [16]

There was plenty for Taylor to do in developing the Chicago Institute of Social Science. Three courses were offered in both the winter and spring terms of 1906, and he organized a summer session on "Humanitarian Progress in Local Institutions." Moreover, he found time to do some lecturing at the New York School of Philanthropy and to observe and compare its program and administration with that of his Institute. Enrollment at the Chicago school rose from 168 students in 1905–6 to 196 during 1907–8. New courses dealing with the effects of urbanization and industrialization were added to the curriculum, and the field work was expanded. When the school rented larger quarters on Adams Street in the fall of 1907, it was necessary to raise tuition fees to $50 for a full course in order to cover the higher operating expenses. In June, 1907, the first certificate was awarded, signifying completion of one year's full-time work at the Institute, and during the following year seven more students earned certificates.[17]

An important addition to the work of the Chicago Institute of Social Science came in 1907 when the Russell Sage Foundation agreed to finance a research department. In the spring of that year Mrs. Russell Sage had established in memory of her late husband a $10 million foundation for "the improvement of social and living conditions in the United States" by means of "research, publication, education, the establishment and maintenance of charitable or benevolent activities, agencies and institutions." The trustees of the fund decided to make grants of $10,000 for investigation and research in social problems to each of the four training schools in New York, Boston, Chicago, and St. Louis. As soon as Taylor learned of this boon, he hired Julia Lathrop of Hull House as Director of Research and made her a co-director of the institute as well. She selected as her assistant, Sophonisba Breckinridge, a young political economy instructor at the University of Chicago and an associate of Jane Addams. The institute formulated plans, which the Russell Sage Foundation approved, for a study of juvenile delinquency.[18]

[16] Victor F. Lawson to Graham Taylor, December 16, 1905; Graham Taylor to Victor F. Lawson, February 6, 1906.

[17] Graham Taylor to the Supervisory Council, Chicago Institute of Social Science, June 25, 1906; Meier, *History of The New York School of Social Work*, pp. 28–30; "Memoranda of Enrollment" (manuscript). Enrollment figures show considerable variation, and it is not always clear whether summer school students are counted.

[18] John M. Glenn, Lilian Brandt, and F. Emerson Andrews, *Russell Sage Foundation 1907–1946* (2 vols.; New York, 1946), I, ii, 30; Edith Abbott, "Sophonisba Preston Breckinridge, Over the Years," *Social Service Review*, XXII (December, 1948), 418, 419; "Memoranda: The Institute of Social Science — 1908" (manuscript); Chicago School of Civics and Philanthropy, *Year Book, 1907–8, with Announcements for 1908–9* (Chicago, 1908), p. 33.

III

In May, 1908, the school changed its name once again. Taylor felt that the increased financial responsibility necessitated incorporation. So in 1908 he secured from the Illinois legislature a charter for the Chicago School of Civics and Philanthropy to promote "through instruction, training, investigation and publication, the efficiency of civic, philanthropic and social work, and the improvement of living and working conditions." Serving on the board of trustees were Taylor, Edward L. Ryerson, Jane Addams, Charles Crane, Allen Pond, and Victor Elting, all of whom were active in the Chicago Commons Association. In addition, Julia Lathrop, Judge Julian Mack, Julius Rosenwald, William Kent, and three prominent Chicago women, Mrs. Joseph T. Bowen, Mrs. Emmons Blaine, and Mrs. William F. Dummer, were named as trustees. Furthermore, the state universities of Michigan, Wisconsin, Minnesota, Illinois, Iowa, Indiana, Nebraska, and Kansas had representatives on the board, the most eminent being Charles Cooley of Michigan and Richard T. Ely of Wisconsin. Taylor was president and Julia Lathrop vice-president of the organization.[19]

The staff soon announced programs for students taking general training as well as for those in the department of social investigation. The former group took six required courses over a two year period and completed field work and a thesis before receiving their certificates. People in the research department studied "Methods of Social Inquiry" in their first year but spent the remainder of their time on investigations under the supervision of Julia Lathrop and Sophonisba Breckinridge. As in the case of the seminary students, Taylor thought that the compulsory field work for people at the School of Civics and Philanthropy was the most valuable part of their training. Their choice of agencies was large, for more than twenty Chicago area organizations participated in the school's program. These included the Illinois Board of Charities, Chicago Bureau of Charities, Relief and Aid Society, Hebrew Charities, Juvenile Court, numerous asylums, hospitals, children's and old people's homes, and, of course, the settlement houses.[20]

---

[19] Chicago School of Civics and Philanthropy, Articles of Incorporation; Taylor, *Chicago Commons*, p. 158; Chicago School of Civics and Philanthropy, By-Laws of Board of Trustees. According to Grace Abbott it was Julia Lathrop "who insisted the word 'Civics' should precede 'Philanthropy' in the name of the school." Grace Abbott, "Grace Abbott on the Beginning of the U.S. Children's Bureau," *Social Service Review*, XXI (March, 1947), 120.

[20] Chicago School of Civics and Philanthropy, *Announcements 1910–1911: Bulletin No. 5, July, 1910* (Chicago, 1910), p. 128; Chicago School of Civics and Philanthropy, *Announcements 1909–1910: Bulletin No. 1, July, 1909* (Chicago, 1909), pp. 18–19; President's Report, May 18, 1911, manuscript; Edith Abbott "Field-Work and the Training of the Social Worker," National Conference of Charities and Correction, *Proceedings, 1915*, pp. 615–21; "Memoranda: The Institute of Social Science — 1908" (manuscript).

Chicago School of Civics and Philanthropy experimented with a number of special courses designed to meet the needs of the community. In the summer session of 1908 Julia Lathrop offered a class for attendants of the insane. As a member of the State Board of Charities, she had been appalled at the ignorance of employees in the state hospitals and poorhouses. Hence her pioneer course at the training school tried to substitute "the educational for the custodial idea in the daily care of the mentally unsound." The attendants learned games, arts, crafts, and hobbies which they could use to reach the patients. Julia Lathrop's instruction in occupational therapy was widely hailed throughout the country, and many institutions required their nurses to enroll.[21] Another innovation was a program for playground supervisors. Directed after 1914 by Neva Boyd, these classes were based on the premise that modern recreation centers were *"municipal settlements"* whose "workers must have . . . thorough training for general social and civic work." So successful was this department that Neva Boyd developed a two-year program and employed a staff of five instructors and fifteen lecturers.[22]

In addition, one of the trustees, Mrs. William F. Dummer, made it possible financially for Dr. William Healy to teach at the school for a number of years. His pioneer studies of problem children led to the establishment of the Juvenile Psychopathic Institute connected with Chicago's Juvenile Court. Moreover, Mrs. Dummer provided the money for a Municipal Department in 1913 which concentrated on problems of local government. During World War I the school offered classes in conjunction with the Red Cross and the State Council of Defense. It also joined forces with the Henry B. Favill School of Occupations of the Illinois Society for Mental Hygiene. Together the two institutions offered special courses for occupational therapists who would work with handicapped soldiers as well as physically disabled and mentally disturbed people.[23]

[21] Jane Addams, "Great Public Servant, Julia C. Lathrop," *Social Service Review*, VI (June, 1932), 280–81; Jane Addams, *My Friend, Julia Lathrop* (New York, 1935), pp. 151–152; Printed announcement of the course for July 7–August 7, 1908; Dr. Albert W. Ferris to Julia Lathrop, May 29, 1908.

[22] Chicago School of Civics and Philanthropy, *Supplementary Announcements 1913–1914: Bulletin No. 20, July 1913* (Chicago, 1913), p. 3; Chicago School of Civics and Philanthropy, *Announcing The Courses of The Summer Session and The Summer Playground School: Bulletin No. 22, January, 1914* (Chicago, 1914), pp. 18–19.

[23] Taylor, *Pioneering*, p. 47; Graham Taylor to Mrs. William F. Dummer, January 29, 1915, and February 4, 1915, Ethel Sturges Dummer Collection, Women's Archives, Radcliffe College, Cambridge, Mass.; Chicago School of Civics and Philanthropy, Board of Trustees, Minutes of Meetings, March 19, 1913; Chicago School of Civics and Philanthropy, *Special Bulletin Announcing a Course for Public Health Nurses: Bulletin No. 28, July 1915* (Chicago, 1915), n.p.; President's Report for 1916–17; Chicago School of Civics and Philanthropy, *Special Courses in Curative Occupations and Recreation: Special Bulletin*, December, 1917.

The research department made a significant contribution to the success of Chicago School of Civics and Philanthropy. In 1908, Julia Lathrop resigned as director of social investigation in order to help organize the National Committee for Mental Hygiene. She continued, however, to lecture at the school and to serve as a trustee. Her capable assistant, Sophonisba Breckinridge, succeeded her in the research department. Meantime, these two had invited a mutual friend, Edith Abbott, to leave the economics department of Wellesley College and join the staff as a social statistician at a salary of $1,500 a year. She quickly accepted, though her older colleagues "considered it an indication of a mild form of lunacy for anyone to leave Wellesley College for an unheard of place called a school of civics and philanthropy." Edith Abbott became Miss Breckinridge's assistant in 1909, initiating a partnership that worked smoothly for the next decade. Together they carried out numerous investigations and supervised publication of the results.[24]

They began with *The Housing Problem in Chicago*, a series of ten pamphlets written between 1910 and 1915. With the help of the Russell Sage Foundation they brought out *The Delinquent Child and the Home* in 1912 and five years later completed a study on *Truancy and Non-Attendance in Chicago Schools*. Other books published under the auspices of the Chicago School of Civics and Philanthropy included Amelia Sears' *The Charity Visitor: A Handbook for Beginners* (1913) and Alice Greenacre's *Handbook for the Women Voters of Illinois* (1913). In 1915 the Russell Sage Foundation decided to discontinue its annual grants to the training schools in St. Louis, Boston, and Chicago, the last payment already having been made to the New York School of Philanthropy in 1912. Through Julia Lathrop, who had been named head of the Children's Bureau in 1912, the Chicago School secured several government contracts for social investigations. This money helped to compensate for the loss of foundation support.[25]

[24] Chicago School of Civics and Philanthropy, Board of Trustees, Minutes of Meetings, October 27, 1908; "Chicago School of Civics and Philanthropy," *Charities and The Commons*, XX (June 20, 1908), 389; Julia Lathrop to Edith Abbott, March 25, 1908, Grace and Edith Abbott Papers, University of Chicago Library; quoted in Addams, *My Friend, Julia Lathrop*, p. 158.

[25] Glenn, *Russell Sage Foundation*, I, 218, 224–25; Chicago School of Civics and Philanthropy, *Announcements 1919–1920: Bulletin No. 43, April, 1919* (Chicago, 1910), p. 52; Chicago School of Civics and Philanthropy, 1918–19 Budget, manuscript; Sophonisba Breckinridge to Julia Lathrop, June 30, 1919. Taylor expressed to Mrs. Dummer his unhappiness about the termination of the Russell Sage Foundation grant: "We can scarcely hope that they will make an exception in our favor, although I could put up a stout argument on the ground of the difference in our situation from that of the New York school with its endowment, the Boston school with its backing by Simmons College and Harvard University, and the St. Louis school with its connection at Washington University. Moreover the wider demands from all the States made upon us and the better prospects we have of meeting them, would I am sure appeal to me as excep-

Throughout this period there was a steady increase in staff and enrollment at the School of Civics and Philanthropy. The annual bulletins listed a faculty of almost one hundred members, though many of them delivered no more than one or two lectures during the year. The brunt of the teaching fell upon Taylor, Alexander Johnson, Charles Henderson, Julia Lathrop, Sophonisba Breckinridge, and Edith Abbott. During 1908–9 there were 164 students in all departments of the school — regular training, playground work, social investigation, summer session, and evening classes. A decade later the enrollment had risen to 683. There was a qualitative as well as a quantitative change in the student body. In place of the full-time charity workers who attended the earliest courses there were students with college degrees or at least some college training who expected to spend two years studying at the Chicago School. A total of 415 certificates were awarded between 1907 and 1920. As the school's reputation spread throughout the country, it drew applicants from a wide area, including more than half the states and several foreign countries.[26]

Since the demand for trained social workers did not slacken, the graduates could choose from a wide range of jobs. In 1908 Taylor established an Exchange for Social Work "to meet the needs of those wishing positions in social work, and to supply the demand of vacant positions." This exchange did a lively business. During 1916, for example, it filled 145 of the 392 openings referred to it. Thirty-one of these jobs were with charity organization societies, 23 in recreation centers, 19 in medical social service, 17 with settlements, 14 in research, 14 with children's agencies and day nurseries, and 7 with charitable institutions. Of the 145 positions filled by the exchange that year, 130 went to former Chicago School students.[27]

IV

As director of the Chicago School of Civics and Philanthropy, Taylor was constantly concerned about finances. Although there was a steady increase in both enrollment and tuition, the fees never covered more than half the cost of instruction, administration, and maintenance. The charge of $50 for a full year's work in 1908–9 had risen to $120 a decade later. But the operat-

tional if I were a trustee of the Foundation. But unfortunately, every one of its trustees is an Easterner." Graham Taylor to Mrs. William F. Dummer, January 25, 1913, Dummer Collection.

[26] Chicago School of Civics and Philanthropy, Statistics for 1908–9, manuscript, Summary of Attendance for 1918–19, President's Report for 1912–13, Registrar's Report for 1913 and 1915–16; Sophonisba Breckinridge, "Preliminary Report Submitted . . . ," p. 10, School of Social Service Administration, University of Chicago, Chicago, Ill.

[27] Chicago School of Civics and Philanthropy, President's Report, October 27, 1908; Registrar's Report, 1915–16.

ing expenses of the school increased even more rapidly. During 1908–9 expenditures came to $12,000, exclusive of the research department which was financed by the Russell Sage Foundation grant. Ten years later the budget exceeded $38,000, about $6,000 of which came from research department contracts.[28]

Approximately half of the operating costs went into faculty salaries. Since lecturers were still paid $10 per class, Taylor found it more and more difficult to attract first-rate people. Writing to a psychiatrist in Kankakee, Illinois, he had to apologize for a "fee . . . so small as to be not worth while mentioning," and, he added, "if you come it will be a pure piece of generosity and scientific interest." Taylor's salary for administering the school, plus teaching and supervising field work, was a mere $2,500 a year. There were times when the financial situation was so precarious that he, Sophonisba Breckinridge, and Edith Abbott were unable or unwilling to draw their salary checks for several months at a stretch.[29]

Another expensive item for many years was rent. A downtown location was convenient for both students and faculty and it provided easy access to the city's libraries, but it was costly. In 1910, after two years in the Rand McNally Building, the school had to move to less expensive quarters in the Northwestern Building. Yet even there the rent was "overwhelmingly disproportionate to the income of the school." In the spring of 1915 one of the trustees, Charles Crane, presented his South Michigan Avenue residence to the Chicago School of Civics and Philanthropy. The board gratefully accepted this generous offer, and that fall the staff made their sixth move in a dozen years. The distance from the city necessitated an immediate enlargement of the library of 3,000 volumes and hundreds of pamphlets, but the comfortable class rooms, the quiet surroundings, and the absence of rent more than compensated for this expenditure. The Crane residence, according to Alexander Johnson, exactly "suited the genius of the institution," for "the very building seemed human to match the president and his faculty." It remained the headquarters of the Chicago School until 1920.[30]

[28] Chicago School of Civics and Philanthropy, *Announcements 1909–1920: Bulletin No. 1, July, 1909* (Chicago, 1909), p. 5; Board of Trustees, Minutes of Meetings, April 27, 1917; Chicago School of Civics and Philanthropy, *Announcements 1917–18: Bulletin No. 35, April, 1917* (Chicago, 1917); Budget for year ending August 31, 1919, School of Social Service Administration. The budget figures show as much variation as enrollment statistics.

[29] Graham Taylor to Dr. Frank P. Norberry, March 7, 1910; Chicago School of Civics and Philanthropy, Report of Executive Secretary, December 24, 1909; Executive Committee, Board of Trustees, Minutes of Meetings, October 30, 1918; Edith Abbott to Julia Lathrop, August 7, 1920, School of Social Service Administration.

[30] Report of Executive Secretary, February 8, 1910; President's Report for 1915–16; Johnson, *Adventures in Social Welfare*, p. 383.

Most of the responsibility for meeting the annual deficit fell upon Taylor. As in the case of the Chicago Commons Association, the trustees were willing to make contributions themselves, but they did not take the initiative in soliciting others. During 1908–9, for example, Taylor received $2,000 from Victor Lawson, $1,000 from Mrs. Dummer, $500 from Ryerson and Crane, $2,000 from Mrs. Bowen, and Julia Lathrop contributed $625 from her Russell Sage Foundation salary. Taylor then had to collect $9,755 to balance the budget. Julia Lathrop's appointment in 1912 by President Taft to head the Children's Bureau was a "great satisfaction" to Taylor, but "a heavy loss . . . at the School. She is the *only* one to help me in raising money & directing the School." By 1915 Taylor was soliciting over $17,000. The following year he described the situation as "quite untenable," due to the expiration of the foundation grant, the high rent of the previous year, and the fact that contributions had not increased fast enough. Taylor reported to Mrs. Dummer in March of 1914 that "not half of the February salaries have been paid nor the rent for the thirteenth floor, due for the month." Acquisition of the Crane residence relieved the rent problem, and both Crane and Rosenwald increased their contributions substantially and agreed "to underwrite a large share of any deficit that may unavoidably accrue." Yet Taylor still considered it necessary to appoint a special committee in the spring of 1916 to raise $36,000 a year for the next three years.[31]

At the same time Taylor appointed a second committee to investigate and report to the board on the possibility of future affiliation with the three large universities in the area: University of Chicago, Northwestern University, and the University of Illinois. As early as 1907 Taylor had discussed merging his social work training program with both the University of Chicago and the University of Illinois. The former institution was cool to the proposal, but the latter actually tried to get state funds to carry out such a plan. When the legislature killed the appropriation bill in the spring of 1909, Taylor gave up the idea of merging with any larger institution. Six years later, however, Sophonisba Breckinridge submitted a report to the board of trustees in which she outlined the academic and financial advantages of university affiliation for the Chicago School. She urged the trustees to reopen negotiations, and several members of the board openly agreed with her. The committee appointed by Taylor in the spring of 1916 was authorized to review the matter and summarize the arguments on both sides.[32]

[31] Breckinridge, "Preliminary Report Submitted," p. 12; Graham Taylor to Lea Taylor, April 28, 1912, in the possession of Lea Taylor; Graham Taylor to Mrs. William F. Dummer, March 18, 1914, Dummer Collection; President's Report, May 5, 1916; Graham Taylor to Mabel Hawkins, August 24, 1916, Hawkins Papers.
[32] President's Statement, May 8, 1918; unsigned letter from Chicago School of Civics

Meanwhile, the school drifted along in the same precarious financial position for two more years. Disturbed by the procrastination of the trustees, Taylor decided to force a showdown in 1918. On April 1, he announced his intention of resigning "in order to free the Trustees from all personal considerations in determining its future, and to secure needed relief from increasing responsibilities, the strain of which I can no longer safely bear." Taylor's reasons were threefold. His wife was desperately ill, and he knew that she had only a few months to live. This burden, added to his labors for the Chicago School and his long hours with the Draft Board, had considerably depleted his own strength. Secondly, the committee to evaluate merger with the universities had taken no definite action since its appointment in 1916, and Taylor felt that its recommendations should be delayed no longer.[33]

Taylor's main reason for resigning the presidency was the hopeless financial position of the school. He confided to his friend Judge Julian Mack:

> While I was not supposed to be responsible for the finances no one else has borne them in mind or has had to face the obligations as they fell due from month to month. The treasurer has never taken any personal concern for them, seldom attends meetings of the Board and pays no attention to communications sent him. . . . There was nothing left to do but for me to assure the payment of current obligations by refusing to draw my own salary, not taking any part of it at one time for fifteen consecutive months.

Under these circumstances, Taylor felt that he should resign and give the board a free hand to select a new director. As he had written to Julius Rosenwald,

> If the president of the School is needed to assume and secure its financial support, I am entirely willing to continue my teaching and leave the trustees absolutely free to choose any one else for president who may be able to take from them and me this burden.[34]

---

and Philanthropy to Victor F. Lawson, February 23, 1909, School of Social Service Administration; David E. Shanahan to Graham Taylor, May 11, 19, 1909, School of Social Service Administration; Breckinridge, "Preliminary Report Submitted," pp. 41–44.

[33] Graham Taylor to Board of Trustees, April 1, 1918; President's Report for 1917–18. There may also have been personal friction between Taylor and Sophonisba Breckinridge at this time, for she had accompanied Jane Addams and Grace Abbott to the 1915 International Congress of Women at The Hague and sympathized with Jane Addams' pacificist position during the war. Edith Abbott, "Grace Abbott: A Sister's Memoirs," *Social Service Review*, XIII (September, 1939), 379.

[34] Graham Taylor to Judge Julian Mack, October 18, 1918; Graham Taylor to Board of Trustees, April 1, 1918; Graham Taylor to Julius Rosenwald, March 4, 1916, Rosenwald Correspondence. The treasurer of the Chicago School of Civics and Philanthropy during this period was Victor Elting.

The Board of Trustees refused to lift the burden from Taylor's shoulders. Widely scattered by their various war duties, they did not meet to consider his resignation until October, 1918, and then only long enough to pass a resolution "that the President be requested to withhold his resignation until the end of the war, and that in the meantime he accept the assurance of the Trustees that they would make renewed efforts to relieve the financial situation." The measure of their success was shown by a surplus of almost $4,000 at the end of the next fiscal year. Cheered by this development and by the large enrollments of 1918 and 1919, Taylor agreed to stay on and was even persuaded to take a two-month vacation in the spring of 1920. The board of trustees named Sophonisba Breckinridge, dean of the school and head of the research department, as acting president during his absence. In April, Taylor set out for California "to arrest a decline in my vitality, which has been running dangerously low of late."[35]

V

Upon his return from the West Coast early in June, Taylor traveled to New Brunswick for the fiftieth reunion of Rutgers' Class of 1870. Reaching Chicago again in a mellow and contemplative mood, he was jolted by recent developments at the School of Civics and Philanthropy. Sophonisba Breckinridge, he learned, had been negotiating with officials at the University of Chicago "over a proposal she had made to them for taking over the School, which, she said, they and Mr. Rosenwald were inclined to favor. I knew nothing whatever of these negotiations, nor did any of the other trustees." Furthermore, Taylor was informed that Dean Breckinridge demanded a budget of $55,000 for the coming year, that in the face of this Crane, Rosenwald, and Lawson had actually reduced their contributions, that no announcements had been printed or distributed for the fall term, and consequently no students had registered.[36]

At an emergency meeting of the board of trustees Sophonisba Breckinridge reported that the University of Chicago was definitely interested in taking over the work of the Chicago School as a graduate professional course. The University insisted, however, that an income of $25,000 a year for five years must be guaranteed the Chicago School by its friends. In view of the academic advantages of university affiliation and the obvious difficulties of raising $55,000 a year for independent maintenance, Sophonisba Breckinridge

[35] Board of Trustees, Minutes of Meetings, October 17, 1918, November 12, 1919; Executive Committee, Board of Trustees, Minutes of Meetings, April 14, 1920; Graham Taylor to Sophonisba Breckinridge, March 30, 1920.

[36] Graham Taylor to "My dear Ken," July 29, 1920; Sophonisba Breckinridge to Graham Taylor, July 3, 1920; Graham Taylor to Julia Lathrop, July 10, 1920.

urged the trustees to ask the university to assume responsibility for the School of Civics and Philanthropy. Taylor was reluctant. He hoped to raise the $55,000 with the help of the American Red Cross and the Russell Sage Foundation, which was willing to make a small contribution to the research department for the year 1920–21. He reviewed "the ideals, standards and services for which the School has struggled for over seventeen years" and pointed out the disadvantages of transferring the program to other auspices. But he admitted that the absorption of a part of its work by the University of Chicago was preferable to its total extinction.[37]

After some discussion it was clear that a majority of the trustees was in favor of turning the school over to the university. Taylor noted with some bitterness in his diary that all of them seemed "glad to be relieved of further responsibility. None making any stand to conserve the whole distinctive life & work costing 18 years of sacrificial struggle." The board appointed a committee of three, Taylor, Breckinridge, and Rosenwald, to carry on further negotiations with university officials and to work out the details of the merger. The president accepted the situation with good grace, convinced as he wrote Julia Lathrop in Washington that there was "neither time nor chance left . . . to do anything but acquiesce and make what effort I can to save as much of the spirit, the fellowship and the method of the School as possible from being lost in the transfer."[38]

Events moved rapidly during the next few weeks. The committee found financial backers for the prospective graduate program under university auspices. Rosenwald and Crane were the largest contributors, promising $5,000 each, while Ryerson and Mrs. Blaine agreed to give $2,500 a piece, and a total of $7,000 was pledged by the Red Cross, Jewish Charities, and United Charities. The University of Chicago spokesmen agreed to maintain all aspects of the school's work except the course for public health nurses and the recreation training program. The former was abandoned, but Neva Boyd arranged to continue her work as the Recreation Training School with headquarters at Hull House. On August 5, the board of trustees formally voted to ask the University of Chicago to establish a graduate professional school for social workers, adding

> that in their judgment such a curriculum can fulfill the demands of the situation only if it be given under conditions of administrative unity characteristic of professional schools, if the classroom work is supplemented by "field work" and skilled placement of graduates, and if the

[37] Board of Trustees, Minutes of Meetings, July 9, 1920; John M. Glenn to Graham Taylor, June 19, 1920; John M. Glenn to Judge Julian Mack, June 3, 1920, School of Social Service Administration.

[38] Taylor, Diary, July 9, 1920; Graham Taylor to Julia Lathrop, July 19, 1920.

high quality of the student body is assured by the provision of scholar-
ships and fellowships.

On August 10, the University of Chicago accepted these proposals and officially established the Graduate School of Social Service Administration. Taylor, meanwhile, was authorized to wind up the affairs of the School of Civics
and Philanthropy.[39]

The closing of the school was a bitter disappointment for Graham Taylor.
He felt that "the struggles and successes of eighteen years" merited "more
permanent loyalty and support." But only Julia Lathrop, Victor Lawson, and
John Glenn of the Russell Sage Foundation seemed to share the president's
viewpoint. The Chief of the Children's Bureau wrote to Taylor in July that
if the trustees had held on for a few more years they could have found support among a "new generation of the young men and women . . . just coming
into active business life and into the control of money." John Glenn found
many defects in the proposed university program. It was "over-elaborate"
and looked "like an attempt to be theoretically comprehensive rather than
practically intensive. . . . I regret exceedingly that the School is going into
the University. I think it would have been better for the future of training
for social work if it could have remained independent." Lawson told Taylor
that he too regretted the "decision and action on the part of our friends more
than I can say . . . I believe a mistake has been made, but you and I are
without responsibility for it."[40]

During the months following the merger Taylor was hurt by further actions which he attributed to Sophonisba Breckinridge and Edith Abbott, both
of whom became associate professors of social economy in the new graduate
school. "Not even the *courtesy* of sending me the list of topics & lecturers
was extended to me, much less any conference or advance notification concerning what is to be," he told his secretary. Worst of all, he was offered no
teaching position in the new program. "Some hollow flattery over what
SPB was pleased to refer to as my name being 'prominently connected with
the School in the past' may be expected & perhaps, after I have been sufficiently disciplined & discredited, some minor course may be offered me, as a
'consolation' appointment!" But Taylor never had the opportunity of turning
down such an appointment.[41]

[39] Board of Trustees, Minutes of Meetings, August 5, 1920; University of Chicago,
Board of Trustees, Resolution adopted August 10, 1920.

[40] Graham Taylor to "My dear Ken," July 29, 1920; Julia Lathrop to Graham Taylor,
July 14, 1920; John M. Glenn to Sophonisba Breckinridge, August 14, 1920, School of
Social Administration; Victor F. Lawson to Graham Taylor, August 13, 1920.

[41] University of Chicago, *Annual Register, 1920–21*, p. 421; Graham Taylor to Mabel
Hawkins, September 4, 1920, Hawkins Papers.

Meantime, he feared that the university officials did not understand the spirit and the methods of his training program. He was caught up in the conflict between privately-sponsored training courses and those affiliated with scholarly institutions, "the social agencies regarding the college schools as academic and impractical, and the colleges regarding the agency schools as underrating theory and principle, and being sufficiently satisfied with mere rule-of-thumb tricks of the trade." Taylor feared that the warm, personal approach of his school would be scuttled at the university and that Breckinridge and Abbott would deliberately emphasize theory and principle at the expense of practical experience. He felt justified in these criticisms when the Graduate School of Social Service Administration decided to take full-time registrants only, thus reversing the long-standing policy of the Chicago School of flexible schedules for part-time students. In the privacy of his diary Taylor sarcastically remarked that the program was being "academicized to death at the university to gratify the pride of S.P.B.!" [42]

In spite of the disappointments Taylor diligently carried out his last assignment from the board of trustees. He presented the school's library to the university. He disposed of the furniture, buying some of it for Chicago Commons and giving "two desks and a noiseless typewriter" to Dean Breckinridge "without charge." Then he prepared a farewell letter to the school's alumnae. In the process, however, he

> accidentally discovered *her* [Sophonisba Breckinridge's] announcement to former students ready for print. . . . It was mean enough to do that without an invitation to me & it was a cold academic notice written in view of the great grand future, with no memory of the past. I *re-wrote* it & ordered my name printed as president & her's as Dean.

Finally, Taylor settled the financial affairs of the School of Civics and Philanthropy, remarking to his secretary as he struggled with "overhanging obligations of nearly $1,000," "so it goes to the end with no one concerned but me." [43]

Yet Taylor could see a brighter side of the picture. He admitted to Victor Lawson that he had had "a hard time closing up the School of Civics and doing away with the last vestiges of it at the Crane residence. It pulled on my heart-strings to do these last things." But, he continued, "I have always felt that any one who would be a winner must also be a good loser. So I am

[42] Eubank, "Schools of Social Work," p. 265; L. C. Marshall to Harry Pratt Judson, March 8, 1921, Harry Pratt Judson Papers, University of Chicago Library; Taylor, Diary, July 21, 1921.

[43] Spencer Dickinson to Allen B. Pond, November 15, 1920; Board of Trustees, Minutes of Meetings, July 21, 1921; Graham Taylor to Victor Elting, March 12, 1921; Graham Taylor to Mabel Hawkins, August 16, September 4, 1920, Hawkins Papers.

thinking more of what has been saved not only at the University but by the continuance of the Recreation Training School as an independent venture." After months of indecision and disagreement in an "atmosphere of suspicion & self-consciousness," he was glad "to breathe the free air of liberty & loyalty which at least *prevails* at the dear old Commons." The sixty-nine year old Taylor was, no doubt, telling the truth when he claimed "a great sense of relief at my release from the wearing financial solicitude which I have borne so long for the School of Civics." [44]

VI

The decision to merge the School of Civics and Philanthropy with the University of Chicago was to some extent a personal victory for Sophonisba Breckinridge and Edith Abbott. These two had grown restless and impatient with Taylor's method of teaching, his educational concepts, and his administration. The older man's frequent use of anecdotes and reminiscences to make the point in the classroom seemed to them a poor substitute for a clearly-outlined, tightly-argued, and statistically-documented lecture. Year after year they objected to his choice of outside lecturers, men like Alexander Johnson, for instance, who thought and spoke exactly like Taylor. Both Breckinridge and Abbott preferred a more scientific, professional approach to social work training. They wanted the high academic standards and strict regulations that were applied to graduate courses at the University of Chicago, where both of them had studied and where Abbott had taught since 1913 and Breckinridge for almost two decades. In addition, they objected to the chronic financial insecurity of the Chicago School because it frustrated their plans for new courses and expansion of program.[45]

[44] Graham Taylor to Victor F. Lawson, October 1, 1920; Graham Taylor to Mabel Hawkins, September 4, 1920, Hawkins Papers.

[45] Interview with Helen R. Wright, December 31, 1953; interview with Katharine Taylor and Lea D. Taylor, December 28, 1953; Helen R. Wright, "Three Against Time: Edith and Grace Abbott and Sophonisba P. Breckinridge," *Social Service Review*, XXVIII (March, 1954), 49–50. Writing in 1948, Edith Abbott claimed that it was "Miss Breckinridge who finally persuaded the University authorities to take over the independent 'School of Civics' and give it the status of a graduate professional school." And Helen Wright, who was a student in the research department at the time of the merger and later became dean of the School of Social Service Administration, testified that it was Sophonisba Breckinridge "who single-handed convinced the University authorities that a graduate school devoted to the education of social workers could be conducted in accordance with the traditions of scholarship of a great university. . . . Probably it was due to faith in her even more than to the persuasiveness of her arguments that the University decided to embark on this new venture." Edith Abbott, "Sophonisba Preston Breckinridge, Over the Years," p. 420; Helen R. Wright, "The Debt of the School of Social Service Administration," *Social Service Review*, XXII (December, 1948), 448. See also Edith Abbott, "Twenty-One Years of University Education for the Social Serv-

Their position was clearly stated by Edith Abbott in a long postmortem letter to Julia Lathrop. Writing in August, 1920, shortly after the final decision had been reached, she summarized events of the past year and expressed the hope that Julia Lathrop would not "withhold . . . cordial approval of the new scheme unless you do really know the facts as to our situation." Last fall, she began, the financial affairs of the school, "which had been very critical ever since the Russell Sage Foundation withdrew its support, became desperate."

> We went through a miserable winter, trying month by month to adjust our expenditures to our possible balance. Dr. Taylor has not had a salary check since last January, and SP and I were without any for several months at a time during the winter. We are not complaining about this, but I mention it only to indicate how uncertain and precarious our income was.

In the midst of these difficulties officials of the Russell Sage Foundation, according to Edith Abbott, hinted that the Chicago School needed to "reorganize and get a live man at the head of it." Though they recommended a candidate, she knew it would never happen because no one with any sense would "come to an institution which paid practically all its faculty the sum of $7,700, and that irregularly."[46]

Abbott and Breckinridge, the letter continued, had a conference with two of the trustees, Jane Addams and Mrs. Emmons Blaine, in which they demanded to know by April 1, 1920, "whether an adequate budget would be assured." When the deadline arrived,

> not even this year's deficit had been met, there were no plans for next year, and Dr. Taylor left to spend the spring in California. I am not criticising Dr. Taylor for leaving. He canceled his salary while he was gone; and . . . it would be difficult indeed to find anyone else in the world who would act as president on a salary of $2,500 and that uncertain. But I only mean to show that we just drifted along.

In June the finance committee told them that they could count on a $55,000 budget for 1920–21. Still Abbott and Breckinridge were skeptical. "We had had previous experiences, however, a good many of them, of budgets voted and then no money coming in, and we had long ago decided that we would not run deficits on promises."[47]

---

ices, 1920–41," *Social Service Review*, XV (December, 1941), 672; Elizabeth Wisner, "Edith Abbott's Contribution to Social Work Education," *Social Service Review*, XXXII (March, 1958), 8–9.

[46] Edith Abbott to Julia Lathrop, August 7, 1920, School of Social Service Administration.

[47] Edith Abbott to Julia Lathrop, August 7, 1920, School of Social Service Administration.

It was at this juncture, Edith Abbott went on, that Sophonisba Breckinridge discovered the university's interest in the school. Though unreceptive to proposals of merger in 1907, 1908, and 1909, the larger institution had come around by the spring of 1920 to the same position which Breckinridge and Abbott held: that social work training should be conducted under university auspices and that it "should not be merely an appendage to the sociology dept. but that it should be a graduate professional work." Encouraged, the two held further conversations with university officials and made tentative attempts to raise the $25,000 guaranty. "Very greatly to our surprise, it appeared to be much easier to get money for the University plan than for the School." [48]

When Taylor returned to Chicago in June of 1920 and was informed of these developments, he

> at first said he cordially approved the plan and asked SPB to draw up a statement for the trustees. Later after talking with Mr. Lawson and possibly with others, he apparently changed his mind, though whenever he was faced with the question of an alternative, he always said the University plan was "the only way out."

Jane Addams, whose "inclinations were for an independent School," wanted to "'go on' for a year or two longer just to make Dr. Taylor happy." But Breckinridge and Abbott, continued the latter, "could not agree. . . . Our obligation is to the work and the students, and I do not think that we had any right to sacrifice them, knowing what we did about conditions at both institutions." [49]

Once the merger decision had been reached, Edith Abbott like Graham Taylor felt a sense of relief. But, "unlike Dr. Taylor, who is, I think, somewhat romantic about what he calls his 'seventeen years of sacrifice," I certainly do not consider my twelve years at the School years of sacrifice. I have worked very hard during this time, but the work has been very rewarding, and always interesting." Having thus explained the role which she and Sophonisba Breckinridge played in the merger, she concluded her long letter to Julia Lathrop with assurances that she was "very happy" about the future plans and felt that they held a great "promise of continual development on a permanently assured foundation." [50]

Julia Lathrop's reply showed that by that time she agreed with Edith Abbott and Sophonisba Breckinridge about the future of the school:

[48] Edith Abbott to Julia Lathrop, August 7, 1920, School of Social Service Administration.

[49] Edith Abbott to Julia Lathrop, August 7, 1920, School of Social Service Administration.

[50] Edith Abbott to Julia Lathrop, August 7, 1920, School of Social Service Administration.

About one thing I am certain: the School is yours and S. P. B.'s in a peculiar sense and your judgment as to the best practicable turn is backed by such generous devotion that I accept it and only feel grateful to you for what you have done and will do to uphold the standards of applied social science.

I fully agree that there is no advantage in postponing the change. I do not see yet just how to cheer up Dr. Taylor but I am sure that delay is not the way. Also I am sure that the only path is ahead on the University Plan. Of course I am sorry, but there is much to be said for the success you have achieved in gaining recognition as a graduate school. That is a genuine triumph which will descend in the history of education.[51]

Taylor may have been somewhat sentimental about his sacrifices for the school, but his total contribution to social work education was substantial and was widely recognized throughout the country. The 415 graduates and the many others who had taken courses at the School of Civics and Philanthropy formed a corps of "splendidly loyal alumni." Frequent testimonials to their efficient work in the field came back to the school's office. The National Conference of Charities and Correction hailed Taylor's leadership by naming him chairman of the first Committee on Training for Social Workers. In this capacity he delivered the group's report to the full conference in 1905. He later helped to establish uniform standards for all the training schools, and his own institution participated in the 1911 and 1915 sessions devoted to social work education. When the American Association of Schools of Social Work was organized in May, 1919, Taylor along with Edith Abbott and Sophonisba Breckinridge were among the seventeen charter members.[52]

During the last few years of the school's existence Edith Abbott and Sophonisba Breckinridge tended to underestimate Taylor's important achievement in establishing and administering an independent training program. Understandably concerned about the financial and academic weaknesses of the Chicago School, they were nonetheless tactless in their dealings with the older man. In the final analysis, of course, their evaluation of the economic plight of the school was correct. Its desperate financial condition ultimately necessitated its surrender to the university. Unlike the New York School of Philanthropy which was generously endowed as early as 1904, the Chicago institution had to depend upon annual appeals to the community. By 1915 when the Russell Sage Foundation support terminated, the school's trustees should

[51] Julia Lathrop to Edith Abbott, August 10, 1920, Abbott Papers.
[52] Graham Taylor to Julia Lathrop, July 10, 1920; "Estimates of the Need and Value of the Chicago School of Civics and Philanthropy Volunteered by Those Best Qualified to Judge" (manuscript); "Standards in Schools of Philanthropy," *Charities and The Commons*, XVIII (1907), 641; Graham Taylor, "Report of Committee on Training for Social Workers," National Conference of Charities and Correction, *Proceedings, 1905*, pp. 436–44; Bruno, "Twenty-Five Years of Schools of Social Work," pp. 153–54.

certainly have looked for contributors outside the Chicago area. Taylor's many obligations to the settlement and the Chicago Theological Seminary prevented him from undertaking this important project. The board failed to do so because they expected somehow to discover new local support. Too late they found, as treasurer Victor Elting expressed it in his *Recollections,* that the "gentle art of giving has never been learned in Chicago by any number of its wealthy citizens." [53]

There were valid academic as well as financial reasons for the merger. Felix Frankfurter outlined the advantages of university connections for social work training programs in a speech before the 1915 National Conference of Charities and Correction. Affiliation was clearly the trend in the postwar years, and by the end of the 1920's only seven schools were operating independently, the other thirty-two were either integral parts of, or closely connected with, a college or university. Edith Abbott and Sophonisba Breckinridge were in complete agreement with the recommendation of Frankfurter, and they were, of course, pleased to see the Chicago merger carried out in 1920. Writing two decades later Edith Abbott reviewed the arguments for university affiliation:

> A few students needed the advanced social science courses that the University offered, and a few needed the elementary courses, and we knew the waste of trying to duplicate this work. We needed some of the courses offered in the Law School and the School of Business; and we needed the cooperation of the medical faculty; and we greatly needed the research facilities of the University, particularly the library; and we needed the protection and stimulus of University scholarship and University educational standards.

"The moving of the old School of Civics to the University," she admitted, "was an act of faith on both sides." But "after twenty-one years I think I can say that we have kept the faith on both sides." [54]

Although some aspects of the merger were handled in a clumsy fashion and caused ill will, the action undoubtedly took place at the right time. University affiliation did enrich the curriculum, raise academic standards, and in the long run preserve the spirit of Taylor's pioneer program. The Graduate School of Social Service Administration, of which Edith Abbott was dean from 1924 until 1942, was a distinct success. During 1920–21 there were only 45 graduate students and 28 undergraduates, but by the end of the five year

[53] Victor Elting, *Recollections of a Grandfather* (Chicago, 1940), p. 124.

[54] Felix Frankfurter, "Social Work and Professional Training," National Conference of Charities and Correction, *Proceedings, 1915,* pp. 595–96; Meier, *History of The New York School of Social Work,* chaps. iv, v; Eubank, "Schools of Social Work," p. 265; Bruno, *Trends in Social Work,* pp. 143–44; Edith Abbott, "Twenty-One Years of University Education for the Social Services, 1920–41," pp. 673, 705.

experimental period there were 90 graduates, 35 undergraduates, and 90 students from other departments enrolled in its courses. The university officials readily assumed full financial responsibility for the work after 1925. Registration continued to increase even during the depression, until it reached the remarkable total of 1,358 people in 1935. Field work, social research, and systematic publication were important aspects of the graduate school's program. Thus the series of monographs initiated by the Chicago School of Civics and Philanthropy became forerunners of an impressive group of University of Chicago Studies in Social Science. Moreover, Sophonisba Breckinridge launched the *Social Service Review* in 1927, a quarterly journal which has become a leading publication in the field of social work.[55]

Even if Taylor had been able to carry the school through the 1920's on an independent basis, the project would probably have foundered in the following decade. And it is quite certain that during the depression none of the three universities in the Chicago area could have salvaged it. Still it was a hard blow for Taylor to lose his independent training program. For years he had juggled his work at the seminary and Chicago Commons so that he could spend the major part of his time and energy on the School of Civics and Philanthropy. "So deeply am I convinced of the fundamental and far-reaching function of this School and the country-wide demand for its work," he told the trustees in 1912, "that I am constrained to make . . . it my life work." It can only be hoped that in his last years he found some consolation in the culmination at the University of Chicago of "the humble educational initiatives adventured by Chicago Commons."[56]

In recent years the university has given appropriate recognition to Graham Taylor. When the School of Social Service Administration celebrated its fiftieth anniversary in 1958, it paid tribute to the Chicago School of Civics and Philanthropy — organized in 1908 — as the starting point of its educational program. Moreover, the new building erected for the school in 1964 has a Graham Taylor lecture hall endowed by Mr. and Mrs. Edward L. Ryerson, Jr. Their gift carries on the Ryerson family tradition of generous support both for Taylor's settlement house and his training school for social workers.

---

[55] "Chicago Brings Gifts," *The Survey*, LIV (May 15, 1925), 250; Edith Abbott, "Twenty-One Years of University Education," p. 673; Thomas V. Smith and Leonard White (eds.), *Chicago — An Experiment in Social Science Research* (Chicago, 1929), p. 212; Taylor, *Pioneering*, pp. 405–6; Wright, "Three Against Time," pp. 50–51.

[56] Graham Taylor to Mrs. William F. Dummer, June 7, 1912; Taylor, *Chicago Commons*, 159.

Seven ⚔ *The Conscience of Chicago*

"To look to the general welfare is . . . part of good citizenship," wrote Taylor in *Charities and The Commons* in 1906. No groups, he warned, especially those with money and the advantage of education, should seek "to isolate themselves from the life of the mass." Instead they must put their knowledge to use in public service.[1] In his own lifetime Taylor practiced what he preached.

He soon discovered, however, that Chicago had two frontiers — one "with its advancing lines of academic research and its picket lines of social pioneers," backed by "the more progressive citizens"; the other, "the frontier in the rear, across which lived and labored the vastly outnumbering multitude of wage-earning people." Taylor had friends in both groups, and, as a result, his life

> swung like a pendulum, almost every twenty-four hours, between the privileged few and the struggling many; . . . between the crowded tenements of the day laborers and the homes and offices of captains of commerce; between industrial wage-earners and their employers; between trade unions and manufacturers' associations; between academic circles and the masses of the people; between the native-born and the foreign-born populations; and in politics and religion, between conservatives and progressives, reactionaries and radicals.[2]

He knew that these varied experiences and wide contacts placed him in an advantageous position for public service, and he made the most of his opportunities. He joined many reform organizations in Chicago and worked with numerous local and state commissions. He spoke in support of various aspects of the progressive movement before hundreds of audiences in the city

[1] Graham Taylor, "The Public Duty of Public Service," *Charities and The Commons,* XVI (August 4, 1906), 473, 474; Graham Taylor, "The Social Obligation of Culture" (manuscript).

[2] Taylor, *Pioneering,* 5, vii–viii.

and throughout the Middle West. In addition, he promoted social, political, and economic reform through the weekly column he wrote for the Chicago *Daily News* for more than three decades. Indeed, it was these good-natured yet persistent pleas for progress which prompted Victor F. Lawson to refer to his star columnist as the "Conscience of Chicago."[3]

Shortly after his arrival in the metropolis Taylor realized that its government was desperately in need of reform. Other Chicagoans agreed with Lincoln Steffens, who said of the city in the 1890's:

> Criminally it was wide open, commercially it was brazen, and socially it was thoughtless and raw; it was a settlement of individuals and groups and interests with no common sense and no political conscience. Everybody was for himself, none was for Chicago.

Foreign visitors were struck by the same thing. George W. Steevens, an Englishman, observed in 1896 that

> nobody in this rushing, struggling tumult has any time to look after what we have long ago come to think the bare decencies of civilisation. . . . In Chicago there is added to this what looks like a fundamental incapacity for government. . . . Wealth every man will struggle for, and even elegance; good government is the business of nobody.

What escaped the attention of many Chicagoans was the fact that bad government had become the exclusive business of a handful of firmly-entrenched aldermen, the "Gray Wolves," who used the city council to secure patronage for their ward machines and bribes for themselves.[4]

For example, in the area Back-of-the-Yards the alderman made a tidy profit by dumping city garbage in his open clay pits. The nineteenth ward boss, John Powers, familiarly known as "Johnny de Pow" to his Irish-Italian constituents, was the tool of traction magnate Charles T. Yerkes. Well-paid for his political services in the council, Alderman Powers spent his boodle buying votes and thus was able to maintain tight control of the Hull House district despite Jane Addams' efforts to oust him. Undoubtedly the most colorful member of the council was John Coughlin, alderman from the first ward which comprised Chicago's notorious vice district. "Bathhouse John" was the proprietor of several fashionable bathhouses, but his real forte was modeling bright-hued velvet waistcoats, reciting poetry, and delivering eloquent if ungrammatical speeches to admiring councilmen and incredulous reporters. His sidekick, Michael "Hinky Dink" Kenna, performed the less dramatic tasks

[3] Lea D. Taylor, "The Social Settlement and Civic Responsibility — The Life Work of Mary McDowell and Graham Taylor," p. 39.

[4] Lincoln Steffens, *The Shame of the Cities* (New York, 1957), pp. 164–65; George W. Steevens, "The Land of the Dollar," in Pierce (ed.), *As Others See Chicago*, p. 400.

of delivering first ward votes and collecting the money from gamblers and brothel-keepers to purchase police protection for the Levee.[5]

Carter H. Harrison, son of the martyred mayor and himself an aspiring politician in the 1890's, was later to describe the city fathers as a "motley crew" of "Saloonkeepers, proprietors of gambling houses, undertakers." Though Chicago was "a great, growing, energetic community," its citizens had brought upon themselves political disgrace. For years, he continued, "from lack of interest, from supineness, from absolute stupidity," they

> had permitted the control of public affairs to be the exclusive appanage of a low-browed, dull-witted, base-minded gang of plug-uglies, with no outstanding characteristic beyond an unquenchable lust for money, with but a single virtue, and that not possessed by all, a certain physical courage that enabled each to dominate his individual barnyard.[6]

The Civic Federation of Chicago took the first effective steps toward cleaning the political barnyard. That organization came into existence in 1894 as a direct result of William T. Stead's castigation of the Black City. The Federation had six committees, one of which was the political department, authorized to establish branch councils in each of the thirty-four wards. Taylor and the Chicago Commons residents promptly launched a Seventeenth Ward Civic Federation in December, 1894. It investigated prostitution and saloons in the area and began a campaign against corrupt ward bosses. By gathering evidence, presenting the facts to independent voters, and making certain that the latter turned out on election day, the local council made considerable headway. When the political action work of the Civic Federation was transferred to the Municipal Voters' League in 1896, Taylor's group co-operated closely with the new organization and won a number of victories in the seventeenth ward.

The Civic Federation, though no longer participating in election contests, continued its campaign for good government. Laws establishing a municipal civil service and regulating primary elections passed the legislature in the 1890's. Thwarted in its attempt to arbitrate the Pullman strike, the Federation arranged a national conference on labor questions and rallied enough support to secure a state arbitration law. To substantiate its charges of exorbitant city contracts, the reform organization proved that streets could be cleaned for $10 a mile instead of the $18.50 paid by the council, and subse-

---

[5] Dedmon, *Fabulous Chicago*, pp. 258–63; Wilson, *Mary McDowell, Neighbor*, pp. 143–44; Addams, *Twenty Years*, pp. 315–22; Lloyd Wendt and Herman Kogan, *Lords of the Levee, The Story of Bathhouse John and Hinky Dink* (Indianapolis, 1943), chaps. i–x.

[6] Carter H. Harrison, *Stormy Years* (Indianapolis, 1935), p. 79.

quently the reluctant aldermen had to hire street cleaners at a much lower figure. In 1899 the Civic Federation sponsored a widely-publicized conference on trusts. It was so successful that the executive secretary, Ralph M. Easley, left Chicago in 1900 to establish the National Civic Federation whose goal was promotion of class conciliation through arbitration of labor disputes. Meantime, the Civic Federation of Chicago spearheaded a drive for revision of the city charter. Taylor and other commission members drew up an excellent document, which was approved by the city voters but was altered so radically by amendments in the state legislature that it brought no substantial improvement. Thereafter the Federation became a self-styled "Tax Sentinel," concentrating upon city and state fiscal problems.[7]

It was the Municipal Voters' League, organized in February, 1896, which eventually freed Chicago's council from the clutches of the "Gray Wolves." Established with the blessing of the Civic Federation, the new organization was headed by a "little, sawed-off giant of reform," George E. Cole. Though he described himself as "a second-class business man in the stationery business," Cole knew instinctively how to fight the boodlers, and he made shrewd use of the Civic Federation's ward councils to gather information and provide campaign workers. He plunged into the 1896 spring aldermanic elections by calling fifty-seven of the sixty-eight councilmen "thieves" and asking the voters to defeat twenty-six of the thirty-four whose terms were expiring. Of that group sixteen were not renominated by their ward machines and four of the remaining ten were beaten at the polls. The following year the League condemned twenty-seven of the thirty-four outgoing aldermen and managed to retire permanently twenty-four of them. In these and subsequent campaigns the League utilized the street railway issue as a strong argument for reforming the council before the valuable franchises came up for renewal in 1903. The voters responded. By 1900 there were enough independent councilmen to defeat Charles T. Yerkes' bold bid for renewal of his franchises. When the unscrupulous traction king sold his Chicago interests and departed from the city, he was admitting defeat at the hands of the Municipal Voters' League.[8]

Graham Taylor, an enthusiastic and active member of the Municipal Voters' League, figured in these events. He served on the executive committee from 1897 until his death, and he became a close friend of George Cole

[7] Sutherland, *Fifty Years on the Civic Front*, chaps. ii–vii; Ginger, *Altgeld's America*, pp. 250–53; Lewis and Smith, *Chicago*, pp. 236–39.

[8] Taylor, *Pioneering*, pp. 56–58; Sutherland, *Fifty Years on the Civic Front*, p. 16; Ginger, *Altgeld's America*, pp. 253–57; Lewis and Smith, *Chicago*, pp. 243–50; Steffens, *The Shame of the Cities*, pp. 169–77.

and his successor, Walter L. Fisher. In addition, Taylor worked in League affairs with Edwin Burritt Smith, William Kent, Allen B. Pond, and Charles R. Crane, all of whom shared Taylor's interest in Chicago Commons and the School of Civics and Philanthropy. Furthermore, it was in conjunction with the Municipal Voters' League that the seventeenth ward reformers were able to elect such outstanding aldermen as Walsh, Smulski, and Dever, and to break the power of Republican boss James H. Burke in that area. Similar victories were won in other wards. When Lincoln Steffens paid a return visit to Chicago in 1903 he found "Johnny de Pow," "Bathhouse John," and "Hinky Dink" still on the council, but most of the other "Gray Wolves" had been driven into retirement. The people of Chicago, he noted with amazement, "have beaten boodling,"

> that is about all they have tried deliberately and systematically to do, and the way they have done that proves that they can do anything they set out to do. They worry about the rest; half free, they are not half satisfied and not half done. But boodling, with its backing of "big men" and "big interests," is the hardest evil a democracy has to fight, and a people who can beat it can beat anything.

Chicago, Steffens decided, was "Half Free and Fighting On." [9]

After 1903, Taylor used his *Daily News* column to promote good government. He gave strong editorial support to the League's candidates in the aldermanic contests, and he himself usually took a stand in the mayoralty battles. In 1897, he favored an independent candidate, John Maynard Harlan, but the voters chose Carter H. Harrison as mayor and re-elected him in 1899, 1901, and 1903. Harrison's Democratic coalition included some notorious political bosses, and hence he was unhappy to see the Municipal Voters' League sweep clean all of the wards. Harrison did, however, help turn the council against the Allen bill which would have allowed Yerkes to retain his monopoly of Chicago's street railways. Lincoln Steffens observed of the second Harrison, "Without ideals, he does only what is demanded of him. . . . Every time Chicago wants to go ahead a foot, it has first to push its mayor up inch by inch." Taylor admitted that Harrison did pave streets and sidewalks, elevate railroad tracks, and appoint park commissioners, but he accused the mayor of making bad police appointments and maintaining a nefarious alliance with "Bathhouse John" and "Hinky Dink." After Harrison's departure in 1905 Taylor wrote:

> He was too politic to be either practical or ever principled throughout. Even the cosmopolitanism of our population never appealed to his imagi-

[9] Taylor, *Pioneering*, pp. 58–70; Steffens, *The Shame of the Cities*, pp. 169, 181, 165–66, 162.

nation. . . . Lacking any wisdom of the Chicago that is to be, he had no
sustained, progressive and comprehensive programme for the city as a
whole. . . . He left office with honor, but he might have left great.[10]

The major issue in the 1905 election was what to do with the street railways. The Democrat, Edward F. Dunne, promised immediate municipal
ownership; the Republican, John Maynard Harlan, preferred to seek the
people's advice in a special referendum. To the readers of the *Daily News*,
Taylor declared: "Untrammeled by party affiliations and absolutely free from
all other considerations except public duty to do as I choose, I deliberately
and heartily favor the candidacy of John Maynard Harlan and am doing all
I can to urge and secure his election." It was Dunne, however, who won.
He failed to deliver the street railways to Chicago and went down to defeat
before the Republican Fred Busse in 1907. Busse, the first Chicago mayor to
serve a four-year term, did eventually reach a solution to the traction problem. Though the city did not own the system, it did get a fair share of the
earnings of the private companies and it did establish effective control over
their operations.[11]

Yet Chicago had not seen the end of Carter H. Harrison. He decided to
run for an unprecedented fifth term in 1911, this time against Charles E.
Merriam, University of Chicago professor and successful alderman. Taylor,
of course, supported Merriam and reminded the voters of Harrison's "old
weakness for dallying with the venders of vice and forming unholy alliances
with illicit and illegal traffickers. In the name of liberty he is promising
license. He is backing up into the future." Chicagoans, nonetheless, rallied to
Harrison and granted him four more years in city hall. Throughout this
period Taylor, along with other members of a Vice Commission appointed
by Busse, worked relentlessly to break up the "unholy alliances" that plagued
Chicago. Two decades later Harrison philosophically described the relationship between himself and Taylor:

> Graham Taylor, the idealist, and Carter Harrison, the practical poli-
> tician, like the East and West of Kipling's poem are "the twain that never
> shall meet!" And it's not all my fault either.
> Had I done the things you would have wanted me to do, I would have
> been "left on third." . . . I kept a little ahead of the procession . . . and
> I was re-elected four times. Finally I moved a little too fast in too many

[10] Harrison, *Stormy Years*, Chaps. v–xxiii; Ginger, *Altgeld's America*, chaps. xi, xii;
Steffens, *The Shame of the Cities*, p. 193; Graham Taylor, "Mayor — With Honor, but
Not Great," *Daily News* (Chicago), April 15, 1905.
[11] Graham Taylor, "Who Shall be Mayor? Why Prefer Harlan to Dunne?" *Daily
News* (Chicago), March 25, 1905; Lewis and Smith, *Chicago*, pp. 314–15; Ginger, *Alt-
geld's America*, chap. xii.

activities and the Hopkins-Sullivan-Brennan-Sweitzer combination got me. The trouble with municipal reform administrations is they are never re-elected.[12]

The 1915 mayoralty election was won by a remarkable Republican, William Hale Thompson. Though he started his political career as second ward alderman under the banner of the Municipal Voters' League, he ultimately became Chicago's most notorious mayor. Elected on a demagogic platform he and his cohorts dipped into the public trough, soon squandering the city's surplus and creating a sizable deficit by 1919. That year Taylor declared editorially: "The defeat of Mayor Thompson is the supreme duty of the hour. It is the test of the voters' loyalty to Chicago." Yet with the help of the gamblers, the Chicago "Boosters," and the Negroes, "Big Bill" won a narrow victory, getting 38 per cent of the vote which was enough to scuttle his three opponents and make him "minority mayor." When William E. Dever, former seventeenth ward alderman, ran against Thompson in 1923, Taylor gave his friend strong editorial support, and throughout Mayor Dever's capable administration he supplied sound political advice. In 1927, Dever and Thompson tangled again. Thompson managed to win another term, in part by promising Irish voters to punch King George V in the "snoot." Taylor had done his best during the campaign to remind *Daily News* readers of Thompson's previous corrupt record. After 1927 he kept them apprised of the mayor's old tricks. For four dismal years William Hale Thompson and his friends connived with bootleggers, racketeers, and murderers, while an international audience watched the amazing spectacle in Chicago.[13]

Throughout this period the vindictive Thompson tried to punish Taylor and Victor F. Lawson for their criticism in the *Daily News*. The mayor bluntly warned Taylor in 1917, "I shall hold you personally responsible for the next false statement that you make regarding me or my administration." Then Thompson changed the building codes, and Taylor had to alter some fire escapes, entrances, and exits to Chicago Commons. The warden told John Palmer Gavit that these petty reprisals had "entailed hundreds of dollars of expense exacted by building inspectors." Thompson's return to

---

[12] Graham Taylor, "On With Merriam, Back With Harrison," *Daily News* (Chicago), April 1, 1911; Harrison, *Stormy Years*, chaps. xxv–xxvii; Carter H. Harrison to Graham Taylor, January 7, 1936. A few weeks later the two elderly antagonists met "to swap yarns," and Harrison concluded, "I have a hunch we are really not far apart — certainly not as far as affection for Chicago and a desire for betterment of its conditions are concerned." Carter H. Harrison to Graham Taylor, March 31, 1936.

[13] Dedmon, *Fabulous Chicago*, chap. xxii; Lewis and Smith, *Chicago*, pp. 250–51, chaps. xvi–xxix; Lloyd Wendt and Herman Kogan, *Big Bill of Chicago* (Indianapolis, 1953), chaps. iv–xxvi; Graham Taylor, "Vote for Chicago to Defeat Thompson," *Daily News* (Chicago), March 29, 1919.

office in 1927 presaged still greater trouble. Nevertheless, Taylor helped organize a Public School Committee and a Civic Advisory Committee "so that the new administration will be watched & not have everything its own way." Furthermore, he kept up the editorial attack and took great satisfaction in shooting at Thompson's "freakish politics" from his "rifle pit in the *Daily News*." Not until the election of Anton J. Cermak in 1931, however, was the aging columnist able to write an end to the "very worst chapter in Chicago's entire history."[14]

Taylor was not as outspoken on national politics as he was on city problems. This was due in large part to his fear that support of any party in a national election would jeopardize his local influence. Writing to a friend in 1916 he proudly declared, "I have never identified myself with any political party organization, not even the Progressive. . . . I have not come out for any presidential candidate, because I wanted to be in a position, as very few are, to help swing the independent vote within and between the parties, especially for the best local candidates." Indeed, during the 1916 presidential campaign he could deplore the partisanship of "so many social and civic workers."

> Many of them have had citywide, statewide and even national influence with people of all parties. . . . What they are saying now for one or the other party in this campaign cannot avoid being taken as partisan. . . . Certainly Chicago is losing more than it gains by the division of some who served the whole city well to a partisan campaigning which could be done as well by others.[15]

Though Taylor eschewed any party affiliation, it is possible to trace some of his national political preferences from comments in his diary,[16] his letters, and his *Daily News* columns. Taylor was clearly sympathetic with the Progressive movement in 1912, and it is almost certain that he voted for Roosevelt. His son, Graham Romeyn Taylor, was interested in the movement, and many of Taylor's friends were active Progressives, including Charles R. Crane, William Kent, Charles Merriam, Raymond Robins, Jane Addams, and Mary McDowell. After the Progressive convention in Chicago in the

[14] William Hale Thompson to Graham Taylor, February 20, 1917; Graham Taylor to John Palmer Gavit, October 28, 1927; Graham Taylor to Graham Romeyn Taylor, May 1, 1927; Graham Taylor, "From Freaks to Sanity in Politics," *Daily News* (Chicago), February 19, 1927; Graham Taylor to Arthur Kellogg, October 28, 1927; Graham Taylor, "Pointers in Thompson's Rise and Fall," *Daily News* (Chicago), February 10, 1923.

[15] Graham Taylor to John Palmer Gavit, November 3, 1916; Graham Taylor, "Some Campaign Gains at National Loss," *Daily News* (Chicago), October 14, 1916.

[16] He hailed James A. Garfield's election in 1880 as "the triumph of Law, Liberty, Intelligence & Loyalty, Morality & Justice," but added, "May God grant it to be all of this." Taylor, Diary, November 3, 1880.

summer of 1912, Taylor wrote to Jane Addams, "I am watching the political developments with keen interest and am considering the best time and way for me to declare for the progressive platform. I have had, and still have, an honest doubt whether it was wise to put a third state ticket in the field, but I am open to conviction." In an editorial for *The Survey* he credited the Progressives with drawing people away "from blind allegiance to the party as an end into a discriminating loyalty to party as a means. . . . The launching of a progressive party cannot fail to develop permanently progressive policies in other parties." But he added, "The progressive movement in American politics and government is far greater than any one party." On this last point he was even more specific in his *Daily News* column for October 19:

> The movement of the hour, however, is greater than the man of the hour. It has moved him more than he has moved it. It is not his movement. He is only one of its men. It would have come — not so fast and so far — but it would have come without him, and it will long survive him.

This editorial column, entitled "The Man and Movement of the Hour," was the closest Taylor came to publicly endorsing Theodore Roosevelt. He was aware, of course, of the efforts of Raymond Robins, Jane Addams, Mary McDowell, and his son to keep the Progressive organization alive in Illinois after the election. But Taylor himself never joined the national Progressive committee, the Progressive State Central Committee, or the Cook County Progressive organization either before or after the election of 1912.[17]

Perhaps the demise of the Progressives encouraged Taylor to take a more forthright stand when President Woodrow Wilson was challenged by Charles Evans Hughes in 1916. To his friend Gavit he confessed in mid-October that he had "really been on the fence, yet more and more inclining toward Wilson."

> I know what a miscellaneous mess constitutes President Wilson's party support. And yet it seems to me that he has had and is likely to have far more control over that mixed Democratic lot than Mr. Hughes' sternest determination and best endeavor will give him over his stiff-necked, bull-headed, abler and closely organized reactionaries.

For the November 4 election edition of the *Daily News* Taylor prepared a strong endorsement of Wilson which Lawson refused to print. As a result Taylor arranged an interview with a Chicago *Herald* reporter in the course of which he announced his decision and gave his reasons. The national

---

[17] Graham Taylor to Jane Addams, August 11, 1912, Jane Addams Papers, Swarthmore College Library, Swarthmore, Penn.; Graham Taylor to Jane Addams, August 20, 1912; Graham Taylor, "Humanizing Politics," *The Survey*, XXIX (October 5, 1912), 10; Graham Taylor, "The Man and Movement of the Hour," *Daily News* (Chicago), October 19, 1912.

Democratic campaign committee then secured a statement from Taylor and circulated it as proof that their candidate would win the backing of an outstanding "Independent, never identified with any party." Both Taylor and his wife greatly admired Wilson's wartime leadership. "I think he will stand next to Lincoln in the history of our country," Taylor wrote to his son.[18]

After Woodrow Wilson fell ill, Taylor's enthusiasm for the Democratic party cooled. He did however, support Democratic presidential candidates in 1920 and again in 1924. Like most of the social workers Taylor jumped on the Hoover bandwagon in 1928. He joined Jane Addams, Julia Lathrop, Edith Abbott, Sophonisba Breckinridge, James Mullenbach, and other civic leaders in praising Hoover's "humanitarian service," his "understanding of the beneficial operation of prohibition," and his awareness "of the need of international understanding and cooperation in promoting the peace and progress of all nations." In 1932, Taylor still clung to Herbert Hoover as "The Man For the Present Crisis," though four years later he referred to the Republicans' candidate, Governor Alfred Landon, as a "hilarious choice." By that time Taylor was impressed with President Roosevelt's "wide and varied administrative experience, his knowledge of national and international affairs, and the courage with which he has tried actually to deal with the still critical situation." So the eighty-five year old Taylor, calling himself "still a middle-of-the-road independent," cast his final presidential ballot for Roosevelt.[19]

II

Taylor did not spare himself from his dictate that public service was a public duty. During his four active decades in Chicago he served on numerous city commissions, the most spectacular of which was the Vice Commission that functioned during Harrison's fifth term. In addition, he played an influential role on the local affairs committees of many clubs and associations. As his reputation spread he was appointed to state commissions that pursued a variety of progressive reforms. Furthermore, he gave support to these same goals on the lecture platform, in the *Daily News*, and in the many articles he contributed to *The Survey*. Far from begrudging the drain on his time and

[18] Graham Taylor to John Palmer Gavit, October 16, November 3, 1916; *Evening Post* (New York), November 6, 1916; Graham Taylor to Graham Romeyn Taylor, January 19, 1919, in the possession of Lea Taylor.

[19] Graham Taylor, "Voting For the Best in a Bad Situation," *Daily News* (Chicago), October 30, 1920; Graham Taylor, "Deciding Votes Between Candidates," *Daily News* (Chicago), November 1, 1924; 1928 newspaper clipping; Graham Taylor, "The Man For the Present Crisis," *Daily News* (Chicago), October 22, 1932; Graham Taylor to Raymond Robins, July 4, 1936.

energy, Taylor welcomed these broader contacts and cheerfully assumed the new burdens with characteristic resilience:

> Starting the day with my teaching . . . stopping for luncheon conferences at one of the clubs or at the "Ways and Means" weekly conference of the Association of Commerce, returning to the cosmopolitan wage-earning neighborhood of Chicago Commons, spending the evenings with groups of working-men or working-women assembled there, or attending elsewhere some larger or smaller public meeting, called to express and attract interest in some industrial, social, or civic situation, my daily life ranged over much of the whole gamut of human vicissitudes.[20]

Taylor's earliest civic service stemmed from his efforts to establish Eckhart Park in the seventeenth ward and a branch library at Chicago Commons. As a result of this activity Carter Harrison appointed him to the Special Park Commission on which he served from 1903 until 1906. Mayor Dunne named him in 1906 to a six-year term on the board of directors of the Public Library. Taylor helped shift the emphasis of the main library from research and reference work to wider public circulation and extensive educational programs. In addition, he argued effectively for more branches and reading rooms connected with the city's recreation centers. Throughout these years he used his *Daily News* columns to lobby for more parks and to urge Chicagoans to take advantage of their Public Library.[21]

Taylor's interest in the city parks prepared him for service on the Chicago Plan Commission. That organization grew out of a special study of long-range urban improvements made by Daniel Burnham for the Commercial Club. The results were published as *The Plan of Chicago*, a book which made such a favorable impression that the city council in 1909 approved of Mayor Busse's idea of a Chicago Plan Commission. Some three hundred citizens, including Graham Taylor, were appointed to the Commission and it was given advisory but not executive power to plan Chicago's physical future. Charles H. Wacker accepted the chairmanship and Burnham was chief architect until his death in 1912. Within twenty years the Commission had reclaimed large areas of the lakefront, built a vast system of parkways, and established an intricate network of inner and outer traffic thoroughfares. As an unofficial publicity agent for these remarkable projects, Taylor was instrumental in rallying civic approval. He carefully explained the plans in his *Daily News* columns and thus helped to mobilize support for each scheme as it came before the council or the voters. In 1927, Wacker wrote to Taylor, "You were one of the first fully to appreciate the significance of the Chicago Plan

---

[20] Taylor, "The Public Duty of Public Service," p. 473; Taylor, *Pioneering*, p. 130.
[21] Taylor, *Chicago Commons*, pp. 58, 153; Graham Taylor, "The Civic Value of Library Work with Children," *Public Libraries*, XIII (July, 1908), 247–48.

and to labor for it. I am sure your influence in shaping public opinion with respect to the Plan has been as wide as any man's."[22]

Without doubt, however, the most dramatic of Taylor's many civic positions was with the Chicago Vice Commission. Carter H. Harrison during his long tenure as mayor from 1897 until 1905 had pursued a "wide-open" policy concerning prostitution and gambling. This was due in part to his conviction that vice could never be completely annihilated and hence segregation was the best way to control it. In part his tolerance was due to the lucrative alliance between his political supporters in the Levee and the proprietors of the brothels and gaming parlors. The first ward Democratic organization, headed by "Bathhouse John" and "Hinky Dink," made a big splash and a good deal of money with their annual ball for the underworld. Starting in the 1890's, these orgies soon grew to such proportions that by 1908 some 15,000 people jammed the Coliseum to catch a glimpse of the well-known leaders of Levee society. During these same years the vice district steadily expanded, destroying adjacent neighborhoods and threatening to poison other areas of municipal life.[23]

The Commons' neighborhood felt the effects of this during Harrison's early years as mayor. In the summer of 1900 it touched a seventeen-year old girl who lived with her mother in the seventeenth ward, attended Chicago Commons, and taught a Sunday school class at the Tabernacle Church. Answering a newspaper advertisement which gave a Madison Street address, she was met at the door of the flat by an elderly woman who said she had rheumatism and needed a companion with her at all times. The young girl was locked in the apartment and her captor, Mrs. Mary Lyons, tried hard to make her entertain a bartender who called frequently. Five days later, the girl managed to slip a note to a seamstress who in turn informed the pastor of the Tabernacle Church. He hurried to the flat, broke down the door, and rescued the girl. Taylor, the pastor, and a representative of the Protective Agency for Women and Children then brought charges against "Mother" Lyons. Meantime the girl was closely guarded at the Commons, and Taylor found it necessary to secure a police guard after thugs from "the Madison Street dens" beat up the church janitor whom they mistook for the pastor. When Mrs. Lyons was tried in the spring of 1901, she attempted to shift

[22] Moore, *Daniel H. Burnham*, II, 10–11, 14–15, chap. xxiii; Lewis and Smith, *Chicago*, chap. xii; Taylor, *Pioneering*, pp. 19–21; Graham Taylor, "The Chicago Plan Fifteen Years After," *Daily News* (Chicago), July 11, 1925; Graham Taylor, "On Planning Beyond the Chicago Plan," *Daily News* (Chicago), December 5, 1925; Charles H. Wacker to Graham Taylor, April 23, 1927.

[23] Dedmon, *Fabulous Chicago*, pp. 263–66; Wendt and Kogan, *Lords of the Levee*, pp. 282–88; Herbert Asbury, *Gem of the Prairie; An Informal History of the Chicago Underworld* (New York, 1940), pp. 243–47.

the blame onto a prominent Chicago businessman who apparently paid the rent on her flat and admitted patronizing her girls. "Mother" Lyons was found guilty and went to jail; the businessman fled Chicago; and the threats of physical violence against the pastor, Taylor, and the Taylor children ceased. The girl was sent away to school for a year with funds which Taylor collected.[24]

Ever since the 1890's the Civic Federation had protested Harrison's policy of tolerating segregated vice. But it achieved little in the way of reform. The idea of a commission to study the whole problem came from the Federation of Churches and was presented to Mayor Busse by Walter T. Sumner, dean of an Episcopal cathedral near the Levee and one of the outraged spectators at the 1908 First Ward Ball. In the spring of 1910 Busse appointed a group of thirty citizens to investigate vice in Chicago and work out a new policy. Dean Sumner was named chairman of the Chicago Vice Commission and other members included Taylor, Julius Rosenwald, Frank W. Gunsaulus of Armour Institute, Mrs. Charles Henrotin of the Federation of Women's Clubs, plus representative clergymen, physicians, and judges. The city council was pressured into appropriating $10,000 for commission expenses, and the newspapers agreed that the delicate investigation was to proceed secretly until a final report was ready for publication.[25]

For more than a year these thirty people, assisted by a small staff of investigators, explored the "bottomless pit of Chicago's underworld." The committees battled against such obstacles as reluctant witnesses, revengeful keepers, angry politicians, and unco-operative policemen. Taylor headed a group authorized to find out where the girls came from and how they were recruited. In the course of his inquiries he visited most of the establishments in Chicago, the small, unorganized, squalid rooms as well as the unbelievably plush houses in the center of the Levee. One of the latter was the Everleigh Club, run by the shrewd sisters Ada and Minna Everleigh, and known from coast to coast as Chicago's leading brothel. Its girls were intelligent, well-groomed, expensively dressed, and they received the select clientele in richly furnished parlors with perfumed fountains and decorous background music.[26]

---

[24] *Tribune* (Chicago), May 17, 1901; *Evening Journal* (Chicago), April 5, 1901; Graham Taylor to Lea Taylor, May 17, 1901, in the possession of Lea Taylor; Interview with Lea Taylor, March 2, 1964.

[25] Lewis and Smith, *Chicago*, pp. 342–43; Walter C. Reckless, *Vice in Chicago* (Chicago, 1933), pp. 2–4; Peterson, *Barbarians in our Midst*, p. 88; Wendt and Kogan, *Lords of the Levee*, pp. 288–90; Asbury, *Gem of the Prairie*, pp. 284–86; *Daily News* (Chicago), March 5, 1910; Fred Busse to Graham Taylor, March 5, 1910.

[26] Taylor, *Pioneering*, pp. 95, 87; Lewis and Smith, *Chicago*, pp. 344–47; Dedmon, *Fabulous Chicago*, pp. 252–56; Peterson, *Barbarians in our Midst*, pp. 87–8; Wendt and Kogan, *Lords of the Levee*, pp. 283–85; Asbury, *Gem of the Prairie*, pp. 247–58.

Taylor and Dean Sumner were somewhat shaken by this scene. As Taylor later described it, they

> found the twenty or more inmates appearing so well in the early evening that it would have been difficult to distinguish them from high-school graduates or college students. They produced the pennants of several colleges, as though they used them to attract or amuse their patrons.

So far as the middle-aged Everleigh sisters were concerned, the reformers had to admit that they too were intelligent and well mannered.

> They extenuated their nefarious trade by saying that it had to be, and that they, as well as others, might profit by conducting it as decently as it could be managed. When asked how they procured inmates, they replied that they always had a waiting list, but insisted upon each one of them answering for herself. Dean Sumner and I were permitted to interview them. . . . few of these inmates failed to claim that they were only there temporarily and would leave the life they were leading when they had earned a competence. Their "madame" somewhat boastfully bade us to persuade if we could, any of them to leave forthwith.

Before departing from the handsomely furnished clubhouse, Taylor

> inquired of the madame how she dared to deal so destructively with both the body and the very life of each inmate. Her hollow, hysterical laughter fittingly accompanied her flippant reply that she was writing what she would call *The Biography of a Lost Soul*.[27]

Through the latter part of 1910, commission members pooled their information and drafted a report. With the help of a $5,000 grant from John D. Rockefeller, they published their findings in a large book entitled *The Social Evil in Chicago*. Organized crime and vice, they asserted, yielded an annual revenue of $60 million with profits exceeding $15 million per year for the people controlling the system. From the testimony of more than 2,400 women they concluded that prostitution stemmed largely from unfavorable home conditions; other factors included low wages, lack of healthy recreation, ignorance of sex hygiene, and the persuasion of procurers. The Commission "unanimously agreed that segregation of commercialized vice was a failure, regulation a false security, and ultimate suppression the only possible remedy." Hence, the report urged Mayor Busse to break up the segregated districts, abolish police protection, and enforce the existing laws that levied $200 fines on keepers, inmates, callers, and owners renting their property for immoral purposes. Furthermore, they asked for the creation of a permanent Morals Commission and a special Morals Court. The essence of the Vice Commis-

[27] Taylor, *Pioneering*, pp. 88–89.

sion's recommendation was summed up in one sentence: "Constant and persistent repression of prostitution the immediate method; absolute annihilation the ultimate ideal."[28]

Yet the reformers got no immediate action on their recommendations. *The Social Evil in Chicago* appeared in April, 1911, just as Busse's term expired and Carter H. Harrison returned to city hall. Unafflicted with "Puritan leanings" and still convinced of the "inevitableness" of prostitution, Mayor Harrison tried to carry on his previous policy by pigeonholing the Commission report. Anticipating this reaction, the reformers established a Committee of Fifteen in May, 1911. It was authorized "to aid the public authorities in the enforcement of all laws against pandering, and to take measures calculated to suppress the white-slave traffic." Taylor was not a member of this watchdog committee, but he did serve on its board of directors from 1911 until his death, all the while employing his *Daily News* column to publicize the recommendations of the Vice Commission and notify Chicagoans of the progress of the Committee of Fifteen. With characteristic optimism he predicted:

> When the public is informed of these facts its opinion will make or unmake city administrations until they conform to the American conscience in placing the public forms of the social evil under the ban of the law, executed by the courts of the state and the police of the city.[29]

The mushroom growth of the vice district, its flagrant abuses, and mounting public protests eventually caused Harrison to alter his policy. In September, 1912, a fervent young evangelist named Virginia Brooks led a huge parade of 5,000 hymn-singing men, women, and children through the Levee. In spite of rainy weather enthusiastic delegations from the Boy Scouts, Campfire Girls, Women's Christian Temperance Union, Epworth League, and Chicago Law and Order Society, accompanied by an impressive Salvation Army band, marched past the darkened bordellos and then adjourned to Symphony Hall where a mass meeting demanded action on the Vice Commission's recommendations.[30]

Ironically Miss Brooks' passionate criticism of the mayor and police was less effective in securing reform than a small brochure published in the same

[28] Chicago Vice Commission, *The Social Evil in Chicago* (Chicago, 1911), pp. 32–33, 262–72, 51–52, 55–65, 25; Taylor, *Pioneering*, pp. 86, 88; Wendt and Kogan, *Lords of the Levee*, pp. 294–95; Lewis and Smith, *Chicago*, pp. 351, 344–46.

[29] Harrison, *Stormy Years*, p. 308; quoted in Taylor, *Pioneering*, pp. 93, 86, Clifford W. Barnes, "The Story of the Committee of Fifteen of Chicago," *Social Hygiene*, IV (April, 1918), 146–47; Graham Taylor, "Vice Commission Facts to Reckon With," *Daily News* (Chicago), April 29, 1911.

[30] *Daily News* (Chicago), September 28, 1912; Wendt and Kogan, *Lords of the Levee*, p. 300; Lewis and Smith, *Chicago*, p. 342; Asbury, *Gem of the Prairie*, pp. 297–298.

year by Ada and Minna Everleigh. A copy of their "audacious advertising" fell into the hands of Carter H. Harrison and even he was shocked by the "full page half-tone illustrations of the various show-rooms, the Japanese Room, the Turkish Room, the Persian Room, the Room of a Thousand Mirrors." What disturbed him most of all, however, was "a caption to the effect that for the visitor to Chicago there were two outstanding points of interest: the Union Stockyards with the packing-houses and the Everleigh Club." Unknowingly the "terrible pair of sisters" had delivered a "solemn warning" to the mayor. Beset on all sides by demands for reform, including a plea from the city council which had finally endorsed the Vice Commission's recommendations, Harrison agreed to abandon his policy of toleration. In a public statement he admitted that

> my ideas of the vice question have been wrong. I have no hesitancy in subscribing to the general indictment of the segregation plan. . . . Chicago is through with the segregated vice idea. There isn't anything that a conscientious person can say now in support of segregation.[31]

The mayor's new policy was repression. He abruptly closed the Everleigh Club and launched a series of raids on other Levee attractions. Scores of madames and inmates were arrested, and city or state police padlocked most of the houses. The leaders of Levee society accepted this action philosophically, though a few tried to retaliate by hastily forming their own Committee of Fifteen which ordered the girls to dress in their gaudiest apparel and invade Chicago's exclusive residential areas asking for shelter. The legitimate committee ignored this sideshow and rejoiced instead in the comforting Chicago *Tribune* announcement that "the open, tolerated, police regulated, segregated district is gone from Chicago. A single, smashing blow . . . has accomplished the task."[32]

Such jubilation was premature, for the raids of 1912 and 1913 did not succeed in driving the oldest profession out of Chicago. The reformers, however, did make progress for a few years. Stricter local and state laws regulated the use of real estate for illicit purposes. The connections among gambling, prostitution, and police protection were thoroughly probed. The city established a Morals Court in 1913 and a Morals Commission two years later. Furthermore, Chicago's war on vice was widely publicized throughout the country and provided direction for other communities. When Taylor looked

---

[31] Harrison, *Stormy Years*, pp. 309, 310, 311; quoted in Taylor, *Pioneering*, p. 93; Wendt and Kogan, *Lords of the Levee*, pp. 296–97; Lewis and Smith, *Chicago*, p. 346; Peterson, *Barbarians in our Midst*, p. 93.

[32] Harrison, *Stormy Years*, pp. 310, 311; Wendt and Kogan, *Lords of the Levee*, pp. 296–301; Lewis and Smith, *Chicago*, pp. 349–50; Asbury, *Gem of the Prairie*, 299–308; quoted in Wendt and Kogan, *Lords of the Levee*, p. 302.

back on these dramatic events from the late 1920's, he credited the Vice Commission and the Committee of Fifteen with proving that "a body of authenticated facts may be trusted to reverse public opinion and turn it from relying upon a refuge of lies." Yet at the very moment Taylor was congratulating his fellow citizens, they were ready to return William Hale Thompson to office and he was ready to subject Chicago to another siege of not only toleration of segregated vice but open encouragement of city-wide vice and crime.[33]

III

Graham Taylor's interest in industrial relations stemmed in part from his civic consciousness and in part from his commitment to the social gospel. Christian principles, he insisted, were applicable to industrial problems. Until men translated their religion "into terms of economic value," it would mean "mighty little to anyone in an industrial age." Moreover, the social settlements ought to be directly concerned with industrial relations. Addressing the National Conference of Charities and Correction in 1896, Taylor said, "From Toynbee's day to this hour the *raison d'être* of the social settlement movement . . . has been the recognition of social democracy." These "households of social democrats" should actively seek to promote co-operation between employers and employees. Some houses would be able to do more than others, but it was clear to the warden of Chicago Commons that "a settlement with no relation to the industrial movement is trying to play Hamlet by leaving Hamlet out."[34]

Taylor also emphasized the need to put industrial problems in historic perspective. He felt that the two most important lessons revealed by the history of labor were "respect for the rights of the industrial classes, and trust in the power of legislation to attain and maintain them." In his teaching at Chicago Theological Seminary, the University of Chicago, and the Chicago School of Civics and Philanthropy he devoted a great deal of time to labor history. During 1896 and 1897 he published a series of articles in *The Commons* tracing the movement from the middle ages to the present. In addition, the pieces he contributed to *The Survey*, many of his *Daily News* columns,

[33] Lewis and Smith, *Chicago*, p. 351; Asbury, *Gem of the Prairie*, p. 289; Taylor, *Pioneering*, p. 94.

[34] Graham Taylor, "The Principles of Christianity Applied to Industrial Problems," *Minutes, National Council of Congregational Churches, 1904*, p. 96; Graham Taylor, "An Industrial Sermon, Being an Address . . . Delivered at the Boston Industrial Exhibit, April 12, 1907," p. 7; Graham Taylor, "The Social Settlement and The Labor Movement," National Conference of Charities and Correction, *Proceedings, 1896*, p. 143; Graham Taylor, "Social Settlements in Industrial Crises," *Daily News* (Chicago), May 23, 1903; Graham Taylor, "Whither the Settlement Movement Tends," *Charities and The Commons*, XV (March 3, 1906), 842.

and the speeches he delivered in Chicago and throughout the country, all attempted to put the industrial problem in historic perspective.[35]

Over the years Taylor spoke to many union gatherings and to organizations of employers. Both capital and labor, he told them, had the right to organize and bargain collectively, but both must seek to understand the other's point of view and both must be willing to compromise. He warned them that narrow economic partisanship was as dangerous as blind political partisanship. He also reminded both groups of their joint responsibility to help assimilate immigrants into the American melting pot. Taylor refused to accept the charge that recent arrivals were lowering wages or the standard of living or that they increased pauperism or delinquency. He strongly urged both capital and labor to practice "an open diplomacy at home" by welcoming the newcomers "who seek the right to live and labor with us."[36]

Taylor knew, however, that honest and inevitable differences between capital and labor would sometimes lead to conflict. This necessitated impartial arbitration, a task which he was willing to perform. Taylor was frequently asked to settle industrial disputes, for both sides realized that he stood between the lines, between the "upper and nether millstone," as he once put it. He soon learned that

> Failure to secure at the beginning . . . the fairest and most explicit understanding as to just what is to arbitrated, the scope of inquiry, the nature of the evidence to be considered relevant and the time within which a decision must be rendered is almost fatal.

He preferred to talk directly with the two parties in conflict rather than render a decision upon evidence submitted to him as the impartial arbiter. For in direct conversations he could remind the disputants that the third and most important party to every struggle was the public, "whose rights the other two parties are bound to respect."[37]

One of the earliest conflicts which Taylor tried to resolve was that between the Building Contractors' Association and the Building Trades' Council

[35] Taylor, "The Social Settlement and the Labor Movement," National Conference of Charities and Correction, *Proceedings, 1896*, pp. 146, 147.

[36] Graham Taylor, "Industrial Faith a Right and a Duty," *Daily News* (Chicago), October 4, 1919; Graham Taylor, "Distribution and Assimilation of Immigrants, Report for the Committee," National Conference of Charities and Correction, *Proceedings, 1913*, p. 30; Graham Taylor, "Foreign Born Citizens as Political Assets," National Conference of Social Work, *Proceedings, 1918*, pp. 452, 456.

[37] Graham Taylor, "Waymarks of Labor Day," *The Survey*, XXII (September 4, 1909), 738; Taylor, "An Industrial Sermon," p. 9; Graham Taylor, "Arbitration of Industrial Differences," *Daily News* (Chicago), April 25, 1903; Taylor, *Pioneering*, p. 143; Graham Taylor, "The Spirit for a Peaceful Reconstruction of Industry "(manuscript).

during 1899 and 1900. His proposal for an impartial investigating commission was approved by the unions but rejected by the contractors on the grounds that there was nothing to arbitrate. By the spring of 1901 the employers had broken up the Building Trades' Council. Meanwhile, construction on the new Chicago Commons building had been resumed in August, 1900. When it was finished Taylor invited the workmen to a housewarming. The Carpenters' Union, however, refused to attend, for, in the words of one orator, "the floor beams cry to the rafters 'scab-built,' 'scab-built'!" Taylor immediately hired a nearby hall, requested the members to hear his side of the story, and in the end won a vote of confidence on this resolution: "That Chicago Commons' building be expurgated from all offense." [38]

During 1903, Taylor was busy arbitrating a shoe workers' strike, a dispute between employers and the union in the Chicago Wholesale Drug Houses, and a third conflict involving the carriage and wagon makers' organization. When the Teamsters' Union, under the erratic leadership of Cornelius P. Shea, suddenly called a sympathetic strike in 1905 and tied up the entire city of Chicago, Mayor Dunne asked Taylor to serve on a Commission of Inquiry to discover the facts. Taylor agreed to do so, but since neither side would testify before the commission, he could only register his disgust for the leaders of both groups in his *Daily News* column. On still another occasion, Taylor agreed to hear the grievances of a shop crew that had been asked to use new machinery which turned out fewer pieces per hour. The union demanded increased pay for piecework. Taylor stood behind each machine off and on for several days and then decided that a small increase should be granted. Almost overnight the new machines disappeared, and the old ones were brought up from storage. The employers, it seemed, had merely been trying out the new equipment, and, faced with the unhappy prospect of having to pay higher wages, they quickly retrieved the old machines.[39]

On the whole, Taylor found labor arbitration a thankless job. Each side "wanted its own way, or no way at all." So his rulings were often considered "an intolerable compromise by both." Taylor sometimes spent weeks on a single case, but he steadfastly refused to accept any pay for his services. Nor would he let either side contribute to the settlement treasury. Labor arbitration, he stoutly insisted, was "a duty of citizenship" which needed no compensation and deserved no reward.[40]

[38] Quoted in Taylor, *Pioneering*, pp. 118, 119.
[39] *The Commons*, VIII (May, 1903), 19; Graham Taylor, "Aftermath of Chicago Teamsters' Strike," *Charities*, XIV (September 16, 1905), 1088–89; Taylor, *Pioneering*, pp. 138–40, 144.
[40] Taylor, *Pioneering*, p. 144.

More satisfying was his service on investigative and legislative commissions. Two Chicago mayors named him to committees dealing with unemployment. He was a member of the Advisory Committee of the Illinois Free Employment Offices from 1915 to 1917. Moreover, Governor Charles Deneen in 1908 appointed Taylor as a representative of the public interest to the Illinois Industrial Commission, a group authorized to investigate and recommend legislation protecting the health, safety, and comfort of employees in factories, stores, mills, and shops throughout the state. The following year the commission submitted a carefully written bill that would guard employees against dangerous machinery, hazardous places of employment, and unsanitary working conditions. Despite stiff opposition in the legislature the measure became law. On the national level Taylor joined the Child Labor Committee in 1904 and was a member of its advisory board in the postwar period.[41]

As a member of the Illinois Mining Investigation Commission, Taylor was directly concerned with a tragic mine disaster in Cherry, Illinois, in 1909. Shortly after the commission had been appointed, its members went to Cherry where a fire had killed 274 men. This was a "never to be forgotten" experience for Taylor, one which he vividly described in articles at the time and recounted in dramatic detail in his autobiography twenty years later. As Lea Taylor knew, few who heard his "first-hand account of that great tragedy . . . would ever forget." Certainly this was true for Albert J. Kennedy, who was

> sitting with Miss Addams in the rotunda office of Hull House, when Graham Taylor appeared without announcement or preamble, fresh from a visit to the scene of the Cherry Mine disaster. For half an hour, through sobs and tears he could not stay, he told of the agonies which the families of the imprisoned men were suffering, and the superhuman toil and bravery of their fellow workmen trying to reach them. I became sensible on that day of yet another dimension in the universe.[42]

Cherry was a dreary, dirty, grim town of some two thousand Italian, Lithuanian, Slavic, and Austrian immigrants, who lived in dwellings that looked to Taylor more like "tents or shacks" than homes. Most of the men were at work in the mine when the fire broke out. It was started apparently by two boys, one under the legal working age, who pushed a cart of hay beneath a

[41] Taylor, *Pioneering*, pp. 159, 160; Earl R. Beckner, *A History of Illinois Labor Legislation* (Chicago, 1929), pp. 417–18, 231–33, 239; Graham Taylor, "Industrial Survey of the Month," *The Survey*, XXII (July 3, 1909), 523–26; Gertrude F. Zimand to Lea D. Taylor, March 30, 1953.

[42] Taylor, *Pioneering*, p. 162, chap. xiii; Lea D. Taylor, "The Social Settlement and Civic Responsibility — The Life Work of Mary McDowell and Graham Taylor," p. 38; Albert J. Kennedy, "Graham Taylor and Amelia Earhart," *Neighborhood*, I (July, 1928), 3.

dripping oil torch. By the time the flames ignited the mine timbers, the boys and the men at the shaft had fled, leaving all the others to their fate. Amateur rescue teams were unable to reach the trapped men, and it was decided to seal the entrances to the mine while the fire burned itself out. Taylor kept vigil with the "little broken family circles" who "sat from early morning until late evening. . . . wistfully looking at the sealed sepulcher of their unburied dead. . . . Their dumb silence of grief was broken only by the undertone of sighs from the women and by the prattle of their little children." When at last the mine was opened, volunteers retrieved the charred bodies and released nineteen survivors who miraculously had sealed themselves off from the smoke and poisonous fumes.[43]

Meantime, the American Red Cross, United Mine Workers, religious groups, social agencies, and other organizations joined hands to help the stricken families. Thousands of dollars poured into the Cherry Relief Commission which was skilfully administered by Taylor's friend and former student, James Mullenbach. The coroner's inquiry, at which Taylor represented the Mining Investigation Commission, placed responsibility upon the mine owners for failing to observe safety measures and to provide trained fire-fighting teams. Within a short time the Illinois Mining Investigation Commission submitted three bills to the state legislature: one regulating fire-fighting equipment, another establishing fire-fighting troops and rescue stations in the mining centers, and the third calling for special mining technical institutes. Eventually the three measures became law. In addition, Senator Shelby M. Cullom of Illinois used the Cherry mine catastrophe to persuade Congress in 1910 to create a Federal Bureau of Mines.[44]

Taylor's role in improving industrial relations and backing progressive legislation was significant. For almost forty years he preached industrial democracy to students, settlement residents, social workers, politicians, clubs and associations, and the reading public. Young ministers left Chicago Theological Seminary to impress upon their parishioners the rights and responsibilities of capital and labor; settlement and social workers argued for honest trade unionism among wage-earners; readers of *The Commons, The Survey*, and the Chicago *Daily News* often heard of their duties as the third party to every industrial conflict. Taylor took pride in the widening effects of this work. He was especially heartened by Mullenbach's later career as permanent arbitrator for the Amalgamated Clothing Workers and Hart, Schaffner and Marx and also by the city-wide impact of his Seminary lectures on industrial arbitration. Taylor never lost his optimistic faith in organized labor's "peaceful

---

[43] Taylor, *Pioneering*, pp. 163, 162, 170, 164, 167.
[44] Taylor, *Pioneering*, pp. 165–66, 171–73; Beckner, *Illinois Labor Legislation*, pp. 300–02.

and evolutionary and triumphant struggle for justice and equity." Nor did he ever shirk his civic responsibility to stand steadfast between the upper and nether millstone. In the words of Robert A. Woods of South End House, Boston, the warden of Chicago Commons was a national leader in carrying out "the original settlement motive of inter-class reconciliation." [45]

<h2 style="text-align:center">IV</h2>

In Lea Taylor's opinion her father's greatest influence on local public opinion was the column he wrote for the Chicago *Daily News*. Many members of the newspaper staff agreed. On completion of Taylor's thirty-fifth year as a weekly columnist, they praised his contributions to the editorial page in these words:

> His articles have breathed the spirit of democracy and sane liberalism. They have pulsated with the sense of justice and brotherhood. In their sequence they have told the story of society's advance toward a better order. They have noted the detours, the obstructions, the gains and losses. They have enlightened and admonished and exhorted, and always with a sturdy faith in the possibility of realizing the good life for all mankind.[46]

Shortly after Taylor's arrival in Chicago in 1892 he found that Victor F. Lawson's *Daily News* was "the most reliable, fair and open-minded, independent and progressive, of all the city newspapers, with few rivals in these respects elsewhere." Three years later, when Taylor was secretary of the newly-formed Chicago Federation of Settlements, he offered to send Lawson "an occasional half column of matter . . . on the work of the settlements." Though Lawson considered it "very wise to keep in close touch with Professor Taylor and to lead in this department of labor and sociology," nothing came of these early negotiations. It was not until 1902 that Taylor was asked to write a weekly column for the *Daily News* on "current events from the settlement point of view." His first article appeared on November 22, 1902, under the title "Social Aspects of Life and Labor." Early in 1903 the format was changed to a pattern which it followed until the 1930's: a two-column spread with the heading "By Graham Taylor" and a descriptive subtitle.[47]

---

[45] Taylor, *Chicago Commons*, pp. 262–65; Graham Taylor, "Class Conflict in America," *American Journal of Sociology*, XIII (May, 1908), 770; Robert A. Woods, "Chicago Commons, its First Quarter-Centennial," *The Survey*, XLII (May 24, 1919), 309.

[46] Lea D. Taylor, "The Social Settlement and Civic Responsibility — The Life Work of Mary McDowell and Graham Taylor," p. 38; "A Salute to a Veteran," *Daily News* (Chicago), November 7, 1937.

[47] Taylor, *Pioneering*, pp. 429, 330; Victor F. Lawson to Charles H. Dennis, December 9, 1895, Charles H. Dennis Collection, Newberry Library.

Throughout these years Taylor met this weekly commitment to the *Daily News* with "unprecedented faithfulness." Sometimes, he admitted, it was "hard to grind out the material irrespective of all else I have to do, or wherever I may be." Yet there were surprisingly few times that illness, travel schedules, or pressure of other work interfered. The compensation for these articles was small, but it did help to augment Taylor's income. For the first fifteen years he received $10 per column. Following a delicate hint to Lawson in 1917, the rate was increased to $18, and in 1937 it reached $20. From time to time Taylor submitted shorter unsigned pieces to the editorial page, and for these he was paid the regular space rates.[48]

Lawson scrupulously observed his agreement never to alter copy without the author's consent. He insisted, however, that the *Daily News* was responsible for all opinions expressed on the editorial page, even those "By Graham Taylor." The paper would be "open to criticism of inconsistency . . . were we to publish . . . contrary views on the editorial page." Taylor did his best to co-operate. In a "cranky crisis" he would revise his manuscript three or four times before dispatching it, and if he still expected trouble, he would send it in a day early so the staff had plenty of time to study it. On the few occasions when Taylor's prose struck Lawson as too "aggressively inconsistent," the two men would meet for lunch and "have it out." Usually they reached a quick understanding and *"came out together* as *Christian men."* Taylor remembered one session in 1920 during the Red Scare when Lawson was watching the editorial page very closely. He took offense at a column in which Taylor discussed the historical role of the church in social crises.

> Upon re-reading it to me over the lunch table, however, he passed each incident as the statement of a historical fact, until we came to the last one. Without quotation, the birth hour of the church was referred to as one in which the new brotherhood of man was proclaimed and exemplified by having their possessions in common and parting them as everyone had need. This he challenged as too radical to be published. But when I assured him that not I, but St. Luke, was responsible for stating that fact in the fourth chapter of the Acts of the Apostles, he laughed merrily, threw up his hands and said, "Let it all go in." [49]

There were only eight times that Taylor's weekly column failed to appear in the *Daily News*. Two omissions were due to delays in cabling copy from

[48] Charles H. Dennis to Graham Taylor, September 11, 1937; Graham Taylor to Victor F. Lawson, February 11, 1913, October 4, 1917; Victor F. Lawson to Graham Taylor, October 12, 1917; Hal O'Flaherty to Graham Taylor, September 29, 1937.

[49] Taylor, *Pioneering*, p. 430; telegram from Victor F. Lawson to Graham Taylor, quoted in a letter from Charles H. Dennis to Graham Taylor, September 15, 1916; Taylor, Diary, February 8, 1917, September 16, 1916, February 4, 1921; Victor F. Lawson to Graham Taylor, September 16, 1916; Taylor, *Pioneering*, p. 433.

abroad — once when he was in Europe before the outbreak of the war and again when he was traveling in the Far East in 1922. The other six occasions resulted from clashes of opinion between editor and columnist. In September, 1916, Lawson rejected an article on a railroad strike because he felt Taylor had made a "fundamental error as to both facts and conclusions." Shortly afterwards he refused to print Taylor's endorsement of President Wilson, though in several other elections Taylor was allowed to back his candidate while the *Daily News* supported the opponent. In January, 1920, Taylor prepared a column criticizing Attorney General A. Mitchell Palmer's treatment of alleged radicals. Lawson objected, and Taylor's copy did not survive the ensuing lunch-table analysis. It was, however, carefully preserved. Entitled "Are We Playing With Two-Edged Swords?" the article warned that violation of civil liberties in the name of national security was a two-edged sword that could "strike back" at the one who used it.

> We may rightly be disturbed by the discovery that some among us want to change the form of our government and threaten to do so by force. Of course, we can neither deny the right to change anything in America by lawful procedures guaranteed by the constitution, nor tolerate the use of force in making any change. But does any one really believe that there are enough revolutionary radicals in America to warrant any uncertainty about the security of American democracy? . . . Need a nation that defeated the German military power be in a panic over the arrest of 5,000 or more aliens accused of revolutionary aims, but not even suspected of having any available means for carrying them out? Does not this very token of fright prompt the courage and persistence of defiance? [50]

Only a handful of articles were rejected, while more than 1,800 columns "By Graham Taylor" were printed in the Chicago *Daily News*. Approximately one-third of these were devoted to "political policies, candidates, and conspiracies," as the author put it, that is, to problems of local, state, and national government. Almost as many dealt with social work, the settlements, and public welfare agencies. One hundred and seventy-seven columns discussed industrial relations, while sixty-two focused attention on religious developments. Taylor's observations while traveling in Europe and the Far East filled ninety-six columns. Half that number praised American social and civic leaders. Taylor felt deeply about his "rare opportunity" to fill a "ministry of understanding and interpretation" with these weekly essays.

[50] Taylor, *Chicago Commons*, p. 289; telegram from Victor F. Lawson to Graham Taylor, quoted in a letter from Charles H. Dennis to Graham Taylor, September 15, 1916; Taylor, *Pioneering*, pp. 430, 432; Graham Taylor, "Are We Playing With Two-Edged Swords?" (manuscript).

And he frequently referred to his position on the editorial page of the *Daily News* as his "civic pulpit."[51]

In drafting these articles Taylor always tried to get "as nearly underneath and inside" his subject as possible and to write "in a constructively critical manner." Edward Price Bell, a *Daily News* colleague, felt he succeeded:

> Of Dr. Graham Taylor himself there is nothing, yet everything, in what he writes. The story is the thing. He wants the reader to hear something he has heard, to see something he has seen, to be moved by something which has moved him. He is a reporter, really, and a vivid one, but a reporter who continually mounts from fact and description into philosophy.

Charles Dennis, Lawson's successor, once told Taylor that he looked forward to the Saturday edition because of the "customary (and invariably beneficial) mental-and-spiritual draft with your reliable name blown in the bottle as a guaranty of its quality."[52]

Yet the quality of these 1,800 editorials was not always even. Some dealt with ephemeral topics; others were repetitious. Taylor usually wrote in a clear, straight-forward style, but he was capable of burying ideas in clumsy, long-winded sentences. Furthermore, his chronic optimism must have tried the patience of many Chicagoans. Jane Addams, for one, observed that Taylor's "personal attitude toward this multitude of readers has been, if I may be permitted to formulate it, a little like that of the good country pastor toward the flock, which is on the whole well meaning and humbly anxious to be good but occasionally needs exhortation."[53]

Though she may have been critical at times of the preacher in Taylor, Jane Addams was quick to recognize that "an astonishing number of people cherish this regular communication with a man whom they profoundly admire and devotedly follow." Many of them told Taylor the same thing. "Business men not a few whom I meet in the clubs and on the streets stop me to say so. Street car conductors, other workingmen and labor leaders ask me questions about what I have written. . . . And one old Negro woman said

[51] Taylor, *Pioneering*, p. 434; Nels F. Nordstrom, "Social Interpretations of Modern Democracy, A Study of Dr. Graham Taylor's Daily News Editorials" (Bachelor of Divinity Thesis, Chicago Theological Seminary, 1936), iv–v; Inscription written by Graham Taylor in Mabel A. Hawkins' copy of *Chicago Commons Through Forty Years*, Christmas, 1937; Graham Taylor, "Response of Graham Taylor," p. 7; Graham Taylor to Victor F. Lawson, February 11, 1913. Nordstrom based his research upon the 1,697 columns appearing between November, 1902, and July, 1935.

[52] Taylor, *Pioneering*, p. 434; Edward Price Bell, "The Marching World," (manuscript); Charles H. Dennis to Graham Taylor, September 11, 1937.

[53] Jane Addams, "Graham Taylor: Pioneer in Sociology," *Chicago Theological Seminary Register*, XVIII (November, 1928), 22.

she had 'clipped and pasted' every one of my articles." These loyal fans probably shared the feeling of Governor Henry Horner, who wrote from Springfield that he followed Taylor's columns because he knew "whether 'for or against' they come from a conscientious and understanding source."[54]

Taylor's friends on the *Daily News* felt the same way. They admired the "passion for service" which kept him "working at high pressure all the time." How he "managed to . . . carry out his multitudinous plans and programs" was a mystery they could never solve. Said one of them,

> the ding of the telephone, directions to his helpers, meetings without number, the rush to catch trolleys and elevated trains, in time for the lecture hours at the Seminary, to say nothing of financial needs, ever enlarging and pressing, amazed me as I found Dr. Taylor equal to all his varied tasks.

Charles Dennis, who had frequent personal and telephone contact with this human dynamo, could not recall a single conversation in which he failed to discover that Taylor "was then on his way to undertake some service for the benefit of this community, or that he had just come from such a service."[55]

This overriding concern for the public welfare was bound to be reflected in the columns "By Graham Taylor," and thousands of readers responded to it. Edward Price Bell had this in mind when he referred to Taylor as "a delightful journalist," but added, "He is also, in his fundamental conceptions, a great journalist. He knows what newspapers ought to be in their ethical substructure. He knows they should be granite for what is right." As a columnist for the Chicago *Daily News*, as a political reformer, as a labor arbitrator, and as a civil servant, Taylor was indeed "granite" for what he considered right. Victor F. Lawson had good reason to call him the "Conscience of Chicago."[56]

[54] Jane Addams, "Graham Taylor: Pioneer in Sociology," p. 22; Graham Taylor to Charles H. Dennis, November 16, 1927, quoted in Taylor, *Chicago Commons*, p. 290; Henry Horner to Graham Taylor, January 28, 1935.

[55] Quoted in Taylor, *Chicago Commons*, p. 291; Sanford, *Origin and History of the Federal Council of Churches*, pp. 55–56.

[56] Edward Price Bell, "The Marching World."

Eight ✕ *Pioneer for Social Justice*

Taylor remarked to his daughter in 1925 that he thought he had squeezed "about as much out of life's machinery & for as long a time of continuous action as any one else." In fact, he traveled in high gear until the last decade of his life, and even then he only slowed to second. Though retired from Chicago Theological Seminary and no longer the director of Chicago Commons, he kept in close touch with both institutions, wrote two more books, and continued his *Daily News* column on a weekly basis until the infirmities of old age finally brought him to a halt. Tall, spare of frame, and endowed with great energy, Taylor also enjoyed remarkably good health and good luck. Except for the sickness in his early childhood and typhoid fever in Hartford, he had no major illnesses. In a lifetime of constant travel his only accident occurred in 1917 when, dashing behind the rear of a street car, he was struck by an automobile and suffered a fractured rib.[1]

He worked at a feverish pace, often writing, dictating, or preparing lectures far into the early hours of the morning. More than once he apologized to his secretary, Mabel A. Hawkins, for "the long days, irregular hours and uneven pressures, which I cannot seem to escape myself or spare those who work with me." The secret of his physical endurance, he thought, lay in the fact that he "did have sense enough to rest when tired out." Since it was almost impossible to do that at Chicago Commons, he would retreat either to the Macatawa cottage or to the home which he began building in 1913 in Ravinia, a suburb north of Chicago. A few days at Macatawa, "away from constant calls, free from bells, . . . make me over in a surprisingly short time," he told his daughter. "How much we miss by staying indoors and in town so much!" During the years that his children were away at school, the family reunions at Macatawa in the summer were an even greater pleasure. Yet he continued to work at the cottage, reporting to Mabel Hawkins

---

[1] Graham Taylor to Lea D. Taylor, January 22, 1925; Percy Alden, "Graham Taylor: An Appreciation," *The Commons*, I (August, 1897), 2; Taylor, Diary, February 28, 1917.

on one occasion that he had answered all the correspondence and "worked off Daily News this morning. I have yet reviews to write, 'Ch[urch] & Com[munity]' copy to prepare, proof of book to read & some reading for my School lectures on Govt. to do — quite enough to occupy half-time until the middle of September — Then the deluge!"[2]

A well-developed sense of humor kept him from taking things too seriously. Taylor's ready wit enlivened many a dull conference and some, though not all, of his articles. His fellow social workers, his friends among the business community, and his students appreciated his ability to note "the humorous, even as he sees the tragic, side of life." Years after his graduation from the seminary, one former student wrote that he could still see Taylor

> standing amidst the old ways and theologies, shaking his fist and shouting, "I tell you, life is larger than logic," looking so fiercely revolutionary for one . . . apprehensive moment, then with a laugh and a gesture brushing the tension into a corner, for you could only cherish the funny side even of scribes and Pharisees.[3]

Taylor knew, as did all of his close associates, that one of the most important ingredients in his successful career was his wife's unfailing courage and devotion. Without her support, he claimed, he would never have taken "the next step onward in the surprising life I have lived." Leah Demarest Taylor deliberately stayed in the background, but she was both an attentive mother to their four children and an intelligent, wise counselor to her busy husband. He conferred with her on every major decision, and he realized that her "gentle incentives & restraints" made his life as "serviceable" and "as happy as it has been." Her death, after a lingering illness through the spring and early summer of 1918, was a hard blow. Of the scores of letters that poured into his office from former residents and staff members the most eloquent was Julia Lathrop's simple telegram expressing gratitude "for her lovely quiet steady generous life."[4]

Taylor remained at his post through 1918 and 1919, struggling with the financial crisis of the Chicago School of Civics and Philanthropy and running Draft Board 39 in addition to his regular teaching and settlement work.

[2] Graham Taylor to Mabel A. Hawkins, August 4, 27, 1913, Hawkins Papers; Graham Taylor to Lea D. Taylor, January 22, 1925; interview with Lea D. Taylor and Katharine Taylor, December 28, 1953; Graham Taylor to Lea Taylor, May 22, 1904, in the possession of Lea Taylor.

[3] S. J. Duncan-Clark, "A Friend of Mankind, Dr. Graham Taylor's Eighty Years," *Daily News* (Chicago), May 1, 1931; Roy E. Bowers to Graham Taylor, September 2, 1930.

[4] Graham Taylor to Graham Romeyn Taylor, March 16, 1938; Graham Taylor to Lea D. Taylor, March 18, 1926; Taylor, Diary, July 22, 25, 1918; Telegram from Julia Lathrop to Graham Taylor, July 26, 1918.

In the spring of 1920, however, he took a two-month trip to California. The following year, after the merger of his training school with the University of Chicago, he made another visit to the West Coast, and this time he chanced to meet a widowed cousin and former childhood playmate from New Brunswick, Isabella Bishop McClintock. He was pleased to find that she still possessed "the same bright mind" and "eager intellectual interests" that had made her so attractive as a young girl. In November, 1921, they were married and shortly afterwards departed on a six-month tour of the Far East.[5]

During the next few years the Taylors divided their time between her home in Pasadena and his in Ravinia. Fall and early winter were usually spent in Chicago, for Taylor kept an eye on developments at the Commons and generally taught a semester course at the seminary. The house in Ravinia was located in a densely-wooded plot adjacent to Helen Taylor Carr's residence. It was Taylor's favorite refuge, a perfect place for "righting up after disturbed, interrupted" work in the city. In these pleasant surroundings he began to write his autobiography, turning himself "inside out . . . so that those nearest and dearest to me will understand every motive." This happy life came to an abrupt end on January 1, 1926, when his second wife died of a heart attack. Once again Graham Taylor found himself alone, facing "the dusk I dreaded to enter."[6]

He did, however, have a measure of financial security in the last decade of his life that he had never experienced before. Somehow he had been able to support his family and educate his children on a meager income consisting primarily of $3,000 a year from the seminary until 1909, and thereafter $1,500 because of his reduced teaching load. His articles for the *Daily News* "never yielded more than about $1,000 a year," while his salary checks from the Chicago School of Civics and Philanthropy were small and extremely irregular. A legacy from Leah Demarest Taylor's family paid for the construction of the Macatawa cottage, and Taylor's brothers helped send at least one of the girls through college. In addition, friends helped in various ways: the Cranes provided steamship tickets when the Taylors made a second trip to Europe in 1911; Julius Rosenwald celebrated his fiftieth birthday by distributing $687,500 in public gifts, $2,500 of which went to Graham Taylor as "a debt of gratitude for the many sacrifices you have made during the many years you have worked for a better Chicago."[7]

[5] Taylor, Diary, April 17, 18, 1921.

[6] Taylor, Diary, December 10, 1910; Graham Taylor to Lea D. Taylor and Katharine Taylor, August 26, 1922; Taylor, Diary, January 1, 1926, September 21, 1921.

[7] Graham Taylor to Edward T. Devine, January 27, 1912; Graham Taylor to Albert W. Palmer, January 4, 1937; interview with Lea D. Taylor and Katharine Taylor, December 28, 1953; Graham Taylor, "Notes of Family Sojourn Abroad," (manuscript), 1911; Werner, *Julius Rosenwald*, p. 104; Julius Rosenwald to Graham Taylor, August 12, 1912.

Taylor's seventieth birthday marked the turning point in his financial affairs. On that occasion the Edward L. Ryersons presented $25,000 to the Commons' endowment fund and specified that the income was to belong to Graham Taylor until his death. "Thus these just & generous friends," wrote the grateful recipient in his diary, "remove the only shadow on my horizon. Now at last my life's hope is realized to be *free* from 'temporal want & worldly care' to serve others, & burden none. A top-notch birthday." Free also "of any temptation to teach . . . longer than I should," he retired from the seminary in 1924. The next year Victor F. Lawson's bequest made it possible for the seminary to pay Taylor a $2,500 annual retirement benefit, enough to cover his living expenses at Ravinia. Furthermore, a share in his second wife's estate plus an unexpected legacy from a distant relative made Taylor's last years free of financial worry. After a family consultation in 1932 he drew up a will leaving the Ravinia property to Lea and the remainder of his estate in a family fund for "you 4 children to dispose of as you may think best."[8]

II

Shortly after Jane Addams described her first *Twenty Years at Hull-House* in 1910, Taylor's friends began urging him to write a similar book. He brushed off the idea at the time, and apparently never gave it serious thought until he had retired from the seminary and turned the settlement leadership over to Lea Taylor. His good friend John Palmer Gavit is the one who finally persuaded him to tackle his "literary remains," though Gavit later admitted, "I did not really expect you to complete it. When I urged you to get down on paper the record of your life and its impressions, I did so . . . chiefly because I thought I saw signs of your getting bogged in the consciousness of the advancing years."[9]

Not suspecting Gavit's motives at the time, Taylor took the bait and actually began writing in the summer of 1923.[10] He expected "to draft a *basic*

[8] Taylor, Diary, May 2, 1921; Graham Taylor to Lea D. Taylor and Katharine Taylor, August 26, 1922; Ozora S. Davis to Graham Taylor, February 19, 1926; Graham Taylor to Albert W. Palmer, January 4, 1937; Graham Romeyn Taylor to Graham Taylor, March 19, 1936; interview with Lea D. Taylor and Katharine Taylor, December 28, 1953; Graham Taylor to Graham Romeyn Taylor, February 14, 1932. In 1937, when Taylor learned that faculty salaries had been cut at Chicago Theological Seminary, he wrote the president and asked to have his own retirement payment reduced from $2500 to $1500 "at once." Graham Taylor to Robert W. Palmer, January 4, 1937, copy in the possession of Lea Taylor.

[9] Graham Taylor to William Rivers Taylor, April 9, 1912; John Palmer Gavit to Graham Taylor, February 8, 1923, April 6, 1930.

[10] By 1930, Taylor was on to his old friend Gavit. He wrote to his son, "Gavit really thought I would only gather the source materials, leaving you, or someone of 'the

copy" in Pasadena, "check up on its omissions & additions while in Chicago & to *revise*, or re-write the *whole* mess or mass in final form *here* next winter & spring." Two years later, in May of 1925, he was still writing, but "getting on so well . . . that I hope to finish my story — in the rough — before returning to Chicago." Yet it was not until January, 1928, that he completed the first version, and then he spent another six months condensing it. In July he wearily pronounced it "as good, and abbreviated, as *I* can make it, after six years of nearly continuous thought and many, many months of consecutive labor upon it."[11]

Lacking confidence in what he had written, Taylor submitted portions of the manuscript to friends for their opinion. Of course, they gave him conflicting advice. Some "criticized omissions as unhistorically misleading, while others warn me not to chronicle but be experiential!" Constructive criticism, however, did come from his son, Graham Romeyn Taylor, and from Gavit, both of whom were seasoned authors. In the early stages, Gavit sent a note of encouragement:

> Go on and get the stuff on paper, just as it comes to you. Don't try to make it consecutive, logical, or anything else. . . . You can arrange and patch and cement afterward.
> Another thing: Just so far as it is humanly possible, forget that you are writing a book, or for publication. . . . tell it to me, simply and directly . . . with frank statement of just how you felt and what you thought within yourself about this, that and the other Son of Belial that you happened to cross swords with at one time and another.

Later on Gavit cautioned him about writing from two different points of view.

> At one point you are writing an autobiography, telling the story of a personality; at the other you are absorbed in the more or less detached and objective history of a period. . . . to have unity and coherence you *must stand at one viewpoint and stay there.*

Many times he objected to his friend's "besetting literary sin": "long sentences," "long paragraphs," and "sesquipedalian words." If you "Squeeze out the preaching and let your story tell itself," promised Gavit, "the publishers will fight for it."[12]

---

younger generation,' to write it up! And you know I thought this might be best." Graham Taylor to Graham Romeyn Taylor, April 12, 1930.

[11] Graham Taylor to Mabel A. Hawkins, July 30, 1923, Hawkins Papers; Graham Taylor to Lea D. Taylor, May 2, 1925; Taylor, Diary, January 6, 1928; Graham Taylor to Graham Romeyn Talyor, July 15, 1928.

[12] Graham Taylor to Graham Romeyn Taylor, January 31, 1928; John Palmer Gavit to Graham Taylor, February 8, 1923, September 3, 1927.

The publishers, however, did not fight for it. Houghton Mifflin, Doubleday, and Harper and Brothers turned it down, and only after further revision did the University of Chicago Press agree to take it. Entitled *Pioneering on Social Frontiers*, the book finally appeared in June, 1930. Taylor divided his story into five sections. The first, "The Civic Front and Rear," was the hardest to write, for he was "stumped" by problems of organization. Eventually he decided to do it "biographically," by which he meant grouping the factual material on civic reform around the leading personalities. His experiences as labor arbitrator and his contacts with labor and industrial leaders here and in England were recounted in the second section, "In the Industrial Arena." Under the heading "Inter-racial Bonds and Breaches" he discussed problems of immigration, work of the draft board, and his European and Far Eastern travels. "The Social Settlement Movement" told the story of Chicago Commons, while the final section, "The Evolving Social Consciousness," analyzed his own social awakening.[13]

As autobiography *Pioneering on Social Frontiers* leaves much to be desired. Taylor never overcame the "self-consciousness" which Gavit complained about, nor did he ever resolve the conflict between the personal and the historical point of view. As a result the reader gets neither a comprehensive view of Chicago reform nor of Taylor's role in that movement. Surveying the final product, Gavit decided that his friend lacked that "capacity for self-appraisal" essential for "honest autobiography." Yet he considered the book a valuable

> history rather of a period than of a person. It is a period . . . to whose character and accomplishment Taylor himself has contributed possibly more than any other one person — the period in which the Protestant churches of America abandoned the old, purely individualistic, theology and began to take account of society as a whole, of the tremendous importance of social environment in determining human destiny.

The author of *Pioneering on Social Frontiers* agreed with these comments. He was satisfied to have written an account "of the *period* & of so many comrades . . . I meant it to be so, for *I* could not write what a biographer might have written."[14]

Reviewing the book for the New York *Times*, Robert L. Duffus called it "the autobiography of a Victorian liberal who has kept pace with the

[13] Graham Taylor to Katharine Taylor, February 1, 1928; Graham Taylor to Graham Romeyn Taylor, January 31, 1928.

[14] John Palmer Gavit to Graham Taylor, February 8, 1923; John Palmer Gavit, "Graham Taylor: His Book," *Saturday Review of Literature*, VII (July 26, 1930), 3; John Palmer Gavit, "At Home with Graham Taylor," p. 237; Graham Taylor to Graham Romeyn Taylor, April 12, 1930.

Georgian century." Taylor's main contribution was "his promotion of the spirit of reasonableness," for though his sympathies were with the oppressed, he was "a middle-of-the-roader when practical remedies are discussed." Speaking for his own generation, Duffus found many things about the book that would annoy "our more restless moderns." "It is not altogether scientific. It lacks a sharp sense of values. It tends to be uncritical. It often substitutes phrases for realities. It has not quite enough salt to suit sophisticated tastes." Yet he felt that Taylor's point of view must not be dismissed lightly. For the Victorian liberal had written a book defending religion, idealism, tolerance, goodwill, and optimism, qualities that had guided his generation of social pioneers. The "restless moderns" of the depression decade could use at least a portion of those old-fashioned virtues.[15]

Judging from the sale of *Pioneering on Social Frontiers*, it was out of tune with the times. Of the 1,538 copies published, only about 1,200 were sold. Taylor admitted that his $400 in royalties did not cover the cost of typing the manuscript. At the time he claimed that he "did not expect more and wrote the book for the sake of the cause." Yet shortly before his death he observed that the volume "should have been published ten years or more before in order to attract the attention of those most interested." As it was, by 1930 "the overlapping remnants of two generations had passed away, and the younger generations knew little and cared less about it all." In short, the Victorian liberal had "waited too late or worked too long."[16]

Taylor's third and final book, *Chicago Commons Through Forty Years*,

[15] Robert L. Duffus, "On Social Frontiers in Chicago," *New York Times Book Review*, July 6, 1930, 4. A Chicago anarchist named Ben Reitman had a different view of *Pioneering on Social Frontiers*. In a letter to Taylor he charged: "Your evaluation of the rich and powerful men is bourgeoise if not servile. . . . Your explanation of the anarchists and the radicals is patronizing but not illuminating. To me your book sounds like a speech before an exclusive lady society where you have to be careful what you say. On the whole your book left me disconsolate. Your optimism if sincere is impossible. . . . you know perfectly well that there is more unemployment, delinquency, perversion, police brutality, than when you, Jane Addams, and Mary McDowell started." Ben L. Reitman to Graham Taylor, June 16, 1931.

[16] S. Walker Findley to Louise G. Wade, April 6, 1954; Graham Taylor to Nathaniel M. Pratt, January 13, 1937; Graham Taylor to Graham Romeyn Taylor, April 12, 1930. Reviewers often compared Taylor's *Pioneering on Social Frontiers* with Jane Addams, *The Second Twenty Years at Hull-House*, which also appeared in 1930. These references made Taylor uneasy. To his son he wrote, " 'Little less useful than Hull House,' Chicago Commons is said to be. How *much* less, as *I always* have known, is measured by the 9,000 copies of The '2nd Twenty Years at H H' printed to meet initial orders, in contrast to the 900 copies sold of the 1st printing of my book, calling for only 500 copies of the second printing! This contrast is as it *should* be, & is mentioned because I am restive under the too close comparisons with J.A. & H.H. recently called forth, which I have never failed to discount, silently, if I could not do so openly!" Graham Taylor to Graham Romeyn Taylor, November 25, 1930.

was, in a sense, a continuation of his autobiography. Condensing the section on the settlement house in *Pioneering* had been a "perplexing problem" for Taylor. But he saved the discarded manuscript and remarked to his son as early as 1930 that some of it could "be included in my story of Chicago Commons later." The fortieth anniversary of the settlement in May, 1934, roused him to action and two years later the book was in print. With some assistance from his son and daughter, Taylor wrote the first thirteen chapters describing the founding and development of Chicago Commons. Lea Taylor discussed the settlement challenge in the depression decade, another staff member described the "Forthgoings of Former Residents," and the Commons secretary, Mabel Hawkins, contributed the final chapter, an account of the fortieth anniversary celebration.[17]

Although the University of Chicago Press asked to see the manuscript, Taylor did not submit it. He felt that few publishers "could afford to issue it" at the price "we wished to distribute it." Furthermore, "consistency demanded that it carry the union label which the press does not tolerate." So Chicago Commons Association advanced the funds to have 1,500 copies printed. Approximately one-third of these were sold at $1.50 each; the others were presented to libraries, former residents, friends of the settlement, and interested social workers. One reviewer thought *Chicago Commons Through Forty Years* lacked "the pithy wisdom and the felicitous phrase of the Hull House papers" and "the penetrating kindliness of Lillian Wald's volumes." But *The Survey* hailed it as "a first-hand notebook" of social welfare work. Meantime, the eighty-five year old author was quite content to think of his final book as a "tribute to cherished associates whose lives and deeds of service through these years have made Chicago Commons what it has been, is, and may become."[18]

III

During the last decade of his life Chicago honored Graham Taylor as one of its distinguished citizens. Dedication of the seminary's Graham Taylor Hall in 1928 gave James Mullenbach an opportunity to pay tribute to his former teacher's lifelong career of "social exploration and endeavor." The City Club, of which Taylor was a charter member, sponsored a testimonial dinner in May, 1930, and the following year the Municipal Voters' League gave him

[17] Graham Taylor to Graham Romeyn Taylor, July 23, 1927, April 6, 1930.

[18] Graham Taylor to Robert Gammon, January 1, 1937; Lea D. Taylor to Louise C. Wade, February 1, April 7, 1954; A. E. Fink, review of *Chicago Commons Through Forty Years*, in *Annals of the American Academy of Political and Social Science*, CXCII (July, 1937), 244; John Palmer Gavit, "A Settlement in Action," *The Survey*, LXXIII (March, 1937), 91; Graham Taylor to Roy Guild, December 16, 1936, Raymond Robins Papers.

an eightieth birthday party. When the Rotary Club surprised the aging civic patriot with its Chicago Merit Local Award in 1937 he accepted with his customary humility, thanking them for the chance to serve Chicago as "an unclassified social democrat" and asking each man to help sow "in this hate-spread world of ours the gospel of peace and good-will." [19]

The gathering which moved him most deeply, however, was the fortieth anniversary of Chicago Commons. Held the first week in May, 1934, it became a city-wide commemoration of Taylor's leadership in the settlement movement. Scores of former residents and seventeenth ward neighbors returned for the four-day reunion. Taylor was especially pleased by Charles Dennis' remarks on "The Civic Influence of Chicago Commons." For forty years, Dennis pointed out, "Chicago Commons has devoted itself to the work of being a good neighbor in a big way." From its center have radiated "progressive ideas and effective applied policies for the benefit of our citizens through improved community practices and better municipal housekeeping." Undoubtedly, many listeners agreed with the *Daily News* editor when he confided that "Keeping in touch with Dr. Taylor is the best way I know to keep one's social consciousness and one's social conscience in tune." [20]

Lea Demarest Taylor shared in these honors. Head resident of Chicago Commons since her father's retirement in 1922, she, of course, frequently discussed settlement policy with him, but the burden of responsibility was hers. Resembling her mother in physical appearance, she had inherited her father's intellectual spirit of adventure and her relationship with him was very close. A few months before his death Taylor asked his old friend Raymond Robins, "Do I not owe it both to the Commons and myself to place Lea first among equals in her distinctive service as head resident through this whole tumultuous decade and for sharing with me as I have shared with her a community of interests very rare in the lives of a father and daughter?" [21]

The passing of two of Chicago's triumvirate of pioneer settlement founders — Jane Addams and Mary McDowell — was a painful experience for Taylor. All three lived to an advanced age. When Mary McDowell remarked at the City Club dinner in 1930 that they ought to feel like an exhibit of

[19] James Mullenbach, "The Pioneer Work of the Church," *Chicago Theological Seminary Register*, XVIII (November, 1928), 14; testimonial statement presented to Graham Taylor by Municipal Voters' League, May 2, 1931; Graham Taylor, "Response of Graham Taylor to Chicago Merit Local Award, presented by Chicago Rotary Club — October 19, 1937" (manuscript); *Daily News* (Chicago), June 7, 1928, May 27, 1930, May 2, 1931, October 26, 1937.

[20] "Notes Taken by Lea D. Taylor of Graham Taylor's Remarks, 1936–38" (manuscript); quoted in Taylor, *Chicago Commons*, pp. 286, 287, 292, 288.

[21] Board of Trustees, Minutes of Meetings, December 29, 1921; Graham Taylor to Raymond Robins, December 30, 1937.

antiques, Taylor quipped that they were more like an exhibition of perennials. He knew, however, that time was running out. Jane Addams was the first to go. Her death in 1935 left Taylor overwhelmed with memories. When the family had first arrived in Chicago, it was "the mistress of Hull-House" who had taken them in, had admitted them "to her personal friendship, and through it to her understanding knowledge of this great city wilderness then so strange to me." She had encouraged and advised him in the establishment of Chicago Commons and the School of Civics and Philanthropy. Though he disagreed with her pacifist stand during the war, his devotion and admiration never diminished. At the simple funeral services held in the courtyard of Hull House, Taylor delivered the final prayer and benediction for his famous neighbor. Scarcely a year later, Mary McDowell passed away.[22]

One of those who attended Jane Addams' funeral, Secretary of the Interior, Harold L. Ickes, noted afterwards in his diary that "Dr. Graham Taylor, who is well over eighty . . . is showing his age." Taylor had begun to feel his infirmities long before. Shortly after his seventieth birthday he resorted to daily naps, "an experience *very strange*, after . . . years of incessant toil, many hours a day." By the time he reached his late seventies he had "to *move* slowly and live regularly to keep . . . my *first* wind up, for I am short on 'second wind'!" During the 1930's when he was in his eighties he spent most of his time at Ravinia, "closely tethered" to his "little cottage in the clearing." His eldest daughter Helen lived nearby, and Lea joined him on weekends, usually bringing social workers or settlement residents with her. Nonetheless, Taylor found it "hard to be out from under so much of what needs to be done at the Commons & in the city to meet this tragic . . . unemployment."[23]

He kept active with his *Daily News* column which he submitted weekly until September, 1937, and thereafter "as the spirit moves me. . . without any fixed date." During 1934, 1935, and 1936, he was working on *Chicago Commons Through Forty Years* and contributing occasional articles and book reviews to *The Survey*. He also corresponded with John Graham Brooks and Francis G. Peabody and sent frequent messages to Raymond Robins who had suffered a crippling accident in Florida. In addition, Taylor often

[22] Graham Taylor, "Jane Addams: The Great Neighbor," *Survey Graphic*, XXIV (July 1935), 338; *Daily News* (Chicago), May 23, 1935; Graham Taylor, "In Memoriam — Mary McDowell, 1854–1936," *Unity*, CXVIII (December 7, 1936), 129.

[23] Harold L. Ickes, *The Secret Diary of Harold L. Ickes, The First Thousand Days, 1933–1936* (New York, 1953), p. 367; Graham Taylor to Lea D. Taylor, July 29, 1923; Graham Taylor to Graham Romeyn Taylor, July 15, 1928; Graham Taylor to Margaret Dreier Robins, December 30, 1937; Graham Taylor to Lessing Rosenthal, November 29, 1937; Graham Taylor to Graham Romeyn Taylor, December 14, 1930.

wrote to the absent members of his family, his son in New York City, his daughter Katharine in Cambridge, Massachusetts, and his brothers Will and Livingston, both of whom had retired from the ministry and spent their summers in Keene Valley, New York. In July, 1938 he made the long journey east to renew the ties which have "kept us three old boy-brothers joyously together as life long play mates and work mates." [24]

But Graham Taylor was soon to depart from that "wonderfully unbroken family circle." He was experiencing recurrent intervals of dizziness and fatigue. His eyesight was failing and his hearing was "just about zero." Early in September he warned the family to "reckon, as I do, on my increasing weakness, with spells of uncontrollable drowsiness." Three weeks later, on September 26, 1938, he died quietly in his sleep. [25]

IV

Graham Taylor was a pioneer for social justice but not a pathfinder. Other men and women, he readily admitted, were the trailbreakers who "led the way and always inspired me to keep abreast of them in the adventures of social and civic faith." His contribution was one of "*broadening* the trails ahead of the rank-and-file." And as John Palmer Gavit observed, Taylor was uniquely fittted for that task because he had the "imagination and vision to find substance in the adventurings of those more recklessly radical then he . . . together with a certain naïve courage to stand forth and fight." Deeply sympathetic with social Christianity and aware of the urgent need for organized welfare work and civic reform, Taylor devoted his considerable talent and energy to promoting these movements. His application of the social gospel, his interpretation of economic problems for two generations of seminary students, his ability to impart his own settlement experience to young social workers, his desire to help the immigrant adjust to unfamiliar patterns of urban life, and his relentless battle for honest municipal government were substantial achievements in a lifetime of social pioneering. [26]

Taylor had the temperament of one who promotes rather than originates

[24] Graham Taylor to Paul Mowrer, August 31, 1937, January 24, 1938; Graham Taylor, "Trail Breaker in Labor Arena," *Daily News* (Chicago), February 19, 1938; Graham Taylor to Raymond Robins, November 8, 1935, Raymond Robins Papers; Graham Taylor to Mr. and Mrs. Raymond Robins, [?], 1937.

[25] Graham Taylor to Livingston L. Taylor and William R. Taylor, July 12, 1938; Katharine Taylor to Graham Romeyn Taylor, Easter, 1937; Graham Taylor to Graham Romeyn Taylor, September 1, 1938; *Daily News* (Chicago), September 27, 1938. Following a funeral service in the auditorium of Chicago Commons, Taylor was buried in New Brunswick, New Jersey.

[26] Taylor, *Pioneering*, p. viii; John Palmer Gavit, "At Home with Graham Taylor," p. 237.

new movements. Seldom an architect of new ideas, he was nevertheless quick to recognize and to utilize promising innovations. In this capacity he was remarkably successful, perhaps because he could temper his own strong idealism with a realistic appraisal of the obstacles that stood in his way. Julius Rosenwald, who worked closely with Taylor on many projects, found him "full of idealism, but always intensely practical, always ready to do the thing that it was necessary to do in order to have a reasonable chance of securing the result." A fellow settlement warden, Percy Alden, had a high regard for Taylor's "sturdy sort of common sense. . . . He never talks without acting, doing, working, for the end he has in view." Taylor's goals were usually moderate, "middle-of-the-road" solutions. By nature he was "a mediator between extremes."[27]

Still another reason for Taylor's role as pioneer rather than trailbreaker was his deliberate decision to work in a variety of reform movements and not restrict himself to one line of endeavor. He was, observed Walter Rauschenbusch, "always in the press of things, taking a hand in whatever was most worth doing." This resulted in commitments by Taylor to many groups, but it precluded the chance to become an outstanding leader in any single one. When he was weighing the Chicago offer in the summer of 1892, one of his Hartford colleagues warned:

> Every man has some limitations. I think that yours lie, if you will allow me to speak quite frankly, in the difficulty of keeping patiently to one or a few lines of effort.

As Taylor's life unfolded his friend's prediction proved accurate. Each new opportunity seemed as challenging to him as the projects in which he was already engaged. Almost invariably he accepted the new responsibility without relinquishing or delegating any of his other duties.[28]

Thus Taylor kept his position as pastor of Hartford's Fourth Congregational Church after accepting the professorship. And though he started his career in Chicago as professor of Christian sociology, he soon added to his academic duties administration of the settlement house, publication of *The*

---

[27] Julius Rosenwald in "Addresses at a Dinner in Honor of Graham Taylor, May 27, 1930," pp. 16–17; Alden, "Graham Taylor: An Appreciation," p. 2; John Palmer Gavit, "At Home With Graham Taylor," p. 237.

In the Introduction to *Religion in Social Action* Jane Addams wrote of her close friend: "Although knowledge of social development gave Dr. Taylor patience with those driven to rebellion, yet his own temperament and training place him in the list of those of the social reformers who believe in a gradual modification of society." Taylor, *Region in Social Action*, p. xxii.

[28] Walter Rauschenbusch, review of *Religion in Social Action*, in *The Survey*, XXXI (January 31, 1914), 527; Waldo S. Pratt to Graham Taylor, July 25, 1892.

Commons, and work with the Civic Federation and the Municipal Voters' League. In 1902, he began the weekly *Daily News* editorials and soon afterwards launched the training school for social workers. As soon as he was free of administrative responsibilities at Chicago Theological Seminary, he plunged into the Chicago Plan Commission, the Vice Commission, and the Illinois Mining Investigation Commission. Meantime, he wrote for *The Survey,* completed *Religion in Social Action,* and directed affairs at Chicago Commons and the School of Civics and Philanthropy. By 1916 Taylor found himself carrying

> the heaviest load of teaching and administration that ever has been piled upon me. I have classes at the University (4 a week) and am on daily duty at the School of Civics not only, but teach . . . divinity students . . . plus the Commons, The Survey and The Daily News.[29]

When Taylor tried to trim his sails he experienced rough going, for all the ventures were closely dependent upon him. To Victor F. Lawson he confided, "My difficulty is that I continue to be so essential to the support and direction of the public trusts." Having involved many other people, he felt he could not "yet let go with honor to them or with safety to these enterprises." Actually Taylor was extremely reluctant to let go. He enjoyed and found stimulating the "many different angles" of his career: "preacher, teacher, social worker, arbitrator of labor troubles, conciliator, and journalist." In each of these roles Taylor acquitted himself well and in some he made notable contributions. But in none of them was he a pathfinder. Perhaps he could have been if he had wanted to stick "patiently to one or a few lines of effort." Percy Alden always claimed that "if the warden of Chicago Commons had been an ambitious man he might have attained to almost any position of honor . . . that the world had to offer." But the warden chose instead to cultivate the "many different angles" of reform.[30]

Taylor was, in addition, too optimistic to be a trailbreaker. He lacked the gloomy despair about society that motivated the extremists. If he lost a battle for reform, he would "bob right up in the same place. Try it over again." This "absolute immunity to discouragement" radiates through most of his writing, particularly the *Daily News* editorials. During the struggle to drive the boodlers out of the city council, he stoutly maintained that all political problems "are soluble by education" and "good citizenship." "Nowhere on earth are the evils of democracy more surely to be overcome by more democracy than right here in Chicago." His newspaper associates described him

---

[29] Quoted in John Palmer Gavit, "At Home with Graham Taylor," p. 237.
[30] Graham Taylor to Victor F. Lawson, October 4, 1917; Charles Dennis in "Addresses at Dinner," pp. 18–19; Alden, "Graham Taylor: An Appreciation," p. 2.

as "an open-minded and clear-visioned optimist." And he himself wrote in a
Daily News column:

> To be optimistic is not to be blind nor false to facts. It is not to blink
> real things. It is not to be without standards and ideals, but on the con-
> trary to have such faith and trust in them as to be confident that they
> will win.[31]

The very qualities which kept Taylor from becoming a trailbreaker — his
preference for reconciling extremes, his eager participation in many areas of
reform, and his unfaltering optimism — uniquely fitted him for pioneering
on social frontiers. Taylor recognized a "three-fold motif" in his life: "a democratic faith, an educational purpose and a religious hope." But Percy Alden
insisted that it was "the same end all through, whether he is lecturing, preaching, or organizing at the Commons. The one object is to educate the civic
conscience, to establish better social conditions, to make it easier for people
to live the true and pure life." Taylor's total achievement as a pioneer for
social justice was impressive. It prompted Alexander Johnson to prophesy
that when "the history of the social movement in the United States . . . from
1880 to 1920, shall be written, the work of Graham Taylor will fill a wonderful chapter."[32]

Taylor's deep faith in social Christianity was perhaps the underlying motive in his life's work. His early conversion to the social gospel involved no
"loosening of his grip on the realities of religion," noted Washington Gladden. "What happened with him was only a change of emphasis, due to the
discovery that religion is not a department of life, but that it included the
whole of life — man in all his relations." Indeed, the term "relationship"
became the key to Taylor's exposition of doctrine. In his evangelical work
in Hartford he "first used this term to interpret religion to men who claimed
to be hostile to it." He told them

> that the Christian religion is essentially the ideal which Jesus had of rela-
> tionship to God as father and to men as brothers; that only in so far as
> any of his followers actually practice those relationships and strive to
> realize them more completely are they really Christian; and that how-
> ever rites and ceremonies, sacraments and creeds, may express and im-

[31] Graham Taylor in "Addresses at Dinner," p. 31; Carl S. Patton, review of
Pioneering on Social Frontiers, in *Chicago Theological Seminary Register*, XX (Novem-
ber, 1930), 42; Alden, "Graham Taylor: An Appreciation," p. 2; Graham Taylor,
"City's Problems Its Citizens' Opportunity," *Daily News* (Chicago), February 24,
1906; "A Salute to a Veteran," *Daily News* (Chicago), November 7, 1936; Graham
Taylor, "On Being Optimistic for Chicago," *Daily News* (Chicago), August 6, 1927.

[32] Graham Taylor, "The Threefold Motif" (manuscript); Alden, "Graham Taylor:
An Appreciation," p. 2; Johnson, *Adventures in Social Welfare*, p. 379.

press religious experiences and aspirations, religion itself is relationship to God and man.[33]

This was the same message which Taylor later expounded to his students in Hartford and it formed the core of his pioneer work in Christian sociology at the Chicago Theological Seminary. Furthermore, religion as "relationship to God and man" was the basic theme of *Religion in Social Action* and it permeated many of his articles and public lectures. That the social gospel would ultimately prevail, Taylor was absolutely certain. In her Introduction to *Religion in Social Action*, Jane Addams explained,

> it is as though Dr. Taylor saw the arid wastes of modern life being slowly flooded by an incoming tide of religion which will in time irresistibly bear away many impediments now blocking the path of social progress. The reader shares the consciousness that these beneficent waters are rising in response to one of those world forces which inevitably draw men's wills into one effective current.

Yet Taylor's optimistic faith in the ultimate triumph of social Christianity did not prevent him from encouraging the "incoming tide." Rather it drove him into still broader fields than teaching and preaching. It forced him to put his own religious convictions into social action.[34]

The success of Chicago Commons won for Taylor in his last decade the epithet, "Grand Old Man of the social settlement movement." The honor was well deserved. For the high standards which Taylor set at the Commons, the inspiration he imparted to resident workers, the role he played in the National Conference of Charities and Correction and the National Federation of Settlements, and the clarity with which he interpreted the settlement movement to the American public were important contributions. Significant also was his training school for social workers. Though absorbed by the university in 1920, the Chicago School of Civics and Philanthropy left an indelible imprint upon scores of young men and women who studied there. As one of them later expressed it, "Dr. Taylor has played the part of Big Brother to many of us youngsters in social work, cheering us, leading us and setting the pace." [35]

The impact of Taylor's settlement house on the seventeenth ward is harder to measure. Statistics are unreliable, and few of the neighbors left written opinions. It is possible, for example, to point out that approximately 4,000

---

[33] Washington Gladden, review of *Religion in Social Action*, in *Congregationalist and Christian World*, XCIX (March 19, 1914), "Literary Section," n.p.; Taylor, *Pioneering*, pp. 442, 443.

[34] Taylor, *Religion in Social Action*, p. xii.

[35] John Palmer Gavit, "Graham Taylor: His Book," p. 3; Eugene T. Lies to Frank McCulloch, April 22, 1919.

people attended Chicago Commons' functions each week during 1904. What is impossible to determine is whether some of these people were counted several times, and whether they were regular participants or only casual visitors. Nor is it possible to know how many of those who stayed away from the settlement were suspicious or even hostile toward the non-immigrant outsiders who had come to help the seventeenth ward.[36]

The neighborhood people who did come regularly to Chicago Commons were rewarded. They acquired skills and developed interests that enriched their lives. In addition, the settlement contacts helped them find new friends and enabled them to adjust more rapidly to American urban life. Those who wrote to Taylor about the Commons usually testified to this effect. One man, for instance, who had grown up in settlement clubs and classes in the 1890's, thanked the warden

> for the opportunities you provided me to learn and employ my spare time. . . . Work such as you have done has kept many from paths that lead to penitentiaries and similar places. It was truly noble of you to so spend your life.[37]

Repercussions of the political reform movement centered at Chicago Commons can be measured with greater accuracy. The Seventeenth Ward Civic Federation and its successor, the Seventeenth Ward Community Club, did break the power of the local bosses. Those organizations, directed by Taylor and Raymond Robins and based at the settlement, managed to control nominations and determine the outcome of most of the aldermanic elections after 1897. When Lincoln Steffens visited Chicago he found it "incomprehensible" that the reformers could carry the seventeenth ward, "in one year for a Republican by some 1300 plurality, the next year for a Democrat by some 1800, the third for a Republican again." Asking Walter L. Fisher of the Municipal Voters' League about this phenomenon, Steffens was informed that the League "did not carry that ward; its own people did it." But the job of rallying the independent vote was performed by the Seventeenth Ward Civic Federation and Community Club, and behind them stood Taylor and his co-workers. In terms of local political reform, Chicago Commons was one of the most successful settlements in the country.[38]

Taylor's efforts to rouse the city-wide independent vote were less spectacular. Most of his *Daily News* columns backed losing mayoralty candidates; not until Dever ran against Thompson in 1923 did he choose a winner. Yet in the long run his editorials supporting not only political reform but a wide

---

[36] *Chicago Commons: A Social Center for Civic Cooperation*, p. 12.
[37] Robert E. Berlet to Graham Taylor, May 1, 1934.
[38] Steffens, *The Shame of the Cities*, p. 181; Davis, Spearheads for Reform, chap. iii.

variety of other worthy projects left their mark. No doubt many Chicagoans felt as did one man in La Porte, Indiana, who assured the columnist that "the public respect and believe 'what Graham Taylor says' . . . I suspect that you fall much short of realizing the extent to which your confidence and public encouragement . . . influences good people everywhere." In time even the precinct leaders had to reckon with the "Conscience of Chicago." A reporter noted in 1931 that among "the rougher politicians" Taylor was "known as 'the professor.' But there is respect in their voices as they pronounce the word," for they have learned that " 'The professor . . . is practical.' " [39]

Taylor generated an enthusiasm for reform that attracted scores of loyal supporters. He welcomed the assistance of one and all. He was, observed Robert M. Lovett, "like a ship carrying every sail set to catch every breeze." The result was an "amazing number of contacts . . . with the high and the low, with the millionaires and the paupers, and with the saints and the sinners." Taylor took them just "as they came . . . getting the best he could out of them," broadening his own understanding of human nature, and at the same time widening the ranks of support for his civic ventures. Surveying Taylor's total achievement, Paul Kellogg of *The Survey* marveled at how much he accomplished and "How many thousands of lives he has touched." But most of all he envied the "rattling good time" that Taylor "has had in the midst of it all." [40]

"Chicago is more civilized because Graham Taylor lived in it," was the moral one reader drew from *Pioneering on Social Frontiers*. But reflecting on the regime of Mayor Thompson then in power, he quickly added, "It would be much closer to the civilized ideal if more people had listened to Dr. Taylor and fewer to the ranters, the demagogues and the inflated supermen that have made the city so colorful and so unhappy." Backsliders never discouraged Taylor in the pulpit or the classroom. And during the last decades of his life, political backsliding in Chicago failed to dim his optimism. At the age of seventy-five he buoyantly reaffirmed the threefold faith that had been "The Keynote of the Whole Adventure."

> I now affirm that this democratic faith in fellow-men, which I followed hither, falters not. No class consciousness of either class in conflict; no aristocracy of any claimants, except those who possess worth and attest it by service; no dictatorship, either beneficent or cruelly despotic, has

[39] C. S. Funk to Graham Taylor, November 18, 1913; "Graham Taylor, Social Pioneer, is 80 Years Old," *Daily News* (Chicago), May 2, 1931.

[40] Alden, "Graham Taylor: An Appreciation," p. 2; quoted in Taylor, *Chicago Commons*, p. 303; Robert M. Lovett in "Addresses at Dinner," 23; Charles Dennis in "Addresses at Dinner," 18; Paul Kellogg to Graham Romeyn Taylor, April 18, 1934, Survey Associates Editorial Research Files.

ever caused me to waver a hair's breadth from my faith in the supremacy of the democratic order of government and social justice. . . .

As strong as ever is my confidence in the educational purpose with which I have sought to express and spread that faith. The teacher sways the scepter of the future, now more than ever. But the teaching in these academic circles fulfilled only part of this educational purpose. Ever on and out has it been carried in teaching youth and adults of our great cosmopolitan neighborhood; still further afield from the platforms of schools and universities, chautauquas, labor unions, industrial plants, clubs, and churches; and yet more wisely on the white wings of the press. . . .

The religious hope for our times, our country, our world, as well as for the soul, is the port of entry toward which I have ever steered my endeavors. It is the hope, shared with all the prophets and apostles, singers and seers, that right is mighty and must prevail, that truth will outlive error, that love abides and cannot fail.[41]

After Taylor's death his four children presented a memorial plaque to the Dutch Reformed Church in Hopewell, New York. It read: "Follower of Christ, Friend of Mankind, and Prophet of the Kingdom of God." Taylor's son preferred "seeker of the kingdom of God among men." That phrase aptly describes the goal of one of America's foremost pioneers for social justice.[42]

---

[41] Robert L. Duffus, "On Social Frontiers in Chicago," *New York Times Book Review,* July 6, 1930, 4; Graham Taylor, "The Keynote of the Whole Adventure," *Chicago Theological Seminary Register,* XXVIII (November, 1938), 8; Graham Taylor, "Response of Graham Taylor," pp. 7–8.

[42] Graham Romeyn Taylor to Paul Kellogg, September 18, 1939, Survey Associates Editorial Research Files.

Bibliographical Essay

The major source materials for this book were Taylor's own writings, the Graham Taylor Collection at the Newberry Library in Chicago, and the personal family letters in the possession of Lea Taylor who lives in Highland Park, Illinois. A complete bibliography of Taylor's writings follows this essay. At the Newberry Library are Taylor's diary and journal, drafts of articles and speeches, lecture notes and course outlines, travel mementos, newspaper and magazine clippings, brochures and correspondence from Chicago Commons, records of the Chicago School of Civics and Philanthropy, copies of the *Daily News* editorials, and hundreds of letters that Taylor wrote or received. This collection covers every phase of Taylor's life and ranges chronologically from his earliest extant letter in 1862 to his thoughts on death and immortality recorded by Lea Taylor during the last months of his life. The documents are described in the author's article, "The Graham Taylor Collection," *The Newberry Library Bulletin*, III (October, 1953). Taylor's writings and the material at the Newberry Library were used in the author's doctoral dissertation, *Graham Taylor, Social Pioneer, 1851–1938*, which is available in Rush Rhees Library, University of Rochester.

Still in the possession of Lea and Katharine Taylor are a large number of family letters. Of particular interest are Taylor's letters to and from his parents, correspondence with his children while they were at college, letters to the family while he and Mrs. Taylor were abroad in 1903 and again in 1911, and letters to his son written in 1918 and 1919. Taylor's daughters kindly granted me permission to use these letters in 1964.

Taylor's schooling at Rutgers and the Dutch Reformed Seminary and his experiences in the Hopewell and Hartford pulpits are discussed at length in his diary. The ministerial journal, which runs from 1873 until 1892, provides many insights. Taylor's letters to and from his father and grandfather, in the Taylor Collection and in the possession of Lea Taylor, explain in detail the parish problems he was trying to solve. Additional information can be found in the Fourth Congregational Church's "Records" at the Connecticut State Library in Hartford and in the Ecclesiastical Society's "Record Book of the Free Congregational Society." Fourth Church publications are useful too, particularly the *Memorial Manual of the Fourth Congregational Church* (Hartford, 1882) and *Five Years' Growth: A Sketch of the Evangelistic Work Centering at the Fourth Church* (Hartford, 1889). Letters from members of the Yoke Fellows' Band and people interested in Taylor's missionary work help round out the picture. Unfortunately, there are only a few sermon drafts in the Taylor Collection, for Taylor destroyed most of them when he was preparing his autobiography in the 1920's. His own account of the ministries in *Pioneering on Social Frontiers* (Chicago, 1930) is brief but revealing.

The Taylor Collection contains a wide variety of material pertaining to Taylor's academic career at the Hartford and Chicago seminaries: course outlines, lecture notes, examination questions, and suggested reading lists. Printed catalogues and year books, Taylor's inaugural addresses, and his *Syllabus in Biblical Sociology* (Chicago, 1900) further define his goals in the classroom. Letters from former students and reminiscent articles, such as J. W. F. Davies, "Graham Taylor — A Tribute From the Alumni," *Chicago Theological Seminary Register*, XVIII (November, 1928), enable one to gauge Taylor's impact upon his scholars. Relations with his Hartford colleagues and his handling of administrative problems can be traced in the Graham Taylor Letters, the A. C. Thompson Correspondence, and the Hartford Theological Seminary's "Record of Faculty Meetings, 1888–1892" in Case Memorial Library, Hartford Seminary Foundation. Comparable source materials for the Chicago experience are the Samuel Ives Curtiss Correspondence, Ozora S. Davis' manuscript "History of Chicago Theological Seminary," and the "Faculty Minutes, 1859–1913" in Hammond Library, Chicago Theological Seminary.

The books of such major figures as Washington Gladden, Walter Rauschenbusch, Richard T. Ely, Lyman Abbott, and Josiah Strong are essential for an understanding of the social gospel. The most useful secondary studies of that movement are Charles Howard Hopkins, *The Rise of the Social Gospel in American Protestantism, 1865–1915* (New Haven, 1940); Henry F. May, *Protestant Churches and Industrial America* (New York, 1949); Aaron I. Abell, *The Urban Impact on American Protestantism, 1865–1900* (Cambridge, Mass., 1943); and James Dombrowski, *The Early Days of Christian Socialism in America* (New York, 1936). For Taylor's interpretation of social Christianity his published articles and, of course, his *Religion in Social Action* (New York, 1913) are indispensable.

The Settlement Horizon: A National Estimate (New York, 1922), by

Robert A. Woods and Albert J. Kennedy is the best survey of the settlement movement in America. Founders of the houses have written about their experiences: Stanton Coit, *Neighbourhood Guilds, an Instrument of Social Reform* (London, 1891); Robert A. Woods, *Neighborhood in Nation Building* (Boston, 1922); Lillian D. Wald, *The House on Henry Street* (New York, 1915); Jane Addams, *Twenty Years at Hull-House* (New York, 1910), and *The Second Twenty Years at Hull-House* (New York, 1930). With the help of her associates Jane Addams described the early work of the settlement in *Hull-House Maps and Papers* (New York, 1895). Howard E. Wilson's biography, *Mary McDowell, Neighbor* (Chicago, 1928), traces the development of the University of Chicago settlement. An unpublished dissertation at the University of Wisconsin, Allen F. Davis' "Spearheads for Reform: The Social Settlements and the Progressive Movement, 1890–1914," discusses the activities of the Boston, New York, and Chicago houses.

Taylor described the founding and growth of Chicago Commons in numerous articles, in abbreviated form in *Pioneering on Social Frontiers*, and in more detail in *Chicago Commons Through Forty Years* (Chicago, 1936). In addition, there is a vast amount of manuscript material in the Taylor Collection. Correspondence with contributors, friends, neighbors, and former residents is augmented by announcements of lectures, club meetings, classes, pageants, parties, and other gatherings. Pamphlets and brochures depicting the expanding activities of the settlement were printed periodically — in 1895, 1899, 1904, 1911, 1919, and so on. Of course the financial records of Chicago Commons Association and the minutes of the meetings of the board of trustees are vital documents.

Relevant information can be found in other manuscript collections. The papers of Mabel A. Hawkins, Taylor's secretary, are now in the possession of Lea Taylor. So too are letters from former residents written at the time of the Commons' fortieth anniversary. Other letters concerning Chicago Commons are located in the Mary McDowell Papers at the Chicago Historical Society; the Jane Addams Papers in Swarthmore College Library; the Raymond Robins Papers at the Wisconsin State Historical Society; and the Lillian D. Wald Papers in the New York Public Library. The Charles H. Dennis Collection and the Victor F. Lawson Collection in the Newberry Library disclose the deep interest of those two newspapermen in Chicago Commons, while the Julius Rosenwald Papers at the University of Chicago highlight the philanthropist's support of both the settlement and the training school. Taylor's dealings with *The Survey* can be traced in the Survey Associates Editorial Research Files at the Columbia University School of Social Work.

The evolution of the Chicago School of Civics and Philanthropy is well documented in the Taylor Collection. Financial records, student registration, course outlines, placement of graduates, the minutes of the meetings of the trustees, and the bound volumes of bulletins issued by the School are all available. Some of Taylor's letters to Mrs. William Francis Dummer, a trustee, are in the Ethel Sturges Dummer Collection, The Women's Archives, Radcliffe College. At the University of Chicago Library, the William Rainey Harper Papers and the Harry Pratt Judson Papers were consulted. Letters of Julia Lathrop, Edith Abbott, and Sophonisba Breckinridge are invaluable for understanding the viewpoint of the faction that wanted the merger. Some of these are in the School of Social Service Administration at the University of Chicago, others are in the Grace and Edith Abbott Papers at the University of Chicago Library, and a few are in the Breckinridge Papers at the Library of Congress. Additional information about the Chicago School of Civics and Philanthropy can be found in the William Kent Papers at Yale University Library. Most useful of the secondary materials on social work education are Frank J. Bruno, "Twenty-Five Years of Schools of Social Work," *Social Service Review*, XVIII (June, 1944); Earle E. Eubank, "The Schools of Social Work of the United States and Canada: Some Recent Findings," *Social Service Review*, II (June, 1928); Ernest V. Hollis and Alice L. Taylor, *Social Work Education in the United States* (New York, 1951); and James E. Hagerty, *The Training of Social Workers* (New York, 1931).

Depicting the Chicago background for Taylor's pioneering required use of the newspapers and material in the Chicago Historical Society library and the Municipal Reference Library at City Hall. Among the scores of books consulted, the following were perhaps the most helpful: Bessie Louise Pierce, *A History of Chicago*, Vol. III: *The Rise of a Modern City, 1871–1893* (New York, 1957); Bessie Louise Pierce (ed.), *As Others See Chicago; Impressions of Visitors, 1673–1933* (Chicago, 1933); Lloyd Lewis and Henry J. Smith, *Chicago, The History of its Reputation* (New York, 1929); Emmett Dedmon, *Fabulous Chicago* (New York, 1953); Wayne Andrews, *Battle for Chicago* (New York, 1946); Ray Ginger, *Altgeld's America: The Lincoln Ideal Versus Changing Realities* (New York, 1958); William T. Stead, *If Christ Came to Chicago!* (Chicago, 1894); Douglas Sutherland, *Fifty Years on the Civic Front* (Chicago, 1943); Lloyd Wendt and Herman Kogan, *Lords of the Levee: The Story of Bathhouse John and Hinky Dink* (Indianapolis, 1943); and Lloyd Wendt and Herman Kogan, *Big Bill of Chicago* (Indianapolis, 1953).

Taylor's correspondence with civic leaders is one measure of his influence as the "Conscience of Chicago." His speeches, articles, and *Daily News* columns pertaining to reform are also important. His praise of comrades in *Pioneering on Social Frontiers* is curiously paralleled by speeches others gave at testimonial dinners for Taylor in the 1930's. Transcripts of these remarks form part of the Taylor Collection. Letters to John Palmer Gavit, Raymond Robins, and members of the family, particularly his brothers and his son, are the best sources for Taylor's last years.

Graham Taylor's Writings

A. BOOKS

Chicago Commons Through Forty Years. Chicago, 1936.
Pioneering on Social Frontiers. Chicago, 1930.
Religion in Social Action. New York, 1913.

B. PAMPHLETS

Books for Beginners in the Study of Christian Sociology and Social Economics. Boston and Chicago, 1895.

The Church and the Industrial Problem (with O. C. Helming and James Mullenbach). Chicago, n.d.

The Church for Brotherhood in Industry (with H. M. Beardsley). Chicago, 1910.

The Church in Social Reforms, an Address Delivered in Boston, Mass., September 23, 1899, Before the International Congregational Council. Boston, 1899.

The Community's Police, an Address Delivered before the Chicago Association of Detective Sergeants on January 19, 1917. Chicago, 1917.

Jane Addams Neighbor and Citizen. Nashville, 1936.

The Practical Training Needed for the Ministry of To-Day [Inaugural Address Delivered October 10, 1888, at Hartford Theological Seminary]. ["Hartford Seminary Publications," No. 2.] Hartford, 1888.

Public Repression of the Social Evil, Address delivered at First National Conference on Race Betterment at Battle Creek, Michigan, January 8–12, 1914. [n.p.], 1914.

A Religious Census of the City of Hartford Made in the Year 1899 Under the Auspices of the Connecticut Bible Socieyt ["Hartford Seminary Publications," No. 10.] Hartford, 1890.

Studies in the English Bible and Suggestions about Methods of Christian Work (with Clark S. Beardslee) ["Hartford Seminary Publications," Nos. 7 and 8.] Hartford, 1889–90.

Syllabus in Biblical Sociology. Chicago, 1900.

Washington Gladden, New York, 1919.

The Work of the American Missionary Association an Evidence of Christianity, Address at Annual Meeting of American Missionary Association, Elgin, Illinois, 1893. Hartford, 1893.

C. COLUMNS

"By Graham Taylor," in *Daily News* (Chicago), November 22, 1902, through July 23, 1938.

"Christian Citizenship," or "Golden Rule Christian Citizenship Clubs," in *The Golden Rule*, IX (October 25, 1894, through September 26, 1895).

"Church and Community," in *The Survey*, XXIX (October 19, 1912) through XXXII (August 15, 1914).

"The Industrial Survey of the Month," in *The Survey*, XXII (April 3, 1909) through XXVI (May 6, 1911).

"The Industrial Viewpoint," in *Charities and The Commons*, XV (February, 1906) through XX (September, 1909).

"Our Present Problem Club: Studies in Social Economics and Civics," in *Young Men's Era*, XX (October 4, 1894) through XXI (March 14, 1895).

"Social and Civic Department," in *Young Men's Era*, XXI (June 20, 1895, through September 12, 1895).

"With the Editor," in *The Commons*, IX (January, 1904), through X (October, 1905).

The articles which Taylor wrote for these columns are *not* included in the following section.

D. ARTICLES

"Academic Clinics Furnished by Settlement," *The Commons*, X (April, 1905), 201.

"Address at the Funeral," *The Advance*, LVII (May 6, 1909), 553.

"Address to Legal Aid Societies' Convention," National Alliance of Legal Aid Societies, *Proceedings of the Cincinnati Convention, 1916*, pp. 123–30.

"After Earthquake and Fire," *Charities and The Commons*, XVI (May 5, 1906), 157–58.

"After Trades Unions — What? A Glance Behind for a Look Ahead," *The Commons*, IX (April, 1904), 105–8.

"The Aftermath at the Cherry Mine," *The Survey*, XXIII (December 11, 1909), 355–56.

"Aftermath of the Chicago Teamsters' Strike," *Charities*, XIV (September 16, 1905), 1088–89.

"Allen B. Pond — Patriot and Architect," *Neighborhood*, II (April, 1929), 109–11.

"American Industrial Society," *The Survey*, XXIII (February 12, 1910), 715–18.

"The American Medical Association," *The Survey*, XL (June 22, 1918), 353–54.

"American Sociological Society," *Charities and The Commons*, XIX (January 11, 1908), 1387–89.

"Are Ye Able?," *Chautauqua Assembly Herald*, XXVII (July 8, 1902), 7.

"Arnold Toynbee and the Settlement Movement for Social Unification," *Chautauqua Assembly Herald*, XXV (July 27, 1900), 5.

"An Aspect of the Housing Problem," *The Commons*, IV (March 31, 1900), 3–4.

"Assertion of the People's Right to the Referendum," *Charities and The Commons*, XVII (March 2, 1907), 973–74.

"At Gary, Some Impressions and Interviews," *The Survey*, XLIII (November 8, 1919), 65–66.

"The Attitude of Settlements Toward Radicalism," *The Commons*, VI (October, 1901), 2–3. Unsigned editorial written by Taylor.

"Basis of Social Evangelism with Rural Application," *Chicago Theological Seminary Register*, VII (January, 1914), 23–27.

"The Belgian Strike," *The Survey*, XXX (May 3, 1913), 204–5.

"Between the Lines in Chicago's Industrial Civil War," *The Commons*, V (April 30, 1900), 1–4.

"A Bluff Well Called," *The Survey*, XXXV (December 4, 1915), 266.

"The 'Bolshevism' of Professor Ward," *The Survey*, XLI (March 29, 1919), 920–21.

"Books on Social Economics," *Chicago Theological Seminary Register*, IV (November, 1910), 6–7.

"Boomerang Investigations," *The Survey*, XXXIV (September 25, 1915), 577–78.

"Bringing Under Law Those 'Above the Law'," *Charities and The Commons*, XV (December 16, 1905), 365–66.

"British Wages and Trade Disputes in 1903," *The Commons*, IX (February, 1904), 54.

"The Brotherhood of Andrew and Philip," in Evangelical Alliance, *Christianity Practically Applied* (New York, 1894), II, 44–46.

"Building a Civic Center Around a Tri-City High School," *The Survey*, XXXIII (October 17, 1914), 65–66.

"Building Progress Stopped," *The Commons*, IV (January 31, 1900), 8.

"The Case of Labor Against Its Traitors," *Charities and The Commons*, XVII (February 2, 1907), 788–90.

"Casting the Horoscope in Illinois," *The Survey*, XXX (July 12, 1913), 499–500.

"Casuistry of Competition — Present and Probably Ethical Effects of Moral Dualism," *The Commons*, I (July, 1897), 12–15.

"Chapters in Rural Progress," *Charities and The Commons*, XX (September 12, 1908), 689–90.

"1848 — Charles Richmond Henderson — 1915," *The Survey*, XXXIV (April 10, 1915), 55–56.

"Chicago as Viewed by Its Intimate Friends," *Chicago Theological Seminary Register*, XX (January, 1930), 8–11.

"Chicago in the Nation's Race Strife," *The Survey*, XLII (August 9, 1919), 695–97.

"The Chicago Commons — Retrospect and Prospect," *Congregationalist*, CXIII (June 21, 1928), 782–83, 788.

"Chicago Keeps On," *Survey Graphic*, XV (August, 1929), 499.

"The Chicago Movement for Social Service Training," *The Commons*, IX (March, 1904), 95.

"Chicago Paper Box Makers Act," *The Survey*, XXVI (May 27, 1911), 332.

"Chicago Reclaims its Daily News," *The Survey*, LV (February 1, 1926), 572–73.

"Chicago Referendum Vote," *Charities and The Commons*, XV (November 11, 1905), 199–200.

"Chicago Rising From Its Fall," *The Survey*, XLVI (June 18, 1921), 397.

"Chicago's Civic Dinner to Jane Addams," *The Survey*, LVII (February 15, 1927), 618–20.

"Chicago's Varied Measures Against Vice and Crime," *The Survey*, XXXIII (February 13, 1915), 535–37.

"Chicago's Welfare Agencies Lead the Way in Many Fields," *Daily News* (Chicago), July 1, 1929.

"The Chimes of a Christian Era," *The Survey*, XLV (December 25, 1920), 467.

"China's Commissioners to Representative Government," *Charities and The Commons*, XV (February 3, 1906), 577–78.

"The Chivalry of the Crowd," *Charities and The Commons*, XVI (June 2, 1906), 293–94.

"Christ in The Common Lot," *Chautauquan Daily*, XXXIII (August 3, 1908), 6.

"Christian Knight-Errantry for Industrial Justice," *Chautauquan Assembly Herald*, XXV (July 25, 1900), 5.

"The Christian Social Spirit," *New Brunswick Seminary Bulletin*, VII (June, 1932), 21–24.

"The Christian Workers' Convention," *Congregationalist*, LXXV (November 20, 1890), 412.

"Christianity and Industry," *Chautauquan Daily*, XXXIII (August 1, 1908), 6–7.

"Christianity and The Social Crisis," *Charities and The Commons*, XXI (October 24, 1908), 122–24.

"The Church," *The Survey*, L (June 15, 1923), 340–41.

"Church and Civic Education — Community Activities as a Means of Education in Civic Righteousness," *Religious Education*, V (October, 1910), 385–90.

"The Church and the Civic Ideal," *The Kingdom*, VIII (June 14, 1895), 134–35.

"The Church and Industrial Discontent," *Christian Century*, XXXVII (March 18, 1920), 9–10.

"The Church as a Center of Rural Organization," *Michigan Political Science Association*, IV (July, 1902), 101–10.

"The Church for Industrial Brotherhood," *The Survey*, XXV (November 5, 1910), 177–78.

"The Church in Social Reforms," *Proceedings, Second International Congregational Council* (Boston, 1899), pp. 143–150.

"The Church Keeps Up With Social Trends," *The Survey*, LXIX (February, 1933), 64–66.

"Church Members and the Industrial Conflict," *Congregationalist and Advance*, CIV (September 4, 1919), 296–97.

"Church Men's New World Vision," *The Survey*, XXIV (June 18, 1910), 479–80.

"The Church Preparing for Social Action," *The Survey*, XXV (March 4, 1911), 916–21.

"The Church's Part in the War Against Vice," *Chautauquan Daily*, XXXVIII (August 22, 1913), 1.

"The Civic Expression of the Common Faith," *Chautauquan Daily*, XXXIII (July 31, 1908), 6–7.

"The Civic Function of the Country Church," *Chautauquan*, XXXVI (December, 1902), 274–78.

"The Civic Martyrdom of Dr. Sachs," *The Survey*, XXXVI (April 22, 1916), 105–6.

"Civic Responsibility," *Young Men's Era*, XX (October 25, 1894), 8.

"The Civic Responsibility and Opportunity of the Young Men's Christian Association," *Proceedings of the Illinois Y.M.C.A. Convention, 1894*, pp. 48–53.

"Civic Significance of the Chicago Election," *The Survey*, XXXIV (April 17, 1915), 61.

"The Civic Value of Library Work with Children," *Public Libraries*, XIII (July, 1908), 247–48.

"Civil Service Success in Chicago Librarianship," *The Survey*, XXIII (October 9, 1909), 71–73.

"Clinical Training in Preparation for Christian Leadership," *The Intercollegian*, XXXIV (January, 1912), 88–91.

"College, Social and University Settlements," (with John Palmer Gavit) *Progress*, IV (1898), 71–76.

" 'The Commons' — the Chicago Seminary Settlement," *The Advance*, XXIX (October 11, 1894), 60–61.

"Community Cafes," *The Survey*, XLII (May 10, 1919), 252.

"Community Development," *St. Louis Lumberman*, January 28, 1914, 78–80.

"Community Secretary," *National Municipal Review*, IV (April, 1915), 281–85.

"Competitive Industrial Order," *Chicago Commons*, I (February, 1897), 11–14.

"A Comradeship of Forty Years," *Chicago Theological Seminary Register*, XXI (May, 1931), 18–22.

"Confession of Faith in the Religious Education Association," *Religious Education*, XXIII (September, 1928), 616–17.

"The Congregational Church and Social Reform," *The New Encyclopedia of Social Reform* (New York, 1908), pp. 272–73.

"Conscience and Competition — Jurisdiction of Ethical over Economic Law," *The Commons*, II (June, 1897), 13–15.

"Cooperation in Training for Public Service," *Chicago Commerce*, IV (November 12, 1909), 20, 22, 24.

"The County: a Challenge to Humanized Politics and Volunteer Co-operation," National Conference of Charities and Correction, *Proceedings, 1914*, pp. 1–14.

"County: a Challenge to Humanized Politics and Volunteer Co-operation," *The Survey*, XXXII (May 30, 1914), 240–44.

"County vs. City Interests in State Legislatures," *Charities and The Commons*, XVIII (May 4, 1907), 142.

"The Crisis in Organized Labor," *The Commons*, IX (September, 1904), 389–91. Unsigned editorial by Taylor.

"Dean Sumner — Chicago's Citizen Clergyman," *The Survey*, XXXIII (January 2, 1915), 348.

"Defending Cook County Against Faction," *The Survey*, XXXII (July 11, 1914), 388.

"Demobilization and Re-employment," *The Survey*, XLI (December 14, 1918), 342–43.

"Democratic Development Since Mazzini," *The Commons*, X (August, 1905), 437–38.

"Deserves Every Token of Grateful Appreciation," *Jewish Tribune and Hebrew Standard*, LXXXIX (November 12, 1926), 3.

"Developing the American Spirit," in *America and the New Era: A Symposium on Social Reconstruction*, ed. Elisha M. Friedman (New York, 1920), 231–45.

"Discussion on Class Conflict in America," *American Journal of Sociology*, XIII (May, 1908), 766–70.

"The Draft, a Great Human Experience," *The Survey*, XXXVIII (August 4, 1917), 404.

"The Draft — a Human Touchstone," *Sunday Herald* (Chicago), February 17, 1918.

"Eastland Disaster," *The Survey*, XXXIV (August 7, 1915), 410–13.

"Eclipse of Religion Under the Shadow of War," *The Survey*, XXXII (September 26, 1914), 630–31.

"Educational Movement for Social Training," *The Commons*, IX (September, 1904), 430–32.

"The Effect of Trade Schools on the Social Interests of the People," *Manual Training Magazine*, IX (April, 1908), 281–84.

"Ella Flagg Young," *The Survey*, XXIV (July 23, 1910), 619–21.

"End of an Industrial Brigand," *The Survey*, XXII (June 12, 1909), 401–3.

"Enforcing English by Proclamation," *The Survey*, XL (July 6, 1918), 394–95.

"England's Revolutionary Strike," *The Survey*, XXVII (October 7, 1911), 976–88. Also published in *City Club Bulletin*, IV (October 11, 1911), 3–15.

"English Settlements Federating," *The Commons*, VIII (September, 1903), 14–16.

"An Epidemic of Strikes in Chicago," *The Survey*, XLII (August 2, 1919), 645–46.

"An Epoch in American Mining," *The Survey*, XXIII (January 29, 1910), 575–77.

"Ethics and Competition," *Chicago Commons*, I (March, 1897), 11–13.

"An Evangelical Church," *Religious Herald* (Hartford, Connecticut), December 25, 1884.

"An Evangelistic Church," *Religious Herald* (Hartford, Connecticut), December 25, 1884.

"The Eve of the Industrial Revolution," *Chautauqua Assembly Herald*, XXII (July 29, 1897), 5.

"The Eve of the Industrial Revolution," *Chicago Commons*, I (November, 1896), 10–13.

"An Evening with Babushka," *The Survey*, XLI (February 1, 1919), 630.

"F. W. Matthiessen: A Trustee for Democracy," *The Survey*, XXXIX (March 16, 1918), 654–55.

"The Factory System," *Chicago Commons*, I (December, 1896), 13–15.

"The Factory System — Its Economic, Social and Ethical Results upon Labor," *Chautauqua Assembly Herald*, XXII (July 30, 1897), 36.

"The Family: The Common Denominator in Social and Religious Work," *The Survey*, XXIX (December 14, 1912), 329–30.

"Fathers and Sons," *Charities and The Commons*, XXI (December 12, 1908), 420–21.

"The Field of Cooperative Undertaking — the Part to be Taken by Government, Business, and Charity," National Conference of Charities and Correction, *Proceedings, 1916*, pp. 156–60.

"Field Work: Its Educational Value and Relation to the Financial Aid of Students," in Evangelical Alliance, *Christianity Practically Applied* (New York, 1894), II, 428–34.

"Fighting Vice in Chicago," *The Survey*, XXIX (October 26, 1912), 94–95.

"Food Prices and Poverty in English Politics," *The Commons*, VIII (December, 1903), 4–6.

"For the Manhood of the Average Citizen as Proved by the Draft Test," *Congregationalist and Advance*, CII (November 22, 1917), 699.

"Foreign Born Citizens as Political Assets," National Conference of Social Work, *Proceedings, 1918*, 452–57.

Foreword, in Hoyt King, *Citizen Cole of Chicago* (Chicago, 1931).

Foreword, in William Burgess, *The World's Social Evil* (Chicago, 1914).

"Four City Commissions at Work for Chicago," *The Survey*, XXXII (August 8, 1914), 489–90.

"The Fourth Congregational Church," in J. Hammond Trumbull (ed.), *The Memorial History of Hartford County Connecticut, 1633–1884* (2 vols.; Boston, 1886), I, 391–94.

"From Serfdom to Wages," *Chicago Commons*, I (October, 1896), 9–11.

"The Frontier in our Rear," *The Advance*, XXXV (May 12, 1898), 636–37.

"The Function of the City Church," *Chautauquan*, XXXVIII (September, 1903), 53–54.

"Graham Taylor on Christianity in China," in *The China Press* (Shanghai), May 13, 1922.

"Half and Half—the Quality of Appointments under Illinois' New Civil Code," *The Survey*, XXXVIII (September 29, 1917), 563–64.

"Hartford," *Minutes, National Council of Congregational Churches, 1886*, pp. 276–79.

"The Hartford Pastors' Mission," *Congregationalist*, XXXIX (April 28, 1887), 2.

"Held to Account for the Eastland," *The Survey*, XXXV (October 9, 1915), 45–46.

"Herbert Spencer's Faith in His Method," *The Commons*, IX (March, 1904), 83.

"The Heresy of Life," *Christian Intelligencer*, XLIX (May 23, 1878), 1–2.

"Holiday Greetings," *The Survey*, LXXIV (December, 1938), 370.

"A Human View of Child Labor," *Charities and The Commons*, XV (January 6, 1906), 434–35.

"Humanizing the Courts in America," *Progress*, IX (October, 1914), 229–31.

"Humanizing Politics," *The Survey*, XXIX (October 5, 1912), 10–11.

"Ideals of the City Club," *City Club Bulletin*, XIII (August 9, 1920), 163–66.

"Illinois Supreme Court Faces Forward," *The Survey*, XXIV (May 7, 1910), 199–200.

"Illinois' Fruitful Legislature," *The Survey*, XLII (July 19, 1919), 592–93.

"In Memoriam — Mary McDowell, 1854–1936," *Unity*, CXVIII (December 7, 1936), 129.

"Industrial Basis for International Peace," *The Survey*, XXII (June 12, 1909), 353–54.

"Industrial Basis for Social Interpretation," *The Survey*, XXII (April 3, 1909), 9–11.

"Industrial Issue at the Bar of the Church," *Charities and The Commons*, XIX (November 2, 1907), 998–1000.

"Industrial Issues at the Chicago Convention, 1908," *Charities and The Commons*, XX (July 4, 1908), 430–32.

"Industrial Peace — with Honor and Democracy," *The Survey*, XXXI (March 7, 1914), 723–24.

"Industrial Survey of the Month — State's Shame on National Exhibit," *The Survey*, XXIII (March 5, 1910), 896–97.

"Industry and Religion: Their Common Ground and Interdependence," in *Merrick Lectures on the Social Application of Religion, 1907–1908* (Cincinnati, 1908), pp. 87–104.

"The Interchurch Steel Strike Report. I: Living and Working Conditions in the Steel Industry. II: Living and Working Conditions in the Steel Industry. III: Is it Within the Province of the Church?," *Congregationalist and Advance*, CV (October 14, 21, 28, 1920), 467–68, 499–500, 530–31.

Introduction, in Caroline M. Hill (comp.), *Mary McDowell and Municipal Housekeeping; A Symposium* (Chicago, 1938).

"Is Religion an Element in the Social Settlement?" *Religious Education*, VIII (October, 1913), 345–48.

"Jane Addams: The Great Neighbor," *Survey Graphic*, XXIV (July, 1935), 338–41, 368.

"Jane Addams — Her Own Confessions of Faith," *Advance*, CXXVII (June 6, 1935), 436–37. Also in *Unity*, CXV (July 15, 1935), 208–9.

"Jane Addams — Interpreter," *American Review of Reviews*, XL (December, 1909), 688–94.

"Jane Addams' Twenty Years of Industrial Democracy," *The Survey*, XXV (December 3, 1910), 405–9.

"Julius Rosenwald, Fellow Citizen," *The Survey*, LXVII (February 1, 1932), 468–69, 501.

"Justice Without Fear or Favor," *The Survey*, XXVI (May 6, 1911), 214–15.

"Knights Errant of Social Chivalry," *Chautauqua Assembly Herald*, XXV (July 23, 1900), 5.

"Labor and Trade," *The Commons*, III (January-April, 1899), 3–5.

"Labor Day, 1908," *Charities and The Commons*, XX (September 5, 1908), 641–43.

"Labor Planks Rejected at Chicago, Adopted at Dinner," *Charities and The Commons*, XX (August 1, 1908), 531–32.

"Labor's Internationalism Tested by the War of Nations," *The Survey*, XXXII (September 5, 1914), 561–63.

"The Labor Movement," *Chicago Commons*, I (September, 1896), 9–12.

"A Laboratory Guide to the Study of Society," *The Kingdom*, VII (October 5, 1894), 396.

"A Letter From Graham Taylor," *Medical Life*, XXXI (July, 1924), 253.

"Lincoln's Soul Goes Marching on in Illinois," *The Survey*, XXIV (September 3, 1910), 750–55.

"The McNamara Case and the Church's Industrial Policy," *Congregationalist and Christian World*, XCVI (December 23, 1911), 914–15.

"The McNamara Confessions," *The Survey*, XXVII (December 9, 1911), 1339–40.

"Machinery and Labor," *Chicago Commons*, I (January, 1897), 11–14.

"*Mary McDowell — Neighbor* by Howard E. Wilson," *The Survey*, LXII (April 15, 1929), 142.

"Mazzini, Prophet and Martyr of Democracy," *The Commons*, X (August, 1905), 436–37.

"Men to Open the Twentieth Century," *Young Men's Era*, XIX (October 5, 1893), 1148–49.

"A Mine Test of Civilization," *The Survey*, XXIII (December 4, 1909), 297–304.

"The Ministry of Today: Its New Opportunities," *University Record*, III (February 17, 1899), 307–10. Also in *The Intercollegian*, XXI (February, 1899), 100–2.

"Mirror of a Man," *The Survey*, LXII (June 1, 1929), 317–18.

"Missions and Social Progress," *The Commons*, I (October, 1897), 14.

"Morals Commission and Police Morals," *The Survey*, XXX (April 12, 1913), 62–64.

"Movements Abroad Emphasizing the Direction of Progress at Home," *The Survey*, XXVII (November 4, 1911), 1161–68.

"Mutualism vs. Individualism," *Chautauquan Assembly Herald*, XXVII (July 10, 1902), 8.

"My Faith," *Chicago Theological Seminary Register*, XXVIII (November, 1938), 7–8.

"National Conference of Charities and Correction and Social Sermon by New President Graham Taylor," *Chicago Commerce*, VIII (August 1, 1913), 30–34.

"The National Conference: Prospect and Retrospect," *The Survey*, XXX (August 2, 1913), 588–90.

"National Front Against Child Labor," *Charities and The Commons*, XXI (January 30, 1909), 741–42.

"National Honesty Tested by Prosperity," *The Commons*, X (July, 1905), 389–91.

"National Movement to Conserve Natural Resources," *Charities and The Commons*, XXI (October 3, 1908), 8–10.

"The Neighborhood and the Municipality," National Conference of Charities and Correction, *Proceedings, 1909*, pp. 156–63.

"Neighborhood and Nation," *The Survey*, XLII (June 21, 1919), 465.

"*Neighbors All* by E. G. Barrows," *The Survey*, LXIV (September 15, 1930), 520–21.

"New Bids and Old Claims for Support," *The Playground*, XIV (August, 1920), 274–77.

"New Crusade for Safety-first," *The Survey*, XXXI (November 1, 1913), 142–43.

"A New Force in Chicago Politics," *The Survey*, XXXVI (April 1, 1916), 34.

"New York's Picket Line," *The Kingdom*, X (October 14, 1897), 34–35.

"New York's Picket Line — Cordon of Settlements Along Manhattan Island," *The Commons*, II (September, 1897), 12–13.

"The New Internationalism," *The Commons*, IX (October, 1904), 453–58.

"The Old Burden of Souls Borne Anew," *Chicago Theological Seminary Register*, III (June, 1910), 12–15.

"On City Evangelization: The Increased Use in City Mission Work of the

Lay Element," (with H. A. Schauffler and Others) *Minutes, National Council of Congregational Churches, 1892*, pp. 239–59.

"On Taking First Sight of the Settlement From a Distance," *The Commons*, VIII (July, 1903), 14.

"On the Vagrant 'Elusive'," *Charities and The Commons*, XVIII (August 10, 1907), 575–77.

"The Organic Growth of Spiritual Life," *Hartford Seminary Record*, I (December, 1890), 61–65.

"Organized Charity and Organized Labor," National Conference of Charities and Correction, *Proceedings, 1905*, pp. 458–62. Also published in *The Commons*, X (October, 1905), 549–52.

"Organized Labor and the Elections," *Charities and The Commons*, XXI (November 14, 1908), 274–76.

"Organized Labor's Political Front Unbroken," *Charities and The Commons*, XXI (October 31, 1908), 149–50.

"Our Labor History — a National Need," *The Commons*, IX (April, 1904), 103.

"Our International Neighborhoods and the New America — Assimilation," National Federation of Settlements, *Seventh Conference, 1917*, pp. 49–50.

"Our New Professorship," *The Advance*, XXV (September 8, 1892), 697–98.

"Our Public Schools in Progress and Reaction," *Survey Graphic*, XXIII (February, 1934), 61–65, 93–94.

"Over-Sectionalizing American Labor," *Charities and The Commons*, XV (November 4, 1905), 140–41.

"Parental Responsibility for Child Labor," *Annals of American Academy of Political and Social Science*, XXVII (March, 1906), 354–56.

"A Permanent Morals Commission for Chicago," *The Survey*, XXXIII (December 12, 1914), 281–82.

"Personal Religion and Progress Through Social Work," National Conference of Social Work, *Proceedings, 1923*, pp. 275–77.

"Pestalozzi and Froebel," *Chautauqua Assembly Herald*, XXV (July 24, 1900), 4.

"Physician — Citizen, an Appreciation of Dr. Henry Baird Favill," *The Survey*, XXXV (March 11, 1916), 704.

"Pioneer Inquiries into Burial Costs," *The Survey*, XXVI (September 2, 1911), 815–20.

"The Police and Vice in Chicago," *The Survey*, XXIII (November 6, 1909), 160–65.

"Police Efficiency the First Effect of Vice Inquiries," *The Survey*, XXVIII (April 20, 1912), 136–41.

"Police Work as a Profession, Not a Job," *Journal of Criminal Law*, VII (November, 1916), 622–24.

"Politics from the Social Settlement Point of View," *The Kingdom*, X (March 17, 1898), 448.

"Popular Value of a Supreme Court Decision," *Charities and The Commons*, XVI (April 7, 1906), 9–10.

"Preparing for Peace," *The Survey*, XXII (May 22, 1909), 275–76.

"The Principles of Christianity Applied to Industrial Problems," *Minutes, National Council of Congregational Churches, 1904*, pp. 87–99.

"The Problem of the One and the Many," *Proceedings of the Indiana Y.M.C.A. Convention, 1896*, pp. 47–56.

"Professional Training for the Police," *The Survey*, XXXVI (August 12, 1916), 503.

"Professionalism: A Peril in Christian Work," *Intercollegian*, XXII (April, 1900), 153–54.

"Professor Scott and the Seminary," *Chicago Theological Seminary Register*, II (May, 1909), 6–9.

"The Progress of the Practical Purpose in Education," *Chautauqua Assembly Herald*, XXVII (July 9, 1902), 1, 3, 7, 8.

"The Public Burden of the Insecurity of Life," *Chicago Medical Recorder*, XXXV (December, 1913), 639–44.

"The Public Duty of Public Service," *Charities and The Commons*, XVI (August 4, 1906), 473–74.

"Public Significance of Labor Day," *Charities and The Commons*, XVIII (September 7, 1907), 641–42.

"Public Spirit in Public Appointments," *Charities and The Commons*, XVI (July 7, 1906), 405–6.

"Race Riot in Lincoln's City," *Charities and The Commons*, XX (August 29, 1908), 627–28.

"Recent Advances Against the Social Evil in New York," *The Survey*, XXIV (September 17, 1910), 858–65.

"Recent Developments in Municipal Activities Tending to Neighborhood Improvement," National Conference of Charities and Correction, *Proceedings, 1904*, pp. 486–95.

"The Red Cross Director," *Charities and The Commons*, XX (June 20, 1908), 396.

"Refusing to Marry the Unfit," *The Survey*, XXVIII (May 18, 1912), 291–92.

"The Relation of Settlements to Politics," *The Commons*, VII (September, 1902), 18–19.

"The Relation of Student Life to the Social Question," *The Association Monthly*, XXXIII (March, 1908), 64–68.

"The Relations of the Young Men's Christian Associations to the Social-Economic Questions of the Day," *Proceedings of the 31st International Convention of the Y.M.C.A., 1895*, pp. 119–26.

"Religion in Social Action," *The Survey*, XXVII (December 2, 16, 1911, January 6, 20, February 3, March 2, 1912), 1277–81, 1360–62, 1557–62, 1601–5, 1679–84, 1833–36; XXVIII (April 6, May 4, June 1, July 6, August 3, September 7, 1912), 28–32, 226–31, 403–8, 540–44, 625–28, 734–40.

"*The Religion of a Democrat* by Charles Zueblin," *Charities and The Commons*, XX (August 22, 1908), 612.

"Religious Education and Social Duty," *Charities and The Commons*, XXI (February 20, 1909), 996–98.

"The Religious Function of the School in a Democratic State," *Chautauquan Daily*, XXXIII (July 30, 1908), 6.

"Report of the Committee on the Administration of the Settlement, and the Future Policy of the Settlement Movement," National Federation of Settlements, *Fifth Conference, 1915*, pp. 9–10.

"Report of the Committee on City Evangelization. Part I: The Social Settlement Movement in Relation to City Evangelization," *Minutes, National Council of Congregational Churches, 1898*, pp. 283–89.

"Report of Committee on Distribution and Assimilation of Immigrants," National Conference of Charities and Correction, *Proceedings, 1913*, pp. 26–35.

"Report of the Committee on Industry," *Minutes, National Council of Congregational Churches, 1910*, pp. 222–33.

"Report of the Committee on Training for Social Workers," National Conference of Charities and Correction, *Proceedings, 1905*, pp. 436–44.

"Report of the Industrial Committee of the National Council," *Minutes, National Council of Congregational Churches, 1913*, pp. 276–78.

"Response," *Chicago Theological Seminary Register*, XVIII (November, 1928), 23–27.

"Response of Graham Taylor to the Greetings of Mayor William E. Dever," *Chicago Theological Seminary Register*, XVII (January, 1927), 6–10.

"Routing the Segregationists in Chicago," *The Survey*, XXIX (November 30, 1912), 254–56.

"The Rudowitz Case," *Charities and The Commons*, XXI (February 6, 1909), 779–80.

"The Science of Relief in Mine Disasters," *The Survey*, XXIV (September 10, 1910), 833–37.

"Seer and Saver," *Social Action*, I (May 1, 1935), 4–5.

"Selective Service Aid for Reconstruction," *The Survey*, XLI (November 30, 1918), 256–57.

"The Settlement as an Influence in Public Opinion: The Social Settlements' Influence upon Public Policies," National Conference of Social Work, *Proceedings, 1923*, pp. 526–29.

"The Settlement as a Way of Life," *Neighborhood*, II (July, 1929), 151–58.

"A Settlement in City Politics," *The Commons*, VIII (May, 1903), 1–3. Unsigned article by Taylor.

"Shall the Pedigree of the Dollar Defeat its Destiny?," *The Commons*, X (September, 1905), 483–85.

"Sharing the Sacred Calling," *Chicago Theological Seminary Register*, VII (May, 1914), 49.

"Shattered Ideals — The War's Greatest Casualty," *The Survey*, XXXVI (June 3, 1916), 267.

"The Shift of Christian Emphasis in the Individual Life," *Chautauquan Daily*, XXXIII (July 29, 1908), 6.

"The Social Advance of the Churches," *The Survey*, XXII (September 25, 1909), 851–55.

"The Social and Civic Responsibility and Opportunity of American Colleges and Their Graduates," Association of American Colleges, *Bulletin*, XI (April, 1925), 63–76.

"Social and Religious Aspects of Industrial Peace and Progress," *Chautauqua Assembly Herald*, XXII (August 2, 1897), 2–3.

"The Social Aspect of Thrift," *The Survey*, XXXVII (October 28, 1916), 83–84.

"Social Aspects of Municipal Elections," *Charities and The Commons*, XV (December 2, 1905), 276–78.

"A Social Center for Civic Co-operation — Chicago Commons," *The Commons*, IX (December, 1904), 585–94.

"Social Christianity Pays Honor to its Pioneers," *The Survey*, XXXIX (November 3, 1917), 111.

"Social Conference of the Friends in England," *The Commons*, VIII (November, 1903), 14–15.

"The Social Conscience," *The Commons*, I (August, 1897), 13–16.

"The Social Emphasis," in F. L. Thompson and Others, *Men and Religion* (New York, 1911), pp. 138–54.

"The Social Extension of the Common Faith," *Chautauqua Assembly Herald*, XXII (August 7, 1897), 6–7.

"The Social Extension of the Common Faith," *The Kingdom*, X (March 17, 1898), 441–43.

"Social Extension of Our Public Schools," *The Commons*, IX (February, 1904), 47–49.

"The Social Function of the Church," *American Journal of Sociology*, V (November, 1899), 305–21.

"Social Incarnation," *Chautauqua Assembly Herald*, XXV (July 24, 1900), 1–3.

"The Social Incarnation," *The Commons*, IX (December, 1904), 581–82. Unsigned editorial by Taylor.

"Social Measures Prompted by the War," *The Survey*, XXXII (September 12, 1914), 587–89.

"The Social Message of the Modern Church," *Charities and The Commons*, XVI (May 5, 1906), 156–57.

"Social Movements for Character Development under Adverse Living and Working Conditions," *Religious Education*, XXIV (February, 1929), 133–36.

"Social 'Overflow' of the War," *The Commons*, III (August, 1898), 2–3.

"The Social Propaganda, Field Notes of the Western Summer Schools and Chautauquas," *Chicago Commons*, I (July, 1896), 2–3.

"The Social Residuum of the War," *The Kingdom*, X (September 22, 1898), 933.

"The Social Settlement," *Chautauqua Assembly Herald*, XXVII (July 8, 1902), 1–3.

"The Social Settlement and Its Suggestions to the Churches," *Hartford Seminary Record*, IV (December, 1893), 55–63.

"The Social Settlement and the Labor Movement," National Conference of Charities and Correction, *Proceedings, 1896*, pp. 143–49.

"The Social Settlement, Religion and the Church," in Jerome Davis (ed.), *Christianity and Social Adventuring* (New York, 1927), pp. 165–76.

"The Social Settlement — Settlement Mediation Between Politics and Religion," *Chautauqua Assembly Herald*, XXVII (July 8, 1902), 1–2.

"Social Settlement, the Church and Religion," *The Survey*, XXX (July 5, 1913), 453–54.

"The Social Settlement Idea for the Churches," *The Standard*, February 7, 1903.

"Social Settlements and the Churches," *The Kingdom*, X (July 7, 1898), 754.

"Social Tendencies of the Industrial Revolution," *The Commons*, IX (October, 1904), 459–468. Also published in *International Congress of Arts and Sciences, Universal Exposition, St. Louis, 1904*, ed. H. J. Rogers (8 vols.; Boston, 1905–7) VII, 682–94.

"Social Under-Tow of the War," *The Commons*, III (June, 1898), 5–6.

"The Social Value of the Household Arts," *Chautauquan Daily*, XXXIII (August 3, 1908), 7.

"Socializing Commercial Ethics," *The Survey*, XXV (January 14, 1911), 640–43.

"Sociological Aspects of the Work," *Young Men's Era*, XX (May 10, 1894), 4.

"Sociological Work in Theological Seminaries," *International Congress of Charities, Corrections and Philanthropy, Chicago, 1893* (Baltimore, 1894), pp. 64–79.

"The Sociological Training of the Ministry," in Evangelical Alliance, *Christianity Practically Applied* (New York, 1894), I, 396–413.

"Some Social Literature," *Chicago Theological Seminary Register*, VI (May, 1913), 6–8.

"Some Things in Common Between Labor and Religion," *Congregationalist and Christian World*, XCI (October 6, 1906), 431–32.

"The Soul of the Settlement," National Federation of Settlements, *Eighth Conference, 1918*, pp. 5–13.

"The Southern Social Awakening," *The Survey*, XXVIII (September 14, 1912), 744–45.

"Spirit of the Settlement House," *The Commons*, VII (January, 1903), 4. Unsigned editorial by Taylor.

"Spiritual Solvents of City Problems," *Charities and The Commons*, XV (March 3, 1906), 753–54.

"The Standard For a City's Survey," *Charities and The Commons*, XXI (January 2, 1909), 508.

"State University Training for Employes of State Institutions," *The Commons*, X (April, 1905), 199–200.

"Story of the Chicago Vice Commission," *The Survey*, XXVI (May 6, 1911), 239–47.

"A Strike That Brought Solidarity," *The Survey*, XXXV (January 8, 1916), 419.

"Strike with Dark Shadows and Bright Lights," *The Survey*, XXVIII (July 20, 1912), 571–72.

"Summer Settlement Tour," *The Commons*, II (August, 1897), 4–6.

"Sunday's Sermon," *Chautauquan Daily*, XXXIII (July 28, 1908), 6.

"Ten-Hour Day for Women Upheld," *The Survey*, XXIV (April 30, 1910), 170–71.

"Ten Years of Progress in Religious Education," *The Survey*, XXIX (March 29, 1913), 902–3.

"This Is Chicago!" *The Survey*, LXIII (November 1, 1929), 160–61.

"Those Who Have Helped," *Neighborhood*, I (July, 1928), 12–14.

"Thoughts on Immortality," *Chicago Theological Seminary Register*, XXVIII (November, 1938), 9–10.

"Time to Assert the Supremacy of Human Interests," *The Commons*, IX (June, 1904), 229–30.

"To Conquer the Industrial Situation," *Christian Register*, XCVIII (September 4, 1919), 849–50.

"To Indiana and Timothy Nicholson," *The Survey*, XLII (July 12, 1919), 565–66.

"Toronto Convention of the American Federation of Labor," *The Survey*, XXIII (February 5, 1910), 684–87.

"Training Center for Social Workers," *The Commons*, IX (January, 1904), 18–19.

"Training for Social Workers," *The Commons*, X (September, 1905), 513–17.

"Trust Conference," *The Commons*, IV (September, 1899), 1–2.

"Two Centuries of Arrested Development," *The Survey*, XXXI (October 4, 1913), 32–33.

"Two Vagrants in Law and Life," *Charities and The Commons*, XIX (October 19, 1907), 895–96.

"Unemployment: Discussion," National Conference of Charities and Correction, *Proceedings, 1915*, pp. 509–14.

"Unemployment in War and Peace," *The Survey*, XXXIII (February 6, 1915), 516–17.

"Unified Government for Chicago," *The Survey*, XXXVII (February 24, 1917), 593–94.

"Unionizing Government Employes," *The Survey*, XXII (May 8, 1909), 226–28.

"The United Cities of America," *Charities and The Commons*, XV (January 20, 1906), 518–19.

"Unity Through Fellowship Achieved by Congregationalists," *The Survey*, XXXI (November 29, 1913), 215.

" 'Unknown Workman, Against the Sky'," *The Survey*, XXIX (February 1, 1913), 563.

"Vitalizing Chicago," *Journal of Education*, LXXXII (August 26, 1915), 150.

"View Points of Labor Abroad," *The Commons*, VIII (October, 1903), 10–11.

"Walter Rauschenbusch 1861–1918," *The Survey*, XL (August 3, 1918), 493–95.

"War a Test of Religious and Social Ideals," *The Survey*, XXXIV (July 31, 1915), 394–95, 401–3.

"The War on Vice," *The Survey*, XXIX (March 8, 1913), 811–13.

"Washington Gladden," *The Survey*, XL (July 13, 1918), 422, 436.

"Washington's Day for Citizenship," *The Survey*, XXV (February 25, 1911), 880–81.

"Waymarks of Labor Day," *The Survey*, XXII (September 4, 1909), 738–39.

"Waymarks of the Labor Movement; From Serfdom to Wages; The Peasant Pioneers," *Chautauqua Assembly Herald*, XXII (July 28, 1897), 2.

"What Must Society Do To Be Saved?," *Young Men's Era*, XIX (November 23, 1893), 1313.

"What the Church May Expect From the Present Sociological Movement," *The Advance*, XXIX (June 30, 1895), 1352–53.

"What to Do About It?," *Chautauqua Assembly Herald*, XXV (July 25, 1900), 5.

"Where There's Common Ground in Civic Progress," *Charities and The Commons*, XVII (November 3, 1906), 188–89.

"Whither the Settlement Movement Tends?," *Charities and The Commons*, XV (March 3, 1906), 840–44.

"Why the City Club of Chicago," *The City Club Bulletin*, XXVI (December 2, 1933), 131.

"Women and Public Service," *Chautauquan Daily*, XXXIII (July 30, 1908), 1–2.

"Women Socializing Politics," *The Survey*, XXXI (February 7, 1914), 595–96.

"The Women's Biennial: Social Sympathy and Public Policies," *The Survey*, XXXII (July 4, 1914), 358–59.

"Women's Voting Significantly Tested in Illinois," *The Survey*, XXXII (April 18, 1914), 69–70.

"Work in the Philippines," *The Living Church*, LXVII (July 22, 1922), 412, 414.

"World Salvage," *The Survey*, XXXV (January 29, 1916), 525–26.

"Writes of His Ins and Outs with the Press," *Press Impressions*, VII (May, 1930), 1–2, 5.

"Wu Ting-fang and a Reunited China," *Review of Reviews*, LXVI (November, 1922), 513–16.

"The Young Men's Christian Association in the Nineteenth Century — A Christian Sociologist's View of Its Services to Society," *Association Men*, XXVI (January, 1901), 110–11.

Index